STRATEGY AS POLITICS:
Puerto Rico on the Eve of the Second World War

STRATEGY AS POLITICS:
Puerto Rico on the Eve of the Second World War

JORGE RODRÍGUEZ BERUFF

LA EDITORIAL
UNIVERSIDAD DE PUERTO RICO

Library of Congress Cataloging-in-Publication Data

Rodríguez Beruff, Jorge.
  Strategy as politics: Puerto Rico on the eve of the Second World War / Jorge Rodríguez Beruff.
    p. cm.

  Includes bibliographical references and index.

  ISBN 0-8477-0160-3

1. Puerto Rico—Politics and government—1898-1952. 2. Puerto Rico—Relations—United States. 3. United States—Relations—Puerto Rico. 4. World War, 1939-1945—Influence. I. Title.
  F1975.R645 2006
  972.9505'2—dc22

                                        2006021317

  ISBN: 978-0-8477-0160-5

Editor / Javier Ávila

Cover photos / Joint Chiefs of Staff, Washington, September, 1942: H. H. Arnold,
                George Marshall, William Leahy and Ernest King.
                Photo: T. Mc Avoy / *Life* Magazine. FDR Library.

                William Leahy, Rupert Emerson, Luis Muñoz Marín. Armistice Day, San Juan,
                November, 1940. *El Mundo* Collection, UPR.

Cover and text design / Yolanda Pastrana Fuentes

LA EDITORIAL
UNIVERSIDAD DE PUERTO RICO

P.O. Box 23322
San Juan, Puerto Rico 00931-3322
www.laeditorialupr.com

TABLE OF CONTENTS

ACKNOWLEDGEMENTS vii

INTRODUCTION ix

Chapter 1
A STRONG AND GUIDING HAND 1

Chapter 2
ABOARD THE U.S.S. HOUSTON 61

Chapter 3
FLEET PROBLEM XX 109

Chapter 4
ICKES'S POWDER KEG 159

Chapter 5
AN OFFICE FULL OF GRIEF 207

Chapter 6
LA LIJA: PACIFYING A COLONY FOR WAR 259

Chapter 7
PEACE AND ORDER IN PUERTO RICO 301

Chapter 8
MOVING MOUNTAINS 349

SELECTED BIBLIOGRAPHY 389

INDEX 419

ACKNOWLEDGEMENTS

This book is based on research that has spanned more than a decade. I began writing the manuscript during my sabbatical in 1996, but could not conclude its revision until nine years later, when it was accepted for publication by La Editorial de la Universidad de Puerto Rico. During such a prolonged period of research and writing, I have incurred a debt of gratitude with many persons and institutions, too many to mention individually here. To all of them my heartfelt thanks.

There are some, however, who must be mentioned. During my research I received small grants from the Institute of Puerto Rican Culture and the *Fondo Institucional para la Investigación* (FIPI) of the University of Puerto Rico that were extremely useful. I also received the support of my department, the Social Sciences Department of the College of General Studies, and its director, Professor Margarita Mergal, in obtaining a sabbatical, without which I could not have written this book. The students Nicolás Quiñones, José Medina and Maribel Véaz assisted me in different stages of the research. I thank them, and I am glad that they have become distinguished professionals. I also learned much from the research of other graduate students who have worked with me on the Second World War period: Carlos Hernández, Miguel Santiago, Gerardo Piñero, Luis López, Josefa Santiago and José Collazo.

I was lucky to have the support of the staff at the following institutions: National Archives (Washington, D.C.); U.S. Army Military History Institute (Carlisle Barracks, PA); Library of Congress Manuscript Division; Naval Historical Center (Washington Navy Yard); U.S. Army Center for Military History (Washington, D.C.); Centro de Investigaciones Históricas; Colección Fotográfica del Periódico El Mundo; Colección Puertorriqueña; Fundación Luis Muñoz Marín; and the Archivo General de Puerto Rico. Whether in the U.S. or in Puerto Rico, I always encountered personnel imbued by a common culture of service to researchers.

My year as Visiting Professor at Rutgers University allowed me to advance considerably in this project. During this period I received the support and intellectual encouragement of Professor Pedro Cabán and Professor John W. Chambers.

Many colleagues read parts of the manuscript and made valuable suggestions that I almost invariably incorporated. I must mention, among them, Rubén Nazario, Juan Giusti, Blanca Silvestrini, Robert Anderson, Juan José Baldrich and Silvia Álvarez. My collaboration with Humberto García on several related projects was an important stimulus for this research.

Special mention must be made of Ángel Collado Schwarz, who read the manuscript as my graduate student and convinced me that it was time to undertake a final revision and have it published. Michael Janeway of Columbia University read the entire draft and provided me with detailed suggestions on all the chapters

My wife, Aura Muñoz Maldonado, gave me her loving support through all the stages of this project. Instead of thanking her again, I simply pledge to devote more time to exploring coral reefs in her company.

In 1940, San Juan and many other parts of the island of Puerto Rico had become a beehive for war-related activity. The first major base construction project was Isla Grande. Then came the expansion of Fort Buchanan and military work on El Morro. Borinquen Field in Aguadilla was hastily readied. On the coasts, near major harbors, a ring of gun emplacements was being built. The number of workers of the Work Projects Administration devoted to defense construction had risen from 18,019 (in 1939) to 32,615. A host of other agencies was also busy in defense-related projects ranging from roads to docks. Ships disembarked soldiers and armaments in the harbor, which was also constantly visited by warships. Military planes from Isla Grande overflew the city in their comings and goings to missions in the Caribbean. Movies, newspapers and the radio were part of the war effort and atmosphere. The Boy Scouts were also patriotically mobilized for the war. And, in apparent harmony with all this, the Governor of Puerto Rico was the recently retired highest ranking U.S. naval officer.

Arturo Morales Carrión, a leading Puerto Rican historian, was a young man in 1940. He witnessed the hectic pace of war preparations and the highly militarized environment of the island. In a seldom quoted article, he reflected on what the recent events meant historically for Puerto Rico. According to him, they posed once again the main dilemma of Puerto Rican history:

> It would seem that the only definite answer which the United States is offering is an old and discredited one: Puerto Rico is to be a formidable fortress, a clenched fist ready to repel foreign intruders in the Caribbean. That was, indeed, the answer that Spain found for three centuries, yet at the very end she was willing to grant a liberal political status which would have permitted Puerto Ricans to assert their individuality, and to

find their own modest path to cultural self-determination. Let it not be said, in full justice to the American sense of democratic equality and fair-play, that the military solution is the only one which the American people can discover for Puerto Rico. If such should prove the case, Puerto Ricans would know that their centuries-old civic struggle has been in vain, and that the fortress reigns forever supreme over the city.[1]

Strategy as Politics is a study of power in a colonial polity during a juncture of looming and, later, actual world war. It centers on the period of about three years (1938-1940) that encompasses the worsening international crisis in Europe and Asia, the outbreak of the Second World War with its immediate impact on the Caribbean, the dramatic collapse of France in the summer of 1940, and the military preparations and international actions of the United States in response to unfolding events.

With regard to Puerto Rican politics, this book deals mainly with the downfall of the Blanton Winship governorship, along with the political practices and alliances it embodied, and the brief, but politically dense, period of Admiral William D. Leahy's governorship (September 1939 to November 1940). During these years, a profound transformation of the pattern of Puerto Rican politics occurred and U.S.-Puerto Rico relations were redefined. These changes created the political conditions for even further transformations, also of a social and cultural character, during the post-Pearl Harbor war years. In many ways, it represents a political watershed.

Among other things, the governing *Coalición* political formation (an alliance between the *Partido Unión Republicana* and the *Partido Socialista*) was torn by a prolonged period of internal strife and factionalism that led to creation of the *Unificación Puertorriqueña Tripartita,* known as *Tripartismo*. Dissidents of both *Coalición* parties joined together with the weakened anti-*Muñocista* leadership of the *Partido Liberal* to put forward a viable electoral alternative to the majority formation. Also a new reformist political party, the *Partido Popular Democrático,* was founded in 1938 as a left alternative to *Coalicionismo* and *Tripartismo*. The unexpected narrow electoral triumph of the *Populares* in the 1940 elections profoundly transformed Puerto Rican politics and forged the post war Puerto Rican economy and society. Soon after the elections, the Roosevelt administration recognized Luis Muñoz Marín as the leader of the dominant party, and subsequently most of his legislative program was to be approved by Governor Guy Swope. Governor Rexford Tugwell, a strong personality with his own views on policy for Puerto Rico, would implement the new legislation and enact far reaching administrative reforms in a relationship with Muñoz Marín that was not always harmonious.

Political developments in Puerto Rico were accompanied, and to a large extent made possible, by changes in the leading policy makers, with a concomitant redefinition of Roosevelt administration's policies toward Puerto Rico. Perhaps the most critical decision was the removal of Ernest Gruening from Puerto Rican policy making. He had hitherto enjoyed broad powers and control over PRRA funds. His appointment as governor of Alaska almost coincided with Roosevelt's unceremonious destitution of Winship and Leahy's assumption of the Puerto Rican governorship. These changes enhanced Secretary of the Interior Harold Ickes's influence over policy.

This was not a mere change of functionaries, but a major shift in Washington's approach to Puerto Rican political conflicts. The new administrators had a clear anti-*Coalición* agenda that opened the door to new political interlocutors. I argue that an important factor for this change had to do with the sharpened perception that a political restructuring was urgently needed to ensure stability and collaboration while the ambitious plans of preparation for war were implemented. Other actors, such as Representative Vito Marcantonio, the American Civil Liberties Union (ACLU) and other liberal groups, were also actively pushing in Washington for a new approach to Puerto Rico.

The dynamics of U.S.-Puerto Rico relations and Puerto Rican politics in the late 30s and early 40s cannot be understood without taking into account the context of international crisis and war, the considerable strategic importance that was attached to the island in U.S. military thinking and planning, and the role it was assigned in U.S. defense preparations, particularly in relation to Caribbean defense. I posit that strategic military considerations had been a major dimension of U.S. policy toward Puerto Rico since 1898 and the military establishment a key policy actor. This pattern was greatly magnified during the Second World War. Although it is not the subject of this book, the same could also be said about the First World War, which resulted in U.S. citizenship for Puerto Ricans and major legislative reform of U.S.-Puerto Rico relations expressed in the Jones Act.

Under conditions of international war and a perceived German threat in South America and in the Caribbean, which could compromise the Panama Canal, military strategy gained even greater prominence, intensely interacting with politics. Strategy and politics became intertwined, to such an extent that it became difficult to determine their borders. John Keegan has recently clarified Karl von Clausewitz's often misquoted dictum about the relationship between war and politics. According to Keegan, the correct translation is that "war is the continuation of 'political intercourse' (*des politischen Verkehrs*) 'with the intermixing of other means' (*mit Einmischung anderer Mittel*)."[2] Perhaps politics or "political intercourse" itself, under war conditions, is to a great extent transformed by that "intermixing" and becomes a continuation of war.

From a methodological point of view, our research seeks to analyze and relate three historical processes: (1) Puerto Rican politics, understood as a distinct sphere of action; (2) U.S. policy-making toward Puerto Rico — i.e., colonial administration; (3) strategic thinking and planning, and actual military policy that was formulated within a regional Caribbean approach. This has meant that I have had to consult many and diverse sources in the U.S. and Puerto Rico.

There are many secondary sources on the war, the U.S. military and the Roosevelt administration. The reader will find most of them cited in the bibliography. However, there is a dearth of studies on Puerto Rican politics of this period. It is, indeed, striking that this crucial period has not attracted the interest of historians, political scientists and researchers of other disciplines. Thomas Mathews's book on the New Deal in Puerto Rico, published in 1970, remains the best study on U.S. policy during the 1930s.[3] However, it does not deal with post-1938 events.

Henry Wells's *The Modernization of Puerto Rico* succinctly discusses the circumstances of the 1940 elections and devotes a chapter to political developments in the 1940s. It should be noted that no mention is made of the governorships of William D. Leahy and Guy Swope. Furthermore, his discussion of the Tugwell-Muñoz period does not take into account the context of the war. Wells just makes brief reference to some of its economic consequences.[4] On the other hand, Gordon Lewis's *Puerto Rico, Freedom and Power in the Caribbean* represents another well known and outstanding contribution to the analysis of Puerto Rican politics, which discusses the period of the war. Unlike Wells, Lewis emphasizes the importance of the context of the Second World War in order to understand internal political processes. However, he also disregards the relevance of the change of U.S. policy during 1939-40, as well as the transitional role of Leahy and Swope. He simply dismisses the latter as "the last of the Farley type appointments."[5] With regard to Admiral Leahy, he utterly misses the circumstances and significance of his appointment, wrongly characterizing it as a mere product of the spoils system:

> Only too frequently the office was used as a rich plum in the spoils system of American politics, while the custodianship of the War Office meant an additional pressure group in the form of elderly retired naval and military gentlemen anxious to spend the twilight of their days south of Miami; as late as 1939 the appointment was given to Admiral Leahy as he made his way to, finally, the American ambassadorship to the French wartime Vichy regime.[6]

Most of the other available secondary sources about this period are memoirs of key participants, such as Luis Muñoz Marín,[7] Rexford Tugwell,[8] George Malcolm,[9] Harold Ickes,[10] William D. Leahy[11] and Ernest Gruening.[12] Some prominent political figures, such a Blanton Winship, Guy Swope and Rafael Martínez Nadal, did not publish memoirs. One of the few political studies that refers to the period is Bolivar Pagán's *Historia de los partidos políticos puertorriqueños, 1898-1956.*[13] But he was also a prominent politician during the 30s and 40s, and his book is far from being a balanced and reliable source.

Humberto García Muñiz has written on the Second World War, but mostly from a regional perspective.[14] Silvia Álvarez Curbelo has written on political discourse during the war, but about a later period than that discussed here,[15] and Mayra Rosario Urrutia has done valuable research on the Anglo-American Caribbean Commission.[16] I hope *Strategy as Politics* will stimulate greater interest in the study of this period, as my previous book *Las memorias de Leahy* (in which I edited the long-lost memoirs of

Admiral William D. Leahy) provoked to a certain extent. That book, I must point out, was a byproduct of the research for *Strategy as Politics* and they complement each other. It must be recognized, however, that a young generation of historians has already undertaken research on unexplored aspects of the Second World War years, producing valuable graduate dissertations. Those historians include José Collazo, Josefa Santiago, Carlos Hernández, Carlos González Morales, Gerardo Piñero and Miguel Santiago, among others.

General history texts on Puerto Rico written by prominent historians such as Fernando Picó, Blanca Silvestrini and María Dolores Luque, Francisco Scarano and Luis Díaz Soler[17] almost invariably glance over the critical years of the Second World War, hardly making more than a perfunctory reference to the impact of the war on the society and polity. Scarano even confuses Admiral William D. Leahy with Senator Patrick Leahy. This may respond to the relative absence of secondary sources, or a tendency toward "Insularism," to use Antonio S. Pedreira's expression, which disregards the importance of international or regional factors.[18] Ironically, another explanation may be the still crucial role of the 1940s in present day political discourse in Puerto Rico, and the way politics still conditions accounts about that decade.

The vast and varied historiographic production on the war in the United States and Europe contrasts with the sorry state of local scholarship. We do not need to go that far. Ken Post's *Strike the Iron, A Colony at War: Jamaica 1939-1945*,[19] Fitzroy André Baptiste's *War, Cooperation and Conflict, The European Possessions in the Caribbean, 1939-1945*,[20] and Bernardo Vega's many works on Trujillo and U.S.-Dominican relations,[21] despite their very different perspectives, are examples of excellent Caribbean academic production that could be emulated in Puerto Rico.

The first chapter of this book examines the role of military factors during the first decades of 20th century Puerto Rican history and in the formulation of U.S. policy towards its new possession. The close personal and political relationship of Franklin Delano Roosevelt and William D. Leahy in its Caribbean dimension is the subject matter of the second chapter. This should provide insights to better understand Roosevelt's decision to entrust Leahy with the governorship of Puerto Rico at the outbreak of the Second World War. The third chapter places both leaders aboard the USS Houston during the Fleet Problem XX maneuvers of 1939. The maneuvers serve as an important starting point to clarifying the situation of Puerto Rico in the strategic framework of the immediate pre-war period. The third chapter also deals with the 1930s political conflicts, and its title is based on a lapidary phrase of Harold Ickes. In that chapter, I take the narration up to the crisis of the Winship administration and the *Coalición*.

The following three chapters are devoted to Admiral Leahy's governorship. The fifth chapter describes the circumstances surrounding Roosevelt's decision to name him governor and the events preceding his arrival in Puerto Rico. The sixth chapter contains an almost blow-by-blow account of Leahy's conflicts with the *Coalición*. The last chapter analyzes political realignments with particular emphasis on the rise of the Popular Democratic Party, the impact of the dramatic events of the war and Leahy's role in war preparations. The chapter concludes with an account of overall military preparations in Puerto Rico and their impact on the economy, the strategic relationship with the Caribbean and the circumstances of Leahy's departure and appointment as Ambassador to Vichy France.

This book is based on a broad research that spanned several years. However, research can be of little consequence, and mostly a private endeavor, if not transformed into readable and actually read text. Thus, the writing process should be just as important as research. Barbara Tuchman, a historian I much admire and who has studied the political implications of war in memorable books such as *The Proud Tower* and *The Guns of August*, stresses in her book of essays, *Practicing History*, the creative and aesthetical dimensions of historical writing:

> As I see it, there are three parts to the creative process: first, the extra vision with which the artist perceives a truth and conveys it by suggestion. Second, medium or expression: language for writers, paint for painters, clay or stone for sculptors, sound expressed in musical notes for composer. Third, design or structure . . . When it comes to language, nothing is more satisfying than to write a good sentence . . .

> As to structure, my own form is narrative, which is not every historian´s, I may say-indeed, it is rather looked down on now

by the advanced academics, but I don´t mind because no one could possibly persuade me than writing a story is the most desirable thing a writer can do.[21]

I agree with Tuchman. I have tried to narrate an interesting story. The readers will decide if I have succeeded.

NOTES

1. Arturo Morales Carrión, "Puerto Rico: the fortress or the city?" Interamerican Quarterly (July, 1940) pp. 36-46.

2. John Keegan, *A History of Warfare* (New York: Vintage Books, 1993), p. 3.

3. Mathews, Thomas. *La política puertorriqueña y el Nuevo Trato* (Río Piedras: Editorial Universitaria, 1970).

4. Henry Wells, *The Modernization of Puerto Rico, A Political Study of Changing Values and Institutions* (Cambridge, Mass.: Harvard University Press, 1969), pp. 129, and Chapter 7.

5. Gordon K. Lewis, *Puerto Rico, Freedom and Power in the Caribbean* (New York: Harper & Row, 1963), p. 97.

6. Ibid., pp. 64-5.

7. Luis Muñoz Marín, *Memorias, 1898-1940* (San Juan: Inter American University Press, 1982); and *La historia del Partido Popular Democrático* (San Juan: Editorial Batey, 1984).

8. Rexford G. Tugwell, *The Stricken Land, The Story of Puerto Rico* (New York: Doubleday, 1947).

9. George Arthur Malcolm, *American Colonial Careerist; Half Century of Official Life and Personal Experience in the Philippines and Puerto Rico* (Boston: Christopher Publisher House, 1957).

10. Harold L. Ickes, *The Secret Diary of Harold L. Ickes*, 4 Vols. (New York: Da Capo Press, 1974).

11. Jorge Rodríguez Beruff, ed., *Las memorias de Leahy, los relatos del Almirante William D. Leahy sobre su gobernación de Puerto Rico (1939-1940)* (San Juan: Fundación Luis Muñoz Marín, 2002).

12. Ernest Gruening, *Many Battles* (New York: Livewright, 1973).

13. Bolívar Pagán, *Historia de los Partidos Políticos, 1898-1956*, 2 Vols. (San Juan: Bolívar Pagán, 1959).

14. Humberto García Muñiz, *La estrategia de Estados Unidos y la militarización del Caribe* (Río Piedras: Instituto de Estudios del Caribe, 1988).

15. Silvia Álvarez Curbelo, "Las lecciones de la guerra: Luis Muñoz Marín y la

Segunda Guerra Mundial, 1943-1946", in Fernando Picó, ed., *Luis Muñoz Marín, Ensayos del Centenario* (San Juan: FLMM, 1999), pp.31-64.

16. Mayra Rosario Urrutia, "La Comisión Anglo-Americana en el Caribe, una estrategia socio-económica con fines de seguridad militar", *Avance de Investigación No. 11*, Centro de Investigaciones Académicas, Universidad del Sagrado Corazón, 1991.

17. Carlos Hernández, "La Segunda Guerra Mundial en Puerto Rico: un análisis historiográfico", manuscript, n.d.

18. On Antonio S. Pedreira and the treintista generation refer to Chapter 4, p. 174, and endnote 36.

19. Ken Post, *Strike the Iron: A Colony at War*, 2 Vols. (Atlantic Highlands, N.J. & The Hague: The Institute of Social Studies, 1981).

20. Fitzroy André Baptiste, *War, Cooperation and Conflict, The European Possessions in the Caribbean, 1939-1945* (Westport, Conn.: Greenwood Press, 1988).

21. For example, Bernardo Vega, *Nazismo, fascismo y falangismo en la República Dominicana* (Santo Domingo: Fundación Cultural Dominicana, 1985).

22. Barbara Tuchman, *Practicing History, Selected Essays* (New York: Ballantine Books, 1982), pp. 48-9.

CHAPTER 1

A STRONG AND GUIDING HAND

The "evangelist" of sea power, Capt. Alfred Thayer Mahan.
U.S. Naval Historical Center.

A STRONG AND GUIDING HAND

The United States became increasingly involved in Central American and Caribbean affairs during the 19th century. The entire region was of great commercial and strategic value to the U.S. The Louisiana and Florida purchases, and later the annexation of Texas, provided the new nation with a long coast in the Gulf of Mexico and with the strategic port of New Orleans. The construction of the Panama railway in the mid 1850s increased U.S. interest in the Central American isthmus due to its expanding role in transoceanic communications.[1] During the pre-Civil War period, military and political forays into the region were mainly sponsored by southern slave-owning interests.[2] The naval aspects of the Civil War, mainly the naval blockade of the South and commerce raiding, served to underscore the strategic importance of the Gulf of Mexico and the Caribbean Sea.[3] The Caribbean, it should also be mentioned, had played an important naval role for Britain during the War of 1812, a topic on which Theodore Roosevelt lectured at the Naval War College in the 1880s.[4] The conclusion of the Civil War gave the U.S. new impetus for the annexation of Caribbean territories and acquisition of naval bases.

Of particular relevance to Puerto Rico was the scheme for overseas expansion formulated by William H. Seward, Secretary of State (1861-1869) to presidents Lincoln, Johnson, and Grant.[5] Within a grand design for expansion "from the Arctic to the isthmus," Seward identified the need for naval stations in the eastern Caribbean and the Pacific Ocean. In 1866, Secretary of the Navy Gideon Welles named a commission of inquiry which called for the acquisition of coaling stations "as colonies under our own flag."[6] Consequently, Seward tried to obtain for this purpose Samaná Bay in the Dominican Republic, the Puerto Rican islands of Culebra and Culebrita, and the Danish island of St. Thomas. The annexation of the Dominican Republic was actively pursued during Grant's administration. A Samaná Bay Company established and obtained a lease on the Dominican bay in 1873, two years after the plan to annex the Dominican Republic had narrowly failed in the Senate.[7] Simultaneously, Seward sought to expand U.S. influence over potential isthmian canal routes in Honduras, Nicaragua and Panama. Though plans to annex Caribbean territories had the firm support of the Navy, they were resisted by Congress. Spain also rejected Seward's offer to purchase Culebra.[8] The "reconstruction" period and the subsequent continual territorial expansion toward the west meant the postponement of Seward's ambitious design of overseas expansion.

An Empty Island?
Puerto Rico in U.S. Strategic Discourse

Captain Alfred Thayer Mahan, the leading U.S. strategic thinker, formulated in the 1880s and 1890s, in what could be conceived as a prolongation of Seward's project, a cogent and persuasive argument for overseas expansion and the acquisition of naval bases in the Caribbean and Central America.[9] Not only did his writings provide a forceful military justification to expansionist political sectors, but they also shaped people's consciousness. Mahan published major works based on extensive research and his ideas became popular through numerous articles in journals and magazines. He was part of a group of imperialist intellectuals that included Frederick Jackson Turner, John Fiske, Josiah Strong, Brooks Adams, Benjamin Kidd, James K. Hosmer, John W. Burgess, and others, who were strongly influenced by contemporary Social Darwinist ideas.[10] Since 1887, Mahan developed a close personal and political liaison with the expansionist sectors in the Republican Party and with Theodore Roosevelt, who wrote a glowing review of *The Influence of Sea Power upon History*.[11]

Mahan's views on the Caribbean and Central America became a persistent paradigm of U.S. strategic thinking that defined the parameters within which strategic debate was to take place during the late 19th and most of the 20th century. With regard to Puerto Rico, Mahan not only provided a powerful strategic argument for its acquisition as a colonial possession (not dissimilar to those of Spanish strategic thinking)[12] but was also personally involved in the formulation of plans for its use as a naval station.

Mahan's first major publication dealt with the strategic significance of the Gulf of Mexico, with special emphasis on the Civil War period.[13] In his 1890 classic study *The Influence of Sea Power upon History*, he argued for the creation of an imperial navy modeled after the British. The acquisition of colonies was part and parcel of this project since in "production, with the necessity of exchanging products, shipping, whereby the exchange is carried on, and colonies, which facilitate and enlarge the operations of shipping and tend to protect it by multiplying points of safety — is to be found the key to much of the history, as well as the policy, of nations bordering upon the sea."[14] Among other things, he attributed Britain's overwhelming naval supremacy to the possession of many strategically located colonies and naval stations, while the lack of these was a crucial factor for U.S. naval weakness. According to him, "the United States has only one link [production] of the three" (i.e., production, shipping and colonies) necessary to become a naval power.[15]

> Having therefore no foreign establishments, either colonial or military, the ships of war of the United States, in war will be like land birds, unable to fly far from their own shores. To provide resting-places for them, where they can coal and repair, would be one of the first duties of a government proposing to itself the development of the power of the nation at sea.[16]

Furthermore, Mahan established an analogy, which he would later elaborate, between the Caribbean and the Mediterranean, and between a future canal in the Central American isthmus and the Suez Canal. The construction of a canal would transform the Caribbean "from a place of local traffic . . . into one of the great highways of the earth."[17] An isthmian canal would consequently mean to the U.S. that it would "not be so easy to stand aloof from international complications."[18] It would enhance the strategic importance of New Orleans and the "United States will have to obtain in the Caribbean stations fit for contingent, or secondary, bases of operation."[19] Significantly, some of the major naval battles among European powers which he analyzed in his book took place in the Caribbean and involved the control of small islands considered strategically important. He predicted that the construction of a canal before the establishment of a clear U.S. naval hegemony over its eastern Pacific and Caribbean approaches would be a strategic disaster.

> The conclusion continually recurs. Whatever may be the determining factor in strifes between neighboring continental States, when a question of control over distant regions, politically weak, –whether they be crumbling empires, anarchical republics, colonies, isolated military posts, or islands below a certain size, –it must ultimately be decided by naval power, by the organized military force afloat, which represents the communications that form so prominent a feature in all strategy . . . Upon this will depend the control of the Central American Isthmus, if that question take a military coloring.[20]

Thus, Mahan favored the acquisition of colonies in the Pacific (e.g., Hawaii), Central America and the Caribbean.[21] To him it was not a question of acquiring a large colonial empire like the British, which could be in contradiction with U.S. institutions, but rather of obtaining naval bases within regions of commercial and strategic interest to the U.S. Colonies were necessary as naval outposts, and not because of their intrinsic commercial and economic value. Their economic value derived mainly from their strategic role in the protection of general U.S. strategic and commercial interests within a particular region.[22] In her book, Barbara Tuchman succinctly describes Mahan's outlook on colonies: "What motivated him was not earth-hunger but sea power."[23] Though his 1890 book reflected still a certain ambivalence regarding colonialism, Mahan's position was subsequently clarified in the sense that he not only favored the acquisition of colonies, but also their administration by the military.

In his influential article "The Strategic Features of the Gulf of Mexico and the Caribbean Sea," published in late 1897, Mahan further elaborated his analogy between the Mediterranean and the Caribbean and stressed the importance of the Central American isthmus. He argued that the strategic value of positions within that space depended on: 1) situation, 2) strength, and 3) resources. Situation, understood as geographic location, in turn, was related to maritime "lines of communication" to the isthmus. On this basis he proceeded to identify positions of strategic value. Cuba's strategic value was strongly emphasized, while, in the eastern Caribbean, Samaná Bay and St. Thomas were mentioned as particularly suited for naval bases.[24]

Mahan could not have overlooked the existence of the islands lying between these last two locations. Since 1894, before war broke out in Cuba, the Naval War College, of which Mahan was a prominent lecturer, had been formulating plans for war with Spain. By 1896, the Office of Naval Intelligence had prepared a plan that included a section on operations in Puerto Rican waters. The Naval War College actively participated in war planning against Spain throughout this period.[25] As noted by a correspondent for *The Times,* a London newspaper, the intense interest of the U.S. military in Puerto Rico, particularly of navy officers, was no secret by July 1898.

> In advance, however, of the expected sailing [of Miles's expedition] appears a short *communiqué,* described as "practically official," that Puerto Rico will be kept by the United States . . . I presume there is not a naval officer in the American service who does not think that the island ought to be permanently annexed for its value as a naval station. Military and naval officers alike would prefer an indemnity in this shape than an indemnity in money.[26]

In two subsequent articles, *The Times* also reported that "strategical reasons" made the annexation of "Puertorico" a certainty due to its "commanding position between the Mona and Anegada passages" and because it "possesses far greater resources than the little island of St. Thomas."[27]

The hasty manner in which the Miles expeditionary force was sent to Puerto Rico, at a time when the military outcome of the war was already decided, can only be understood as a maneuver designed to obtain military possession of the island before a peace treaty was signed.[28] It should be noted that General Miles later opposed the annexation of the Philippines but favored retaining Puerto Rico.[29] Also, it is significant that Theodore Roosevelt wrote from Cuba to Henry Cabot Lodge, the leading Congressional spokesman of the imperialist sector of the Republican Party, that, "you must prevent any talk of peace until we get Porto Rico and the Philippines." By May 1898, Lodge informed

Roosevelt that "the administration is now fully committed to the large policy we both desire."[30]

U.S. naval officers were already formulating concrete plans for the future military use of the island long before the Puerto Rican campaign ended. For example, Capt. Francis J. Higginson, the commander of the naval force that brought Miles to Puerto Rico, suggested, in a letter to Admiral Sampson dated only a week after the invasion, that a naval station should be established in Culebra.

> I also recommend that island Celebra [sic] be taken by the Navy. I doubt if there is any defences there and it could be easily captured and held. The Marines at Camp McCalla might be transferred to this place to capture and hold it for the use of the Navy as a coaling station and dock yard.[31]

Just a few days later, Mahan, then a member of the Naval War Board,[32] submitted a long official memorandum to the Secretary of the Navy, John D. Long, regarding the most desirable locations in the Pacific and the Caribbean to establish naval stations once the war ended. He recommended that naval stations in the Caribbean be located: "1: Upon the circumference or entrance to the sea; 2: In the neighborhood of the Isthmian Canal." Mentioned as potential bases in the Caribbean were: 1) an eastern port of Cuba (Nipe, Santiago and Guantánamo), 2) San Juan, and 3) either Samaná, St. Thomas or Culebra. It is worth quoting his reference to Puerto Rico, as the island he failed to mention in his 1897 article had suddenly become a prized location for a naval station, while St. Thomas was now "too small and too distant," only valuable in relation to Puerto Rico.

> For the former [upon the entrance to the sea] Porto Rico is advantageously situated and the harbor of San Juan would be apparently best adapted for the purposes of a coaling station . . .
>
> With reference to the position of the United States in the Caribbean Sea, *assuming the Island of Porto Rico to belong to us*, it is the opinion of the Board that the further acquisition of a strong neighboring position would substantially strengthen the general military control conferred by Porto Rico . . .

There are a couple of points in the vicinity, either of which would appear to answer as the second and stronger of the fortified positions referred to above; they are the Island of St. Thomas and the Bay of Samana . . .

Without Porto Rico, St. Thomas is too small and too distant from United States territory, but with Porto Rico the group of islands would form a territory susceptible of defense and valuable for military and commercial control . . .

The Board has just heard of another position that might perhaps be useful as the second strong place instead of St. Thomas or Samaná Bay. It is called "Great Harbor," in the Island of Culebra, 55 miles easterly from San Juan, Porto Rico, and 23 miles westward from St. Thomas.[33]

In *Lessons of the War with Spain*, Mahan once again expressed his views concerning Puerto Rico's strategic importance. It was now the Malta of the Caribbean.

Puerto Rico militarily, is to Cuba, to the future isthmian canal, and to our Pacific coast, what Malta is or may be, to Egypt and the beyond . . . it would be very difficult for a transatlantic state to maintain operations in the western Caribbean with a United States fleet based upon Puerto Rico and the adjacent islands.[34]

As Ronald Spector has explained, Mahan's doctrines of sea power, and their corollary regarding the need for naval stations, became dominant within U.S. naval circles before 1898. They expressed, among other things, the technological transition from the old wood and sail navy to a new navy based on steam and armor-plated heavy battleships. The modernization of the U.S. navy was already well underway when *The Influence of Sea Power Upon History* was published.[35] Referring to Great Britain, Daniel R. Headrick describes how the development of the steamship Red Sea route to India in the 1830s provoked the acquisition of new colonies. For example, the island of Socotra and, later, Aden, were seized to provide the coaling needs of the *Hugh Lindsay* steamer. Control over Egypt and eventual construction of the Suez Canal were also related to these developments.[36] Maurice de Brossard, the French naval historian, has made a similar point regarding all modern navies and colonial acquisitions in Asia and the Pacific.[37]

The need for naval stations and, consequently, for the retention of Puerto Rico under U.S. control, was also cogently argued by Commander R. B. Bradford in a February 1899 article. He had played a role in persuading president McKinley that a coaling station in Manila presupposed colonial control over the entire Philippine archipelago and not just the island of Luzon, as Manila existed only due to its relationship with the rest of the Philippines.[38] He based his argument for the "acquisition of foreign islands" as naval stations on the requirements of the new naval technology of a navy that aspired to have global reach.

According to Bradford, the new battleships required regular maintenance of their hulls. Their large machinery and coal needs restricted cargo space, while the new rapid-fire guns consumed huge amounts of munitions. Above all, they required large quantities of coal to be able to operate far from their home base. The blockade of Santiago had required a large number of steam colliers, but colliers were expensive, and coaling in the high seas was inconvenient. Bradford pointed out that Dewey could not have returned to the U.S. after the battle of Cavite without taking Manila. To reinforce Dewey with a small naval force, eleven colliers and 40,000 additional tons of coal had been required. Thus, a large fleet was not enough. A fifty-battleship navy could not operate on the coast of China without several intermediary bases, not even with steam colliers.

Concerning the Caribbean, he emphasized that a naval attack against the U.S. would come from the east and could not be repulsed without coal supply stations. He reproduced Mahan's arguments almost verbatim.

> And now let us turn to the south and glance at the map of the West Indies and the Caribbean Sea, located at our very doors. The building of an isthmian canal in the near future is a certainty: it will be a highway between our Atlantic and Pacific coasts, and must be guarded as an army defends its line of communication over which pass its supplies and sinews of war. In [the] future our maritime interests cannot be greater in any part of the world away from our coasts than in the vicinity of the Caribbean Sea and the Isthmus of Panama. It is of paramount importance that we have coaling-stations and depots for supplies located near all the strategic points in the West Indies.[39]

The "strategic points" were related to the maritime passages to the future canal. With regard to the Yucatán and Windward passages, Bradford remarked that the U.S. would have bases in Cuba "now and in the future." Puerto Rico, on the other hand, will be the guardian of the Mona and Anegada passages, without excluding traditional aspirations to control Samaná Bay and St. Thomas as well.

> The next important position is the Mona Passage, between Hayti and Porto Rico. The port of Mayaguez, at the west end of Porto Rico, can be made a fair coaling-station: Samana Bay, Santo Domingo is a better one. Passing on eastwards, next comes the Virgin Passage, which may be controlled by ships supplied from ports at the east end of Porto Rico.[40]

Other contemporary authors –military and civilian– strongly concurred with Bradford's assessment. Edwin Van Dyke Robinson, citing William H. Seward and A. T. Mahan, argued in favor of the acquisition of a large number of bases in the Caribbean and the Pacific to protect an isthmian canal. The list was basically the same as the one contained in Mahan's 1898 memorandum to Secretary Long. Of these, "Cuba is obviously the most important," while "Porto Rico is useful but not vital."[41] Similarly, W. V. Judson, also citing Mahan as the leading authority, underscored in 1902 the importance of Caribbean naval bases. He argued that "no matter how strongly the isthmian canal may be fortified it would, in war, serve us no useful purpose -indeed, through war we might lose it entirely- if our fleet could not control its approaches."[42] Puerto Rico was considered superior to St. Thomas as it could resist a blockade, provided food production and the loyalty of the population were promoted.

Although Major William A. Glassford dissented regarding Puerto Rico's strategic value vis-à-vis St. Thomas, he significantly pointed out that "having acquired the island . . . it is necessary to retain it" and that, therefore, it was necessary to examine "its value as a military post."[43] Finally, Captain William H. Beehler stressed in 1905 that the construction of the Panama Canal and the rise of Japanese naval power, demonstrated in the Russo-Japanese war of that year, required the construction of a fifty-battleship navy by 1914, with one of the five squadrons, composed of nine battleships each, to be based in the Caribbean. Thus, the construction of the Panama Canal, of a large blue-water navy based on battleships, and the acquisition of naval stations and island possessions both in the Atlantic and Pacific — as necessary conditions to commercial expansion and world power status— became strongly associated in navalist discourse during the late 19th and early 20th century.

Eugene P. Lyle's 1906 article, "Our Experience in Porto Rico," illustrates how the navalist perspective shaped even contemporary civilian views on the island. His article, a textbook case of the White Man's Burden argument, painted a dreadful picture of the U.S. colonial experience in Puerto Rico. He complained of the natives' "pathetic impracticality." They were also "tricksters," "Spigs," [i. e. Spiks] "public plunderers," "an ingrate people," and "children," for which "the ugly fact of the Puerto Rican's hard name remains."[44] Additionally, the mixing of races "should be regarded with as much horror in Porto Rico as it always has been in the South." He specifically complained of the politicians, the teachers (they "betrayed us"), the mayors, and the workers.

The accompanying photographs depicted all the U.S. had done for "ungrateful" Puerto Rico: American schools, primary manual training, an American Catholic bishop, trolley cars, Puerto Rican infantry soldiers, a splendid naval station at Culebra, tobacco production, and large sugar mills, among others. Despite all this, the U.S. colonial administration was also judged highly deficient due to congressional neglect, "incompetent or tactless American officials," "absenteeism" of sugar producers, legislative restrictions on large landholdings, the maritime shipping monopoly, and so on. His main prescriptions for a better colonial policy consisted of intensified efforts at Americanization through education, and racial segregation for the "regeneration of a people." Economically, Puerto Rico was a liability as "the increase in our trade is not in proportion to what the island costs us." Inevitably, the author rhetorically asks why the U.S. should hold the island, answering that the reason is only strategic and that an "empty island" would have been preferable.

> The true answer to the question is that we are getting an island that we need. Our problem would be simple enough, and we ourselves would be much happier, were there no trade at all, which is to say, were there no islanders. We were not

yearning to make Porto Rico a training school for Americanization when we took it over. We simply have to have the
island for strategic purposes. And, for the same reason, we
could not afford to let anybody else have it. Spain had Porto
Rico because of the opportunities it gave to exploit the natives. But we, on the other hand, give the natives full value
for the strategic advantages that come from the occupation. It
is a fair bargain. . .

We need Porto Rico to guard the approaches to the Canal. We
have not St. Thomas. We have not Santo Domingo. But between the two we must control the two passages that open
the Canal to fleets from Europe . . .[45]

By 1899 and 1901 respectively, the area of Isla Grande in San Juan
harbor and a large portion of Culebra had been expropriated for naval
purposes by a presidential decree. The Treaty of Paris had ceded to the
U.S. additional military real estate in San Juan consisting of the Spanish "Crown Lands." U.S. occupation of Cuba was not ended until
Guantánamo had been ceded. Military control over the isthmus of
Panama was obtained in 1903 and, in 1917, St. Thomas was bought
from Denmark. It is significant that U.S. protectorates, semi-colonies
and colonies in the Caribbean corresponded with those countries to
which greater strategic importance was attached, i.e., mainly Panama
and Nicaragua in Central America, and the "northern tier" islands of
the Caribbean (Cuba, Haiti, the Dominican Republic, Puerto Rico and
the Virgin Islands).

Thus, one would be mistaken to argue, as has a Puerto Rican historian, that Puerto Rico passed into U.S. control due to a request to president McKinley made by a Puerto Rican delegation.[46] Arturo Morales
Carrión, on the other hand, while mentioning existing commercial interests, places great emphasis on strategic considerations: "Naval supremacy
was the key element, and in an age of steamships this implied coaling
stations at key places."[47] Likewise, Thomas McCormick has persuasively
explained, with regard to the Pacific, the considerable weight of strategic military considerations in the acquisition of an insular empire.[48] David
Challener has developed a similar argument, but applied it more broadly
to early U.S. expansionism.[49]

The Mahanian geostrategic paradigm on the Caribbean and Puerto Rico also became dominant in the U.S. Army during the 20th century, as Army War College documents demonstrate. Army thinking understandably added a new element to Puerto Rico's strategic value. Apart from its geographic location, it was also seen as a source of military personnel. Colonel Guy V. Henry, Jr., the son of former military governor of Puerto Rico, General Guy V. Henry, participated in the drafting of a document entitled "Intelligence Summary of the Estimate of the United States" for the 1920-1921 General Staff College course. The document stressed the importance of defending the "West India islands" and the role played by Puerto Rico in wireless and cable communications. It argued that Cuba and Puerto Rico could provide their own garrisons. In the case of Puerto Rico, the study estimated that there were 222,762 white and 52,238 black males of military age, of which more than 100,000 were fit for combat service and over 20,000 for limited military service. It recommended that the existing garrison of 80 officers and 2,811 men should be trebled to 238 officers and 6,038 men. With regard to Haiti and Santo Domingo the document stated that "the population consists mainly of negroes and mulattoes" and "the available manpower would be of little military value except in the form of labor troops."[50]

The suitability of Puerto Ricans as combat troops was always a controversial issue in Army War College discussions and strongly colored by racial considerations. Colonel S. C. Vestal lectured in 1924 on "The use in battle of allies, auxiliaries, colored troops, and troops raised in the insular possessions." He argued that "troops raised after the outbreak of war in disaffected territory and territory occupied by backward races are almost invariably loyal to the foreign power." However, large numbers of trained reservists in dependent territories posed obvious dangers. In case of war or insurrection, colonial troops should be used on a fifty-fifty basis with U.S. troops. For use abroad, "native units" should be employed "on the principles recommended for negro troops."[51] A 1935 study considered Puerto Rican "whites" suitable for military service, but not the "colored inhabitants," whose use "should be restricted to employment as common laborers."[52] Other documents recommended using colored troops as "labor in the tropics." In 1938, a Major Joseph L. Ready claimed that "the Puerto Rican negro is like the other West Indian negroes, an excitable, lazy, inefficient person of low intelligence and very little courage."[53]

The 1920-1921 course at the Army War College produced another document entitled "Survey of the Vital Strategic Areas of the United States and Its Possessions" that stressed the "vast importance" of the Panama Canal and the consequent need to control all the entrances to the Caribbean Sea. It remarked that all the Larger Antilles, except Jamaica, were "possessions or protectorates" of the U.S. and that Trinidad should be seized if necessary. Regarding Puerto Rico, it was pointed out that it was important on account of:

> (1) Vieques Sound as a Fleet Rendezvous, covering Anegada Passage and the passages south towards Trinidad.
> Considerable military assistance would be forthcoming, particularly in Porto Rico, with her two infantry regiments, one regular army, and the other national guard.

> The strategic importance of the West Indies as an outpost covering the Panama Canal is apparent. The controlling factors are the passes through the Islands and naval bases. The present weakness is in the possession by a possible enemy of Jamaica and Trinidad.[54]

Twelve years later the perception regarding the strategic importance of Puerto Rico and of the entire Caribbean region had not changed. In a lecture entitled "The Caribbean Sea," General W. W. Harts used Mahan's concept of the American Mediterranean.[55] All the islands of the north were "bound to us by definite treaty, by ownership or interest. They contribute to our commercial and naval strength in these waters." European ownership of Caribbean islands was considered a problem and, consequently, British and French islands should be purchased in exchange of war debts. The following passage evokes an updated Mahan.

> Cuba, freed from the rule of Spain by America in 1898, Porto Rico, also our prize in that war, the Virgin Islands bought in 1917 from Denmark, have together become the potential guardians of the American interests in the Caribbean. They are the watch-towers of future American expansion in trade. The present economic life of the United States is bound up in the continued dominance of our commerce over these waters.

> The Panama Canal has added a new meaning to this sea as
> the Suez Canal brought earlier to the Mediterranean. New
> lines of commerce since the Isthmus of Panama was pierced
> have filled the West Indian waters with streams of valuable
> and growing traffic. These lanes of trade have multiplied un-
> til now the Caribbean is the crossways of a world commerce
> of uncalculated value.[56]

Similar views were expounded by Navy Commander C. E. Van Hook
in a 1934 memorandum to the Assistant Commander of the Army War
College. The best locations for advanced fleet bases were Samaná Bay
and Vieques Sound, while Guantánamo and Culebra "offer the best fa-
cilities for subsidiary bases and should be developed during peace time."
In addition to the strategic value of Caribbean possessions, Van Hook
underscored that U.S. protectorates ("nominal republics") ensured access to additional bases in case of an emergency. These were "Cuba, Haiti,
San Domingo (sic), Panama and Nicaragua." He also included, among
U.S. possessions, the "Nicaraguan Canal Zone" and the Little and Great
Corn Islands. A notation in the document indicated that the Army's War
Plans Division, Judge Advocate General and Bureau of Insular Affairs,
the Navy's War Plan Division of the Office of the Chief of Naval Operations, and the State Department concurred with its views.[57]

By 1940, an Army War College study called Puerto Rico the "hub
of a wheel." Together with Guantánamo and the Virgin Islands, it was
considered of "strategic importance in the defense of our continental
coast and the Panama Canal."[58] The document mentioned the creation
of the Puerto Rico Department of the Army in July 1939 and recommended augmenting all Army forces in Puerto Rico to war strength to
form a reinforced triangular division. It cited the Commanding General of the Puerto Rico Department as recommending that intelligence
activities specifically aimed at the Nationalist Party should be strengthened, but noted that this party "is now in decadence and should not
furnish any material hazard to the military effort in an emergency."[59]
The possibility of imposing Martial Law was discussed, but it would be
decreed only if civilian cooperation was not forthcoming. It also expressed
prevalent military opinion regarding the combat value of Puerto Rican
military personnel.

Combat value. Officers of the United States Army who have
served with the 65th Infantry, with white American Officers
and native Puerto Rican enlisted men, are in disagreement
concerning the combat value of the native troops. All of these
officers who have been consulted agree on one point with reference to these troops and that is that they are apparently good
parade ground troops, neat in appearance and shoot their
weapons well.

It will be observed that the officers are generally well educated, both as regards civilian and military schooling.[60]

Another document highlighted the huge defense construction project
that was under way in Puerto Rico, specifically mentioning the dredging of
San Juan harbor, and the construction of a submarine base, a dry dock, fifteen auxiliary airfields and twelve National Guard armories. The author,
Lieutenant Philip S. Wood, also expressed concern with the possibility of
sabotage and the consequent need of assuaging pro-independence leaders.

This in turn brings us to the requirement which concerns sabotage . . . There is not a large European Foreign element in
Puerto Rico and, as far as I know, there is not an existing organization of nationals sympathetic to Black [Germany]. As
in all Latin countries, politics thrive on the Island, but the bulk
of the peon class is led by a comparatively small group of
political leaders. As to the amount of sabotage to be expected,
I believe this would depend much on the type of promises
that might be made to the Independencia leaders in regard to
granting freedom of the Island in the event of a coalition victory. I question the reception that a Black promise would have
and am inclined to the belief that while the talk of Independence in Puerto Rico has much popular appeal, on the other
hand, the local *políticos* are astute enough to realize that they
will get more from the United States than they would from a
problematical Black granted independence.[61]

The Military in the Founding of the Colonial State

Franklin Delano Roosevelt's decision to name an admiral, albeit
recently retired, to the governorship of Puerto Rico in 1939 did not represent a departure from established styles of colonial governance with

regard to the political role of the military. At most, it signified a shift from army to naval political preponderance. The U.S. military not only attached great strategic value to Puerto Rico, as we have seen, but were also conspicuously involved in colonial administration, despite the formally civilian character of the political institutions. Furthermore, strategic military considerations had exercised a powerful influence in shaping U.S.-Puerto Rico relations in other historical junctures before the Second World War.

After the 1898 invasion, the island was governed by U.S. Army officers from August 1898 to May 1900.[62] This period of military government, though brief, was of great significance, since the Spanish administrative structure was dismantled and substituted with new political and legal institutions. With a few adjustments, the latter would be inherited by the subsequent civilian regime established by the Foraker Act of 1900.[63] The Foraker Act itself closely followed the recommendations of military officers and the War Department.

In a sense, the military were the "Founding Fathers" of the new colonial state. H. K. Carroll, who was entrusted by president McKinley in 1898 to head a commission of inquiry into Puerto Rican conditions under the military regime, underscored the "revolutionary" character of military rule and the continuity it would have with subsequent civil administration.

> When Congress gives Porto Rico civil government the change will not be revolutionary. The revolution has already been anticipated under the military *régime*. The military governors have exercised much the same powers which Spanish governors-general had, but in a different way and with a different end in view . . . The American military governors have administered both insular and municipal affairs, decreed changes in the codes, and reorganized the courts.[64]

It must be remembered that the U.S. Army had no previous experience in the administration of overseas territories. General Guy V. Henry, in an article on his governorship of Puerto Rico, emphasized this lack of previous colonial experience.

> It was an entirely new duty for American Army officers. There was no precedent in the experience of those so suddenly

placed in charge of this our first real colony, upon which their policy could be based.[65]

Thus, the manner in which the military went about this task of setting the foundations of the new colonial state was influenced by two previous experiences in the control of civilian populations: 1) their participation in the pacification and administration of Indian peoples, and 2) the involvement of the army in the repression of the urban working-class movement from the 1870s to the 1890s.

As Walter Williams has argued, many of the officers (and some civilians as well) who were directly involved in the administration of new colonies had previously participated in the Indian campaigns and the administration of Indian affairs. The model for the Division of Insular Affairs of the War Department—later the Bureau of Insular Affairs—was the Bureau of Indian Affairs.[66] The Mexican War and the recruiting of black troops (186,017 men) during the Civil War (a Bureau of Colored Troops was established in 1863) also placed the Army in contact with other subordinate ethnic groups.[67] Finally, the regular army was increasingly used to quell labor unrest in mines and eastern cities during the late 19th century.

> Between 1870 and 1900, the National Guard was mobilized some 150 times to cope with industrial disputes (though, significantly, not once did it serve under federal authority, as the Constitution allows). Only when the militia proved ineffectual did Federal troops intervene –in eight states during the Great Strike of 1877, in eleven states during the labor disturbances of 1894, and in the Couer d'Alene mining region of Idaho on three occasions during the 1890s.[68]

The career of General Nelson A. Miles was emblematic of many high-ranking army officers who participated in the war of 1898.[69] Miles began his military service during the Civil War as a First Lieutenant by raising a company of seventy men. He rose rapidly to the rank of general, commanding a black regiment and participating in the military government during the "reconstruction." The enormous federal army (a total of 2,666,999 enrolled) was almost completely demobilized after the war, eventually reverting to a compact professional frontier force of about 24,000 men mostly deployed in a chain of forts.[70]

In 1869, Miles was sent to the west to participate in the Red River wars. For over twenty years, Miles served in frontier posts and intermittently fought almost all rebellious Indian tribes. He negotiated several settlements which restricted the tribes to reservations. Miles married the niece of General William Tecumseh Sherman, then commander of the Division of the Missouri, who had directed the war against the Sioux. Sherman's attitude to Indians was not uncommon among military officers. He stated that: "We must act with vindictive earnestness against the Sioux, even to their extermination, men, women and children."[71] His campaign in the South during the Civil War had also been ruthless in the treatment of the civilian population.

In 1890, Miles was named commander of the Division of the Missouri and of the military forces which participated in the Wounded Knee massacre of December of that year. General John R. Brooke, later military governor of Puerto Rico, was commander of the Department of the Platte. Major Guy V. Henry, also to serve as governor of Puerto Rico, was the officer dispatched by General Brooke with reinforcements (the Ninth Cavalry, a "colored" unit) to relieve the embattled Colonel Forsyth. Forsyth's unit, the Seventh Cavalry, formerly commanded by the notorious George Armstrong Custer, had just killed 84 Indian men and boys, 44 women, 16 children and injured 51 others, of which 7 later died, according to official figures. The soldiers lost 25 men and 35 wounded. Some accounts estimate a much higher number (300) of Indian deaths.[72] Military historian Russell F. Wiegley has underscored the genocidal character of the post-Civil War Indian campaigns, calling them the "Annihilation of a People."[73] Brooke and Miles also commanded operations against the Indians immediately following the Wounded Knee massacre. Thus, we find three officers, later to play important military and political roles in Puerto Rico, involved in the repression of the Indians.

Like these three officers, Brigadier General George Davis, the last military governor, began his military career during the Civil War and was subsequently aide to General Sheridan and military instructor at Fort Leavenworth. He also served as an engineer in the Nicaragua Canal Construction Company in 1890. Davis is the only ranking army officer in Puerto Rican administration about whom we have no record of a direct involvement in the Indian wars.[74] Other army officers such as

General Leonard Wood, involved in colonial administration, did have a background of participation in the Indian campaigns. Wood, for example, was a Harvard-educated Army doctor who entered military life by fighting Apaches in Arizona and pursuing Geronimo. He later became military governor of Cuba, governor of the Moro province of the Philippines, Army Chief of Staff, governor of the Philippines, and candidate for the presidential nomination of the Republican Party.[75]

In May 1894, the Pullman railway workers in Chicago, with the support of Eugene V. Debs's American Railway Union, went on strike to protest salary cuts. The General Managers Association responded by dismissing workers who expressed support for the strike, bringing to a halt rail traffic in Chicago. The Cleveland administration sided with the rail managers and urgently summoned General Miles to a meeting at the White House. Attorney General Richard Olney persuaded Cleveland, against Miles's objections, to use regular troops to suppress the strike.[76]

On July 4, Miles took charge of the military operation in Chicago, ordering the dispersal of "mobs . . . even if firearms have to be used." The next day he requested permission to fire at the strikers, mostly foreign-born immigrants, a request he would later repeat. The repression of the strike was a ruthless affair, with additional military forces brought in from Forts Riley and Robinson. A total of 12,000 regular troops joined other security forces (mainly the state militia and the police) in Chicago during the Pullman strike. Miles firmly aligned himself with the railway owners, called Debs a "dictator," and openly displayed nativist prejudices against foreign workers. He saw in the Chicago disturbances the seeds of the Paris Commune and blamed them on "anarchists and socialists." His views were starkly expressed in a *North Atlantic Review* article.

> Men must take sides either for anarchy, secret conclaves, unwritten law, mob violence, and universal chaos under the red or white flag of socialism, on the one hand, or on the side of established government, the supremacy of law, the maintenance of good order, universal peace, absolute security of life and property, the rights of personal liberty, all under the shadow and folds of "Old Glory," on the other.[77]

The repression of the urban working class movement made the military keenly concerned with internal security and the need to construct effective security institutions capable of dealing with civilian unrest. Anarchism became a *bête noir* for ranking Army officers such as Miles.

The campaigns against the Indians and the administration of Indian affairs were manifested among the officer corps in a paternalistic racism. They considered themselves, simultaneously, conquerors and protectors of the Indians.[78] The inexorable march of "progress," an agent in the Army, required the forceful repression of Indian resistance and their confinement in reservations. Once defeated, it was the army's role to protect the "savages" from themselves and from exploitative civilian "special interests." The Indian nations were defined as "wards" of the federal government and, particularly, of the Army, which was entrusted with their guardianship. Paternal tutelage of subject Indian nations became an important dimension of "military honor" for "Indian fighters."

General Miles's autobiographical accounts contain extensive references to Indian society, culture and leaders. They express few regrets of the army's conduct during the Indian wars, while uttering admiration for the Indians' resilience, courage, and attachment to traditional ways.[79] One of Miles's biographers has noted:

> On the one hand, he advocated just treatment for Indians; on the other, he rejected traditional tribal values and urged the tribes' assimilation into white-dominated society. He fought for the abolition of slavery, worked to assist freedmen, and spoke to black groups. But he refused to accept blacks as equals and left his black regiment at the earliest opportunity after the Civil War.[80]

It is interesting to note that a biographical note published on occasion of Guy V. Henry's death, significantly entitled "Guy V. Henry: A Knightly American," celebrated this paternalistic attitude with regard to Puerto Rico. "General Henry never for a moment conceived of Porto Rico as belonging to us for our own sakes. The acquisition of the island meant to him the assumption of a trust on behalf of the inhabitants."[81]

A similar point of view was expressed in 1898 by Captain A. T. Mahan, who believed that army and navy officers, who were accustomed to "dealing with men who are our dependents," were better equipped than civilians to exercise "guardianship" over the new dependencies.[82] Mahan defined the paternal protection of alien subjects, still in "race-childhood," as a corollary of sea power.

> But, where the relations are those of trustee to ward, as are those of any State which rules over a weaker community not admitted to the full privileges of home citizenship, the first test to which measures must be brought is the good of the ward. It is the first interest of the guardian, for it concerns his honor. Whatever the part of the United States in the growing conflict of European interests around China and the east, we deal here with equals, and may battle like men; but our new possessions, with their yet minor races, are the objects only of solicitude . . .

> Sea power, as a national interest, commercial and military, rests not upon fleets only, but also upon local territorial bases in distant commercial regions. It rests upon them most securely when they are extensive, and when they have a numerous population bound to the sovereign country by those ties of interest which rest upon the beneficence of the ruler; of which beneficence power to protect is not the least factor. Mere just dealing and protection, however, do not exhaust the demands of beneficence towards alien subjects, still in race-childhood. The firm, but judicious remedying of evils, the opportunities for fuller and happier lives, which local industries and local development afford, these also are a part of the duty of the sovereign power.[83]

The insistence of the military governors on the need to establish highly centralized state structures under the tight control of the federal government, with extremely restricted institutional spaces for the representation of Puerto Rican political forces, was related to this racist ideology. It may also explain the rejection of full annexation and extension of U.S. citizenship. An immature people required an indeterminate period of authoritarian rule under what Elihu Root called a "strong and guiding hand" to learn republican civic virtues. General Davis justified his recommendation for a "strong central power" with the following explanation:

> Three-fourths of the people living in Porto Rico are of the very
> lowest class of those rated as civilized, and their moral senses
> are blunted. The process by which their moral consciences
> may be developed is one of slow application and develop-
> ment. Meanwhile, a strong central power should exist,
> equipped to cope with these masses of ignorant, half-starved
> inhabitants, and to protect the persons and property of the
> well-disposed whether poor or rich.[84]

According to Morales Carrión, most of the "revolutionary" institutional changes under military government were undertaken by General
Henry, while the report submitted by General Davis substantially shaped
subsequent colonial policy toward Puerto Rico. The former described
his approach to colonial administration as "giving [the people] kinder-
garten instruction in controlling themselves without allowing them too
much liberty." He thought that Puerto Rico should be administered by
the military "for some time to come."[85]

In an account of his governorship, Henry mentioned four important
policy issues that confronted him: "unequal taxation oppressing the poor;
the financial question; the necessity for an insular police; and the extreme laxity of morals."[86] The latter two issues were related to "law and
order," and internal security. The concern for internal security may explain the urgency felt for rapidly establishing native police and military
forces which could serve as buffers between the regular army and the
population. Difficulties encountered by the U.S. military in establishing
control over the civilian population also contributed to the establishment of native police and military entities.

When the Spanish security forces (the *Guardia Civil* and the *Orden
Público*) were disbanded in October 1898, irregular bands of armed peasants, known as the *partidas sediciosas*, sprang up in the countryside.[87]
General Brooke, in command of the island, ordered General Henry, in
charge of the district of Ponce, to dispatch troops to the interior of the
island to suppress the *partidas*. Four companies of the First Kentucky
Volunteer Infantry were sent into the mountains, but their lack of knowledge of the language and the people made them ineffective. Later Henry
established military commissions in San Juan, Ponce, Mayagüez, and
Arecibo to try the rural bandits and sent a full regiment of cavalry to the

interior. These efforts also proved unfruitful.[88] General Davis explained the problem in the following terms:

> The difficulties encountered by the U.S. Army in stopping these outrages were very great. All was strange to the officers and men — the country, the people, the laws and the language.
>
> It was sometimes impossible for the troops to follow the marauders to their haunts or to discover them, and it was very difficult to apprehend the criminals.[89]

General Henry recommended dealing with internal security by establishing a military garrison with Puerto Rican troops under U.S. officers and a police force similarly organized.

> In regard to the military on the island, it will be necessary to maintain some troops there, as is now done in the western part of the United States, simply as permanent posts of regular soldiers; but the force should mainly consist of Porto Ricans — possibly, for a time, officered in the higher grades by regular army officers. The success of the battalion already organized by an act of Congress has been assured, and there is no reason why it should not be duplicated.
>
> The maintenance of law and order in the island should be placed principally in the hands of the insular police, whose work during my stay in Porto Rico met with my own and the people's entire approval. The insular police is made up of young men of good family, and the record already established by the force proves its efficiency.[90]

Civilian functionaries involved in the administration of the new colonies shared the racist paternalism of the military. Elihu Root, in his 1899 Annual Report as Secretary of War, argued that Puerto Rico had to "slowly learn" the lessons of self-government, which was not a "matter of intellectual apprehension" but required a change of "character and habits of thought and feeling." Meanwhile, it would require "a course of tuition under a strong and guiding hand."[91] William Howard Taft, sent by Root to the Philippines as head of the Second Philippines Commission, wrote to John H. Harlan that *filipinos* were no more than "grown up children" who would need fifty or a hundred years to understand "Anglo-Saxon liberty."[92] When Theodore Roosevelt visited Puerto Rico in 1906, after observing the progress of the construction work of the Panama Canal, remarked that "there is something pathetic and childlike about the people."[93] The ubiquitous metaphor of childhood became a justification for a strong colonial tutelage with a prominent political role for the military. As Efrén Rivera has explained, this racist outlook was enshrined as legal doctrine in the *Insular Cases* that defined the juridical status of the new territories.[94]

This was the official position of the War Department, expressed by Secretary Elihu Root, in the Congressional debate on the Foraker Act. The War Department proposals were based on the reports of Generals Brooke, Henry, and Davis, and of the Insular Commission that had been named in 1899 by the former Secretary of War Russell Alger. General Davis had suggested emulating the Crown Colony arrangement imposed by the British in Trinidad, under which it was governed by a Governor and an Executive Council of five members and three appointed natives.[95] H. K. Carroll's recommendations for broader self-government were not heeded.

Root's conception of civil government was endorsed by President McKinley and transmitted to Congress in his message of December 5, 1899. In McKinley's proposal the only sphere of Puerto Rican elected representation would be the municipalities, whose power had already been severely undermined. During the hearings Henry G. Curtis, head of the War Department's Insular Commission, and General George Davis argued against self government. General Roy Stone even suggested there should be no elections at all in four to five years.[96]

As María Eugenia Estades has argued, though the Foraker Act departed in some ways from Root's scheme, it bore the imprint of the military and the War Department.[97] Representative Sereno Payne later claimed it had been written by Root. It vested legislative powers in an Executive Council composed of functionaries named by the President. Most of the legal system was also under the control of the president or the governor. The powers of the elected assembly, the only significant concession to self-government, were extremely limited. Representative Jones, during the discussion of the law, stated that it concentrated power on a carpetbag executive council and a carpetbag governor, and that it constituted "a scheme for despotic government."[98] It was, indeed, a highly centralized and authoritarian arrangement. In addition, it left the military in control, not only of the military forces, but also of the "civilian" police.[99]

Furthermore, the first civilian governor appointed by McKinley under the Foraker Act, Charles Allen, was strongly related to the military establishment. Before coming to Puerto Rico, Allen had been serving as Assistant Secretary of the Navy, a post he reluctantly relinquished at the president's behest. He came to Puerto Rico accompanied by a naval aide.[100] Allen was a strong promoter of sugar investments and thought that "every acre of rich sugar land should be developed."[101] He later became president of the Appleton National Bank and of the American Sugar Refining Corporation.

More broadly, the centralized and authoritarian political institutions established by the military and the War Department were the political framework under which Puerto Rico was rapidly transformed into a sugar monoculture plantation economy. It should be noted that Secretary of War Root had previously served as a lawyer of the sugar trust and that sugar was considered one of the few strategic commodities in which the U.S. was not fully self-sufficient.[102] Sugar interests had been instrumental in reorganizing the economy and annexing a strategically valuable island such as Hawaii. Sidney Mintz has underscored this connection between military rule and sugar in the Caribbean.[103]

The liaison of the governorship with the military continued after Allen's departure. Two other Assistant Secretaries of the Navy, Beekman Winthrop and Theodore Roosevelt Jr., served as governors of Puerto Rico. Winthrop, who replaced Allen's successor William Hunt in 1904, came to Puerto Rico after serving as judge in the Philippines during the military suppression of the Aguinaldo rebellion. He had been recommended to William Howard Taft by Theodore Roosevelt. After leaving Puerto Rico in 1907, he was named Assistant Secretary of the Navy. Winthrop was succeeded in this post by Franklin Delano Roosevelt. Governor Theodore Roosevelt Jr. (1929-1932) had previously occupied the post of Assistant Secretary of the Navy. He was also a Lieutenant Colonel in the reserve and would die in combat during the Normandy invasion of the Second World War.[104] Three other military officers with previous colonial experience occupied the governorship during the century: Colonel

George Colton (1909-1913), General Blanton Winship (1934-1939), and Admiral William D. Leahy (1939-1940). But even a governor with a civilian background, such as Horace M. Towner (1923-1929), saw Puerto Rico from the perspective of the Mahanian paradigm. During the debate on the 1917 Jones Bill, which made Puerto Ricans U.S. citizens, he stated the following:

> We are never to give up Porto Rico for, now that we have completed the Panama Canal, the retention of that island becomes very important to the safety of the canal, and in that way to the safety of the Nation itself. It helps to make the Gulf of Mexico an American lake. I again express my pleasure that this bill grants these people citizenship.[105]

A contemporary observer, journalist Eliseo Combas Guerra, made an incisive description of the military atmosphere that pervaded the Governor's Mansion in 1938 under General Winship.

> Here in the Palace of Santa Catalina khaki predominates . . . Winship is a retired general . . . The interim governor Colom is a Colonel of the National Guard . . . The nervous Walter Wilgus and his namesake, the champion Walter Cope, served as lieutenants during the last war . . . And I, as Second Lieutenant of the Reserves, "honoris causa" . . . place my column at the service of the fatherland . . .[106]

Constructing the Internal Security Structures

During the period of military government, new police and military forces were organized with Puerto Rican recruits and under the command of army officers. The police were organized by Lieutenant Frank Fletcher, who was named Chief of Insular Police, and had a Puerto Rican Assistant Chief, Luis Berríos. According to General Davis, the police was built along military lines: "While this force was not part of the Army, it was in reality a military body and subject at all times to the orders of the military governor."[107] Davis also emphasized that the new police force was modeled after the Spanish security forces since "Anglo-Saxon countries do not tolerate the existence of such a police force, but all Latin countries are accustomed to maintain a similar body."[108] It was a gendarmerie or constabulary force.

S. S. Tuthill noted that General Henry took the initiative to create this native force "as the marauders must be captured by men as familiar with the people and the country as the criminals were" and that he "doubtless had in mind his experience with the Indians."[109] He also underscored the collaboration of the towns and large property owners with the police, "for whose protection the force was formed."[110] By the end of the military regime, the force comprised 475 officers and men. It was kept under the command of military officers until after World War II.[111]

In March 1899, soon after the establishment of the Insular Police and also on the initiative of General Henry, a battalion of native troops was established. It was used to repress the *partidas sediciosas*.[112] A second battalion was authorized in February 1900, and the two battalions were designated as the Porto Rico Regiment, U.S. Volunteers Infantry. The Porto Rico Regiment became the only native military force -apart from the militarized police force- for two decades. By 1900, the regiment comprised about 900 officers and men, compared to a U.S. regular army garrison of 700. It was reorganized in May 1901 and renamed as the "Provisional Regiment." In 1908, it was assimilated into the regular army under the name Porto Rico Infantry Regiment, U.S. Army, and a third battalion was added in 1916.[113] The formation of the police and the army regiment in Puerto Rico had the similar purpose of pacifying the countryside, as had the establishment of the *Guardia Rural* in Cuba under U.S. Army auspices during 1899.[114]

The place the military occupied in the symbolic pecking order of the colonial state can be glimpsed from the 4th of July parade held in 1906. Its organizing Executive Committee consisted of four Puerto Ricans and six members from the U.S., including Colonel H.K. Bailey. The Parade Committee was composed of three military officers and two civilians, all from the U.S., and was presided over by Colonel Bailey, who was the Grand Marshall. The program of the parade was the following: 1) a detachment of mounted police, 2) a detachment of policemen on foot, 3) the Grand Marshall and his aides, which included an officer each from the Army, the Navy, and the USMC followed by a Mister Lewis J. Proctor and four Puerto Ricans, 4) the Grand Army of the Republic, 5) the band of the Porto Rico Battalion, 6) the Marines, 7) a battalion of the Porto Rico Regiment, 8) the sailors of the *USRC Algonquin*, 9) the police band, 10) a police battalion, 11) musicians, 12) the Fire Department, 13) civic groups (Masons, Elks, Odd Fellows, and workers of the *Federación Regional* and *Federación Libre*), 14) music of the *Beneficencia*, 15) pupils of the *Beneficencia*, 16) citizens on foot, and 17) citizens in cars.[115]

Still, the U.S. military structure in Puerto Rico was relatively small until the First World War. In Puerto Rico the U.S. did not have to face an uprising as in the Philippines. The main internal security concerns before 1917 were rising labor agitation and strikes by tobacco and sugar workers. These were controlled mainly by the police, with the Porto Rico Regiment serving as an internal security reserve. The Navy, although acquiring large tracts of land in San Juan and Culebra, did not develop major base facilities in Puerto Rico during this period, apart from naval communications installations.[116] Consequently, military expenditure in 1901 and 1910, for example, was less than $300,000 and less than one percent of the Gross National Product.[117] However, World War I produced a major increase and restructuring of the military institutions which was to endure into the 1930s.

Since 1905, persistent efforts had been made by different governors to create a National Guard. In 1906, an attempt was made to create such a force but it did not have congressional approval and was disbanded.[118] Governor George R. Colton, a military officer himself, was particularly insistent in this regard. In 1910 he argued that such a force would not only contribute to internal security, but also constitute an important instrument for "Americanization." In a memorandum prepared by J. R. Pierson, a U.S. businessman residing in San Juan, and forwarded by Colton to the Bureau of Insular Affairs (BIA), the rationale for such a force was explained in the following terms:

Militia in Porto Rico

FIRST: Militia composed of *enlisted native Porto Ricans* (with American and Porto Rican militia officers, or regular officers detailed upon request of the Governor of Porto Rico), would have the following good results.

(a) It would strengthen loyalty and patriotism.

(b) It would give the young business men of Porto Rico the same opportunity that American citizens have to serve their country, and also a knowledge of the U.S. military tactics, which could be of great benefit to the Federal Government in case of need in the tropics, of acclimated troops.

(c) As the drills will be conducted in English this would be of assistance and encouragement to the Puerto Ricans to learn the English language . . .[119]

Plans for the formation of a National Guard had to be kept in abeyance until 1916, due to the existence of legal obstacles relating to Puerto Rico's definition as a non-incorporated territory, as well as to the absence of a clear policy decision by the BIA.[120] In 1916, the BIA finally approved the scheme and detailed a U.S. Colonel for that purpose. Large strikes by sugar workers in 1915 and 1916 were possibly a factor in the decision to create this additional military force. By April 1917, the Puerto Rican legislature had approved a Military Code of Puerto Rico drafted by the BIA. However, once the U.S. entered the war, the BIA decided to postpone the creation of the National Guard in order to recruit the largest possible number of Puerto Ricans into the regular army. With the conclusion of the war, Governor Yager, using the argument of growing labor agitation, once more demanded the final constitution of the force. The National Guard -consisting of one regiment of infantry and a squadron of cavalry- was formed in November 1919.[121]

U.S. involvement in 1917 in World War I enhanced Puerto Rico's military importance, both due to its perceived naval importance in the Caribbean and as a potential source of military personnel. The approval of the Jones Act, which reformed the governmental structure and extended U.S. citizenship to Puerto Ricans, cannot be understood without taking the war into account.[122] U.S. citizenship and measured political concessions were expected to strengthen the loyalty of the population. Furthermore, Puerto Ricans, hitherto citizens of Puerto Rico or "nationals," could not be drafted within the legal framework of the National Defense Act of 1916. Arturo Morales Carrión has accurately explained the context of this decision:

> Much of the world was at war, and defense considerations now impinged on many decisions of the Administration. Beyond the moral duties of the self-imposed tutor, there was the strategic imperative, the great basic consideration which had led to the 1898 landing.[123]

In March 1917, Woodrow Wilson signed the Jones Act, and by April 5 the U.S. officially entered the war.

The following month a selective service law was passed and made applicable to Puerto Rico, with Selective Service Boards being organized by June.[124] That same month, 11 officers and 1,389 soldiers of the Porto Rico Regiment were sent to Panama to garrison the Canal Zone. A total of 18,000 Puerto Ricans were drafted or recruited during World War I. War Department plans to train the draftees in the U.S., particularly in a camp in South Carolina, created a sharp controversy of overt racial connotations in the U.S. and Puerto Rico.[125] Also, a Home Guard of 1,500 men was organized under the command of Lieutenant Colonel Orval P. Townshend for the duration of the war.[126] Governor Yager and the main Puerto Rican political parties represented in the House of Delegates, including leaders of the pro-independence sector of the *Partido Unión*, demanded that military forces be brought up to brigade size once the war ended.[127]

Though this demand was not met, the large pool of trained military personnel was organized in 1922 into reserve units comprising a brigade, three regiments, and several companies. Also, the *American Legion* was established in September 1919 by a small number of veterans, reaching a membership of 1,500 by 1931.[128] Likewise, compulsory ROTC programs were formally established in the University of Puerto Rico,[129] as well as the *Citizens Military Training Camps* (CMTC), for the military training of youths. The latter were military summer camps where about 300 to 400 young people trained yearly. They were an important source for recruitment into the 65th Infantry Regiment (as the Porto Rico Regiment was named after World War I) during the 1920s and 1930s.[130]

During the 1920s, the War Department began to consider plans to substantially reduce its military forces in Puerto Rico. These plans met with the entrenched opposition of Governor Horace Towner (1923-1929). In 1926, Towner argued that Puerto Rico was a "special case" since military demobilization could worsen unemployment and sharpen social conflicts.[131] With the onset of the economic crisis in 1929, the War Department decided to completely demobilize the 65th Infantry Regiment. Towner once again opposed the plan, now with greater vehemence. He argued that it would jeopardize U.S. influence in the Caribbean at a critical juncture and leave 7,500 people without sustenance, fostering pro-independence feelings.

> Here at this strategic juncture where the influence and prestige of the United States for the whole Caribbean region is involved, it would seem to me the height of folly to abandon it. I suggest on this line the Department of State be consulted. I am sure the proposition would not find much favor there . . .

> The effects of the presence of the Regiment as an Americanizing agency . . . [are] very great. The independence demand had almost ceased to be heard but there are signs of its revival. The removal of the Regiment would strengthen greatly that sentiment. The training of the CMTC and ROTC has been especially helpful. They know what the U.S. means and what the flag stands for, and the general educational influence is far stronger than in the United States.[132]

Though the scheme to disband the 65th Infantry was abandoned, by 1931 the War Department considered eliminating one of its three battalions. This, too, was opposed by the BIA. In 1933, Governor Robert Gore proposed an ambitious plan for providing military training to 60,000 Puerto Rican youths as a means of "Americanizing" them. He also asked for the strengthening of existing military forces. However, by 1933, a year of intense political and labor conflicts, War Department funds had dropped from $1.7 to $1 million.[133]

Despite fiscal limitations, a complex security structure had been established by the 1930s that embraced several military and police organizations. The 65th Infantry Regiment, the main regular army garrison, comprised two active and one reserve battalion. The National Guard had a regiment (the 295th Infantry) with two active battalions. Another regiment was formed in 1923 (the 296th Infantry) and reorganized in June 1936 (soon after the assassination of police chief Col. Francis Riggs by two nationalist youths) bringing it to two-battalion strength. By late 1939, the 65th Infantry had about 1,800 men, and the National Guard regiments an additional 4,000 (including the reserve battalions of both forces).[134] To this must be added the CMTC program based in Fort Buchanan and the compulsory ROTC program at the Río Piedras and Mayaguez campuses of the University of Puerto Rico.

The police, under military control and organized along military lines, was increased by 200 in 1934 to deal with the large number of strikes by sugar workers and other groups. By 1935, it had 665 men. Another 200 policemen were recruited immediately after Police Chief Colonel Francis Riggs's death in early 1936. The police was armed with fifty machine guns and trained by National Guard officers. Thus, political conflicts in the 1930s led to the strengthening of both the National Guard and the police.[135]

Army officers from the U.S. commanded the 65th Infantry, the National Guard, and the police, and, from 1934, a retired army general held the governorship. The first native police commander was Army Colonel Enrique de Orbeta (considered by U.S. functionaries a "fine Spanish gentleman" rather than a Puerto Rican). He was named in 1936 after the assassination of Colonel Francis E. Riggs. In 1939, Colonel Luis R. Esteves was made Inspector General of the National Guard, the first native officer to hold that post. Major John A. Wilson had held that post uninterruptedly from 1919 to 1938.

A number of military and civilian agencies—mainly the Military Intelligence Division (MID), the Office of Naval Intelligence (ONI), the Federal Bureau of Investigations (FBI), and the Insular Police—carried out intelligence activities that emphasized political surveillance of pro-independence groups.[136] Finally, semi-official groups, such as the American Legion, played an important political support role to the security forces. During the intense political and social conflicts of the 1930s, the existing security structure was often utilized by the state in internal repression, particularly under Governor Blanton Winship.

Aside from the security structure that was constructed during the first three decades of U.S. control in Puerto Rico, the most important mechanism of continued military influence over colonial administration was the War Department's Bureau of Insular Affairs (BIA). In 1909, concerned about conflict with the Puerto Rican leadership of the *Partido Unión*, the Taft administration decided to place Puerto Rico again under the jurisdiction of the army. This arrangement was maintained until 1934, when President Franklin Roosevelt transferred jurisdiction over the island to the Department of the Interior.

The Bureau of Insular Affairs and Colonial Policy

The Foraker Act did not satisfy the aspirations of the main political forces of Puerto Rico, the *Partido Republicano* and the *Partido Federal*, that had fully collaborated with the new metropolitan authorities. General Guy V. Henry had distanced Luis Muñoz Rivera and the *Partido Federal* (which he considered the "Spanish party") from the government, and Governor Charles Allen followed an openly antagonistic policy towards this force. This led to an electoral boycott in 1900 by the *federales*, the largest political force on the island. On the other hand, the new colonial administration openly favored and relied heavily on the *Partido Republicano* of José Celso Barbosa (which General Henry called "the Radical party, representing the masses"). But neither party was granted the broad "self-governing" institutions and U.S. citizenship they demanded.[137] Renowned intellectual Eugenio María de Hostos remarked soon after the approval of the Foraker Act that it "only gives force of law and appearance of constitutional procedure to the fact of the subjection of Puerto Rico by the armed forces of the United States."[138]

By 1904, the *Partido Unión* was founded out of the elements of the *Partido Federal* and discontented elements from the *Partido Republicano*. Its program emphasized self-government and protection of Puerto Rican production to be achieved either through statehood or "an independent nation under a U.S. protectorate."[139] Attempts by the *unionista* leadership to obtain concessions from Theodore Roosevelt had no effect. The *Partido Republicano*, on the other hand, demanded statehood, U.S. citizenship, and "organized territory" status as a transitional arrangement toward statehood that would permit self-government.[140]

The *Partido Unión* obtained a two to one victory in the 1908 elections, gaining control over the House of Delegates and a majority of municipalities. A conflict developed between *unionismo*, within which the pro-independence wing gained ascendancy, and Governor Regis H.

Post, regarding the control of municipalities and the legislative powers of the House of Delegates. Post warned Luis Muñoz Rivera in a document that "an anti-American tendency has begun to emerge in the country."[141] He also asked president Taft to intervene against the *unionista* assembly.[142]

This situation was made more complex by rising labor agitation and strikes. The strikes of 1905 to 1906 had led to a severe restriction of workers' rights to organize and hold public meetings. A labor meeting in April 1906 in Ponce, attended by 6,000 persons, had been forcibly broken up by the Insular Police. During 1908, trade union organization gathered significant momentum.[143] Although a close relationship existed between labor leader Santiago Iglesias and Samuel Gompers' American Federation of Labor, the more radical expressions of the labor movement were a source of concern in Washington. Furthermore, the U.S. was confronting similar political difficulties in the Philippines, where the *Partido Nacionalista* of Manuel Quezón had gained dominance in legislature in 1907 with a platform of "immediate independence" and was involved in a bitter conflict with the administration of Governor Cameron Forbes.[144]

It was in this context that Puerto Rico was brought, in 1909, under the jurisdiction of the War Department's Bureau of Insular Affairs. Taft, in his message to Congress of May 10, 1909, claimed that the Puerto Rican situation was of "unusual gravity" and that the people were "ungrateful." He asked Congress to limit the budgetary powers of the House of Delegates. The Olmsted Amendment to the Foraker Act incorporated Taft's recommendation and authorized the president to place Puerto Rican affairs under the executive agency of his choosing.[145] On July 15, 1909, the president once again placed the island by executive decree under the administration of the BIA.[146]

This brought Puerto Rico under the same arrangement as the Philippines, which had been kept under the BIA when the civil administration was established in 1902. Colonel Frank McIntyre, former Chief of the BIA, later argued that in the case of Puerto Rico, this step had been requested by Governor Beekman Winthrop, who had worked with the BIA during his period in the Philippines.[147] When the Jones Act was approved, Woodrow Wilson signed a new executive order on March 21, 1917 maintaining Puerto Rico under the BIA.[148]

Other developments confirmed that the formal involvement of the War Department in the governance of Puerto Rico represented a hardening of colonial policy. In 1910, Representative Olmsted presented a bill that had the support of the Taft administration. It broadened the authority of the BIA over colonial policy, eliminated the 500 acre restriction on land tenure (as demanded by sugar interests), and sought to close the door to eventual independence. According to Truman Clark, "it was designed to lodge even more areas of the Puerto Rican government in the Bureau of Insular Affairs."[149] It passed the House but died in the Senate.

Upon the resignation of Governor Post in late 1909, Taft named a military officer, Colonel George R. Colton, to the governorship. Colton had been in charge of the customs receiverships in the Philippines and the Dominican Republic. He had been the principal agent of the BIA (which took charge of Dominican customs) and had become deeply involved in Dominican politics during the 1905 intervention. Challener calls him "the Army's man in the Dominican Republic."[150]

Colton and the BIA's "strong and guiding hand" played a major role in weakening and bringing into line the *Partido Unión*, as well as repressing the more radical elements in the labor movement. With the tacit agreement of Santiago Iglesias, Colton used the police to persecute anarchists and radical working class leaders. He stated that anarchist societies had no place in Puerto Rico or in any other territory under the American flag.[151] Mass arrests of alleged anarchists in Caguas, Fajardo, Aguas Buenas, and Humacao were carried out in 1911, and the May Day celebration was replaced by an official Labor Day.[152] Colton also openly intervened in municipal politics, naming ninety assemblymen and nine mayors between 1912 and 1913.[153] The role played by Colonel Colton had many common elements with the policies of General Winship two decades later.

The Bureau of Insular Affairs and the Secretary of War became key policy makers in the colonial administration of Puerto Rico and other territories and protectorates. As they did not form part of the government structure created by the Foraker and Jones Acts, and their actions were not as overt as those of the governor and other U.S.-appointed officials, their importance has been relatively overlooked by historical and political analysts.[154] Truman Clark, however, in his analysis of U.S. policy in Puerto Rico, has noted that the BIA was "the nearest thing the United

States ever had to a colonial office; and in the affairs of Puerto Rico, from 1909 until 1934, it held more power than any other agency of the United States."[155]

U.S. colonial administration of "non-contiguous" territories was shared by the BIA, the Central Division of the Office of the Chief of Naval Operations, and the Interior Department. Incorporated territories destined to become states (Hawaii and Alaska) were administered by the Department of the Interior. Small islands that served as naval enclaves — mainly Samoa, Guam, other possessions in the Pacific, and the Virgin Islands — were placed under naval administration. Of these, the Virgin Islands were eventually transferred to the Department of the Interior in the early 1930s. Finally, the Philippines, Puerto Rico, the Canal Zone, the customs receiverships in the Caribbean, and the occupation governments of protectorates such as Cuba, Haiti, the Dominican Republic, Nicaragua, Veracruz, and others, were under the responsibility of the BIA, which shared this responsibility with the State Department. The BIA often had jurisdictional controversies with the State Department, as in the case of the Dominican Republic. Thus, the BIA was fundamental in overall U.S. Central American and Caribbean policy.

In a 1932 article, General Frank McIntyre, former BIA Chief, tried to play down the power of the BIA vis-à-vis U.S. "non-incorporated" territories. The BIA was under severe criticism in Congress and the press for its role in colonial administration, as it created the "impression" U.S. territories were still under military rule. Quite possibly, McIntyre's arguments regarding the BIA's limited powers and its being above politics and exploitative "special interests", were important ideological mechanisms that justified the BIA's considerable influence.[156] Another reason he gave for retaining colonial policy under the War Department was national defense requirements: "It should go without saying that the requirements of national defense must not be lost sight of in considering the administration of territories *originally acquired for that particular purpose*."[157] He vehemently defended the BIA's record in colonial administration.

> Imperfections may of course be pointed out, but it should be remembered that the supervisory department is not given the power of a dictator. The head of the department may advise and admonish. Unfortunately there have been instances when

advice was not followed and admonition was not heeded. Yet the work of the War Department in the Philippines, in Porto Rico, in the Canal Zone, in Cuba and elsewhere has been well done. If it has fallen short of perfection there remains the satisfaction of remembering that many expert critics predicted that it could not be done at all.[158]

With regard to Puerto Rico, the BIA performed a number of crucial functions. It: 1) advised the president and Congress on colonial policy, 2) coordinated Puerto Rican policy with the Puerto Rico Resident Commissioner, 3) was the official conduit for communications of the governor with the Secretary of War, the president, and other federal agencies, 4) issued directives to the governor on specific issues, 5) drafted legislation to be submitted by the governor to the Puerto Rican legislature, 6) intervened in the appointment of officials to the government of Puerto Rico, circulating personnel with colonial experience from other territories, 7) intervened in political disputes among the Puerto Rican leadership, and mediated in their relationship with the president and federal agencies, 8) centralized information in Washington regarding the island, 9) conducted legal studies through the War Department's office of the Judge Advocate General, 10) collaborated with U.S. non-governmental groups (notably the American Federation of Labor) and corporations with interests in Puerto Rico, 11) monitored specific developments in labor, social and economic policy, and 12) carried out, with other federal agencies, intelligence activities on Puerto Rican politics.[159]

The long periods of incumbency of the military officers who were chiefs of the BIA, the information and network of contacts it possessed, and the power of the military establishment it represented endowed this office with a political clout that went beyond the formal "supervisory" role it claimed to have. The Secretary of War and the Chief of the Bureau were normally present in all important meetings on Puerto Rican policy, including those of the president with delegations of Puerto Rican politicians.

These powers, however, were not absolute and depended on the collaboration of other actors. The nominations of governors Emmet Montgomery Reily (1921-1923) and Robert Gore (June 1933-January 1934), for example, were strictly payments of political debts. Reily provoked the opposition of the BIA as he bypassed the War Department

and corresponded directly with President Harding. He also ignored the
BIA's advice in key decisions. War Department opposition to Reily was
a major factor in his departure from the governorship.

During the debate of the Jones Act in 1917, Congressman John Sharp
Williams remarked that "it was about time we were recognizing the fact
that Porto Rico ought not to be governed by the War Department as if it
were still a military occupation of it."[160] In his 1932 article, General Frank
McIntyre quoted a critical publication of 1921 that made a similar point.

> It has been noted that with the exception of Alaska and Ha-
> waii the administration of our colonies and dependencies is
> under the jurisdiction of our military establishment. However
> effective such administration is mechanically, it is always sub-
> ject to the criticism that the people involved feel that, to a
> certain extent, they continue to live under a military govern-
> ment. It is believed that the separation of such questions from
> the military and naval establishments would do much to im-
> prove the feelings of the people of our dependencies and pos-
> sessions toward the American Government.[161]

In 1932, Luis Muñoz Marín identified Congress and the War Department as the two main Washington power centers concerning Puerto Rico.

> There is a traditional axiom of the warrior, which is also an
> old imperial tactic: divide and rule. The colonial system of
> government in Puerto Rico is designed with diabolical subtlety
> to produce this division, to stimulate, determine and manage
> it. An irresponsible authority, from the seats of Congress or
> the desks of the Department of War of the United States, has
> in its hands to reward or punish the public actions of the
> Puerto Ricans.[162]

Roosevelt named Robert H. Gore to the governorship of Puerto Rico
in June 1933 at the latter's request. He had the support of James A. Farley,
Postmaster General and Chairman of the Democratic National Committee, who managed political appointments in Puerto Rico. Gore had been
an important fundraiser for Roosevelt in Florida during the 1932 campaign and had consistently supported him since 1920 through his three
Florida newspapers (*Ft. Lauderdale Daily News, Sun Record,* and *Sun News*).

He also owned, according to Ruby Black, "the largest mail-order insurance company in the world."[163] His letter requesting the Puerto Rican post was extremely revealing.

> I do want to be governor general of Porto Rico. I have a reason. I go to Florida each winter because I can not stand the cold dry atmosphere of the north due to a rhinitis condition of my throat and nose. Moreover, I have nine children and six of them are still in school, and I want them to have the opportunity to learn Spanish which I believe is going to be important in view of our possibilities in South and Central America.
>
> Moreover, I want to go to Porto Rico as governor general because it gives me the opportunity to do some real constructive work for this country and for the people of those islands.[164]

Gore's governorship, during one of the worst periods of the depression, was a major fiasco. Ernest Gruening has called him a "worse than inept governor."[165] Pedro Albizu Campos, leader of the Nationalist Party, openly challenged him.[166] Gore managed to immediately alienate the Liberal Party. Luis Muñoz Marín conducted an untiring campaign to force his removal.[167] Labor agitation by sugar workers culminated in the launching of an island-wide strike by early December 1933.[168]

Much of the lobbying efforts in favor (the *Coalición* leaders) and against Gore (mainly Muñoz Marín and the Liberal Party) were directed at Secretary of War George Dern and the Acting Chief of the BIA, Creed B. Fox.[169] Other efforts were directed at Eleanor Roosevelt.[170] By late October 1933, the BIA had begun to distance itself from Gore. On November 1 of that year, Ruby Black informed Muñoz that the governor was "on the way out" and about two weeks later cabled him that he should "cease all attacks on Gore at Derns (sic) suggestion stop Don't touch Teddy Roosevelt again strictly confidential."[171] By January 8, 1934, Gore resigned supposedly because of health reasons.

During the crisis with Gore and the high level of political and labor agitation in Puerto Rico in late 1933 and early 1934 that the decision to name General Blanton Winship was made. After his blunder with Gore, Roosevelt could hardly disregard the opinion of the War Department about the governorship of Puerto Rico. Powerful representatives of sugar corporations, such as Jorge Bird Arias and former governor James Beverley, alleged to the War Department that a "state of anarchy" existed in Puerto Rico and asked for a "strong man" as governor. Beverley even suggested the name of General Winship.[172]

Apart from his extensive colonial experience,[173] Winship's hard-line attitude towards Puerto Rico was known, as he had recommended, as Judge Advocate General of the Army, the prosecution of the Nationalist Party leadership for a bond issue of the Republic of Puerto Rico offered in Wall Street.[174] Other considerations, such as the ongoing Cuban crisis, may have influenced in this decision. In any case, as Ernest Gruening has emphasized, the decision was made by the Secretary of War and President Roosevelt following the BIA's advice, which corresponded to the president's naval proclivities.

> Puerto Rico had recently suffered a worse than inept governor, Robert Gore, appointed through Jim Farley's effort as a reward for a campaign contribution and the unwavering six Puerto Rican votes for Roosevelt at the Chicago convention. Gore was forced to resign after six months and Roosevelt wisely decided not to pay campaign debts with the office again. The Insular Bureau of the War Department, still in charge, secured the appointment, in February 1934, of Major-General Blanton Winship, just retired as Judge-Advocate General.

> I had, after Gore's departure, forwarded to the President, Muñoz Marin's recommendation that a qualified Puerto Rican, Martin Travieso, be named governor . . . But Roosevelt was imbued with a strong naval tradition; the Caribbean was an American lake. Winship was a decent, able man, but the obsolescence of appointing almost any non-Puerto Rican to that difficult and delicate post, and especially a military man who would convey a proconsular aura, had not yet dawned on the nation's executive conciousness.[175]

Soon after Winship's nomination in January 1934, the Roosevelt administration began an overall review of policy toward Puerto Rico. This had been insistently requested by Luis Muñoz Marín, but was also in response to the serious internal political and economic crisis. This review had two important dimensions: first, a consideration of urgent social and economic policy measures necessary to stabilize the Puerto Rican economy and prepare it for the impact of the new sugar quota system contained in the Jones-Costigan Act.[176] Second, it was part of an overall revision of the administration's policy towards territories and possessions.[177] Eleanor Roosevelt's trip with Rexford Guy Tugwell and J. Franklin Carter in March 1934, the creation of the Puerto Rico Policy Commission (the Chardón Commission), and President Roosevelt's visit to Puerto Rico (and other territories) in July were part of this process.

The two main decisions that came out of these initiatives were the transfer of Puerto Rico from the BIA to the newly created Division of Territories and Island Possessions of the Department of the Interior, and the creation of the PRRA (Puerto Rico Reconstruction Administration) to coordinate emergency assistance to the island. Both institutions were placed under Ernest Gruening, named by Roosevelt in May 1934 to the post of director of the new division in the Interior Department. This made Gruening a key player in federal policy toward Puerto Rico and in internal politics (due to his control of the huge PRRA bureaucracy) from 1934 to 1939. A former managing editor of the liberal journal *The Nation*, and friend of Muñoz Marín, he had a background of anti-imperialist militancy in the 1920s and early 1930s. Highly critical of U.S. interventionism and military rule in the Caribbean, he was now placed in the role of colonial administrator, and he had to collaborate with a military governor who had actively participated in those interventions.[178]

It may seem paradoxical that while an army general was named governor in January, a few months later BIA control over Puerto Rico had ended. The major political decisions made in 1934 possibly reflected a transaction between two broad political sectors in the administration which related to different political forces in Puerto Rico. On the one hand, the War Department, the sugar interests, and the governing *Coalición*, favored a strong hand response to the mounting economic and political crisis, and the perceived internal threat to colonial order posed by the radical demands for independence of the Nationalist Party, the militance of the sugar workers, and generalized popular unrest.

On the other, a sector of the administration represented by persons such as Eleanor Roosevelt, Harold Ickes, Charles Taussig, Rexford Guy Tugwell, Ernest Gruening (who subsequently allied himself with Winship and the *Coalición*), and others, favored a revision of political and economic policies as a means of stabilizing the internal situation. This sector sympathized with the reformist proposals being put forth by Luis Muñoz Marín, Carlos Chardón, Chancellor of the University, and the opposing Liberal Party. The Nationalist Party was totally devoid of interlocutors in the administration, as independence was never seriously contemplated as an option by Roosevelt, and also the Nationalists pursued a strategy of open confrontation.

The transaction politically favored the first sector as Winship (and later Gruening) strongly aligned himself with the *Coalición*, and the sugar interests and economic reforms were postponed in favor of emergency economic assistance, and the political role of the military was prolonged through the presence of General Winship in the governorship and of Colonel Francis E. Riggs as chief of police.

The War Department, however, strenuously opposed Roosevelt's decision to place Puerto Rico under the Department of the Interior. Harold Ickes first mentioned the president's plan on March 7, 1934. His scheme included creating Advisory Committees for each territory and a Central Council under the Chairmanship of the Bureau Chief, and it was linked to the planned presidential inspection tour of Caribbean and Pacific territories.[179] By April 12, Ickes had drafted and submitted to Roosevelt an Executive Order creating the Division of Territories and Island Possessions and placing Puerto Rico (as well as the Philippines) under its jurisdiction.

Director of the Budget Lewis W. Douglas submitted this draft to Secretary of War George H. Dern on April 21.[180] Dern consigned his opposition to the plan in a letter to Douglas dated only two days later. He argued that Ickes had not discussed the plan with him, that it would increase costs without increasing efficiency, and that it would not place Puerto Rican affairs in good hands. The letter mentioned six arguments, ranging from international and colonial experience to "being above politics," and it explained why colonial administration should be retained by the War Department and the army officers of the BIA. Dern also extensively explained why the critical political situation in Puerto Rico made "it desirable to retain the administration of civil government under the War Department." His arguments illustrated the War Department's concerns with "public order" and political instability:

1. Puerto Rico presents a special problem. It contains a mixture of races with a Spanish cultural background and with characteristics very similar to other Latin-American areas. There is always the possibility of internal disturbance which may at times reach serious proportions as demonstrated by recent events.

2. The fact that civil government has for the past twenty-five years been administered under the War Department has undoubtedly had a very stabilizing effect as regards public order without in any way infringing upon the autonomy granted to the Island under the Organic Act.

3. Changing the administration at a time when conditions are so unstable, as has been indicated by recent incidents, might serve as an incitation to future disturbances. This point transcends in importance even the question of economy.[181]

By May 28, 1934, Roosevelt settled the issue in a curt note to Dern informing him that "after the most careful consideration of all angles, I am more and more certain that Puerto Rico should be treated in the same way and under the same form of government as Hawaii, Alaska and the Virgin Islands," and therefore he would sign the Executive Order the following day.[182] A few days later a *Washington Herald* editorial condemned the decision, calling it the result of "sinister machinations of the Sugar lobby against Puerto Rico."[183]

NOTES

1. David McCullough, *The Path Between the Seas: The Creation of the Panama Canal, 1870-1914* (New York: Simon and Schuster, 1977), Chapter 1.

2. Robert E. May, *The Southern Dream of a Caribbean Empire, 1854-1861* (Baton Rouge: Louisiana State University Press, 1973). Also, Frederic Rosengarten, Jr., *William Walker y el ocaso del filibusterismo* (Tegucigalpa: Editorial Guaymuras, 2002).

3. Luis Martínez Fernández, *Torn Between Empires, Economy, Society, and Patterns of Political Thought in the Hispanic Caribbean, 1840-1878* (Athens: The University of Georgia Press, 1994), pp. 153-70; also, Thomas D. Schoonover, *The United States and Central America, 1860-1911, Episodes of Social Imperialism & Imperial Rivalry in the World System* (Durham: Duke University Press, 1991), Chapter 1.

4. Ronald Spector, *Professors of War, The Naval War College and the Development of the Naval Profession* (Newport: Naval War College Press, 1977), p. 32. Theodore Roosevelt subsequently published his study: *The Naval History of the War of 1812* in *Works*, Vol. VI (New York: Charles Scribner's Sons, 1926). See, also, David McCullough, *Mornings on Horseback* (New York: Simon and Schuster, 1981), pp. 76, 207, 232, 235, 247-48, 250, 262. According to Merck, Mahan's sea power doctrines lent relevance to Roosevelt's book from 1894 onwards, when it was reprinted several times. He also notes that this book was instrumental in getting him the post of Assistant Secretary of the Navy under McKinley. Frederick Merck, *Manifest Destiny and Mission in American History* (New York: Vintage Books, 1963), p. 237.

5. Ernest N. Paolino, *The Foundation of the American Empire, William Henry Seward and U.S. Foreign Policy* (Ithaca: Cornell University Press, 1973); also, Walter LaFeber, *The New Empire, An Interpretation of American Expansion, 1860-1898* (Ithaca: Cornell University Press, 1963), pp. 24-32. Also, Frederick Merk, op. cit., Chapter 9.

6. D. W. Meinig, *The Shaping of America, A Geographical Perspective on 500 Years of History*, Vol. II (*Continental America, 1800-1867*) (New Haven: Yale University Press, 1993), p. 555.

7. Diómedes Núñez Polanco, *Anexionismo y resistencia, relaciones domínico-norteamericanas en tiempos de Grant, Báez y Luperón* (Santo Domingo: Alfa y Omega, 1999).

8. Wilfrid Hardy Calcott, *The Caribbean Policy of the United States 1890-1920* (New York: Octagon Books, 1977), pp. 34-39; Hans-Ulrich Wheler, *Der Aufstieg der amerikanischen Imperialismus* (Göttingen: Vandenhoeck & Ruprecht, 1974), pp. 14-16; Ramiro Guerra y Sánchez, *La expansión territorial de los Estados Unidos* (La Habana: Editorial Universitaria, 1964), pp. 288-91; Luis Martínez Fernández, op. cit., pp. 164-70.

9. Jorge Rodríguez Beruff, "Cultura y geopolítica: un acercamiento a la visión de Alfred Thayer Mahan sobre el Caribe", *Op. Cit., Revista del Centro de Investigaciones Históricas*, No. 11 (Río Piedras: 1999), pp. 173-190.

10. H. W. Brands, *Bound to Empire, The United States and the Philippines* (Oxford: Oxford University Press, 1992), pp. 8-16; Hans-Ulrich Wheler, op. cit., pp. 43-73; and, Walter LaFeber, op. cit., Chapter 2.

11. Roosevelt wrote that, "Captain Mahan has written distinctively the best and most important, an also by far the most interesting, book on naval history which has been produced on either side of the water for many a long year." Cited in H.W. Brands, op. cit., pp. 13-4.

12. See, Julio Albi, *La defensa de las Indias (1764-1799)*, (Madrid: Ediciones de Cultura Hispánica, 1987), Chapter 2.

13. A. T. Mahan, *The Gulf and Inland Waters* (New York: Charles Scribner's Sons, 1883).

14. A. T. Mahan, *The Influence of Sea Power Upon History, 1660-1783* (London: Sampson Low, Marston, Searle & Rivington, n.d.), p. 28.

15. Ibid., p. 84.

16. Ibid., p. 83.

17. Ibid., p. 33.

18. Idem.

19. Ibid., p. 34.

20. Ibid., p. 416.

21. See, for example, A. T. Mahan, "Hawaii and Our Future Sea Power," *The Forum*, Vol. 15 (March 1893), pp. 1-11.

22. In 1890, he distinguished between colonies and "purely military naval stations" remarking that "such colonies the United States has not and is not likely to have." A. T. Mahan, *The Impact of Sea Power Upon History, 1660-1783*, p. 83. However, by the late 1890s he abandoned the ambivalence toward the colonial enterprise that can be found in this text, as the acquisition of naval stations was seen to require colonial control.

23. Barbara W. Tuchman, *The Proud Tower, A Portrait of the World Before the War, 1890-1914* (New York: The Macmillan Co., 1966), p. 150.

24. A. T. Mahan, "Strategic Features of the Caribbean Sea and the Gulf of Mexico", *Harper's Monthly*, Vol. 95 (October 1897), pp. 680-91.

25. For the formulation of war plans against Spain, see, Ronald Spector, *Professors of War, The Naval War College and the Development of the Naval Profession* (Newport: Naval War College Press, 1977), pp. 88-97. For the 1896 war plan, see, Lieut. Wm. W. Kimball, Staff Intelligence Officer, "War with Spain - 1896", June 1, 1896, E 43, R.G. 313, U.S. National Archives.

26. "The War", *The Times*, July 22, 1898.

27. "The War", *The Times*, August 1, 1898, and "Times Leader," *The Times*, September 17, 1898.

28. "Such a movement, Miles pointed out to Secretary Alger, would secure a foothold in Puerto Rico before Spain sued for peace, as she was likely to do, now that she had lost both her fleet and Santiago." Graham A. Cosmas, *An Army for Empire, The United States Army in the Spanish-American War* (Columbia: University of Missouri Press, 1971), pp. 230-31.

29. Robert Wooster, *Nelson A. Miles and the Twilight of the Frontier Army* (Lincoln: University of Nebraska Press, 1995), p. 269.

30. Cited in H. W. Brands, op.cit., p. 31.

31. Capt. Francis J. Higginson to Admiral William T. Sampson, August 2, 1898, E 37, R.G. 313, U. S. National Archives.

32. The Board was created by Secretary of the Navy John D. Long in April 1898 to advise on the conduct of the war. It initially consisted of Assistant Secretary Theodore Roosevelt, Rear Admiral Montgomery Steard, Capt. A. S. Baker, Capt. A. S. Crowninshield, Chief of the Bureau of Navigation, and Commander Richardson Clover, Chief Intelligence Officer. Roosevelt, Baker, and Clover left in May. Capt. Mahan reported to the Board on 9 May, which consisted only of Mahan, Sicard and Crowninshield. "Mahan was less impractical than the Secretary had expected him to be, for on his advice and that of his colleagues Long made the decisions on which naval operations were based." See Henry P. Beers, "The Development of the Office of the Chief of Naval Operations," *Military Affairs*, Part I (Spring 1946), pp. 53-55.

33. A. T. Mahan to John D. Long, [August 15-20], 1898, in Robert Seager II and Doris D. Maguire, eds., *Letters and Papers of Alfred Thayer Mahan*, Vol. II, Naval Letter Series (Annapolis: Naval Institute Press, 1975), pp. 582, 584-7. Author's emphasis.

34. A. T. Mahan, *Lessons of the War With Spain and Other Articles* (Boston: Little, Brown and Company, 1899), p. 29.

35. In 1883 the construction of four steel vessels was authorized. Congress appropriated funds for thirty more ships between 1885 and 1889. The Naval War College was established in 1884 and the decision to build large British-

Admiralty class battleships was taken in 1889. See, Ronald Spector, "The Triumph of Professional Ideology: The U.S. Navy in the 1890s," in Kenneth J. Hagan, ed., *In Peace and War, Interpretations of American Naval History, 1775-1978* (Westport: Greenwood Press, 1978), pp. 174-7; Walter LaFeber, op. cit., pp. 58-61. See, also, Mark Russell Shullman, *Navalism and the Emergence of American Sea Power, 1882-1893* (Annapolis: U.S. Naval Institute Press, 1994).

36. Daniel H. Headrick, *The Tools of Empire: Technology and European Imperialism in the Nineteenth Century* (Oxford: Oxford University Press, 1981), Chapter 10.

37. He argued that naval coaling stations had to be found in imperial routes for technological reasons, leading to the acquisition of colonial enclaves in the Far East by England and France, and the active search by Japan and Germany of strategically located islands in the Pacific Ocean. See, Maurice de Brossard, *Histoire maritime du Monde*, Volume 4 (Paris, Editions France-Empire, 1974), Chapter 1. See, also, Bernard Brodie, *Sea Power in the Machine Age* (Princeton: Princeton University Press, 1941).

38. Bradford's report to McKinley was dated September 1898. See, Thomas McCormick, "Insular Imperialism and The Open Door: The China Market and the Spanish-American War," *Pacific Historical Review*, Vol. 32, No. 2 (May 1963), p. 163.

39. R.B. Bradford, "Coaling Stations for the Navy," *Forum,* Vol. 26, No. 6 (February 1899), pp. 738-9.

40. Idem.

41. Edwin Van Dyke Robinson, "The West Indian and Pacific Islands in Relation to the Isthmian Canal," *Independent*, No. 52 (March 1, 1900), p. 254.

42. Ibid., p. 61.

43. Major William A. Glassford, *The Strategic Value of Saint Thomas, A Military Essay on "Porto Rico and a Necessary Position in the West Indies"* (New York: Journal of the Military Service Institute, January 1904), p. 3.

44. Eugene P. Lyle, Jr., "Our Experience in Porto Rico," *The World's Work*, Vol. 11, No. 3 (January 1906), pp. 7082-94.

45. Ibid., pp. 7093-94.

46. This historian the accepts explanation popularized by Roberto H. Todd. If Todd's explanation were correct, Puerto Rico would have been the first country invaded by the mechanism of "petition" to the U.S. President. See, Carmelo Rosario Natal, *Puerto Rico y la crisis de la Guerra Hispanoamericana* (Hato Rey: Ramallo Brothers, 1975), p. 192 *passim*.

47. Arturo Morales Carrión, *Puerto Rico, A Political and Cultural History* (New York: W. W. Norton and Co., 1983), p. 134.

48. Thomas McCormick, op. cit., pp. 155-169.

49. Richard D. Challener, *Admirals, Generals, and American Foreign Policy, 1898-1914* (Princeton: Princeton University Press, 1973), particularly the "Introduction" and Chapter 6.

50. Course at General Staff College 1920-1921, "Intelligence Summary of the Estimate on the United States," Committee No. 25, Intelligence Course No. 35, General Staff College File No. 183-25, U.S. Army Military History Institute, Carlisle Barracks, PA, pp. 18-21.

51. Colonel S. C. Vestal, C.A.C., "The use in battle of allies, auxiliaries, colored troops, and troops raised in the insular possessions," Lecture delivered at the Army War College, Washington Barracks, D.C., April 30, 1924, Command Course No. 46, 1923-1924, U.S. Army Military History Institute, Carlisle Barracks, PA.

52. Course at the Army War College 1934-1935 (Manpower), Supplement No. 2 to Report of Committee No.1, Subject: Manpower of Hawaiian Islands, Alaska, Puerto Rico, the Philippines and it use, U.S. Army Military History Institute, Carlisle Barracks, PA, p. 11.

53. Course at the Army War College 1938-1939 (G-1), Report of Committee No. 2, Subject: Manpower in Philippine Commonwealth and Certain Insular Possessions and Territories, October 28, 1938, Oral Presentation by Maj. Joseph L. Ready, Inf., U.S. Army Military History Institute, Carlisle Barracks, PA, p. 5.

54. Course at the Army War College 1921-1922, "Survey of the Vital Strategic Areas of the United States and Its Possessions," Army War College No. 224-1, U.S. Army Military History Institute, Carlisle Barracks, PA, p. 29.

55. General W.W. Harts, "The Caribbean Sea," ms, May 8, 1933, The Army War College No. 306-19, U.S. Army Military History Institute, Carlisle Barracks, PA.

56. Ibid., pp. 2-3.

57. Course at the Army War College 1933-1934, "Naval Defense of the Caribbean Area," Army War College No. 407-79, Memorandum for the Assistant Commander prepared by Comdr. C.E. Van Hook, USN, 5 May, 1934, U.S. Army Military History Institute, Carlisle Barracks, PA, pp. 1-5. See, also, Course at the Army War College 1934-1935, Report of Committee No. 1, Army War College No. 2-1935-1, "The Caribbean Area," U.S. Army Military History Institute, Carlisle Barracks, PA.

58. Course at the Army War College 1939-1940, War Plans Course, "Studies of Overseas Departments and Alaska, The Puerto Rican Department," Committee

No. 1, Army War College No. 5-1940-5A, U.S. Army Military History Institute, Carlisle Barracks, PA, p. 1.

59. Ibid., p. 12, 14.

60. Ibid., p. 11.

61. Course at the Army War College 1939-1940, War Plans Course, "Studies of Overseas Departments and Alaska," Report of Committee No. 2, Group No. 5, Puerto Rican Department, Oral Presentation of Lieut. Philip S. Wood, Inf., U.S. Army Military History Institute, Carlisle Barracks, PA, p. 7.

62. Major General John R. Brooke (August-December, 1898), Major General Guy V. Henry (December 1898-May 1899), Brigadier General George W. Davis (May 1899-May 1900).

63. This process of dismantling or reshaping the Spanish colonial institutions, as Fernando Picó has noted, was also undertaken from "below," and responded to demands to redress grievances of the population. See, Fernando Picó, "La revolución puertorriqueña de 1898," paper presented at the *Simposio 95+3*, October 14, 1995 History Department, University of Puerto Rico.

64. H. K. Carroll, "What Has Been Done for Porto Rico Under Military Rule," *American Review of Books*, No. 20 (December 1899), p. 711. See, also, Carroll's *Report on the Island of Porto Rico: Its Population, Civil Government, Commerce, Industries, Production, Roads, Tariff, and Currency, with Recommendations* (Washington, D.C.: Government Printing Office, 1899).

65. Brigadier General Guy V. Henry, "Our Duty in Porto Rico," *Munsey's*, No. 22 (November 1899), p. 233.

66. Walter L. Williams, "United States Indian Policy and the Debate over Philippine Annexation: Implications for the Origins of American Imperialism," *Journal of American History* (March 1980), pp. 810-831.

67. Russell F. Weigley, *History of the United States Army* (New York: The Macmillan Company, 1967), Chapter 9 and p. 212.

68. Bruce D. Porter, *War and the Rise of the State, The Military Foundations of Modern Politics* (New York: The Free Press, 1994), p. 268.

69. The biographical literature on General Miles is extensive. See, for example, Charles B. Erlanson, *Battle of the Butte, General Miles' fight with the Indians on Tongue River* (n.p., 1963) and *General Miles, The Red Man's Conqueror and Champion, General Miles Campaign Against Lame Deer*, (n.p., 1969); Virginia Weisel Johnson, *The Unregimented General: A Biography of Nelson A. Miles* (Boston: Houghton Mifflin, 1962); J. T. Marshall, *The Miles Expedition of 1874-1875: An Eyewitness Account of Red River War, by Scout J. T. Marshall* (edited by

Lonnie J. White) (Austin: Encino Press, 1971); and Newton F. Tolman, *The Search for General Miles* (Mew York: Putnam's, 1968).

70. Russell F. Weigley, *History of the United States Army*, Chapters 10, 11.

71. Russell F. Weigley, *The American Way of War, A History of United States Military Strategy and Policy* (Bloomington: Indiana University Press, 1973), p. 158.

72. Dee Brown, *Bury My Heart at Wounded Knee* (New York: Holt, Rinehart & Winston, 1970), p. 44.

73. Russell F. Wiegley, *The American Way of War*, Chapter 8, "The Annihilation of a People: The Indian Fighters;" see, also, the extremely useful analysis of the geopolitical dimensions and forms of administration and control over subject peoples developed during territorial expansion towards the west in C. W. Meinig, op. cit., Part I Chapters 5, 9, Part III Chapter 7, and Part IV Chapter 3.

74. See a biographical note in Tomás Sarramía, *Gobernadores de Puerto Rico* (San Juan: Publicaciones Puertorriqueñas, 1993), p. 211.

75. H. W. Brands, op. cit., pp. 122-123.

76. Richard Olney, before becoming Attorney General, was a well paid railroad lawyer in New England. In 1895 he became Secretary of State and played a central role in the Venezuela boundary dispute with Great Britain. Olney was an outspoken supporter of expansionism and considered himself a precursor of the "large policy" of 1898. See, Walter LaFeber, op. cit., pp. 255-83.

77. Cited in, Robert Wooster, *Nelson A. Miles and the Twilight of the Frontier Army* (Lincoln & London: University of Nebraska Press, 1993), p. 201.

78. That is reflected in the title of a book on Miles. See, Charles B. Erlanson, *General Miles, The Red Man's Conqueror and Champion, General Miles Campaign Against Lame Deer* (n.p., 1969).

79. See, for example, N. A. Miles, *Personal Recollections and Observations of Gen. N. A. Miles, Embracing a Brief View of the Civil War; or from New England to the Golden Gate, and the Story of his Indian Campaigns...* (Chicago and New York: The Werner Co., 1896), and, *Serving the Republic, Memoirs of the Civil and Military Life of Nelson A. Miles* (New York: Books for Libraries Press, 1971), first published in 1911.

80. Robert Wooster, op. cit. (Lincoln & London: University of Nebraska Press, 1993), p. 272.

81. "Guy V. Henry-A Knightly American," *American Review of Books*, No. 20 (December 1899), p. 710.

82. Captain A. T. Mahan, "Remarks to the New York State Chapter of the Colonial Order," November, 1898.

83. Captain A. T. Mahan, "The Relations of the United States to Their New Dependencies," *The Engineering Magazine*, Vol. 16, No. 4 (January 1899), pp. 523-4.

84. George W. Davis, *Report of the Military Governor of Porto Rico on Civil Affairs* (Washington, D.C.: GPO, War Department, Division of Insular Affairs, 1902), p. 105.

85. Cited in, Arturo Morales Carrión, op. cit., p. 145.

86. Brigadier General Guy V. Henry, "Our Duty in Porto Rico," *Munsey's*, No. 22 (November 1899), pp. 242.

87. For an excellent analysis on the *partidas* and the military's response to them, see, Fernando Picó, *1898: La guerra después de la guerra* (Río Piedras: Editorial Huracán, 1987).

88. S. S. Tuthill, "The Insular Police of Porto Rico," *The Independent*, No. 51 (July 20, 1899), pp. 1922-1924.

89. Davis, op. cit., p. 97.

90. Brigadier General Guy V. Henry, op. cit., p. 248.

91. Cited in Truman R. Clark, *Puerto Rico and the United States, 1917-1933* (Pittsburg: University of Pittsburgh Press, 1975), p. ix.

92. Ralph Eldin Minger, *William Howard Taft and United States Foreign Policy, The Apprenticeship Years, 1900-1908* (Urbana: University of Illinois Press, 1975), p. 34.

93. Arturo Morales Carrión, op. cit., p. 163.

94. Efrén Rivera, "The Legal Construction of American Colonialism, The Insular Cases (1901-1922)," *Revista Jurídica de la Universidad de Puerto Rico*, Vol. 65, No. 2 (1996), pp. 284-300.

95. See, Arturo Morales Carrión, op. cit., p. 153.

96. Lyman J. Gould, *La Ley Foraker: Raíces de la política colonial de los Estados Unidos* (Río Piedras: Editorial Universitaria, 1975), pp. 80-85.

97. For an excellent discussion of the role of Root and the military in the formulation of the Foraker Act, see, María Eugenia Estades, *La presencia militar de los Estados Unidos en Puerto Rico, 1898-1918* (Río Piedras: Ediciones Huracán, 1988), Chapter 4.

98. Carmen I Rafucci, *El gobierno civil y la Ley Foraker* (Río Piedras: Editorial Universitaria, 1981), p. 102.

99. Lyman J. Gould, op. cit., pp. 80-97; Truman R. Clark, op. cit., pp. 5-11.

100. Roberto H. Todd, *Desfile de Gobernadores de Puerto Rico, 1898-1943* (Madrid: Ediciones Iberoamericanas, 1966), pp. 43-47.

101. Arturo Morales Carrión, op. cit., p. 160. Also, for the background of the first governors, see, Truman R. Clark, op. cit., pp. 18-20.

102. José Antonio Herrero, *La mitología del azúcar: un ensayo en historia económica de Puerto Rico, 1900-1970* (Río Piedras: CEREP, 1971), p. 4.

103. Sidney W. Mintz, *Sweetness and Power, The Place of Sugar in Modern History* (London: Penguin Books, 1985), p. 188.

104. Roosevelt was portrayed as a selfless military hero in the classic 1962 film *The Longest Day*, about the Normandy invasion.

105. José A. Cabranes, *Citizenship and the American Empire, Notes on the Legislative History of the United States Citizenship of Puerto Ricans* (New Haven: Yale University Press, 1979), p. 94, footnote 459.

106. Eliseo Combas Guerra, *En torno a la Fortaleza, Winship* (San Juan: Biblioteca de Autores Puertorriqueños, 1950), p. 208.

107. General George W. Davis, op cit., p. 100.

108. *Ibid.*, p. 99.

109. S. S. Tuthill, *op. cit.*, p. 1923.

110. Idem.

111. José E. Martínez Valentín, *La presencia de la policía en la historia de Puerto Rico, 1898-1995* (Caguas: J. E. Martínez Valentín, 1995), pp. 63-70.

112. General George W. Davis, op. cit., p. 100.

113. Coronel Tenny Ross, USA, "El ejército en Puerto Rico", in Eugenio Fernández García, *El libro azul de Puerto Rico* (San Juan: El Libro Azul Pub. Co., 1923), pp. 104-10.

114. Federico Chang, "Los militares y el ejército en la república neocolonial, las primeras tres décadas", in Juan Pérez de la Riva, Oscar Zanetti, Francisco López Segrera, et al., eds., *La república neocolonial*, Vol. I (La Habana: Editorial de Ciencias Sociales, 1975), pp. 187-92.

115. "Programa Oficial de las fiestas con que el pueblo de Porto Rico celebra el 4 de julio de 1906," n.d. The program included the following advertisers: San Juan Light and Transit, The American Grocery and Ship Supply Co., Pillsbury Best and Studebaker represented by John M. Turner, New York and Porto Rico Steamship Co., American Colonial Bank of Porto Rico and West India Oil Co.

116. María Eugenia Estades, op. cit., Chapter 5.

117. *Informes Económicos al Gobernador* (selected years), Junta de Planificación, Gobierno de Puerto Rico.

118. Héctor Andrés Negroni, *Historia militar de Puerto Rico* (San Juan: Comisión Puertorriqueña para la Celebración del Quinto Centenario, 1992), pp. 377-8.

119. J.R. Pierson to George R. Colton, 9 April 1910, File 21212, Record Group 350 (BIA), U. S. National Archives.

120. Documents on this legal controversy are in File 21212 (National Guard), R.G. 350, National Archives.

121. *La Democracia*, 27 November 1919.

122. José A. Cabranes argues, against all evidence, that the 1917 political reform was not connected to strategic considerations. See, his, *Citizenship and the American Empire* (New Haven: Yale University Press, 1979).

123. Arturo Morales Carrión, *Puerto Rico, a Political and Cultural History* (New York: Norton, 1983), p. 193. Another important analysis on the citizenship question is Efrén Rivera Ramos, *The Legal Construction of Identity* (Washington, D.C.: American Psychological Association, 2001), Chapter 7.

124. Governor Yager, in his public statement on the Jones Act, denied it had any connection with the war. For his statement, see *Puerto Rico Progress*, April 13, 1917. Other contemporary documents indicate that U.S. citizenship and its relation with the draft was an important issue for U.S. functionaries in Puerto Rico and Washington, including Governor Yager. See, for example, Governor Arthur A. Yager to General Frank McIntyre, July 20, 1917, File 723, R.G. 350, National Archives; and, "Circular Letter No. 334 to all Officers of the Department of Justice in Charge of the Civil Registers of the Island," June 16, 1919, cited in *Report of the Adjutant General of Porto Rico on the Operation of the Military Registration and Selective Service Draft in Porto Rico* (San Juan: Bureau of Supplies, Printing and Transportation, 1924), pp. 10-11.

125. Governor Manning, senators Tillman and Smith, and the entire congressional delegation of South Carolina, opposed the training of negro troops, particularly Puerto Ricans, in that state. See, "Objects to Negro Camp, South Carolina Delegation Particularly Opposed to Porto Ricans," *The New York Times*, August 27, 1917. Governor Yager and the Puerto Rican political leadership also

insisted during the months of September-November 1917, that training should be carried out in Puerto Rico. See, documentation in File 723, Part 1, R.G. 350, National Archives. The Puerto Rican troops to be sent to Camp Jackson, South Carolina, were classified as "white" by the army. Black troops were destined to Camp Viton, Haphauwk, New York.

126. Héctor Andrés Negroni, op. cit., p. 387.

127. "Patriotic Resolution of the House," *La Correspondencia*, February 17, 1917. Also, Governor Arthur Yager, Cablegram, April 18, 1917; General Frank McIntyre to Secretary of War, November 26, 1917; Speaker José de Diego to Resident Commissioner Córdova Dávila, November 26, 1917; in File 723, Part 1, R.G. 350, National Archives.

128. The period of greatest growth in the American Legion membership was from 1929 to 1931. See, File 27634 (American Legion), R.G. 350, National Archives.

129. Héctor Andrés Negroni, op. cit., pp. 392-94.

130. The CMTC originated in the Plattsburg summer camps sponsored by Leonard Wood in 1915. They were associated with the "preparedness movement" of the 1910s, the conservative National Security League and the National Association for Universal Military Training "whose advisory board included both Root and Stimson." See, Russell F. Weigley, *History of the United States Army*, Chapter 15; and George F. James, *Eight Years of the CMTC, 1921-1928* (Chicago: Military Training Camps Association of the U.S., 1928).

131. Governor Horace Towner to BIA Chief Frank McIntyre, May 5, 1925, File 723, R.G. 350, U.S. National Archives.

132. Governor Horace Towner to General Parker, BIA, September 17, 1929, File 723, R.G. 350, U.S. National Archives.

133. Though Gore's plan was not implemented, Puerto Rico was apparently treated as a "special case" during the early 1930s. Army expenditure increased steadily from 1928 to 1931. National Guard funds also recovered after a drop in 1928. Major cuts in military expenditure were made in rivers and harbors works and in naval funds. See, "Expenditure of U.S. Government Department in Porto Rico;" "War Department Expenditures in Porto Rico;" Letter from J.J. Cheatham, Paymaster General of the Navy to Chief of Bureau of Insular Affairs, February 25, 1931, File 28042, R.G. 350, National Archives.

134. Course at the Army War College, 1939-1940, "Mobilization," Supplement No. 10 to Reports of War Department Group, Subject: Mobilization Plans, Overseas Department, Appendix Puerto Rico Forces, p. 52, U.S. Army Military History Institute, Carlisle Barracks, PA; Marion D. Francis, "History of the Antilles Department, Section II, Chapter I, War Plans and Defense Measures Prior to Organization of the Caribbean Defense Command, July 1, 1939-29 May 1941,"

Historical Section, Adjutant's General Office, Antilles Department, San Juan, Puerto Rico, October 1946, pp. 109-114; and, Héctor Andrés Negroni, op. cit., pp. 378-81.

135. Sonia Carbonell, "Blanton Winship y el Partido Nacionalista, 1934-1939," Master's dissertation, History Department, University of Puerto Rico, 1984, pp. 24, 68, 108.

136. María Eugenia Estades, "Colonialismo y democracia: Los informes de la División de Inteligencia Militar del Ejército de los Estados Unidos sobre las actividades subversivas en Puerto Rico, 1936-1941," Paper presented at the XVIII International Congress of the Latin American Studies Association, Atlanta, 10-12 March 1994. The FBI significantly increased its intelligence activities after February 1936. See, Sonia Carbonell, op. cit., p. 69.

137. Carmen I. Rafucci, op. cit., pp. 126-35.

138. Cited in, ibid., p. 133.

139. Reece B. Bothwell González, *Puerto Rico: cien años de lucha política*, Volume I-1 (Río Piedras: Editorial Universitaria, 1979), pp. 286-89.

140. Ibid., pp. 295-99.

141. Roberto H. Todd, op. cit., p. 87.

142. Arturo Morales Carrión, op. cit., p. 165.

143. Gonzalo F. Córdova, *Santiago Iglesias, creador del movimiento obrero de Puerto Rico* (Río Piedras: Editorial Universitaria, 1980), pp. 58-62; also, Gervasio L. García and Angel Quintero Rivera, *Desafio y solidaridad* (Río Piedras: Ediciones Huracán, 1982), pp. 52-58.

144. H. W. Brands, op. cit., pp. 88-95.

145. Arturo Morales Carrión, op. cit., pp. 167-69; also, Truman Clark, op. cit., pp. 12-13.

146. The BIA was called Division of Insular Affairs before 1902. Its named was changed when the Philippines civil government was established. Major General Frank McIntyre, "American Territorial Administration," *Foreign Affairs*, Vol. 10, No. 2 (January 1932), p. 297.

147. Ibid., p. 297.

148. Truman R. Clark, op. cit., p. 27.

149. Truman R. Clark, op. cit., pp. 19-20. On the 1909 legislative crisis and the response of the Taft administration, see, also, Carmen I. Rafucci, "El Senado de

Puerto Rico: la lucha por un espacio político puertorriqueño," in Carmen I. Rafucci, Silvia Álvarez Curbelo and Fernando Picó, eds., *Senado de Puerto Rico 1917-1992, ensayos de historia constitucional* (San Juan: Senado de Puerto Rico, 1992), pp. 23-49.

150. On Colton's role in the Dominican Republic, see, Richard D. Challener, op. cit., pp. 134-42.

151. Cited in Rubén Dávila Santiago, *El derribo de las murallas, orígenes intelectuales del socialismo en Puerto Rico* (Río Piedras: Editorial Cultural, 1988), p. 181.

152. Ibid., pp. 196-216.

153. Truman R. Clark, op. cit., p. 11.

154. For example, in the organizational charts prepared by Blanca Silvestrini and María Dolores Luque de Sánchez of the structures created by the Foraker and Jones Acts, the BIA (nor, for that matter, the entire Federal sphere) is not depicted. See, *Historia de Puerto Rico: trayectoria de un pueblo* (San Juan: Cultural Puertorriqueña, 1987), pp. 392, 413.

155. Truman R. Clark, op. cit., pp. 12-13. It should also be noted that Thomas Mathews, in a study of another period of U.S.-Puerto Rico relations, also underscores the salient role of the War Department and the BIA in Puerto Rican policymaking. See *La política puertorriqueña y el Nuevo Trato* (Río Piedras: Editorial Universitaria, 1970), particularly Chapters 1-5.

156. General Frank B. McIntyre, op. cit., pp. 293-303.

157. Ibid., p. 295.

158. Ibid, p. 303.

159. It is striking that an analysis on the role of the BIA is still to be written. See, however, Truman R. Clark, op. cit., pp. 12-13, 168-170; Thomas Mathews, op. cit., Chapters 1-3; Arturo Morales Carrión, op. cit., Chapters 8, 9; Frank B. McIntyre, op. cit.; and Bureau of Insular Affairs Files, War Department Records, Record Group 350, National Archives. Also, Kenneth Munden and Milton Greenbaum, "Records of the Bureau of Insular Affairs Relating to Puerto Rico, 1898-1934, A List of Selected Files" (Washington, D. C.: National Archives, March 1943), pp. vii-xi.

160. Truman R. Clark, op. cit., p. 22.

161. General Frank McIntyre, op. cit., p. 301.

162. Carmen I. Rafucci, *El gobierno civil y la Ley Foraker*, p. 41. Author's

translation. It is interesting to note that in his criticisms, Muñoz left out the White House then occupied by Franklin Delano Roosevelt.

163. Ruby Black, Press Articles on Robert Gore, April 29, and May 5, 1933, Ruby Black Collection, Centro de Investigaciones Históricas, University of Puerto Rico.

164. Robert H. Gore to President Franklin D. Roosevelt, April 22, 1933, FDR Library, FDR Papers -PPF- Container 740, Folder Gore.

165. Ernest Gruening, *Many Battles, The Autobiography of Ernest Gruening* (New York: Livewright, 1973), p. 191.

166. Pedro Albizu Campos, *Obras escogidas*, Vol. I (San Juan: Editorial Jelofe, 1975), pp. 236-240.

167. See the extensive documentation and correspondence on Gore and the anti-Gore campaign of Muñoz Marín in the Ruby Black Collection, April 1933 to January 1934, Centro de Investigaciones Históricas, University of Puerto Rico.

168. Taller de Formación Política, *Huelga en la caña, 1933-1934* (Río Piedras: Huracán, 1982), Chapter 3.

169. See, documentation on various meetings in Washington, particularly during the months of October-November 1933, in Ruby Black Collection, Centro de Investigaciones Históricas.

170. See, Dorothy Bourne to Eleanor Roosevelt, November 2, 1933, FDR Library, FDR Papers -OF 400-, Container 22, Folder P.R. This report, critical of Gore and calling attention to political "unrest," was forwarded by President Roosevelt to the Secretary of War on November 13, with the notation "for your eyes only" and asking for its return. See, also Luis Muñoz Marín to Mrs. Franklin D. Roosevelt, December 8, 1933, FDR Library, Eleanor Roosevelt Papers, Series 100, Container 1272, Folder 1933 Mo-Mu.

171. Ruby Black, Press Release November 1, 1933, and cablegram to Luis Muñoz Marín, 17 November 1933, Ruby Black Collection, Historical Research Center.

172. Thomas Mathews, op. cit., pp. 110-1, 140-1.

173. Winship, born in Macon, Georgia, participated as a Captain of the 1st Georgia Volunteers in the war of 1898 and served until 1901 in the Philippines. He had studied at Mercer University and obtained a law degree from the University of Georgia in 1893. In 1906, he participated in General's Enoch Crowder's government in Cuba, remaining there until 1909. He served as judge advocate general of the Army of Cuban Pacification. During the occupation of Veracruz in 1914, he was placed in charge of civil affairs. In 1919-1920, Winship served as

judge advocate general of U.S. occupation forces in Germany. From 1928 to 1930, he served as legal adviser to Henry L. Stimson, Governor General of the Philippines. In 1931 he was named judge advocate general of the army, a post he occupied until his retirement in November 1933. *Webster's American Military Biographies* (Springfield, MA: G. & C. Merriam Co.), p. 486; and, The Adjutant's General Office, Official Army Register (Washington, D.C.: GPO, 1940), p. 1192.

174. Ibid., p. 141.

175. Ernest Gruening, op. cit., p. 191.

176. The Jones-Costigan Act establishing sugar quotas was presented in Congress in February and signed into law by Roosevelt the following May, 1934.

177. Harold Ickes, entry for Wednesday, March 7, 1934, op. cit., p. 151.

178. Ernest Gruening, op. cit., Chapters 7-9 and 14.

179. Harold Ickes, *The Secret Diary of Harold L. Ickes, The First Thousand Days, 1933-1936* (New York: Simon and Schuster, 1953), pp. 151, 157.

180. L.W. Douglas to Attorney General, April 23, 1934, FDR Library, FDR Papers, OF 400, Container 23, Folder P.R.

181. George H. Dern, Secretary of War to Lewis W. Douglas, Director of the Bureau of the Budget, April 23, 1934, FDR Library, FDR Papers, OF 400, Container 23, Folder P.R.

182 The President to George Dern, Secretary of War, May 28, 1934, FDR Library, FDR Papers, OF 400, Container 23, Folder P.R.

183. "Puerto Rican Affairs," *Washington Herald*, June 7, 1934.

CHAPTER 2

ABOARD THE
USS HOUSTON

Roosevelt and Leahy aboard the "USS Houston" in 1939.
El Mundo *Collection, UPR, and U. S. National Archives.*

ABOARD THE USS HOUSTON

On March 1, 1939, while traveling aboard the cruiser *USS Houston* near the coast of San Juan, President Franklin D. Roosevelt told Admiral William D. Leahy, Chief of Naval Operations (CNO), that he should prepare himself upon retirement to assume the governorship of Puerto Rico. Roosevelt had toured the Caribbean in the summer of 1934 on the Houston, visiting Haiti, Puerto Rico, the U.S. Virgin Islands, Colombia, and Panama.[1] He cruised the Caribbean again during the summer of 1938 aboard the *USS Philadelphia*.[2]

The President and Admiral Leahy were returning to the United States after reviewing the first major fleet maneuvers held entirely in the Caribbean, Fleet Problem XX, which had taken place mainly in the Puerto Rico-Virgin Islands zone. The two men watched the lights of the fortress-city of San Juan from the unseen cruiser and discussed the island's future, a metaphor on the asymmetry of power in a colonial relationship.

> The President then informed me that the Governor of Puerto Rico, Blanton Winship, who had occupied the office several years, wished to be relieved.
>
> Mr. Roosevelt asked me if I would accept the appointment when I should be overtaken by the inevitable statutory Navy retirement age. This was a complete surprise offer, but without consulting my lady who was in Washington, I replied that he well knew I would undertake anything at least once if he wished me to do so.[3]

Leahy's autobiographical account of his role during the war, *I Was There*, begins precisely when he was recalled by Roosevelt from the post of Governor of Puerto Rico and named Ambassador to Vichy France; this conversation is one of the few events from his period in Puerto Rico recalled in the book.

Quite possibly Roosevelt's offer was of his own initiative since, apparently, it had not been previously discussed in official circles related to policy-making toward Puerto Rico. The offer was welcome news to Harold Ickes, Secretary of the Interior, one of the main functionaries responsible for Puerto Rican policy. The need to find a replacement for Governor Winship, another military officer, had been a subject of intense discussion both in Congress and in the Executive.[4]

> After Cabinet I waited to have the President sign some PWA books and he then brought up the question of Puerto Rico, telling me that he had a "crazy" idea about it. I knew what was coming but all that I said was that I hoped he was going to tell me what I was hoping to hear. Then he said that he had concluded Winship had been Governor of Puerto Rico long enough. I applauded this statement. He went on to discuss Admiral Leahy as a possibility for Governor and I gave no indication that anyone had ever mentioned this to me before.

> The President said that he had never known Winship particularly well and that he had felt for some time that there was no real community of interest either between Winship and himself, or Winship and myself. In this I concurred. I remarked Senator Nadal really controlled Puerto Rico, and that he and Winship seemed to have an understanding as a result of which each would give the other what he wanted. I also told him I had a very good opinion of Admiral Leahy from what I had seen of him, and that any change would be for the better. I also said that my opinion of naval officers was much better than my opinion of army officers so far as dealing with civilian populations was concerned. So, unless something happens we will be soon rid of Winship, and, unless I am wrong, we will be in much better hands in Puerto Rico with Admiral Leahy serving there as Governor.[5]

Sumner Welles, Assistant Secretary of State for Latin America, strongly concurred with Ickes on Roosevelt's choice of Leahy for the governorship of Puerto Rico.[6] Roosevelt had told Leahy rather disingenuously that Winship "wished to be relieved," which was clearly not so, and certainly the Puerto Rican leadership of the *Coalición* wanted Winship in power.

The fateful conversation aboard the *Houston* was not simply one between a president and his immediate subordinate. They were also friends who had first been acquainted in the early 1910s, during Roosevelt's tenure as Assistant Secretary of the Navy (1913-1920) under President Woodrow Wilson. At the time, Leahy was an officer in the Navy Department's Personnel Division and reported directly to Roosevelt. He later became Captain of the secretary's personal dispatch vessel, the *Dolphin*, which Roosevelt and his family often used.

> He found himself drawn more and more to the young, athletic Roosevelt, generally held to be a man with a bright future in politics. Franklin and Eleanor lived only three blocks from the Leahys at 1733 N Street, and in the rose garden in the back the assistant secretary and his wife entertained, as their office required them to do, the officials and leaders of Washington . . . The Leahys received their share of invitations, for the Roosevelts were determined to get to know the officers in Washington. Even though Leahy was comparatively junior, he was performing an important job and was working under the eye of the brilliant young assistant secretary . . .
>
> In Leahy, FDR found a man of integrity, sound judgement, and common sense. Their association developed into a friendship which extended beyond the office. Leahy was formal, respecting their different offices and ranks. The genial FDR always called him "Bill." Leahy would answer, "Mr. Secretary" or "Mr. Roosevelt."
>
> . . .The most frequent user of the Dolphin was the assistant secretary, so the friendship that had developed between the two men had an opportunity to deepen during days at sea.[7]

Leahy's personal admiration and loyalty to Roosevelt were unswerving throughout the latter's long political career. Not surprisingly, Roosevelt, upon reaching the presidency, promoted Leahy's career and named him Chief of Naval Operations in late 1936. He became one of Roosevelt's closest and most trusted military advisors during the pre-war and war years. His decision to name such a trusted and high-ranking naval officer Governor of Puerto Rico on the eve of the war reflected the strategic importance the President attached to Puerto Rico and the Caribbean, as many commentators duly noted.

Roosevelt and Leahy, due to their common naval background, also shared a considerable knowledge of Caribbean and Central American affairs, strongly colored by the dominant geostrategic navalist perspective formulated by Captain Alfred Thayer Mahan.[8] As Richard D. Challener emphasized in his classic study, *Admirals, Generals and American Foreign Policy, 1898-1914*, ". . . the political ideas of the leaders of the United States at the beginning of the twentieth century were virtual mirror images of the *Weltanschauung* of Alfred Thayer Mahan."[9] The Caribbean and the Central American isthmus occupied a central position in Mahan's strategic thinking, followed by his concern for the Asia-Pacific region.[10] Additionally, their careers had brought both of them into close contact with regional politics and had cast them as key players in Caribbean military and political developments. In Puerto Rico's case, they were both crucial political figures from the point of view of metropolitan policy-making during the 1930s.

Franklin Delano Roosevelt, Navalism and the Caribbean

As a member of the Roosevelt clan, and cousin of President Theodore Roosevelt, Franklin Delano grew up in a political milieu where navalist and expansionist ideas were the dominant outlook on international affairs. Theodore Roosevelt's liaison with Captain Alfred Thayer Mahan, his admiration for his geopolitical thinking, and his advocacy for a powerful navy are well known.[11] Mahan's writings were a main source of guidance for cousin Theodore's policies, first as Assistant Secretary of the Navy and later as President. Theodore Roosevelt's passionate support of the war against Spain, his promotion of a large imperial navy, the creation of the White Fleet, the decisive naval intervention in the Venezuelan blockade of 1902, and his "taking of Panama," among other things, cannot be understood without reference to the tenets contained in the writings of the "evangelist of sea power."[12] Close political associates of his cousin, such as the influential Supreme Court Justice Oliver Wendell Holmes and Senator Henry Cabot Lodge, shared these views. In 1895, for example, Cabot Lodge stated that:

In the interests of our commerce and of our fullest development we should build the Nicaragua Canal, and for the protection of that canal and for the sake of our commercial supremacy in the Pacific we should control the Hawaiian Islands and maintain our influence in Samoa. England has studded the West Indies with strong places which are a standing
menace to our Atlantic seaboard. We should have among these
islands at least one strong naval station, and when the Nicaraguan canal is built, the island of Cuba, still sparsely settled
and of almost unbounded fertility, will become to us a necessity. Commerce follows the flag, and we should build up a
navy strong enough to give protection to Americans in every
quarter of the globe and sufficiently powerful to put our coasts
beyond the possibility of successful attack.[13]

Roosevelt was introduced to Mahan's writings in his youth.[14] In 1898,
as a student in Groton, he cited Captain Mahan as an authority during a
debate on the desirability of annexing the Hawaiian islands. The naval
aspects of the issue figured prominently in his speech. His comments on
colonial possessions were premonitory of the situation he would have
to deal with in Puerto Rico three decades later.

We do not want to own any of these tropical countries or to
go there ourselves. By the Monroe Doctrine we are only supposed to keep foreign powers from these countries but not to
govern them or own them. Now if we once go in for foreign
colonies we must stick to that policy and not only are foreign
colonies expensive, but they are dangerous children and may
bring political difficulties upon the mother country at any
moment.[15]

During his incumbency as Assistant Secretary of the Navy Later,
Roosevelt's public expressions closely followed Mahan's geopolitical
outlook and he demonstrated no qualms regarding colonial rule over
"tropical countries." He actively sought advice and support during this
period from both his cousin Theodore and Mahan, with whom he maintained correspondence on naval matters until the latter's death in 1914.[16]
He was also close to Cabot Lodge. Despite the evident differences between the Latin American and Caribbean policies of the two Roosevelts
as presidents, and their different party affiliations, mahanian navalist

and geopolitical doctrines were never abandoned by Roosevelt, not even during his "Good Neighbor" period in the early 1930's. They were always an integral part of his outlook on international relations, shaping his views on military strategy and Caribbean affairs. Roosevelt's high position in the Navy Department during U.S. interventions in Central America and the Caribbean, his close relationship with his cousin, his ardent promotion of the Navy, and the network of supporters he constructed among Washington's political elite[17] were clearly a boon to his political career.

The Roosevelt family inherited a privileged relationship with the Navy and U.S. Marine Corps (USMC). Four members of the Roosevelt family —Theodore Roosevelt, Franklin Delano Roosevelt, Theodore Roosevelt Jr., and Henry Latrobe Roosevelt— were Assistant Secretaries of the Navy. Franklin Delano was both the youngest and longest serving Assistant Secretary. Theodore Roosevelt Jr., who served as Governor of Puerto Rico (1929-1932) and the Philippines, and Harry Latrobe Roosevelt, who participated in the 1915 Haitian intervention, were also high ranking officers in the Marine Corps. Roosevelt's son, James Roosevelt, also joined the marines, reaching the rank of Colonel by the late 1930's.

The armed forces of the United States underwent a transformation during the late 19th and early 20th century that Walter Millis termed euphemistically "the managerial revolution,"[18] but which was closer to a deepened militarization of the U.S. federal state, especially concerning foreign policy. The "managerial revolution" radically altered the armed forces within the state structure and the dynamics of civil-military relations. The navy made a transition from a modest wood and sail establishment (mainly guided by doctrines of coastal defense) to a large steam and steel naval force of 65,000 officers and men, with a budget of $144 million by the time Roosevelt became Assistant Secretary in 1913.[19] Mahan's sea power doctrines, which called for the creation of a large fleet resembling the British Royal Navy, became dogma to the new naval establishment. Similarly, the regular army, previously a small frontier force of about 25,000 men, underwent a significant expansion and a profound restructuring that transformed it into what Cosmas has called "an army for empire."[20]

Both armed services rapidly broadened their political role in the for-mulation of foreign policy[21] and in the administration of newly acquired territories in the Caribbean and Asia-Pacific regions,[22] consequently blur-ring the distinctions between traditional civilian and military spheres.[23] They also developed considerable clout within the political system. Roosevelt's period as Assistant Secretary of the Navy was an important factor in propelling him to the national political arena (he had previ-ously been a member of the New York State legislature), becoming the vice-presidential candidate of the Democratic Party in the 1920 elections.[24] Links to the military power structure and experience in colonial admin-istration became valuable assets in the careers of other contemporary civilian politicians of both parties, as the case of William Howard Taft exemplifies.[25]

The predecessor of Roosevelt in his post in the Navy was Beekman Winthrop, who served as governor of Puerto Rico (1904-1907) during the presidency of Theodore Roosevelt. As Assistant Secretary of the Navy, Roosevelt played the role of a Young Turk who frequently sided with proponents of a big ship building program and an aggressive naval policy, such as Rear Admirals Bradley A. Fiske and William F. Fullam.[26] During the first major crisis with Japan after coming into office, in May 1913, he proposed a course of action that was considered dangerous and pro-vocative both by Josephus Daniels, Secretary of the Navy, and President Woodrow Wilson.[27]

Daniels was a former Interior Department functionary of pacifist persuasion who, during the first phase of the Wilson presidency, sought to reduce the considerable power wielded within the Department of the Navy by the admirals who controlled the four Divisions (operations, ma-terial, personnel and inspection),[28] and to moderate the demands for a large fleet (forty-eight battleships) made by the General Board under the direction of Admiral Dewey.[29] Roosevelt felt no qualms in occasionally providing ammunition to Daniels's navalist critics in Congress, such as Representative Augustus P. Gardner.[30] He also courted the Navy League with success.[31] It became an important source of political support.

Assistant Secretary Roosevelt was a big-navy, a "battleship man." He demonstrated this by his immediate friendliness toward the Navy League of the United States, and the purport of his first important speech, an address of welcome to the League convention in April 1913. The main objective of the League was a larger navy, and its membership was studded with representatives of the steel, shipping, export and international financial interests; Roosevelt was on the best of terms with its president, Colonel Robert M. Thompson, chairman of the board of the International Nickel Corporation, and with one of its vice-presidents, Herbert Satterlee, son-in-law of J. P. Morgan.[32]

After the sinking of the *Lusitania* by a German submarine on May 7, 1915, the Woodrow Wilson administration shifted toward a policy of large-scale rearmament and naval preparation for war. It was precisely the course that Roosevelt had consistently advocated. He played a crucial role in the carrying out of the ambitious plans of naval rearmament leading up to the direct involvement of the United States in the European conflict in 1917.[33] Robert Greenhalgh Albion, a leading analyst of naval policy, considers that the two decisive periods of naval expansion during this century began in 1915 and 1940, respectively; these two periods followed upon a first decisive cycle of expansion in the 1880s and 1890s. It is significant that Franklin Roosevelt played a crucial role in both, first as Assistant Secretary of the Navy, and later as president (as his cousin had been in the 1890s and early 1900s).

> Two dates, exactly a quarter century apart, stake off an especially unstable period in our internal naval policy. On 21 July 1915, President Wilson, suddenly converted to preparedness, directed the Secretaries of War and Navy to draw up plans for rapid rearmament. On 19 July 1940, with the United States again gravely concerned about the war in Europe, President Franklin D. Roosevelt signed the tremendous "Two Ocean Navy Bill," which would carry our naval strength to unprecedented heights.[34]

The affinity young naval officers such as Leahy felt for Roosevelt went beyond personal considerations. They saw in Roosevelt a promising civilian politician who shared their views on international relations and national security, and was staunchly pro-navy.[35] He cultivated relationships with other young officers such as Lieutenants William F. Halsey, Jr., Ernest J. King, Chester Nimitz, and Harold Stark, who would later play prominent military roles as his commanders during the Second World War.[36]

Bruce Porter points out that "Franklin Roosevelt's own views of government had been profoundly shaped by his service as Assistant Secretary of the Navy under Wilson, and he evoked the analogy of World War I extensively" into his term as president.[37] In a 1932 election speech, Roosevelt explained his reformist proposals of the New Deal as a response to an "emergency at least equal to that of war."[38] A large part of New Deal civilian leadership had previously served in Wilson's wartime administration, particularly in the War Industries Board.[39] A recent study highlights the broader connections between the war experience, the military, and New Deal reformism.[40]

According to a statement made when he was in San Juan in 1934, Franklin Roosevelt had first visited Puerto Rico "thirty years ago",[41] when he was in his early twenties and his cousin was President of the United States. Since Theodore Roosevelt traveled to Puerto Rico in November 1906, it is possible he accompanied his famous cousin on this trip.[42] In 1905, Theodore Roosevelt had given away his brother Elliot's daughter, Eleanor, in marriage to the young Franklin Delano.[43]

The construction of the Panama Canal increased Roosevelt's interest in the Caribbean. He first visited the Canal Zone in 1912, when he wrote to his mother, "I can't begin to describe it and have become so enthusiastic that if I didn't stop I would write all night . . . I only wish you could see this wonder of the world, greater than the Tower of Babel or the Pyramids."[44]

The breadth of the U.S. naval presence and U.S. Marine Corps activities in the Caribbean, together with the interventionist policies of the Wilson administration,[45] brought Roosevelt into closer contact with the region during his period as Assistant Secretary of the Navy.[46] In a 1917 letter to author Stephen Bonsal, he claimed the Caribbean was "the American Mediterranean," a concept long found in Mahan's writings.[47] He also candidly stated that "we have simply got to control those islands as a whole - the sooner the better- the next step is to purchase the Dutch interests."[48] By the 1930s he had revised his views and no longer wanted all the islands, but remained convinced of the need for military bases.

In April 1914, an incident provoked by the *Dolphin*, the dispatch ship Leahy would later command, led to the decision by Wilson to take the Mexican port of Veracruz. The occupation of the city was a bloody affair. Roosevelt openly called for a full-fledged invasion of Mexico.[49] He continued to be directly involved in naval aspects of Mexican policy, particularly around Pershing's "Punitive Expedition" from 1916 to 1917. Haiti and the Dominican Republic were also objects of his attention. He personally issued orders in July 1914 to deploy seven hundred marines in Guantánamo in preparation for an invasion of Haiti. After the invasion took place during the following July, Roosevelt closely followed Haitian and Dominican developments (the Dominican Republic was invaded in 1916) and USMC activities in those countries. His friend Leahy also participated in the Haitian operation as Chief of Staff to Admiral Caperton, commander of the naval forces, and later participated in the landing of marines in the Dominican Republic.[50]

Following the interventions in Haiti and the Dominican Republic, Roosevelt toured the Caribbean from January to February 1917 to have a firsthand look at the occupation.[51] The trip began in Havana, where he met President Mario García Menocal, and proceeded by rail to Santiago. In Haiti he was met by the "maverick" marine Smedley D. Butler and by his cousin, USMC Major Henry Latrobe Roosevelt ("Harry"), Butler's quartermaster officer. Among other things, he visited the fortresses of La Citadel, Sans Souci, and Fort Rivière. The latter was site of a "major victory" of the Marine Corps against a badly armed band of *caco* rebels.[52] Through his marine cousin Harry, he actively explored investment possibilities in Haiti.[53] Roosevelt gave unqualified support to the USMC, and particularly to Butler's activities in Haiti. From that country he went on to the Dominican Republic. He was in Santiago de los Caballeros when the U.S. entered World War I, and was ordered to return to Washington.[54] Bernardo Vega has documented Roosevelt's intense involvement in military and political affairs in the Dominican Republic.[55]

Roosevelt's role in Haitian politics became an issue in the 1920 election campaign, as he claimed to have drafted the 1918 Haitian constitution and to have administered a couple of Caribbean countries.

In August [1920] the former assistant secretary of the Navy and Democratic vice-presidential candidate, Franklin Roosevelt, boastfully raised the matter of U.S. control in the Caribbean, and the Republican presidential candidate, Senator Warren G. Harding, took up the issue. As president, he declared in a direct reference to Roosevelt's claim to have written the 1918 Haitian constitution, "I will not empower an Assistant Secretary of the Navy to draft a constitution for helpless neighbors in the West Indies and to jam it down their throats at the point of bayonets borne by United States marines." Utilizing damning evidence from *The Nation* and other periodicals, Harding lambasted the Democrat's Caribbean policy and in effect committed his future administration to withdrawal from Santo Domingo.[56]

Roosevelt also actively participated in the policy debate on naval bases in the Caribbean during the mid-1910s.[57] Although the U.S. had acquired Caribbean territories and established several naval bases, it did not develop any of these as a major naval base in the region. An important policy debate developed in naval and political circles regarding where to establish the main Caribbean naval base. Sites such as Colón (Panama), Guantánamo (Cuba), Samaná Bay (Dominican Republic), Culebra (Puerto Rico), and St. Thomas (Danish Virgin Islands) were considered. Eventually the discussion centered on Guantánamo versus Culebra.[58] Roosevelt aligned himself with the proponents of Culebra, making an eloquent defense of the Puerto Rican island, which he considered a "Caribbean Helgoland." To him the only comparable location was the still Danish island of St. Thomas.

> Mr. Butler. Now, Mr. Secretary, following on the subject which Gen. Estopinal has questioned you about, in your judgement, is it not advisable that somewhere about the Gulf of Mexico or the Caribbean Sea there should be established a large naval station?

> Mr. Roosevelt . . . There have been many recommendations for the fortification and improvement of Guantanamo, but nothing has been done; and now the opinion seems to be swinging away from Guantanamo in favor of Culebra island, which is just to the eastward of Porto Rico. The best parallel I can give is that of Germany. You all know the island of

Helgoland and the part it has played in the defense of the German coast. What we need is a Helgoland somewhere in the West Indies; preferably pretty well out to the eastward. As I say, at the present time Culebra Island is favored. There has been no special board appointed on that, because, frankly, it would take a good deal of money to fortify an island of that kind.

Mr. Butler interposed: *Culebra?*[59]

In line with contemporary naval opinion, Roosevelt also favored the acquisition of several other small islands in the Caribbean[60] and the Gulf of Fonseca in Central America.[61] By 1917, the U.S. had purchased the Danish Virgin Islands. Leahy, Commander of the *Dolphin*, was commissioned to help install the first U.S. governor of those islands, Rear Admiral James H. Oliver.[62]

During most of the 1920s, Roosevelt was active in internal Democratic Party politics, obtaining the governorship of New York in the 1928 elections. This kept him away from direct involvement in the formulation of foreign policy. He had recanted from his previous enthusiasm for U.S. interventionism in the Caribbean and Central America. Military intervention, he now perceived, damaged relations with Latin America and should be undertaken only multilaterally in extreme cases. This, however, did not signify in any way an abandonment of the Mahanian geostrategic paradigm, just a recognition of the problems that interventionism had engendered.[63]

The Caribbean and regional naval policy loomed large from the very beginning in Roosevelt's agenda as president. The first major crisis his recently inaugurated administration had to face was the 1933 revolution in Cuba. The Cuban crisis was emblematic of the contradictions and political instability created, in part, by U.S. regional policy since 1898. Defusing the Cuban situation without resorting to overt military intervention (i.e., landing of Marines), and resolving other urgent problems in U.S. Caribbean relations, were necessary conditions for the general improvement of relations with Latin America.

Although the main thrust of U.S. policy in Cuba consisted in the "mediation" conducted by Sumner Welles and the "non-recognition" stance toward the Grau government, there were also important military and naval components of the Cuba policy. Internally, they had to do with wooing Fulgencio Batista and his military supporters away from radical civilian leadership.[64] Externally, they consisted of the prolonged naval encirclement of Cuba and a naval presence in its harbors by over 30 warships as a form of pressure on the Grau government and, later, in support of the Batista-backed Carlos Mendieta presidency.[65] Roosevelt, it should be mentioned, had sent to Cuba three trusted advisors, all directors of the American Molasses Company: Charles Taussig, Adolph A. Berle, and Rexford G. Tugwell.[66] They would continue to play important advisory and policy-making roles in the Caribbean throughout the thirties and forties. The other two urgent regional issues, the renegotiation of the Panama Canal Treaty and the termination of USMC occupation of Haiti, also had evident military implications.

Sumner Welles argued that Roosevelt was particularly well equipped to direct the very active Caribbean diplomacy in the first stages of the "Good Neighbor" policy.

> President Roosevelt, unlike all his predecessors, had been long familiar with the nations of Central and South America from both personal knowledge and experience. He had, long before he assumed office, visited Venezuela and Colombia. During his eight years as Assistant Secretary of the Navy, he had occasion to visit Panama and Cuba, and he had not only visited, but voyaged extensively through, the Dominican Republic and Haiti, for whose people he had developed a peculiar regard. Finally, while not fluent in the Spanish language, he could understand it and read it with ease.[67]

In 1934 Roosevelt again cruised the Caribbean, this time aboard the *USS Houston*, to review the political situation and to inspect military arrangements in the region.[68] One purpose of this trip was to visit U.S. territories in the Caribbean and Hawaii, and to announce the administration's "tropical policy."[69] During that tour, he again visited Haiti to complete the arrangements with President Stenio Vincent to end the occupation of that country.[70] He also met the presidents of Colombia and Panama, Enrique Olaya Herrera and Harmodio Arias, respectively. Arias and Vincent had previously visited Washington to discuss the strained relations between the U.S. and their countries.

In the case of Puerto Rico, Roosevelt had sent in advance a fact-finding mission composed of Eleanor Roosevelt, Rexford G. Tugwell, and John Franklin Carter in March.[71] He also asked Charles Taussig for a memorandum on Puerto Rico and the Virgin Islands.[72] In fact, Roosevelt's visit was part of a major policy review on Puerto Rico that probably began after the disastrous experience with Governor Robert H. Gore, his first nominee. The President continued to closely follow events in Puerto Rico after 1934, as the abundant White House documentation and Eleanor Roosevelt's personal involvement attest.

Roosevelt explained the naval implications of his trip in his address to the crew of the USS Houston. According to him, it amounted to an inspection of America's "first line of defense." Both the navy and the territories visited were part of this line.

> As far as the Navy goes, I am very proud of it. I have felt myself a part of it for so many years. We are improving the Navy. We got pretty far behind but, as you know, our Navy building program is larger today than it has been at any time since the close of the war.
>
> It is going to take three or four more years to bring the service up to treaty parity but we are going ahead with that object in view.
>
> I am glad to say both Congress and the country understand what we are doing in building up the Navy and about its use. The Navy is not only the first line of defense and upon this particular cruise of ours we have very nearly covered three-fourths of the first line of defense. Starting up on the northeast coast, swing down to Puerto Rico and the Virgin Islands, then to the Canal, out to Hawaii, and back to the coast, we are covering nearly all of this first line of defense.[73]

During his visit to Puerto Rico, Roosevelt visited military installations and reviewed defense plans.[74] He was also presented with a plan drafted by retired naval officer Virgil Baker and submitted by Filipo de Hostos, President of the Chamber of Commerce, for the construction of a large naval base in Ensenada Honda, Ceiba.[75] Roosevelt Roads Naval Station would be constructed there during the Second World War and thus named by the Navy in order to honor the President.

Regarding the Dominican Republic, Roosevelt's administration followed a two-track policy that, as the European conflict escalated, eventually supported Dictator Rafael Leonidas Trujillo. The State Department, headed by Secretary Cordell Hull and Assistant Secretary Sumner Welles, maintained an official policy that, if not openly antagonistic, at least sought to maintain Trujillo at arm's length. Open support for Trujillo's military dictatorship would have entailed serious complications in Latin America in the issue of credibility of the "Good Neighbor" policy, and also with Roosevelt's liberal supporters in the U.S..[76] However, another important element in Dominican policy during this period was the involvement of the Navy Department and the USMC. The Navy was consistently supportive of Trujillo. He had cultivated a network of old military cronies who had access to the highest levels of Roosevelt's administration, including the president himself.

Military members of the Roosevelt clan played prominent roles in the "naval track" of Roosevelt's policy. Theodore Roosevelt, Jr., the former president's son and former governor of Puerto Rico, attended Trujillo's inauguration in 1930 and became a key figure in Trujillo's lobbying efforts in Washington during the Hoover administration. He had been Roosevelt's successor in the post of Assistant Secretary of the Navy (1921-1924). In 1933, Henry Latrobe Roosevelt, Assistant Secretary of the Navy under Roosevelt, and Kermit Roosevelt, a son of Theodore Jr., visited the Dominican Republic and openly endorsed Trujillo.[77] Henry tried to obtain a military mission for the Dominican Republic, but Cordell Hull vetoed the proposal. Other high ranking USMC officers, such as General George Richards, approached Roosevelt on behalf of Trujillo. Finally, USMC Colonel James Roosevelt, Roosevelt's son, visited the Dominican Republic in February 1938, an event that was effectively exploited by Trujillo and generally interpreted as a major shift in U.S. policy.[78]

In May 1938, Roosevelt sent a friendly telegram to Trujillo while fishing near the entrance of Samaná Bay in the USS Philadelphia.[79] On February 1939, Fleet Problem XX provided the U.S. with a further opportunity to strengthen military and political ties to Trujillo, who visited the U.S. for the first time in July of that year and had a warm reception by the navy and the USMC. The following year he, along with Haiti President Stenio Vincent, was invited to observe the naval maneuvers in Culebra and St. Thomas. On that occasion, he was received with full honors. Vice Admiral Ellis commented, rather hyperbolically, that Culebra should be renamed "Trujillo's island."[80]

It may seem surprising to find Roosevelt in a "fishing expedition" off the coast of the Dominican Republic in May 1938, given the rapidly deteriorating situation in Europe and Asia. On March 12 and 13, Hitler annexed Austria as a province of the German Reich. By May, German military preparations for the invasion of Czechoslovakia had begun, provoking a partial mobilization of the Czech army. Simultaneously, fighting between the Japanese North China Army and the Nationalist Army had intensified in China.[81]

However, Roosevelt's presence in the Caribbean in 1938 was apparently related to these international developments. Samaná Bay in the Dominican Republic had been visited by German warships in 1934 (the cruiser *Karlsruhe*), 1936 (the *Emden*) and in March 1938 (the *Schliesen*). Destroyer *USS Mugdorf* shadowed the *Schliesen* while it remained in Samaná. The U.S. henceforth sought to establish a naval presence in the Dominican Republic, particularly in Samaná Bay. There was also considerable anxiety at this time regarding German activities and influence on the Dominican Republic.[82]

Developments in Latin America were also a source of great concern throughout 1937 and 1938. "Fifth-column" activities by Nationalist Spain, Germany, and Italy were closely monitored and considered a major security threat. During this period, fascist "subversion from within" was seen as more menacing than conventional military threats emanating from Europe or Asia. In a study of the situation, David C. Haglund explains that "If one month could be singled out as a turning point in American perceptions of the danger to the south, it would be April 1938."[83] One month before, the Cárdenas government in Mexico had decreed the expropriation of the oil companies, precipitating a major crisis in Mexican-U.S. relations.[84]

Additionally, Fleet Landing Exercises (known as Flex) were carried out in Culebra in 1937 (Flex 3) to test USMC amphibious landing theories and equipment, which were later extensively applied in the Pacific campaign. According to Abbazia, Flex 4 exercises carried out in Culebra in 1938 were particularly important since they revealed major flaws in the planning and execution of amphibious landings.[85] Although we cannot ascertain Roosevelt's presence in Culebra in 1938, it is likely his cruise had the additional purpose of reviewing naval preparations and training in the Caribbean. In fact, he did visit Panama and the Canal Zone soon after his fishing trip to the Dominican Republic.[86] The "Vinson Act" authorizing a significant increase of the fleet was approved on May 17, 1938. It was precisely during May that Roosevelt instructed his CNO, Admiral William D. Leahy, to carry out Fleet Problem XX in the Caribbean, using the inauguration of New York World's Fair as an excuse for shifting the fleet to the Atlantic.[87]

Roosevelt would not only participate in Fleet Problem XX, but would also extensively cruise the Caribbean in 1940 aboard the *USS Tuscaloosa* to "inspect at first hand the tentative sites of a number of naval bases which the United States had gained permission to construct in British territory."[88]

Yerxa summarizes Roosevelt's prominent role in naval policy and war planning from 1938 to 1941 in the following terms:

> [Roosevelt], a former Assistant Secretary of the Navy in the Wilson administration, created a new Atlantic Squadron, diverted naval strength from the Pacific to the Atlantic, pushed for more naval bases in the Caribbean, supported Anglo-American cooperation in the Atlantic-first strategy, and generally took an active role in directing naval operations. But although the Caribbean became a paramount concern for the President and naval planners, the years of relative neglect left the Navy unprepared for war in the region.[89]

William D. Leahy's Naval career: Administrator and Diplomat

William Leahy came from an Irish immigrant family who settled in the United States in 1836. Leahy's father, Michael, served in the Civil War in the 35th Wisconsin Infantry Regiment. Michael Leahy subsequently studied law in Ann Arbor, Michigan, graduating in 1868, and briefly serving as a Populist in the Wisconsin State legislature. Leahy's childhood years were spent in Wausau, Iowa. His family later moved to Ashland.

According to Linda McClain, Leahy was traditional and conservative, an outlook that "was intensified by a career in the traditional and conservative Navy, and was to remain a lifelong characteristic of William D. Leahy."[90] He wrote in his diary that "[P]ride of ancestry has been and is of value to us in that it makes repugnant any deviation from traditional ideals and gives strength with which to resist temptation to drift into a lower order of human society."[91] Contrary to his father's wish that he should study Law, Leahy sought an appointment at the U.S. Military Academy at West Point. Unable to secure it, he accepted an appointment to Annapolis for the following year.

> In those years, the Naval Academy cadets were a generally homogeneous group with similar upper middle class backgrounds in commerce, industry or the professions, and they studied mostly technical subjects, with little in the way of history or world affairs. The result was a tendency for the Academy to produce officers who were conservative in a political as well as military sense, largely provincial yet technically prepared. They were also strongly apolitical and all the military services shared a common tradition of civilian supremacy. Leahy had all these characteristics and a self-proclaimed, lifelong disdain for politics as well.[92]

Leahy's naval career really began in the Caribbean, specifically in Cuban waters, as gunner of the *Oregon* battleship in the Battle of Santiago. He had studied from 1893 to 1897 in the Naval Academy, graduating fourteenth in a class of forty-seven. The Class of 1897 "furnished the highest percentage of flag officers to graduate from the Naval Academy."[93] His first assignment was to the *Oregon*, then based on the West Coast. The *Oregon* sailed down the coast of South America, past the Strait of Magellan, and northwards to the Caribbean from March to May 1898, eventually arriving off Santiago de Cuba on 30 May. The *Oregon* fired the first shot at Cervera's *Infanta María Teresa*. Leahy's battery fired thirteen-inch shells at the *Colón*, forcing its Captain to run aground and surrender. Leahy was euphoric at this first battle experience "jumping up and down, slapping his leg with his cap, and yelling his head off."[94] It would also be his last naval battle, as the rest of his career would mostly consist of duty in the newly acquired colonial empire and in naval administrative posts in Washington.

Leahy's next assignment was in the gunboat *Castine*, but when he reached Ceylon he was ordered to return to the Naval Academy for examinations for promotion. He visited Hawaii, Guam, and the Philippines aboard the cruiser *Newark*, from which he was again transferred to the *Castine*. This ship was deployed in Shanghai in 1900 to protect the "International Settlement" during the Boxer Rebellion.[95] Immediately after the mission in Shanghai, the *Castine* sailed to Amoy to evict, in agreement with the British, a large Japanese force occupying the island. Later the *Castine* was assigned to Manila to participate in the repression of the Philippine Insurrection. Leahy served in the Philippines from 1900 to 1902. He observed first-hand the mistreatment of the Philippine people by the U.S. Army during the ruthless repression of the Aguinaldo rebellion.

Although he recorded no opposition to U.S. policies in the Philippines, the assassination of a native priest, "Padre of Molo," and the plight of a fifteen-year-old who was condemned to death, offended his sensibility and sense of military honor that called for making "less bitter the defeat of the vanquished."[96] Gerald Thomas explains Leahy's conflict with the U.S. military:

> The duality and conflict between Leahy's acceptance of America's unhindered right to use any necessary military measures to promote her own interests versus his sensitivity to the suffering of those who were the victims of American policies continued to the end of his career.[97]

In 1904, Leahy was assigned to the *Boston*, bound for duty in Panama, where the construction of the Canal was getting underway. The mission of the *Boston* was to ensure the progress of construction efforts. He thought Panama was "a ridiculous Republic" and "a potentially rich and productive country, and the resources of this particular part of America will begin to develop when it comes completely under the control of the United States."[98] He remained in Panama until February 1905, returning briefly in the summer. From 1905 to 1912, he performed a number of tasks that included teaching duties at Annapolis, cruises to Japan and South America, and working as naval aide to president Taft. He also increased his knowledge in the field of naval gunnery.

By 1912 Leahy was back in Central America, this time participating in the intervention in Nicaragua. The U.S. had intervened in 1909 and 1910 to remove from power President José Santos Zelaya, considered antagonistic to U.S. interests. In 1911, the U.S. had installed the conservative Adolfo Díaz in the presidency. The 1912 intervention by the Taft administration was designed to retain the puppet Díaz in power despite the opposition of the Nicaraguan Constituent Assembly, the Liberal Party, and sectors of the army. Leahy's ship, the *California*, was ordered in August 1912 to proceed to Corinto with Admiral W. H. H. Sutherland on board.

During this operation, Leahy was placed in command of a naval contingent in Corinto charged with the protection of the railway line to Leon. He was also entrusted with a military district that included Corinto to Paso Caballos.[99] There he collaborated closely with USMC Major Smedley Butler, whom he would later meet again during the Haitian and Dominican interventions, and whose exploits he recorded profusely in his diary.[100] His attitude toward the Nicaraguan intervention was critical.

> [L]ater orders from Washington directed us to take a definite stand on the side of the existing government which has resulted in disarming the rebels and supporting a weak unpopular tyrannical government, against which the people will in self defense take up arms as soon as we leave the country.[101]

Leahy also took note of the brutality of Adolfo Díaz's forces after the success of the intervention: "The party that had come into power through our efforts seemed unable to understand why we would not permit them to rob and execute their late antagonists."[102]

After Nicaragua, Leahy was assigned to the Navy Department in Washington, where he reported for duty in December 1912. His first post was in the Division of Operations under Lieutenant Commander Thomas T. Craven. In August 1913, he was named assistant to the Secretary's aide for Personnel, Rear Admiral Henry T. Mayo. This brought him into closer contact with the Secretary of the Navy, Josephus Daniels, and his Assistant, Franklin Delano Roosevelt. The latter is mentioned for the first time in Leahy's diary during this month.[103] Soon afterwards Admiral Mayo was assigned to the Naval Academy, leaving Lieutenant Commander Leahy as the only officer in the Personnel Division and entrusted him with administrative responsibilities normally carried out by an admiral. Even though he thought Daniels was "not in sympathy with the Navy," he developed a lasting friendship with the young Assistant Secretary.

As we have seen, Roosevelt could hardly be suspected of not harboring pro-Navy sentiments. The Assistant Secretary tried to put Leahy in command of the destroyer tender *Melville*, but was overruled by Daniels, who instead assigned Leahy in 1915 to the *Dolphin*, the secretary's personal dispatch vessel.[104] This brought him into even closer contact with Roosevelt and his family, thus strengthening a personal and political bond that would last until Roosevelt's death.

In 1916, Leahy was ordered to sail the *Dolphin* to the Caribbean to serve as the flagship of Rear Admiral William B. Caperton, the commander of the naval forces involved in the intervention of Haiti. This operation had begun in the summer of 1915. Colonel L. W. T. Waller and Major Smedley Butler were in command of the USMC forces in Haiti. Waller had been in the Philippines at the time Leahy was there. Butler's career had many parallels with Leahy's as he had been in the Battle of Santiago, in China during the Boxer Rebellion, in the Philippines during the Aguinaldo rebellion, in Panama, in Veracruz, in Nicaragua, and now in Haiti.[105] Leahy was named Chief of Staff to Admiral Caperton, thus able to actively participate in the negotiations that took place with the Haitian political leadership. In this task he displayed diplomatic abilities that would later be an asset to his career.

> The best the department could do for him [Caperton] was the small and ancient Dolphin, only conditionally classed as a warship even when she was commissioned back in 1885, and for many years a sort of glorified naval yacht for Washington bigwigs . . . One consolation came in the form of Dolphin's young skipper, Lieutenant Commander [later Admiral of the Fleet] William D. Leahy, who took over as the admiral's chief of staff. Leahy's unusual ability pleasantly surprised the admiral, though Leahy himself recorded that his inadequate mastery of the French language forced him into a crash study program. Furthermore, the admiral noted that Leahy and his officers were cordial and accommodating which was more than he could say of "the Tennessee crowd."[106]

This time Leahy expressed no misgivings regarding the outcome of military intervention despite the high-handed tactics of the marines: "Our occupation performed miracles in improving the condition of the poor inhabitants who were poverty and disease-stricken beyond words."[107]

From Haiti, the *Dolphin* proceeded to the Dominican Republic to take part in the landing of marines in Santo Domingo, which began the prolonged military occupation of that country (1916-1924). As Chief of Staff to Admiral Caperton, Leahy once again participated in talks with Dominican leaders that were the prelude to the occupation of Santo Domingo by the marines. Seven companies of marines landed on May 12 and 13 from the *Culgoa*, and companies of sailors from the *Memphis*, the *Prairie*, the *Dolphin*, and the *Castine*. Although political instability was the justification for the intervention, the occupation forces refused to recognize a Dominican president selected by the Senate. Instead, the country was placed under direct naval administration.[108] Leahy noted in his diary that "The Dominicans definitely do not like us, differing from the Haitians in that some of the latter were in favor of our efforts to stabilize their government and their finances . . . They are proud, intelligent, inefficient, and unfriendly toward Americans."[109] After the Dominican operation, the *Dolphin* sailed back to the U.S., stopping in Veracruz and Puerto Mexico, where Leahy found "the local populace to be bitterly resentful as the result of Wilson's interventions."[110]

By April 1917, Leahy was back in the Caribbean helping install the U.S. governor of the recently purchased Virgin Islands. These islands, long coveted by the Navy for their geostrategic location, were also placed under naval administration. Roosevelt had planned to attend the inauguration ceremonies of Rear Admiral James H. Oliver, but U.S. entry into World War I cut short his Caribbean cruise. After the Virgin Islands mission, the *Dolphin* remained in the Caribbean for several weeks searching for the suspected German raider *Nordskav*, which was finally located in St. Lucia. It turned out to be a normal merchant vessel.[111]

After some assignments in Europe and Washington, Leahy was made commanding officer of the *USS Shawmut*, the flagship of Mine Squadron One.[112] The squadron held maneuvers in Cuban waters during early 1922, during the intervention led by General Earl Crowder, the Cuban post-war sugar crisis, rising student unrest in the University of Havana, and social agitation.[113] Interestingly, General Blanton Winship, whom Leahy would later succeed as Governor of Puerto Rico, was a member of Crowder's military staff. From Cuba, Leahy sailed the *Shawmut* to San Juan, where he visited the governor. He noted that "San Juan is in appearance the nearest approach to a Spanish city, and the few people that I spoke to on the streets did not understand English."[114] During the remainder of 1922, Leahy fulfilled other missions in Central America and Panama.

From 1923 to 1926, Leahy performed administrative duties in the Bureau of Navigation of the Navy Department, and was in command of another battleship, the New Mexico, which carried out exercises in Panama and the Caribbean, ending in the naval base of Guantánamo. By 1927 Leahy had reached the important administrative post of Chief of the Bureau of Ordnance (BuOrd), one of the eight bureaus of the department. His recognized expertise in naval gunnery was a key factor in this assignment. It made him part of the "Main Navy," which not only referred to the Navy Office Building in Washington, but also to the group of naval officers who had reached the top of the hierarchy. Furthermore, this post was particularly strategic in developing contacts with political circles in Washington.

> It was the Bureau of Ordnance which, above any other billet, allowed officers to make strategic contacts with Congress and a disproportionate number who became CNO's or fleet commanders in the inter-war period had that background.[115]

Leahy strongly disagreed with the naval policy of the Hoover Administration in the London naval conference of 1930, which he considered favored Britain and Japan. Hoover's negotiator, Admiral William V. Pratt, with whom Leahy had frequent disagreements, became CNO in September. Consequently, he chose to leave his Washington post to become Commander Destroyers, Scouting Force, in the summer of 1931. By this time he was already foreseeing war in Europe as "inevitable," while blaming the "pacifist influences" of the Hoover administration for U.S. naval unpreparedness.

> Another war in Europe seems inevitable, and while predictions of future diplomatic developments are always inaccurate, appearances now point to the probability of an alliance of Germany and Italy against France with Great Britain neutral.[116]

Soon after Roosevelt's election, Leahy was back in Washington as Chief of the Bureau of Navigation (BuNav), another crucial post in the Navy Department. He would serve under Secretary of the Navy Claude S. Swanson, and Assistant Secretary Henry Latrobe Roosevelt. He was also named member of a board (known as the Roosevelt Reorganization Board) chaired by the Assistant Secretary to review the command structure of the Navy. Admiral William S. Standley, an old acquaintance of Roosevelt during his days as Assistant Secretary, substituted Admiral Pratt as CNO.

Roosevelt soon responded to demands for naval construction by assigning "238 million dollars for a program of 34 vessels which could not be secured through regular naval appropriations."[117] These funds were funneled through the Public Works Administration (PWA) as a job-creating measure. They allowed work to begin on the *Yorktown* carrier, the heavy cruiser *Vincennes*, the Mahan class of destroyers and a host of other vessels. Furthermore, the Vinson-Trammell Act of March 27, 1934 authorized building up the Navy to treaty strength.[118] Though this naval expansion was modest compared to the huge naval construction project launched in 1940, it was certainly privileged treatment compared to Roosevelt's neglect of the Army.[119]

Leahy's post as Chief of BuNav placed him in a position of considerable power within the naval structure, as personnel matters were under his control. He sought to enhance his power vis a vis the office of the CNO, provoking a dispute with Admiral Standley.

> Leahy was serving as Commander of Destroyers, U.S. Fleet, when his old friend Roosevelt (with whom he had kept in touch) became President in the 1932 election, but he returned to shore in 1933 to head the most powerful of all the Navy bureaus, Navigation, which, despite its title handled personnel matters. In that post, his power to select officers for key slots gave him a tremendous influence on the WW II Navy. He tended to assign conservative admirals, members of the so-called "Gun Club" clique of big gun battleship officers, to key fleet billets and his aides and proteges went far in the Navy.
>
> During his two years at BuNav, he had become known as one of the Navy's most skillful line negotiators and ablest executives.[120]

In the summer of 1935, Leahy was given command of the Battleship Divisions of the Battle Force with the rank of Vice Admiral. He participated in that year's fleet exercises, entertaining aboard his flagship, the *USS Houston* a party that included Roosevelt, Secretary of the Interior Harold Ickes, and WPA Administrator Harry Hopkins.[121] As in the days of the *Dolphin*, he took Roosevelt on a fishing trip from the Pacific through the Panama Canal and ended in Charleston. Leahy was promoted in March 1936 to Admiral and placed in command of the Battle Force. That gave him command of a total of 78 combat ships, 2,762 officers and 30,370 enlisted men. He had already been chosen by Roosevelt to become CNO if he won the 1936 elections, a post he occupied on January 2, 1937.[122]

The office of the Chief of Naval Operations had been established by legislation in 1915. It was the culmination of a prolonged process of administrative reorganization in the Navy Department during the late 19th and early 20th century toward the creation of a general staff and the centralization of administrative power. It also signified a redistribution of power between the appointed civilian functionaries and the line officers, in favor of the latter. Throughout most of the 19th century the Navy was organized under the "bureau system," which diluted the power of the naval administrators and enhanced the power of the Secretary.

The creation of the Naval War College, the Office of Naval Intelligence (ONI), and the General Board were important steps in the evolution of a general staff. Additionally, the demands of colonial administration, both of island possessions and occupied countries, and of an enlarged foreign policy role, required a larger and more effective administrative structure. During the Taft administration, Secretary of the Navy George L. Meyer established, above the bureaus, four administrative divisions entrusted to line officers. However, Josephus Daniels, Wilson's Secretary of the Navy, believed that the division system placed too much power in the hands of the admirals and did not reappoint officers to head the divisions as the posts became vacant. The only head of the division that retained his post was Admiral Bradley A. Fiske (Operations). Fiske and a group of naval officers secretly enlisted the support of Congressman Richmond P. Hobson to draft a law creating the office of the Chief of Naval Operations, which was eventually passed despite Daniel's opposition. He argued that the law was "a plan to prussianize the American Navy."

Albion explains the considerable power the CNO came to wield by the 1930s.

> From that time [the Far Eastern crisis of 1931] until the outbreak of World War II, the Chief of Naval Operations to a large extent supplanted the Secretary as the Navy's chief spokesman in politico-military matters.[123]

By 1937, the CNO ruled over a large and complex bureaucracy. It exercised jurisdiction over the following administrative divisions: (1) War Plans Division, (2) Central Division, (3) Technical Division, (4) Intelligence Division, (5) Secretarial Division, (6) Communications, (7) Inspection Division, (8) Fleet Training Division, (9) Fleet Maintenance Division, (10) Naval Districts Division, and (11) Ships' Movement Division. Although several navy-ruled territories had been transferred to the jurisdiction of the Department of the Interior in 1931, the Central Division was still entrusted with "Island Governments," and "International Affairs." The Intelligence Division, best known as the Office of Naval Intelligence (ONI), was responsible for foreign intelligence and followed developments in Puerto Rico, among other countries.[124] At this time, only Britain had a slightly larger naval establishment than that of the United States.[125]

Leahy's power as CNO was further enhanced by the fact that Roosevelt had not named an Assistant Secretary of the Navy after the death of Henry Latrobe Roosevelt in 1936. In addition to this, Secretary of the Navy Claude Swanson was chronically ill during most of this period and often could not discharge the responsibilities of this post. Harold Ickes noted that Leahy regularly attended cabinet meetings in 1937.[126] In fact, Roosevelt formulated naval policy directly with his CNO Leahy. They met twice a week in early 1938.[127] The only other presidential advisor who would develop such a close relationship with Roosevelt was Harry Hopkins after 1941. Leahy was also responsible for negotiations on naval affairs with the Congressional leadership, particularly with the House and Senate Naval Affairs Committees. Thus, the post of CNO required not only administrative skills, but also considerable political acumen.

> It was in fact Leahy's role as an adviser to the President that made his tenure as CNO unparalleled. Few, if any, of his predecessors could claim to have been not only the senior officer

for all naval affairs, but also the de facto Secretary of the Navy and a cabinet-level adviser on international and defense affairs in a crucial time for the nation's defense.[128]

It should be noted, however, that despite Leahy's personal and political links to Roosevelt, he was politically conservative and felt no sympathies for the reformist thrust of New Deal policies. He once made his criticisms known to the president and was told to remain within the bounds of professional military affairs. "FDR then directed him to limit his attention to his own area of competence, and thereafter the Admiral kept a strict silence on political questions."[129]

Thus, it is not surprising that later he would not be favorably impressed by Luis Muñoz Marín's outspoken support for the New Deal or by his reformist program. Muñoz, however, did not seem to mind Leahy's conservatism given his performance as governor of Puerto Rico.

> I don't know whether admiral Leahy is a conservative or a liberal in his fundamental ideas. But his keen intelligence and his solid character are a guarantee of good order and government in Puerto Rico. I have only spoken to him one or three times. I have never asked or received any favors from him, nor do I intend to do so. But my observation of his public acts and of his reactions to particular situations — always following a clearly defined idea of what government must be in Puerto Rico — leads to these conclusions. This obvious fitness of governor Leahy is having a marked effect on public morale and is restoring confidence in government.[130]

Leahy also held strong anti-Soviet views much before the outbreak of the Cold War and had used bureaucratic mechanisms in the mid-thirties to prevent the construction of a battleship for the USSR. He had some first-hand knowledge of the Russian revolution, as he was detached to Constatinople in 1921 as commander of the *St. Louis*.[131] Constantinople was a center of White Russian activities in South Russia, in which the U.S. became involved.[132] During the Truman era, Leahy consistently favored a hard-line stance toward the Soviet Union. He was a leading architect of the Cold War policy of containment and of the new security structure built for this purpose.[133]

Leahy's tenure as CNO was particularly significant since the first steps toward naval preparation for war were taken from 1937 to 1939. As soon as he took office, he announced the construction of two new battleships, the *North Carolina* and the *Washington*, to replace the aging *Arkansas*, *Texas* and *New York*.[134] During the summer of 1937, the Italian invasion of Ethiopia, German and Italian intervention in the Spanish Civil War, and the Chinese invasion of Manchuria combined to provoke concern in Washington regarding the deteriorating international situation. Roosevelt's "Quarantine Speech" of October 5, 1937 was a response to these developments. It was interpreted as an abandonment of the policy of neutrality and elicited an extremely negative response from the press and public opinion.[135] Leahy, persuaded that war was inevitable, supported Roosevelt's strong stance.

The sinking by Japanese planes on December 12, 1937 of the U.S. gunboat *Panay*, deployed near Nanking to protect Standard Oil interests, provoked more decisive measures of preparation for war. Leahy advised Roosevelt to respond to the attack by establishing, with the help of the British navy, a naval blockade of Japan, a drastic step likely to precipitate war. The crisis was defused through diplomatic means. However, the Roosevelt administration initiated secret naval conversations with Great Britain. Captain Royal Ingersoll, Chief of the War Plans Division, was ordered to travel to Britain in late December. As CNO, Leahy would play a crucial role in the U.S.-British naval negotiations that took place in 1938 and 1939.[136]

In early January 1938, Roosevelt asked the congressional leadership to support a second program of naval expansion, the Vinson-Trammell Act, which would increase the navy by 20%. This legislation was approved by March, although with fewer resources than the president had requested. It provided for 24 cruisers and several other vessels, and an increase in the Army and air forces. It also created the Hepburn Board,[137] which would review requirements for naval bases in the Pacific and the Atlantic. Roosevelt signed on May 17, 1938 the law assigning $1.1 billion to the Navy over a period of three years.[138] Leahy played an important role in lobbying for this legislation and was entrusted with the task of carrying out naval rearmament.

In the autumn of 1938, Roosevelt ordered Leahy to begin reconditioning old World War I destroyers moored in Philadelphia and San

Diego, and to establish a new cruiser squadron in the Atlantic. By September 6, 1938, the Atlantic Squadron was created with 14 ships. Its mission was "to discover and to turn back a sudden raid into the Caribbean" until reinforcements could be brought from the Pacific. The creation of the Atlantic Squadron was the first major step for naval preparations in the Atlantic. A main objective of the Fleet Problem XX maneuvers of 1939 was to prepare the naval forces in the Atlantic, formed by the new Atlantic Squadron to which the existing Training Detachment had been attached.[139]

The Munich agreement of September 30 accelerated the process of rearmament. It was interpreted in Washington as demonstrating British unreliability, hence increasing the likelihood of war. Haglund argues that concern with developments in Latin America during 1938 also played a major role in precipitating military measures.[140] By October 1938, Roosevelt decided to launch a massive expansion of airplane construction and announced a further increase of $300 million in military expenditure for hemisphere defense.

Also, U.S. war plans began to be revised from 1937 to 1938 in the light of the new international circumstances. In 1937, the Joint (Army-Navy) Board instructed military planners to revise Plan Orange, the war plan against Japan, considering the possibility of war in both oceans. The Joint Board approved a new Plan Orange in 1938.[141] That year Roosevelt created a State-War-Navy Standing Liaison Committee composed of the Assistant Secretary of State (Sumner Welles), the CNO (Leahy) and the Army's Chief of Staff (Malin Craig). The attention of the committee focused mainly on the situation in Latin America and the Caribbean.[142] On November 12, 1938, the Joint Board ordered the preparation of plans for "hemispheric defense." This process culminated in 1939 with the preparation of the five Rainbow Plans, which guided U.S. grand strategy during the war. The war plans prepared during this period placed great stress on the strategic importance of the Caribbean. Leahy prominently participated in this process of strategic planning and in the intense public debate that developed regarding U.S. strategy and military preparations.[143]

Another important aspect of war preparations in which the CNO was involved was the hectic "military diplomacy" undertaken in 1939 toward the Caribbean and Latin America. After returning from Fleet

Problem XX, Leahy, Sumner Welles and Army General George C. Marshall participated in Senate Foreign Relations Committee hearings to urge arms supplies to South American countries. Leahy also asked for the construction of warships destined to South American navies.[144]

General Anastasio Somoza of Nicaragua was invited to Washington in May 1939. *The Washington Star* reported that "not in years has Washington seen such a display for a visiting head of state" and that Somoza was known in Nicaragua as "el Yanqui." Among the dignitaries in the White House reception were "The Chief of Staff of the Army and Mrs. Craig, the Chief of Naval Operations and Mrs. Leahy, the Commandant of the Marine Corps and Mrs. Holcomb."[145] Cuba's de facto president General Fulgencio Batista had already been given a hero's welcome in Washington in November 1938.[146] General Leonidas Trujillo of the Dominican Republic also was invited to Washington in June 1939. He was received with less official pomp than Somoza and Batista, but he privately conferred with Roosevelt and Cordell Hull. The USMC and the Navy admired Trujillo. General Breckinridge called him "the Fourth Immortal, Duarte-Sanchez-Mella and Trujillo Molina."[147] Another important visitor to Washington in June 1939 was the Brazilian Army Chief of Staff, Major General Pedro Aurelio de Goes Monteiro, accompanied by a group of high ranking officers. Leahy participated in the military conversations, later maintaining regular communication with the Brazilian military.[148] The Caribbean and Brazil were the regions of greatest military concern during this period.

Negotiations with Great Britain also had a Caribbean dimension. During the visit of the British monarchs in June 1939, Roosevelt stated that since 1936 he had been considering establishing a system of naval bases in Newfoundland, Bermuda, Jamaica, St. Lucia, Antigua, and Trinidad. He argued that 1938-1939 naval maneuvers (mainly Fleet Problem XX) had demonstrated the viability of a naval patrol against submarines and raiders that would relieve the Royal Navy from "these responsibilities." Roosevelt again brought up the issue in a meeting with British Ambassador Lindsay. He requested bases in Bermuda, Trinidad, and St. Lucia "before war broke out."[149]

Simultaneously, secret naval talks were being held in Leahy's house with the participation of Commander T. C. Hampton, Naval Attache

Capt. L. C. A. Curzon-Howe, of the Royal Navy, and Rear Admiral Robert L. Ghormley, Chief of the War Plans Division for the U.S. Navy.[150] U.S. demands for naval bases in British colonies in the Caribbean must have been an important part of the discussions on naval collaboration in the Atlantic. These negotiations, later carried out by Roosevelt with Churchill[151], would eventually lead to the "destroyers-for-bases" agreement of 1940.

On August 1, 1939, Leahy turned over the office of CNO to Admiral Harold Stark. Roosevelt attached a handwritten note to Leahy's retirement papers that said "Dear Bill: I just HATE to see you go."[152] The international situation had deteriorated badly since Roosevelt's decision in March to name Leahy Governor of Puerto Rico, and by late August war was imminent. Leahy recalled a conversation with the President in his writings: "If we should become seriously involved in the European difficulty it would be necessary for him to recall me [Leahy] from Puerto Rico and assign me to duty of assisting him in coordinating his work with that of State, War and Navy Departments."[153] Leahy sailed for Puerto Rico just two days after the German invasion of Poland.

The press, both in Puerto Rico and in the U.S., interpreted Leahy's nomination to the Puerto Rican governorship as part of U.S. defense plans. *The Washington Post* commented that he had been "Chosen to head the island's government because of the plans for establishing huge naval and air bases there to make Puerto Rico the Gibraltar of the Caribbean."[154] *The New York Times* said that "the fact that San Juan, P.R., is to be made a major link in the Atlantic defensive chain is also considered a prime reason for the appointment of Admiral Leahy as Governor of Puerto Rico."[155] *El País* of San Juan called him "the ablest brain in U.S. forces" and noted that "recently prominent in defense considerations has been stubby little Puerto Rico island. President Roosevelt, viewing naval maneuvers this spring, was impressed by the island's potentiality as guard for the Panama Canal Zone."[156]

According to Leahy's account, Roosevelt gave him oral instructions to closely monitor defense preparations in Puerto Rico and the Caribbean.[157] From his civil post, he continued to advise the Roosevelt administration at the highest levels on strategic affairs.

During that summer of despair for the Western Allies, in 1940 Leahy discussed past and future preparations for sea defenses with the Acting Secretary of the Navy at the President's request. He also held talks with Rear Admiral Raymond A. Spruance and an Admiral Greenslade on the war situation in the Caribbean, and with CNO Admiral Harold R. Stark on the naval situation in particular.[158]

Leahy was even present in the discussion between Roosevelt and Admiral James O. Richardson, on whether to retain the fleet in Pearl Harbor, that sealed the fate of naval forces destroyed during the Pearl Harbor attack.[159] His abilities as administrator and diplomat were required in Puerto Rico to launch the ambitious defense plans for the island and the Caribbean region that were formulated during 1938 and 1939. Contrary to notions that the Puerto Rican governorship was a sinecure for third-rate retiring functionaries or a nice tropical assignment used to reward political supporters, at least in 1939, it was entrusted to the highest ranking naval officer and closest military advisor of the President.

NOTES

1. "Trip of the President, Summer 1934, June 29, 1934 to August 2, 1934," FDR Library, FDR Papers, OF 200, Container 5, Folder 200 F.

2. Bernardo Vega, *Trujillo y las fuerzas armadas norteamericanas* (Santo Domingo: Fundación Cultural Dominicana, 1992), p. 212.

3. William D. Leahy, "A Sailor's Adventure in Politics," unpublished ms, Leahy's Papers, Wisconsin Historical Society, p. 1.

4. Representative Vito Marcantonio of New York had maintained a constant campaign denouncing Winship's repressive policies and corrupt practices. Winship was also under fire from the *American Civil Liberties Union* (ACLU) for his role in the Ponce Massacre of March, 1937, and from liberal journals such as *The Nation*, in which Oswald Garrison Villard wrote scathing reports on his mismanagement, corruption and militaristic style of governing. Within the Executive branch, Harold Ickes, the Secretary of the Interior, was actively seeking his removal. In Puerto Rico, not only the Nationalist Party, but also Luis Muñoz Marín and his followers, kept up a relentless campaign against Winship, Ernest Gruening and the governing *Coalición*. A constant flow of letters with serious charges against Winship reached the White House and the Interior Department, particularly during 1937 and 1938. For an interesting example of this correspondence see Jaime Benítez, "Non-Rational Politics and Waste in Puerto Rico," FDR Library, FDR Papers, OF 400, Container 24, Folder P.R. It was referred by FDR to Harold Ickes with a memorandum dated 27 November 1938, which read, "Please read this and return. It should not be shown to anyone else."

5. Harold Ickes, "Secret Diary," ms, Library of Congress Manuscript Division, entry for Saturday, March 18, 1939, pp. 3307-08.

6. Linda Mc Clain, "The Role of Admiral W. D. Leahy in U.S. Foreign Policy," Ph. D. dissertation, University of Virginia, August 1984, p. 32.

7. Henry H. Adams, *Witness to Power, The Life of Fleet William D. Leahy* (Annapolis: Naval Institute Press, 1985), pp. 31-32.

8. On Mahan, see, for example, Philip A. Crowl, "Alfred Thayer Mahan: The Naval Historian", in Peter Paret, ed., *Makers of Modern Strategy, from Machiavelli to the Nuclear Age* (Princeton: Princeton University Press, 1986), pp. 444-80.

9. Richard D. Challener, *Admirals, Generals and American Foreign Policy, 1898-1914* (Princeton: Princeton University Press, 1973), p. 15.

10. According to Yerxa, "Without question, Alfred Thayer Mahan considered the Caribbean-Canal area as the most important region within the strategic purview of the United States Navy. In the last year of his life, 1914, he asserted that the

'Caribbean Sea and Panama Canal form together a central position: ...the most important within the sphere of action of the United States.'" Donald A. Yerxa, "The United States and the Caribbean Sea, 1918-1941", Ph. D. dissertation, University of Maine, 1982, p. 13.

11. "Widely read and respected at home and abroad, friend and confidant of Theodore Roosevelt and Senator Henry Cabot Lodge, Mahan exerted a potent influence upon the current of affairs." Julius W. Pratt, *A History of United States Foreign Policy* (New York: Prentice-Hall, 1955), p. 370. See, also, Wilfrid Hardy Callcott, *The Caribbean Policy of the United States, 1890-1920* (New York: Octagon Books, 1977), pp. 70-72.

12. As Margaret Sprout called Mahan in an important essay. See Margaret I. Sprout, "Mahan: Evangelist of Sea Power", in Edward Mead Earle, ed., *Makers of Modern Strategy* (Princeton: Princeton University Press, 1971), pp. 415-45.

13. Henry Cabot Lodge, "Our Blundering Foreign Policy," *Forum* (March, 1895), p. 17.

14. "National strategic thinking came naturally to him; at age fifteen he had been given a copy of Mahan's *The Influence of Sea Power Upon History* for Christmas, and was repeatedly to make clear how fully he absorbed its message." Eric Larrabee, *Commander in Chief, Franklin Delano Roosevelt, His Lieutenants, and Their War* (New York: Harper and Row, 1987), p. 3.

15. Elliot Roosevelt, ed., *F.D.R. His Personal Letters, Early Years* (New York: Duell, Sloan and Pearce, 1947), pp. 162-63.

16. FDR maintained correspondence with Mahan and Theodore Roosevelt from May to July, 1914. On 28 May, he wrote Mahan that, "When the canal is finally opened next winter there will undoubtedly be a great deal of pressure brought to bear –political and sectional– to have the fleet divided, and have one half kept on the Pacific and one half on the Atlantic." Consequently, he asked for Mahan's help in convincing the "'average man on the street' the military necessity of keeping *The Fleet* intact." In another letter he points out that "the only other person I have written to in regard to the possible division of the Fleet is my cousin, the ex-president..." (June 16). He also confidentially explained to Mahan his role in the Japanese crisis of the previous summer. Mahan agreed to write an article along the lines suggested by FDR, "The Panama Canal and the Distribution of the Fleet," which was published in the *North American Review*. It was Mahan's last publication. Shortly before his death that same year, Mahan visited the Navy Department but was disappointed in not finding the Assistant Secretary. According to Freidel, he died "without having met his greatest disciple." FDR Library, FDR Papers - Assistant Secretary of the Navy - Container 137, Folder: Correspondence with A. T. Mahan.; and Frank Freidel, *Franklin D. Roosevelt, The Apprenticeship* (Boston: Little, Brown and Company, 1952), pp. 234-35.

17. Among these were the Supreme Court Justice Oliver Wendell Holmes, Henry Adams, Senator Henry Cabot Lodge, Representative Augustus P. Gardner (Cabot Lodge's son-in-law), Army Chief of Staff General Leonard Wood, former Secretary

of War Elihu Root, J. P. Morgan, and the French and British Ambassadors. See Frank Freidel, op. cit., pp. 167-69, 298-99. Several of these were members of the Republican Party and ardent critics of Woodrow Wilson's "pacifism" and internationalism. Cabot Lodge, for example, led the successful campaign against the League of Nations.

18. Walter Millis, *Arms and Men, A Study in Americal Military History* (New York: G. P. Putnam's Sons, 1956), Chapter 3, "The Managerial Revolution." Many of the politically relevant actors in this process of naval and military expansion and restructuring (Theodore Roosevelt, Alfred Thayer Mahan, Elihu Root, Leonard Wood, and Henry Cabot Lodge, among others) were in different ways associated with FDR in the 1910s.

19. Frank Freidel, op. cit., p. 163.

20. Graham A. Cosmas, *An Army for Empire, The United States Army in the Spanish-American War* (Columbia: University of Missouri Press, 1971).

21. According to Healy, "In a study of post-Spanish War Cuban policy some years ago, I found that United States Army officers who commanded the first Cuban occupation exercised an important influence on the decisions which collectively determined the future status of Cuba, while then-Secretary of War Elihu Root held a pivotal position in shaping resultant policy. In short, the army and the War Department constituted the vital center which produced long-range Cuban policy. Similarly, the navy (including the Marine Corps) was at times deeply involved in the formation, as well as the implementation, of United States policy in the Caribbean." David Healy, *Gunboat Diplomacy in the Wilson Era, The U.S. Navy in Haiti, 1915-1916* (Madison: The University of Wisconsin Press, 1976), p. 5.

22. The Bureau of Insular Affairs in the War Department and the "insular desk" (established in 1922) of the Policy and Liaison Section, Planning Division, of the Office of the Chief Naval Operations were institutional expressions of this power. Insular affairs were under the Assistant Secretary of the Navy since 1900. Military matters were assigned to the Chief of Naval Operations in 1919.

23. "...the fact remains that the military dimension of American foreign policy did begin to assume greater significance and importance after the Spanish-American War... In these altered national circumstances the role of military men and military power in protecting and advancing America's position in the world was therefore an issue which assumed a new and different perspective." Challener, op. cit., p. 10.

24. It is no coincidence that FDR's British counterpart during the Second World War, Winston Churchill, was First Lord of the Admiralty during 1911-1915.

25. Ralph Eldin Minger, *William Howard Taft and United States Foreign Policy, The Apprenticeship Years, 1900-1908* (Urbana: University of Illinois Press, 1975).

26. Frank Freidel, op. cit., p. 222.

27. The crisis was provoked by a Japanese diplomatic protest against a California law which prohibited Japanese and Chinese immigrants from owning land. Naval officers close to FDR, such as Admiral Bradley A. Fiske, suggested preparation for war against Japan. Ibid., pp. 222-23. "...it was Roosevelt, who shared the fears of the admirals and endorse their plans, to whom the militants turned. It was he who was entrusted by Fiske and Fullam with the task of putting their recommendations before the recalcitrant Secretary. Young FDR, needless to say, was pleased to cooperate." Richard Challener, op. cit., p. 371. Challener explains (ibid., pp. 367-79) that this constituted a major crisis in civil military relations, as the General Board of the Navy, the Army's Chief of Staff General Leonard Wood, and the Joint (Army-Navy) Board placed considerable pressure on Woodrow Wilson to take aggressive action against Japan. It was Josephus Daniels who led the opposition in the Cabinet to the military's position.

28. Henry H. Adams, op. cit., pp. 30-36.

29. Frank Freidel, op. cit., pp. 221-22.

30. Ibid., p. 241.

31. James MacGregor Burns, *Roosevelt: the Lion and the Fox* (New York: Hartcourt, Brace, 1956), pp. 51-52.

32. Frank Freidel, op. cit., p. 172.

33. Ibid., Chapters 13-17.

34. Robert Greenhalgh Albion, *Makers of Naval Policy, 1798-1947* (Annapolis: United States Naval Institute Press, 1980), p. 220. Albion does not mention that the other period of significant naval expansion of this century occurred during the presidency of another Roosevelt, cousin Theodore.

35. "The close ties that Roosevelt felt with the Navy extended far down into internal policy and into surprisingly minor details. The Navy derived considerable benefit from this flattering attitude, which aroused some jealousy in other branches of the Government. It had its price, however; naval officers were sometimes heard to mutter, 'I wish to God he'd be absorbed into the Army for a change.' His love of the Navy was possessive, and he expected to be informed of everything that went on, however small." Ibid., p. 386.

36. Frank Freidel, op. cit., pp. 164-165. See also, Eric Larrabee, *Franklin Delano Roosevelt, his Lieutenants, and their War* (New York: Harper and Row, 1987), p. 24-25.

37. Bruce D. Porter, *War and the Rise of the State, the Military Foundations of Modern Politics* (New York: The Free Press, 1994), p. 277.

38. Idem. See, also, William E. Leuchtenburg, *Franklin D. Roosevelt and the New Deal* (New York: Harper Torchbooks, 1963), p. 41-42.

39. Ibid., p. 278. Bernard Baruch headed the powerful War Indutries Board. A host of other war bureaucracies were created during Wilson's war administration, such as Food Administration, National War Labor Board and War Labor Policies Board, War Trade Board, and War Financial Board. See Gerd Hardach, *Die Erste Weltkrieg, 1914-1918* (Munich: Deutscher Taschenbuch Verlag, 1973), Chapter 4.

40. "One of the most striking features of the response to the Depression was the way people looked back to the war for models of national unity and cooperation in a time of a crisis. It seemed only natural that the National Recovery Administration, the spearhead of Roosevelt's program, was entrusted to a general, Hugh Johnson. In its parades, its emblems and its oratory the NRA had a quasi-military character. And far from resenting programs like the CCC [Civilian Conservation Corps] as an intrusion on their professional concerns, some army officers felt a patriotic duty to help overcome the Depression." Geoffrey Peret, *A Country Made by War* (New York: Vintage Books, 1990), p. 355.

41. He mentioned then he had been in Puerto Rico thirty years ago. See, "The President's Radio Address at San Juan, Puerto Rico, July 7, 1934," FDR Library, FDR Papers, PPF 1820, Speech # 175.

42. I, however, have found no record of this early trip of Franklin Roosevelt to Puerto Rico.

43. David McCullough, *Mornings on Horseback* (New York: Simon and Schuster, 1981), pp. 368-69.

44. FDR to Sara Roosevelt, April 22, 1912, *F.D.R., His Personal Letters*, Elliot Roosevelt, ed., (3 vols. in 4; New York, 1947-1950), II, 184-187, cited in Lowell T. Young, "Franklin D. Roosevelt and America's Islets: Acquisition of Territory in the Caribbean and in the Pacific," *The Historian*, Vol. 35, No. 2 (Feb. 1973), p. 206.

45. "The Wilson administration announced a friendlier policy toward Latin America, but actually used the Navy and the Marines in oppressive occupation of Haiti and Santo Domingo." Robert Greenhalgh Albion, op. cit., p. 330.

46. USMC activities, and administration of insular possessions and occupied countries, were under the jurisdiction of the Assistant Secretary of the Navy during Wilson's administration.

47. Alfred T. Mahan, "Strategic Features of the Caribbean Sea and the Gulf of Mexico," *Harper's Monthly*, Vol. 95 (October 1897), pp. 680-91.

48. Lowell T. Young, op. cit., p. 206.

49. "Sooner or later, it seems, the United States must go down there and clean up the Mexican political mess. I believe that the best time is right now." Cited in Frank Freidel, op. cit., p. 232.

50. Henry H. Adams, op. cit., pp. 33-35.

51. For a general account of the trip see Frank Freidel, op. cit., 277-85. For a discussion of the naval aspects of the Haitian invasion see, David Healy, *Gunboat Diplomacy.*

52. In that battle 51 *caco* rebels were killed, no prisoners were taken and the Marines suffered only one casualty: a soldier was injured by a rock. Hans Schmidt, *Maverick Marine: General Smedley D. Butler and the Contradictions of the American Military History* (Lexington: The University of Kentucky Press, 1987), pp. 81, 82-3; and Hans Schmidt, *The United States and the Occupation of Haiti* (New Brunswick: Rutgers, 1971), pp. 84-85.

53. "After FDR's departure, his cousin Harry, on duty with the gendarmerie, surveyed investment possibilities -port development, sisal and sugar plantations, cattle, cotton, coffee and the like- and reported his findings unofficially to FDR and McIlhenny [Chairman of the U.S. Civil Service Commission, later named financial advisor to Haiti, author's note]. While nothing materialized from these purely private pursuits, FDR and McIlhenny were actively interested until the end of McIlhenny's tour in 1922, when FDR proposed setting up a Haitian-American import-export company. Also involved was McIlhenny's friend, the banker and Haiti mogul Roger L. Farnham." Hans Schmidt, *Maverick Marine...,* p. 90.

54. Bernardo Vega, *Trujillo y los militares norteamericanos...,* p. 167.

55. See ibid., and Bernardo Vega, *Nazismo, fascismo y falangismo en la República Dominicana* (Santo Domingo: Fundación Cultural Dominicana, 1985).

56. Bruce J. Calder, *The Impact of Intervention, The Dominican Republic during the U.S. Occupation of 1916-1924* (Austin: University of Texas Press, 1984), p. 202. For a critical Haitian appraisal of FDR's and USMC roles in the approval of the constitution, see, Suzy Castor, *La ocupación norteamericana de Haití y sus consecuencias (1915-1934)* (México: Siglo XXI Editores, 1971), pp. 49-53.

57. Donald A. Yerxa, op. cit., p. 105.

58. For an account of this debate with special reference to Puerto Rico, see, María Eugenia Estades Font, *La presencia militar de Estados Unidos en Puerto Rico, 1898-1918, Intereses estratégicos y dominación colonial* (Río Piedras: Huracán, 1988), pp. 44-58, 180-187. Also Donald A. Yerxa, op. cit., pp. 98-112.

59. FDR Library, Congressional Record, 64th Congress "Statement of Hon. Franklin D. Roosevelt Assistant Secretary of the Navy," pp. 3488-89.

60. These were the Swann islands, the Corn islands, and the Danish Virgin Islands.

61. Lowell T. Young, op. cit., pp. 206-208.

62. Henry H. Adams, op. cit., p. 35; Donald A. Yerxa, op. cit., p. 52.

63. According to Gellman, FDR revised his views on military intervention in Central America and the Caribbean during the 1920s. His new outlook was contained

in an article entitled "Our Foreign Policy" that was published in *Foreign Affairs* in 1928. See Irwin F. Gellman, *Good Neighbor Diplomacy: United States Policies in Latin America, 1933-1945* (Baltimore: Johns Hopkins University Press, 1979), p. 11; and, Robert Dallek, *Franklin D. Roosevelt and American Foreign Policy, 1932-1945* (New York: Oxford University Press, 1979), pp. 15-20.

64. Welles considered Batista a "brilliant and able figure." Sumner Welles, *A Time for Decision* (New York: Harper and Row, 1944), p. 197. His version of the 1933 crisis is in pp. 193-202. For a detailed analysis of Roosevelt's relationship with Batista, which began during this period, see Irwin F. Gellman, *Roosevelt and Batista, Good Neighbor Diplomacy in Cuba, 1933-1945* (Albuquerque: University of New Mexico Press, 1973). A Cuban account of events is Lionel Soto, *La revolución del 33*, 2 Vols. (La Habana: Editorial de Ciencias Sociales, 1977). See also, Luis E. Aguilar, *Cuba 1933: Prologue to Revolution* (Ithaca: Cornell University Press, 1972).

65. The naval presence of the Caribbean Special Service Squadron was maintained from September 1933 to early 1934. Yerxa, op. cit., pp. 291-301,

66. They were in Cuba in 1932 "to study the situation." They were all members of Roosevelt's 'Brain Trust'. Taussig was the president of the American Molasses Company, Berle the legal advisor and Tugwell vice-president. All were prominently involved in policy-making toward Puerto Rico and the Caribbean during the thirties and forties. Hugh Thomas, *Cuba, The Pursuit of Freedom* (New York: Harper and Row, 1971), p. 598.

67. Sumner Welles, op. cit., p. 191.

68. On this trip see, Irwin F. Gellman, *Good Neighbor Diplomacy* . . . , pp. 38-39. The official itinerary of the trip, which in fact was delayed, is "Trip of the President, Summer 1934", FDR Library, FDR Papers - OF 200 - Container 5, Folder 200F.

69. "It is the President's intention in Puerto Rico to speak briefly and outline our tropical policy - the policy of the United States towards its tropical territories. For his use in this connection he requests a memorandum from the State Department. He would also like a brief statement for use at St. Thomas - something to correct the 'poorhouse' impression." Stephen Early, Assistant Secretary to the President to Secretary of State, March 31, 1934. FDR Papers, OF 200, Container 5, Folder 200F.

70. Hans Schmidt, *The United States and the Occupation of Haiti*..., Chapter 11.

71. Information on this trip is available in the Ruby Black Collection, Centro de Investigaciones Históricas, University of Puerto Rico; see period 4-11 March 1934. Rexford G. Tugwell prepared an extensive report based on this visit. A Round Table Conference at la Fortaleza, the Governor's Palace, attended by Eleanor Roosevelt and Rexford. G. Tugwell, laid bare the profound differences of opinion that existed in Puerto Rico, particularly with regard to agricultural policy. "Round Table Conference at La Fortaleza", March 10, 1934. FDR Library, Eleanor Roosevelt

Papers, Series 100, Container 1315, Folder 1934. It is also discussed in Thomas Mathews, *La política puertorriqueña y el Nuevo Trato* (Río Piedras: Editorial Universitaria, 1970), pp. 158-170.

72. Charles Taussig to FDR, June 28, 1934, FDR LIbrary, FDR Papers, OF 400, Container 23, Folder P.R.

73. "President Roosevelt Address to Crew of *USS Houston*, Saturday Morning, July 21, 1934". FDR Library, FDR Papaers, PPF 1820, Speech # 175.

74. General Blanton Winship revealed a few years later that, "The value of Puerto Rico in hemisphere defense has long been known to President who made an inspection of various strategic positions during his visit to the island in 1934... The President then studied, on the ground, charts of various navy studies for use in the entire area between Puerto Rico and the Virgin Islands for Panama Canal and American coast line defenses. While the naval plans were then more advanced than the army's, the President also made an inspection of army properties and studied reports on a projected enlargement of its activities." See, "Roosevelt Has Analyzed Puerto Rico for Defense," *The New York Times*, 10 May 1939, p. 19.

75. Virgil Baker to Filipo de Hostos, 11 June 1934, and Filipo de Hostos to the President of the United States, 13 June 1934. FDR Library, FDR Papers, OF 200, Container 5, Folder 200F.

76. Irwin F. Gellman, *Good Neighbor Diplomacy...*, pp. 35-36. Also Bernardo Vega, *Trujillo y las fuerzas armadas...*, Chapters 7-8.

77. Henry Latrobe Roosevelt had fought in Santiago de Cuba. As a Marine he was deployed in the Philippines, Panama and Haiti. By, 1917 he had reached the rank of Major in the Haitian *Garde*. He had been an important source of information for FDR on Haitian business possibilities. Kermit Roosevelt became a Middle East expert for the Central Intelligence Agency. On the latter, see, H. W. Brands, *Bound to Empire, the United States and the Philippines* (New York: Oxford University Press, 1992), p. 156.

78. Trujillo decorated James Roosevelt while *Fleet Problem XX* was being staged. See Bernardo Vega, *Trujillo y las fuerzas armadas...*, Chapters 5-9.

79. In the brief telegram, FDR informed Trujillo that he had been fishing in Dominican territorial waters near the entrance of Samana Bay aboard the *USS Philadelphia*, escorted by *USS Fanning*, and that he regretted not being able to visit him. Trujillo answered that he hoped that in a future occasion FDR could be his "distinguished guest." Bernardo Vega, *Trujillo y la fuerzas armadas...*, pp. 212-13.

80. Ibid., p. 242.

81. E.H. Carr, *International Relations Between the Two World Wars, 1919-1939* (New York: Harper Torchbooks, 1966), pp. 267-73.

82. Bernardo Vega, *Nazismo...* , pp. 83-95. Vega's book provides a detailed analysis of German activities in the Dominican Republic in the 1930s and 40s, and U.S. policy regarding fascist influence.

83. David C. Haglund, *Latin America and the Transformation of U.S. Strategic Thought, 1936-1940* (Albuquerque: University of New Mexico Press, 1984), p. 79.

84. E. David Cronon, *Josephus Daniels in Mexico* (Madison: University of Wisconsin Press, 1960), Chapter 8.

85. "The Flex landings off Puerto Rico did much to demonstrate the feasibility of the amphibious theories being developed by the Marines, but lack of suitable assault craft, vital transports, tankers, and auxiliaries, necessary communications equipment, and other important gear meant that the state of the art still lagged well behind the hopes of the Marines." Patrick Abbazia, *Mr. Roosevelt's Navy, The Private War of the U.S. Atlantic Fleet, 1939-1942* (Annapolis: United States Naval Institute, 1975), pp. 25-31; Culebra exercises were crucial to the development of USMC amphibious landing tactics since the 1920s. See, Samuel Eliot Morison, *The Two Ocean War* (Boston: Little, Brown and Co., 1963), p. 16.

86. FDR Library, FDR Papers, Official File 200: Trips of the President, Boxes 40, 41, 42/43.

87. Yerxa, op. cit., p. 332.

88. During that trip he visited Jamaica and several of the smaller Antilles, as Antigua and St Lucia. "Log of President's Inspection Cruise Through the West Indies, 3-14 December, 1940." FDR Library, FDR Papers, OF 200, Container 69, Folder "Cruiser USS Tuscaloosa", p. 1.

89. Yerxa, op. cit., pp. 326-7.

90. Lina McClain, op. cit., pp. 7-8.

91. Cited in Henry H. Adams, op. cit., pp. 6-7.

92. Linda McClain, op. cit., p. 8

93. Henry H. Adams, op. cit., p. 11.

94. Ibid., p. 17.

95. The Boxer rebellion was crushed, in August 1900, by an international army of 19,000 men which took Peking. See, Julius W. Pratt, op. cit., pp. 434-41.

96. Henry H. Adams, op. cit., pp. 20-21; "The sight of a fifteen-year old Filipino 'suspect' weeping and hysterically protesting his scheduled execution saddened Leahy, not enough to protest, but enough to prompt him to sadly return to his ship, the *Leyte*,

and leave the executions to the soldiers of the 38th American Infantry Regiment." Gerald E. Thomas, "William D. Leahy and America's Imperial Years, 1893-1917," Ph. D. dissertation, Yale University, 1973, p. 151; also Henry H. Adams, op. cit., p. 45.

97. Gerald Thomas, op. cit., p. 154.

98. Adams, op. cit., pp. 23-24.

99. For Leahy's role in the Nicaragua intervention of 1912 see, Gerald Thomas, op. cit., pp. 101-125; also Henry Adams, op. cit., p. 29.

100. "During this time Leahy worked closely with the spectacular marine, Major Smedley Butler. He spent more time describing Butler's exploits than he did his own. They had to work together keeping a railroad running between Corinto and the interior. Butler and his marines managed the interior terminal, while Leahy and his troops were responsible for the rail head at Corinto." Henry Adams, op. cit., p. 29. For an account of Butler's role in the Nicaraguan interventions of 1910 and 1912 see, Hans Schmidt, *Maverick Marine...*, Chapter 5.

101. *Leahy Diary*, September 1912, cited in Gerald Thomas, op. cit., p. 113.

102. *Leahy Diary*, October 1912, cited in ibid., p. 122.

103. Linda Mc Clain, op. cit., p. 11.

104. Henry H. Adams, op. cit., p. 32.

105. For Butler's colonial career see Hans Schmidt, *Maverick Marine...*, Chapters 1-7.

106. David Healy, op. cit., p. 192.

107. Cited in Henry Adams, op. cit., p. 33.

108. For an account of the intervention, see, Bruce Calder, op. cit.

109. *Leahy Diary*, May, 1916, cited in Gerald Thomas, op. cit., p. 140.

110. Ibid., p. 142.

111. Henry H. Adams, op. cit., p. 35.

112. Ibid., p. 40.

113. Julio Le Riverend, *Historia económica de Cuba* (La Habana: Editorial de Ciencias Sociales, 1985), pp. 615-20; also, Hugh Thomas, op. cit., Chapters 46-48.

114. Henry H. Adams, op. cit., p. 40.

115. Linda Mc Clain, op. cit., p. 13.

116. Henry H. Adams, op. cit., p. 70.

117. Robert Greenhalgh Albion, op. cit., p. 252.

118. The limits had been set by the London Naval Disarmament Conference of 1930. See, Philip T. Rosen, "The Treaty Navy, 1919-1937," in Kenneth J. Hagan, *In Peace and in War, Interpretations of American Naval History, 1775-1978* (Westport: Greenwood Press, 1978), Chapter 12, pp. 221-236.

119. "President Roosevelt had initiated a naval rebuilding program as early as 1934, after Japan withdrew from the Washington and London naval limitations agreements. Roosevelt's tastes were nautical, and perhaps partly for that reason he was much slower to sympathize with Army requests for rebuilding." Russell F. Weigley, *History of the United States Army* (New York: The Macmillan Co., 1967), p. 417.

120. Linda Mc Clain, op. cit., p. 13.

121 A trip Roosevelt used to attempt to resolve feuding between Ickes and Hopkins. See, Robert E. Sherwood, *Roosevelt and Hopkins, An Intimate History* (New York: Harper & Brothers, 1948), pp. 77-9.

122. Henry H. Adams, op. cit., pp. 83-89.

123. Robert Greenhalgh Albion, op. cit., p. 267.

124. For a general analysis of the evolution of the navy's administrative structure and the office of the Chief of Naval Operations, see, Henry P. Beers, "The Development of the Office of the Chief of Naval Operations," *Military Affairs*, Part I (Spring 1946), pp. 40-68; Part II (Fall 1946) pp. 10-38; and Part III (Summer 1947) pp. 88-237. Also Robert William Love, Jr., ed., *The Chiefs of Naval Operation* (Annapolis: Naval Institute Press, 1981).

125. In 1936, the U.S. Navy had a total tonnage of 1,078,000 compared to Britain's 1,192,000 tons. Japan had 748,000, France 548,000 and Italy 411,000. See, Samuel Eliot Morrison, *The Battle of the Atlantic, September 1939-May 1943*, Vol. I (Boston: Little Brown and Co., 1947), p. lix.

126. Linda Mc Clain, op. cit., pp. 14-15

127. Ibid., p. 22.

128. Linda Mc Clain, op. cit., pp. 31-32.

129. Linda Mc Clain, op. cit., p. 8.

130. Luis Muñoz Marín to Ruby Black, January 8, 1940, Ruby Black Collection, Box 5, 1940, Centro de Investigaciones Históricas, University of Puerto Rico.

131. Henry H. Adams, op. cit., pp. 42-45.

132. One of the U.S. Army officers in South Russia, Lieutenant Colonel Francis E. Riggs, would command the police in Puerto Rico in the 1930s. As we shall see, his assassination had profound political repercussions. On the Allied intervention in South Russia, see, George A. Brinkley, *The Volunteer Army and Allied Intervention in South Russia, 1917-1921* (Notre Dame: University of Notre Dame Press, 1966); for Riggs participation refer to pages 34, 177, 178 and 329 (n. 81).

133. David McCullough, *Truman* (New York: Simon & Schuster, 1992), passim. Also, Henry H. Adams, op. cit., Chapters 16-18.

134. Henry H. Adams, op. cit., pp. 90-91.

135. William L. Langer and Everett Gleason, *The Challenge to Isolation, 1937-1940* (New York: Harper and Row, 1952), pp. 11-12.

136. Henry H. Adams, op. cit., pp. 100-4; also, James R. Leutze, *Bargaining for Supremacy, Anglo-American Naval Collaboration, 1937-1941* (Chapel Hill: University of North Carolina Press, 1977), pp. 19-28.

137. I refer to this report in the following chapter.

138. John Major, "The Navy Plans for War, 1937-1941," in Kenneth J. Hagan, op. cit., p. 241.

139. Patrick Abbazzia, op. cit., pp. 30-31.

140. For example, the attempted coup of the Integralista party of Brazil against the Vargas government in May 1939 and the constant flow of alarming information of fascist activities throughout Latin America. David G. Haglund, op. cit.

141. James R. Leutze, op. cit., p. 29.

142. William L. Langer and Everett Gleason, op. cit., p. 41.

143. See, for example, Joseph S. Edgerton, "Defense of Neighbors Held Essential to Safety of U.S., 'Continental' Plan Advocated to Make Sure Enemy Would Not Seize Weak Country for Basis of Attack," *Washington Star*, November 27, 1938. The newspaper sources cited in this part are found in Leahy's Papers, Manuscript Division, Library of Congress, "Scrapbook."

144. "Welles and Military Chiefs Urge Arms-Making for Americas," *Washington Star*, March 22, 1939; and "Leahy Supports Ship-Aid Proposal," *Cincinnati Post*, March 22, 1939.

145. Blair Bolles, "Capital Greets Nicaragua's Head With Pomp, Planes, Soldiers and Crowds Provide Dazzling Reception," *Washington Star*, May 5, 1939.

146. Batista had removed from power the constitutional president Miguel Mariano

Gómez and installed the puppet Laredo Bru. He was invited to Washington by the Army's Chief of Staff Malin Craig. He met FDR, Cordell Hull, and his friend Sumner Welles. He visited West Point and participated in the Armistice Day celebrations. Although Cuban affairs were generally discussed, FDR stressed his concern over "totalitarian influences" in Cuba. This visit strengthened Batista's power in Cuba. Irwin F. Gellman, op. cit., pp. 167-8; also, Hugh Thomas, op. cit., pp. 711-12.

147. Bernardo Vega, *Trujillo y las fuerzas armadas...*, pp. 232-239.

148. "Brazilian Army Chief Is Feted At Banquet," *Washington Post*, 22 June 1939.

149. James R. Leutze, op. cit., pp. 42-4.

150. Ibid., p. 37.

151. Francis L. Loewenheim, Harold D. Langley and Manfred Jonas, eds., *Roosevelt and Churchill, Their Secret Wartime Correspondence* (New York: Da Capo Press, 1990), pp. 104-114.

152. Henry H. Adams, op. cit., p. 117.

153. William D. Leahy, "A Sailor's Adventure in Politics," p. 2.

154. "Leahy Faces Hard Task in Puerto Rico, Critical Problems Await Arrival of Retired Naval Operations Chief," *Washington Post*, May 28, 1939.

155. "Leahy to Succeed Governor Winship," *The New York Times*, May 13, 1939, p. 4.

156. "Leahy Called Ablest Brain in U.S. Forces," *El País*, June 21, 1939.

157. William D. Leahy, "A Sailor's..." p. 14.

158. Linda Mc Clain, op. cit., p. 35.

159. Idem.

C H A P T E R   3

FLEET PROBLEM XX

*FDR meets Admirals Leahy, Bloch, Kalbfus and Andrews of Fleet Problem XX
in Culebra, February, 1939. El Mundo Collection, UPR.*

FLEET PROBLEM XX

Puerto Rico –particularly the capital city of San Juan– was engulfed in a war atmosphere during the Fleet Problem XX maneuvers of February 1939 and just before President Roosevelt offered Leahy the governorship. The outbreak of full-scale war in Europe was still seven months away; formal declaration of war by the U.S. would take almost two more years. However, headlines, news dispatches and articles on the European and Asian conflicts, the Fleet Problem XX maneuvers, defense plans for the island, and statements by FDR and other U.S. politicians on the international situation, tended to eclipse Puerto Rican politics in the pages of *El Mundo*, Puerto Rico's leading daily. The ubiquitous physical presence of the U.S. military left no doubt regarding the seemingly inexorable course of events.

A strong dose of war movies was being dispensed in the main cinemas, and public schools were already moving toward "war education." In early February, a local cinema was showing the Paramount film *Men with Wings* with Fred McMurray, Ray Milland, and Louise Campbell. The advertisement showed an air battle scene, presumably of World War I, between biplanes.[1] This was followed by a 20th Century Fox film, *Submarine Patrol*, a "drama of heroism and courage" in which "these creatures learnt what is necessary to be called men in the infernal baptism of turbulent waters, fire and shrapnel."[2] It was about an anti-submarine vessel that had to be readied in 24 hours to hunt German submarines during World War I.[3] Simultaneously, the Martí Cinema began showing the "rollicking riot of roaring romance," *Join the Marines* with June Travis and Paul Kelly, and made by Republic Pictures. Its title was translated into Spanish as "Vámonos con la Marina" (let's go with the Navy). This film was shown with a serialized documentary entitled "¡Guardacostas Alertas!" (Coast Guard Alert!).

A few days later, the Martí Cinema began showing *Brother Rat*, a Warner Brothers movie starring Priscilla Lane and Wayne Morris. It was set in the Virginia Military Institute. Joseph, its main character, was "going to be a general. Which –next to being a 'Brother Rat', is better than anything– but less fun." The title was translated as *Los Soldados Mandan* (soldiers rule), a particularly meaningful title in the Puerto Rican circumstances.[4] The propaganda campaign spearheaded by Hollywood during 1939 provoked an interesting response by a psychologist in *El Mundo*. He argued in a well-documented article that war propaganda had a negative effect on people's emotions and that he could not tell his patients to relax since he knew that "the men that took the United States into the war in 1917 were victims of emotional propaganda." The author made particular reference to Warner Brothers' film *Confessions of a Nazi Spy*. Its premiere was attended by Walter Cope, personal secretary to Governor Leahy, and by Brigadier General Edmund L. Daley, commander of the Army's Puerto Rico Department. The promotion of the film said: "Your neighbor could be a spy that is selling [out] the fatherland! Perhaps a foreign government is paying him to commit treason!"[5]

Cigarette vendors were also in a fighting mood. Chesterfield ran a quarter page advertisement with George Brent, Olivia de Havilland, and John Payne that said: "these three stars will be admired and applauded in *Wings of the Navy* a Cosmopolitan film distributed by Warner Bros., soon to be shown in your cinema."[6] Camel also advertised with a smoking navy captain.[7] Even Mexican actors had to begin donning military uniforms to compete with the cascade of war films coming out of Hollywood.[8]

In 1937, the acting Commissioner of Education in Puerto Rico, H. A. Martin, had issued a directive instructing teachers to explain the benefits the U.S. derived from well organized armed forces and the sacrifice made by soldiers in defending its territorial integrity. They were also to explain the different military organizations, especially mentioning Regiment 365 stationed in San Juan, the National Guard, and the Army Reserve. He emphasized the celebration of Armed Forces Day.[9] Commissioner José Gallardo, in a letter dated October 30, 1939, ordered the celebration of Veterans' Day and honoring all soldiers who had given their lives for democracy.[10] Another letter from Gallardo instructed teachers and students to make arrangements to participate in National Guard exercises in Vega Baja.[11] Gradually, the public educational system was oriented toward activities in support of military preparations and the war effort.

The Boy Scouts celebrated their 20th anniversary in February with a campaign under the slogan "Scouting Promotes American Ideals."[12] Charlie Chan and Dick Tracy were busy pursuing foreign devils with German names and "oriental" faces. Modern airplanes and "high technology" were important characters in these comic strips. WNEL radio ("The Link of the Americas") advertised with the phrase "News of the War," illustrated with two firing cannons and infantry soldiers marching under a flag.[13] The "Queen" of the University of Puerto Rico was shown escorted by a uniformed ROTC student as she passed through a tunnel formed by swords held by other ROTC students. In many ways, war was already manifesting itself as a cultural phenomenon.[14]

But real war was more pervasive. Throughout the month of February, the press followed the last stages of the Spanish Civil War on a daily basis. Maps depicting the military situation and photographs from the front line and the Spanish-French borders were prominently displayed. Spanish events were reported in *El Mundo* by Ralph Heizen, and occasionally by Julius C. Edelstein.[15] Romualdo Real, a *Falange* sympathizer and prominent member of the *El Mundo* staff,[16] wrote columns on the Spanish and European situation from Nationalist-controlled Tenerife in the Canary Islands. He apologetically expounded the ideas of Primo de Rivera,[17] and praised the statesmanship of British Prime Minister Neville Chamberlain and French Prime Minister Daladier for their agreement with Hitler in Munich.[18] Real also virulently attacked Indalecio Prieto, the Republican leader,[19] while arguing that he opted for the "historic Spain" against the "loyal" "Hispano-Bolshevik Republic."[20]

The Spanish Civil War was not a distant event to be observed in the "international stage." *El Mundo* printed a sympathetic story by Emilio S. Belaval of a young lady of a prominent Puerto Rican family who was a member of the *Falange*. It included her picture in fascist uniform.[21] The raising of the Nationalist flag in the *Casa de España* by three local young *falangistas* –Carmencita Durán, Amalia de la Haba, and María Antonia López– was also reported with a prominent photograph.[22]

Japanese-Chinese hostilities in China were an additional source of war news that furnished images of widespread destruction.[23] F. Sotomayor Rabat, in a column entitled "La muerte de un gigante" (Death of a Giant), said that Japanese military victories in China should concern Puerto Ricans as "...Uncle Sam would not hesitate in throwing [us, North American citizens] the uniform in case of a conflict..."[24] He painted a dismal picture of the international situation.

> In view of the international tension, a horrible noise from all sides thunders in our ears: Czechoslovakia... Tunisia... Corsica... Suez... Ukraine... Hungary... Gibraltar... Maginot... Mediterranean... Spain... Pyrenees... Gibraltar... Ceuta... Malta... Pantellería... Danzig... China... Bolshevism... and many more names that smell as powder and already have the scent of blood.[25]

On February 2, the main headline of El Mundo reported that the German Press had denounced a "regime of terror" in Puerto Rico.[26] The report referred to an article published in Das Schwarze Korps, the official organ of the national socialist "storm troopers," which claimed that the U.S. was using OGPU (Soviet secret police) methods in Puerto Rico and that "Governor Winship, who enjoys Washington's high esteem, attempts to model [him]self as far as possible on his prototype Stalin." It also described the 1937 Palm Sunday massacre of Nationalists in Ponce, claiming that the police "turned machine-guns on crowds with a coldbloodedness of gangsters." This had immediate repercussions in Washington as liberal journalist Oswald Garrison Villard used his column "Issues and Men" in The Nation to launch a scathing attack on Governor Winship, whom he called an "autocratic, dictatorial type." He also argued that the German indictment was "in the main... a correct one."[27] Villard was a strong Roosevelt supporter who could hardly be suspected of fascist sympathies. The Puerto Rican House of Representatives, on the other hand, responded to the German report by issuing a strong condemnation of the German press.[28]

The German attack on U.S. policy in Puerto Rico was apparently elicited by a secret meeting in the White House between the president and the Senate's military affairs committee. In this meeting FDR informed the congressmen that war might be inevitable, and favored supporting Britain and France in that case to enable them to harden their stance toward Germany. He also asked for support for rearmament and defense measures.[29] Just before the *Das Schwarze Korps* article was published, Hitler had reacted to reports of this meeting, promising in a speech that foreign criticisms would be answered.[30] Thus, Puerto Rico became part of the intense propaganda war that was being waged, and Governor Winship's repressive policies a source of international embarrassment. But the incident did not conclude then, as Rafael Martínez Nadal, President of the Puerto Rican Senate and close political ally of Winship, claimed that the U.S. exercised "fascist control" over Puerto Rico. His statement was reported by *The New York Times*.[31]

Another war-related issue that made headlines during February was the U.S. plan to establish bases in Puerto Rico.[32] Vice Admiral F. R. Harris and two other naval officers arrived in San Juan in early February to go over the arrangements for the construction of a dry dock in the San Juan Harbor. They paid a visit to Governor Winship at La Fortaleza.[33] The construction of a dry dock for military purposes had been planned in 1918, but the project was abandoned after the conclusion of World War I. The dry dock to be constructed in 1939 was 75 feet larger than a similar one built in Callao, Perú, with the purpose of accommodating cruisers of the Memphis and Philadelphia class. The $2,000,000 contract was awarded to E. H. Latham & Co. of Columbus, Ohio, and the construction of the huge floating door entrusted to Sucesores de Abarca of San Juan. Representative Vito Marcantonio would later denounce as illegal a $75,000 fee paid to Frederick R. Graves, a friend of Governor Winship, for the drawing of the plans.[34] Though the project was presented as a local initiative, it was evident to contemporary observers that it was essentially a military project related to strategic plans for the San Juan harbor.

> As a spot for the investment of private capital, a $2,000,000 drydock at San Juan is not attractive. There is not the slightest doubt but that the military value of the new graving dock at San Juan, to enable the Navy to recondition vessels quickly and conveniently in time of emergency, was the deciding factor in the discussions that led to the final approval of the drydock project.[35]

The large harbor dredging projects undertaken during 1939 were also militarily related. Standard Dredging Co. of New York was awarded a $539,000 contract to double the deep water area of the harbor, while F. Benítez Rexach was paid $350,000 to dredge the Martín Peña channel for the use of barges and to fill a swamp.

> The first is a project of military significance because the harbor of San Juan, capable of accommodating the regular traffic of the port, did not offer sufficient deep water anchorage for the fleets of naval vessels that would, presumably, use the port as a base in time of war.[36]

The Martín Peña project was said to have the purpose of connecting that area, where navy warehouses might be built, to the harbor.[37] However, most of the reports published during the early part of the month focused on the discussion in congressional and naval circles of the Hepburn Board recommendation to establish a naval air and submarine base in the Isla Grande area of San Juan. The Isla Grande site had been a Pan American Airways installation since 1928, but since 1936 the Navy and USMC had begun using it for yearly exercises.[38] On February 3, another headline tied the question of military bases to the island's political status. It read: "Navy decided to establish here permanent bases, the plan is already drafted without taking into account the eventual political fate of the island." It informed the public about a hearing in the House Naval Affairs Committee with Captain Arthur L. Bristol, Jr., where the issue of independence was discussed. Bristol stated that "probably the United States would retain the naval station no matter what is the course of political events."[39] By mid-February the Naval Affairs Committee favorably recommended legislation providing for the construction of naval bases, which included $9,138,000 for the installation to be built at Isla Grande. It was the largest assignment for a base construction contained in the bill. By February 22, the House had approved the law, except for the assignment for a base in the island of Guam.[40]

However, reports published in *El Mundo* clearly showed that defense plans went beyond the recommendations of the Hepburn Board and that Fleet Problem XX would serve to identify additional bases in Puerto Rico and the Caribbean.[41] On February 27, a letter from Resident

Commissioner Santiago Iglesias was reported in a front-page article with the headline "Puerto Rico constantly acquires more importance in U.S. defense programs." It reported a statement to the House Military Affairs Committee by General H. H. Arnold, Commander of Army Air Forces, regarding the need to establish air bases in Puerto Rico, Hawaii, Alaska, and the continental United States. The editors included a note stating that the Puerto Rican base had already been approved by the House.[42] Significantly, the article said that the Resident Commissioner was very optimistic about "the concessions and privileges that the island will obtain as a result of its importance in national defense programs."[43] Another article in the same paper stated that Santiago Iglesias had submitted a project to make Puerto Rico an "incorporated territory."[44] Clearly, the governing *Coalición* was trying to jump on the military bandwagon and cash in politically on Puerto Rico's enhanced strategic importance. It was to suffer a strong disappointment.

In March, Governor Winship confirmed that this was not an isolated move by Iglesias, but a strategy to bolster the *Coalición*'s and his own already shaky standing in the Roosevelt administration. In a radio address through the Columbia Broadcasting System, he emphasized defense plans for Puerto Rico and demanded special concessions, while dismissing the difficulties he had faced with the Nationalist Party and the pro-independence movement.

> [Puerto Rico] now is deemed essential to provide complete protection, both for the Atlantic seaboard of the United States and for the Panama Canal and South America, and Puerto Rico has been termed the keystone in our national defense.

> Strategically located in the Caribbean Sea, fourteen hundred miles south and east of New York, about one thousand miles east of Panama, and less than six hundred miles from the north coast of South America, Puerto Rico is ideally situated, not only for the large proposed naval airbase but also as a full-fledged base for naval vessels. In addition, plans have been advanced to guard against possible seizure by enemy forces...

> Now, in view of our newly recognized importance to the United States, we have every reason to hope that the Federal

government and the people of this great country will do everything in their power to aid our little territory in attaining a
more stable economic position.[45]

The same day that FDR and Leahy cruised near San Juan at the conclusion of the fleet maneuvers, *El Mundo* reported in its main headline
that "plans exist to make Puerto Rico an inexpugnable fortress." The
article claimed that defense plans for the construction of bases and fortifications would transform the island into the "Hawaii of the east" and
that $25,000,000 had been earmarked for this purpose.[46] The previous
day, Senator Morris Sheppard, Chairman of the Senate Military Affairs
Committee, had called Puerto Rico, Panama, Hawaii, and Alaska "vital
links" in U.S. defense plans.[47] Upon his arrival in Charleston, FDR said
that Fleet Problem XX had confirmed the need for naval bases in San
Juan and the U.S. Virgin Islands.[48]

Another Country

By mid-January 1939, San Juan began to experience the impact of
the Fleet Problem XX maneuvers. A flotilla of 47 planes (including 18
USMC "Drummonds") landed in the Isla Grande airfield on January 17.
They had flown from Quantico, Virginia, to Port-au-Prince, Haiti, and
on to San Juan. A few days earlier the transport ship *Capella* had brought
supplies to build a tent camp at Isla Grande and the area had been sealed
off.[49] Air maneuvers over San Juan, consisting of a mock attack on the
city, soon began.[50] Forty-eight more planes arrived on January 23. These
flew from bases in California to Panama, and then directly to Puerto
Rico. Air maneuvers were also held that day over San Juan. *El Mundo*
published a picture of 18 planes flying in formation over El Morro.[51] It
stated also that the 65th Infantry Regiment and the Puerto Rican National
Guard would take part in the maneuvers, carrying out an "enemy" attack in the Ponce area. A total of 140 ships, 600 planes, and 58,000 men
would participate in Fleet Problem XX.[52]

The naval aspect of the maneuvers was also conspicuous to
sanjuaneros. The *Phoenix* cruiser arrived in San Juan harbor on February
12.[53] The *Wyoming* and *Memphis* battleships soon followed, and a host of

other vessels also moored at San Juan.[54] Warships were deployed in other Puerto Rican harbors. On January 15, several warships cruised near the coast of San Juan.[55] The sight of these huge and technologically advanced war machines –wonders of industrialism– must have overshadowed the modern sugar mills that had long dominated the social landscape. The press reported that an attack on Puerto Rico by a "Black Fleet" (U.S. forces) was likely to occur.[56] However, it was the "White Fleet" (the German) which carried out diverse raids. The summary of events of Fleet Problem XX shows that many combat operations took place in San Juan and adjacent waters. For example, the summary of events for February 25 read,

> From a position about one hundred miles north of San Juan the carriers of the White Raiding Force launched an attack on the air base at San Juan. The first attack at 0700, a flight of 17 dive bombers, engaged for two minutes the Black Marine Plane Squadron with machine guns. This resulted in the loss of five fighting planes to Black [i.e. U.S.]and an unknown number of planes to White. Fleet Problem XX culminated in a major naval battle in the waters between Culebra and St. Thomas.[57]

Fleet Problem XX culminated on February 27 with a large naval battle in the waters between Culebra and St. Thomas. However, Fleet Landing Exercise (Flex) 5, carried out in Culebra, did not conclude until March 11.[58] Rear Admiral Raymond A. Spruance, later to become the first commander of the 10th Naval District established in San Juan, participated in the Culebra exercises. New landing craft used in the Pacific campaign were tested during Flex 5.[59] On March 12, a large number of Navy planes again participated in air maneuvers over San Juan that were watched "by hundreds of persons who invaded the roofs of Old San Juan."[60] This meant that, in early 1939, Puerto Rico was subjected to two months of intense and uninterrupted military exercises. It was a dress rehearsal of what would later occur in 1942 during the "Battle of the Caribbean."

But the military display was not limited to the skies and waters of Puerto Rico. San Juan was also "invaded" by thousands of military and naval personnel of at least three countries, the U.S., Venezuela, and Finland. To these must be added the mobilized local military units of the 65th Infantry Regiment, the National Guard and other military and paramilitary institutions, then comprising more than 2,000 men. Puerto Rican Army Colonel Luis R. Esteves, who had been trained at West Point, was promoted to Brigadier General in early February and simultaneously placed in command of the Puerto Rican National Guard.[61] He was the first Puerto Rican to reach the rank of general officer. The next day, activities for a "National Defense Week" began. These ran parallel to Fleet Problem XX maneuvers until February 22. The original plan for this defense week consisted in a massive "attack" on the capital city to be staged by the 65th Infantry Regiment, the National Guard, the American Legion, and regular Army and Navy units. This exercise was abandoned.[62] Instead, plans were made for an air show over San Juan with 20 planes piloted by Puerto Rican reservists, followed the next day by a military parade with the 65th Infantry Regiment and the National Guard.[63] The main speaker at the parade was former Governor of Puerto Rico James R. Beverley. His speech emphasized looming threats to U.S. and world security, and called for rearmament and military preparedness. E. Combas Guerra graphically described the unprecedented spectacle that could be seen daily on the streets of San Juan:

> In these days, when we go out on the street, we get the impression of being in another country. The only thing now seen in this capital city are sailors, aviators, cadets and Finnish sailors, Venezuelan cadets, soldiers, national guardsmen, boy scouts... We feel a pleasant sensation when we find someone dressed as a civilian, as if we had returned to reality... Thousands of sailors fill our sidewalks daily, our cafés, our buses, our cinemas, our hotels, our parks and even our carnival... By night we see various scenes of revelry... North American and Finnish sailors –those that have two black bands behind their caps– have become good friends, despite their lack of knowledge of their respective languages...[64]

Puerto Rico in the Hepburn Board Report

The U.S. Navy had not conducted a major study on base requirements since 1923, when the Rodman Board Report was prepared. Naval war planning during the pre-World War I period had mainly focused on a possible German threat to U.S. possessions in the Caribbean and to the

Panama Canal. Germany, in fact, had elaborated a very detailed plan for the occupation of Puerto Rico.[65] In the Asia-Pacific region, Plan Orange dealt with war against Japan. Britain was also considered a potential enemy, but, given the extent of U.S.-British collaboration, war with Britain was highly unlikely. During World War I, naval collaboration with Britain was further enhanced. Even the possibility of a major German naval attack in the Atlantic-Caribbean region was remote as long as Britain maintained naval supremacy in the North Sea. In such circumstances, Germany's naval operations would have to rely mainly on submarine warfare.

After World War I, the U.S. enjoyed an even more favorable strategic environment. Germany's naval power had been eliminated. Britain accepted U.S. naval and military supremacy in the Caribbean, while the U.S. practically placed British and other European colonies in the region under its security umbrella. In addition, the Washington Naval Conference (1921-1922) had placed strict limits on the size of the navies of the U.S., Great Britain, Japan, France and Italy.[66]

Thus, the presidencies of Harding, Coolidge, and Hoover (known as the Republican Restoration) were characterized by great parsimony in naval expenditures. Strategic concern after World War I understandably shifted from the Atlantic back to the Pacific and to Japan's naval might.[67] It was FDR who began to reverse the trend in 1933 in the direction of renewed naval expansion. Dexter Perkins relates this "strategic vacuum" to changes in U.S. Caribbean policy during the late twenties and early thirties.

> Per contra, it is significant that with the defeat of Germany, the Caribbean policy of the United States underwent a substantial revision. The sea power of the Reich had been destroyed; there was no European state that could or would challenge the position of the United States in the waters controlling the approaches to the Canal, and this fact explains why the Monroe Doctrine underwent substantial revision in [the] late twenties and early thirties. The Roosevelt corollary was gradually abandoned...[68]

The Rodman Board Report reflected the post-World War I situation. It stressed the great strategic importance of the Panama Canal and the entire Caribbean geo-strategic space. However, it did not consider that threats to the region warranted the construction of a major base for the U.S. fleet. If eventually required, it could be constructed in Panama. The report did not recommend a major expansion beyond the existing base system.[69]

The Hepburn Board was created by the Naval Expansion Act of May 17, 1938. The senior member of the board, Admiral A. J. Hepburn, had been Leahy's classmate. The board consisted of two rear admirals, three captains and one commander.[70] The report was submitted to CNO Leahy on December 1, 1938 and to Congress the following month by Claude Swanson, Secretary of the Navy. While agreeing with the strategic outlook contained in the Rodman Board Report, it stressed: (1) that the greatest need for additional bases was in the Atlantic-Caribbean region as "the United States Fleet has been based in the Pacific during recent years, when the expansion of the air force has been most rapid, the growth of air bases, to serve the fleet, has been almost wholly in that area."; and (2) that air and submarine bases were urgently required.[71] Regarding Puerto Rico it said:

> In its study of the Caribbean the Board found only one site capable of being made into an air base suitable for the normal operation of patrol planes. This is at Isla Grande, in the harbor of San Juan, Puerto Rico... In addition to its suitability for patrol planes, the site offers [a] suitable area for the construction of a landing field and facilities for the training of one or more carrier groups. A base for patrol planes situated this far eastward in the Caribbean will be of major strategic importance. The Board understands that negotiations are in progress to have the site transferred by the insular government to the jurisdiction of the Navy.[72]

Consequently, the report recommended, "(a) Facilities for one carrier group (planned with a view to expansion to two carrier groups), (b) Facilities for two patrol-plane squadrons (original plans for this station must provide for immediate emergency expansion for at least four patrol-plane squadrons), (c) Facilities for complete engine overhaul, (d) Construction of breakwater at harbor entrance, [and] (e) Berthing at pier for one carrier."[73] The expansion and construction of air and naval facilities in Guantánamo and the U.S. Virgin islands were also proposed, but in a scale smaller to those of Isla Grande. Similarly, the board advised the creation of a submarine base at Isla Grande.

> 128. [...] The Board previously in this report has recommended the establishment of an air base in San Juan. Necessary wharfage for submarines can be readily provided at the air base without interference with air activities.

> 129. The Board recommends that submarine berthing be provided at Isla Grande and that an adequate supply of fuel be established.[74]

The only two other sites in the Caribbean mentioned as possible submarine bases were Key West and the U.S. Virgin Islands. However, new construction was recommended only in the case of San Juan.

The board prepared four lists of new bases: air, submarine, destroyers, and mines. Each list was further divided into Category A (for earliest completion) and B (for later completion). No Caribbean bases for destroyers and mines were proposed. On the lists for air and submarine bases, Isla Grande appeared in Category A. On the air bases list, Isla Grande appeared in fourth place of a total of fifteen, followed by Panama. On the submarine bases list, it occupied second place (after Guam) of five sites. Additionally, the Isla Grande project was the most costly ($9,300,000) of all that were eventually approved by Congress in late February 1939.[75] The board left no doubt of the importance it ascribed to the San Juan bases. The final commentary of the report said:

> There are certain projects, however, which the Board has no hesitation in selecting because of their immediate strategic importance as being necessary for accomplishment at the earliest predictable date and without regard of the expansion contemplated by the Act of May 17, 1938. These items are: Kaneohe Bay, Midway Island, Wake Island, Guam, Johnston Island and Palmyra Island in the mid-Pacific are; Kodiak and Sitka in the Alaskan area; and San Juan, Puerto Rico, in the Atlantic area. In addition, the immediate increase of training facilities at Pensacola, Fla., is mandatory.[76]

The importance of Isla Grande was further demonstrated by the congressional decision to reject a major base construction in Guam.

The Isla Grande project, when considered in historical perspective, was the largest investment the U.S. made in military infrastructure in Puerto Rico since it obtained control of the island in 1898. The Hepburn Board Report highlighted the prominent role that was being assigned to Puerto Rico in U.S. Atlantic-Caribbean strategy. Ironically, it would be very rapidly superseded by naval demands for even more bases and installations in the island as a result of Fleet Problem XX. The Army, particularly the Air Corps, also had plans for the construction of major facilities in Puerto Rico.[77] The *Economic Review* journal, in a June 1939 article, took note of the rapid increase of military construction plans for Puerto Rico and their potentially favorable impact on the economy.

> Recent moves on the part of the military and naval authorities in Puerto Rico make the general outlines of the Government's plan clear enough. The notion that Isla Grande Airport, Pan American Airway's terminal, would be the center of operations, has gone into discard. It seems clear that the Army will locate its principal flying fields, shops and training quarters at some distance from the capital city and that the Navy will base no more than a squadron of reconnaissance planes at San Juan proper. It is also clear that the port of San Juan, regardless of where the military establishments are built, will be the heart of the military circulation system as far as supplies are concerned, and unquestionably the strategic moves of both the Army and Navy mean greatly increased tonnages at San Juan's docks. They also mean the establishment of considerable personnel at San Juan...[78]

The urgency for Caribbean bases is understandable in view of the intense strategic debate that was taking place in the US, and the "lessons" derived from the fleet maneuvers of 1939.

The Caribbean in U.S. Strategic Debate and War Planning

From 1938 to 1941 (when the U.S. finally became belligerent), an intense strategic debate took place in civilian and military circles regarding the defense policies the U.S. should adopt in view of impending (and, later, actual) war in Europe and Japanese expansionism in the

Asia-Pacific region. This debate was, to a large extent, conducted in public. It signified the gradual waning of the pacifist and neutralist consensus of the pre-1938 period, during which intellectual and political critics of U.S. participation in World War I had been extremely influential.[79] Opposition to war, a large military establishment, and "foreign entanglements" had brought together, since the 1920s, diverse and powerful political forces in Congress, academia, the press, and a vast network of peace groups.[80] These forces -as the sharp negative reaction to FDR's "Quarantine Speech" and proposed military measures against Japan as a reaction to the *Panay* incident had demonstrated- became a formidable political obstacle to rearmament and measures for decisive war preparation.

The new strategic debate that began in 1938 tended to underscore U.S. military weakness and its unpreparedness for both continental and hemispheric defense. Although the Caribbean had always figured prominently in U.S. strategic thinking, its crucial importance for US defense plans was considerably magnified after 1938. The Caribbean became the object of analysis in a deluge of articles and books. In fact, military control of the Caribbean geo-strategic space and its relationship to both continental and hemispheric defense plans became an almost obsessive preoccupation of strategic analysts. In prevalent discourse, many Caribbean islands suddenly became "Gibraltars," "Maltas," "bulwarks," "ramparts," "keys," "capstones," "strongholds," "sentinels," "watchdogs," "outposts," and "defense problems." Within the Caribbean, the geo-strategic importance of the Puerto Rico-Virgin Islands' zone was also greatly stressed. Parallel to this intellectual and political discussion, war planning was revised also to reflect the renewed importance ascribed to the region.

Among the strategic proposals that were publicly discussed in 1938, George Fielding Eliot's book *The Ramparts We Watch: A Study of the Problems of American National Defense* –which by 1939 was in its sixth printing– had particular implications for military policy toward the Caribbean.[81] This book appeared during the Sudeten crisis of September 1938. Eliot had also written with R. E. Dupuy another book that was published in 1937, *If War Comes*, which dealt with similar issues.[82] Eliot was a former major of army intelligence.

In a broad analysis of U.S. military security and strategy, he proposed a policy of "hemispheric security" based on a balanced expansion of naval and military forces, but placing great emphasis on the navy's role. He also sharply criticized undue reliance on the expansion of air power.[83] It is interesting to note that the epigraph of the first chapter is a quotation from an FDR speech on the deteriorating international situation, while the chapter on naval policy is headed by a statement by Admiral Leahy on the importance of battleships.[84]

Regarding the Caribbean, his argument closely followed known tenets of Mahan's geopolitical outlook, underscoring the vital importance of the Panama Canal, and the need to ensure naval control of the entire region and access to bases. Additionally, the control of the Caribbean was considered essential to the defense of Brazil and the South Atlantic. According to Eliot, Dutch, French, and British possessions in the region should not be allowed to fall under the control of a hostile power, while existing bases (Panama, Guantánamo, Puerto Rico-Virgin Islands) should be developed and strengthened. He also called for the acquisition of additional bases and expressly mentioned as possible sites Jamaica, Curaçao, Trinidad, Barbados and St. Lucia, all European possessions. In this regard, he proposed considering a barter of the Philippines for the British Caribbean territories, or condoning the British and French war debts in exchange for their Caribbean possessions, an old aspiration of some military sectors that had been rejected in 1936.[85]

Eliot placed great emphasis on the importance of the Puerto Rico-Virgin Islands area. In a map of the Caribbean region, he drew a square over the zone and named it the "Eastern Outpost."[86] The vital Mona and Anegada passages could be controlled from these islands and air and naval power projected toward the Atlantic and the Lesser Antilles.

> On the Mona passage we have Puerto Rico, a large island of considerable local resources with several good harbors, none of them unfortunately, able comfortably to accommodate battleships. There are no fixed defense or even mobile heavy guns here, nor is there an air base. Just east of Puerto Rico and belonging to it is the islet of Culebra, whose Great Harbor is adequate for a fleet anchorage, though difficult to defend by fortification. A few miles further eastward, however, we possess a harbor of quite different characteristics. The island of Saint Thomas, one of the American Virgins, with its fine and easily protected port of Charlotte Amalie, is now our

easternmost Caribbean possession. Together with Puerto Rico and Culebra, it forms an outpost which extends the influence of Guantanamo 700 miles to seaward and it watches the Anegada Passage, 70 miles distant, which is the principal commercial route for European traffic directed upon Panama.[87]

Eliot proposed increasing the Puerto Rican garrison to about 1,500 men and providing it with coastal artillery.[88] With an additional base in Barbados or Trinidad and one or more auxiliary bases in the Lesser Antilles, the U.S. could seal all potential entry points to the Caribbean and project naval force toward the South Atlantic as far as the strategically important Brazilian "salient."[89] It is striking how closely actual U.S. military planning followed Eliot's recommendations.

In late October 1938, *Life Magazine* published an article entitled "America Gets Ready to Fight Germany, Italy and Japan," which included a half-page photo of Admiral Leahy standing in front of a world map. The map had a large arrow connecting the region of Dakar in Africa with the "Brazilian bulge" and a caption that read, "it is only 2,000 miles from Africa to South America." It also included a map of the Caribbean indicating naval bases and maritime routes with the caption, "Caribbean is strategic key to the Western Hemisphere," and indicated that "the region above is the part of his map which Admiral Leahy studies with most concern." It also said that "From the strategist['s] viewpoint, America's long soul-searchings over 'imperialism' in the Caribbean are sentimental twaddle. America *must* control the Caribbean or some other power may control America." The *Life Magazine* article cited Eliot's books *The Ramparts We Watch* and *If War Comes* as authoritative sources on the Caribbean, emphasizing his recommendation of additional bases in several European possessions.[90]

It is also interesting that when a review of Eliot's book, written by Walter Millis, was published in *The Washington Post* in November 1938, it was accompanied by a prominent photograph of Leahy.[91] The fact that Millis, though calling Eliot a "militarist," sympathetically reviewed his book ("a brilliant clarification of our strategic problem"), is an indication of how broad the emerging consensus on defense policy was by late 1938. Millis was a leading critic of U.S. expansionism and militarism and had published a widely read indictment of U.S. participation in World

War I.[92] Another article by *The Washington Star* on defense preparations cited both Leahy and Eliot as the main authorities on hemispheric defense, advancing quite similar proposals.[93] All this indicates the semi-official character of Eliot's views, as well as Leahy's apparent support for his scheme.[94]

A host of other writers followed Eliot's lead. Wilbur Burton published an article in *Current History* in December 1938 entitled "Panama: Defense Problem No. 1." He argued that the "isthmian connection between the Atlantic and the Pacific — whether via Panama, Nicaragua, or Tehuantepec— far transcends commerce: it is vital for national American well-being." According to the author, the main potential threat to the canal were "airplanes operating from floating carriers *or from nearby land bases.*"[95] Harold Sprout argued that the U.S. should aim, as a "minimum requirement," at the "indisputable military control of all marine approaches to North America and Northern South America out to a distance greater than the effective operating radius of a hostile fighting fleet or carrier based airplanes." He connected this strategic aim to the recommendation of the Hepburn Board Report for bases in Puerto Rico and the Virgin Islands, noting that "the locus of the 1939 fleet maneuvers gave further emphasis to this new orientation."[96] Norman J. Padelford developed a similar argument in "An Atlantic Naval Policy for the United States," stressing the need for an Atlantic fleet, naval and air bases, and air power.

> The Bahamas, the Greater and Lesser Antilles, and Venezuela are vital to the United States. Here lie the keys to the security of the Panama Canal and the Central American states. From here come indispensable petroleum, tropical foods, and raw materials required by American industry and consumers.[97]

This article was profusely illustrated with photographs of Santo Domingo (Dominican Republic), La Guaira (Venezuela), Cartagena (Colombia), San Juan (Puerto Rico), La Citadel (Haiti), and Guantánamo (Cuba).

In "Island Bulwarks," published in March 1940 by Colonel Cary I. Crockett, the situation in Hawaii and Puerto Rico was reviewed and the dire social and economic difficulties of the latter stressed. This article was also accompanied by several photographs of the San Juan Harbor, Spanish fortifications, and country scenes. A caption of a photograph of the Puerto Rican countryside read: "A crowded land brings social evils that may affect national defense," while a town scene depicting *jíbaros* riding donkeys elicited the comment: "An American scene in Puerto Rico, where hunger may grow into violent unrest."[98] By 1941, Lieutenant Commander Ephraim McLean wrote: "When all the new bases have been constructed and manned by units of our Army and Navy, Mahan's dream will have come true, for the Caribbean will then be an American lake."[99] The prolific defense analyst and *New York Times* military affairs correspondent, Hanson W. Baldwin, also underscored the importance of Caribbean bases. He proposed, among other things, the deployment of long-range bombers in Puerto Rico.[100] An April 1939 article by Oswald Garrison Villard in *Harper's Magazine*, calling for "sanity" in defense policy, appeared anachronistic amidst the barrage of publications in favor of "preparedness."[101]

National Geographic, a reliable barometer of U.S. geostrategic interests,[102] also published extensive articles focusing on particular countries or subregions. In December 1939, the main article by E. John Long was entitled "Puerto Rico: Watchdog of the Caribbean, Venerable Domain Under American Flag Has New Role as West Indian Stronghold and Sentinel of the Panama Canal." The first section had the heading "The Island's Strategic Location" and quoted the co-pilot of the clipper plane that brought him to Puerto Rico as saying, while pointing to a map of the Caribbean:

> Now do you see? About 1,000 miles to the Panama Canal, 1,000 miles to Miami, 700 to Bermuda, 550 to Caracas on the mainland of South America, 650 to Trinidad. This is the hub of a wheel. Put enough planes here, and enough land to guard your bases, and Puerto Rico becomes the 'Gibraltar of the West Indies,' or the 'Hawaii of the Atlantic.'[103]

Interspersed with numerous photos of Puerto Rican scenery and everyday life, the author included several pictures of fortifications, battleships, bases, and military exercises. Interestingly, a detailed analysis on the Puerto Rican situation by Earle K. James published just two years before by *Foreign Policy Reports* did not refer to strategic questions.[104]

National Geographic also devoted its main article of the January 1941 issue to the British West Indies. Its title was "British West Indian Interlude." The map of the Lesser Antilles had the title "Like a Curving Shield the West Indies Guard the Panama Canal," while the section with photographs read "West Indies Links in a Defense Chain."[105] The article was followed, in the same issue, by a brief report by Edward T. Folliard on Martinique. It discussed the French military presence in Martinique and Guadeloupe.[106] Other journals such as *Harper's Magazine, Survey Graphic, Hemisphere, Foreign Affairs* and *Inter American-Quarterly* were also stricken by the Caribbean fever.[107]

Books such as Carleton Beals's *The Coming Struggle for Latin America,* J. Fred Rippy's *Caribbean Danger Zone,* and Walter A. Roberts's *The Caribbean: Our Sea of Destiny,* as their tiles suggest, were part of the debate.[108] For example, Beals's 1938 book, which went through several printings, dealt with the threat to U.S. security posed by the growing fascist influence in Latin America and the Caribbean. He devoted much attention to Puerto Rico, arguing that U.S. policy toward the island undermined Roosevelt's claim to defend democracy in the hemisphere and exposed a weak flank to German propaganda. In this he coincided with the arguments on Puerto Rico expounded by other liberals such as Oscar Garrison Villard.

> Puerto Rico is not considered part of Latin America except in Latin America itself. For Latin America, Puerto Rico is *terra irredenta*. What we do in Puerto Rico is ever sharply scrutinized by other countries.
>
> Actually the little island is ruled over by an appointed governor, safely protected, none ever quite so generally hated as the present Governor Winship. It is ruled over by American sugar companies, monopolizing the land in violation of the constitutional proviso limiting holdings to 500 acres. It is ruled over by a Congress made up mostly of lawyers and others representing the large American interests. It is ruled by a brutalized constabulary. . .
>
> . . .Branded as "agitators" even by Secretary Ickes, harassed, jailed and murdered by the police, the Nationalists have retaliated, and violence has grown into violence, and bitterness

into hatred. In this matter we have displayed the same dull colonial stodginess of any other imperialist power.

The head of the Nationalist Party, Pedro Albizu Campos (with whose partially medieval views I do not sympathize), has been railroaded to Leavenworth by a packed American jury.[109]

The 1940 book edited by William H. Haas, *The American Empire*, on the other hand, reviewed US policy toward all its overseas territories.[110] It elaborated on the acute problems and scant economic value of the U.S. Virgin Islands and Puerto Rico. With regard to the former, the editor stated in the concluding chapter that "although their prospects for the present may prove disappointing, we have the assurance that no other nation can readily avail itself of their strategic features." The book discussed the predominantly strategic military interests in continued U.S. control over Puerto Rico: "Recent developments in Puerto Rico also point to its increasing military importance to the United States. For the present at least, this outweighs all other considerations." Haas ruled out both independence and autonomy as a solution to the island's main problems, overpopulation and poverty.[111] The chapter on Puerto Rico, written by Rafael Picó and William Haas, outlines the serious economic and social ills of the island and flatly states: "That autonomy or even complete independence would solve all Puerto Rican problems is far from true." According to the book, either option only advocated making elective the post of governor.[112] This is particularly illuminating given Picó's alignment with the emerging Popular Democratic Party.

The revision of U.S. war plans which began in 1938 also reflected the growing importance assigned to the Caribbean and the Atlantic. Throughout the 1930s, naval forces in the Caribbean-Atlantic region amounted to a few ships of the Training and Special Service Squadrons. Plan Orange (war against Japan) only dealt with a possible threat to the Panama Canal from the Pacific. In November 1938, the Joint (Army-Navy) Board instructed the Joint Planning Committee to revise war plans in light of the new international circumstances.

The document drafted by Army Colonel Frank S. Clark and Navy Captain Russell S. Crenshaw and issued in April 1939 described a strategic situation very similar to that of Fleet Problem XX: a fascist insurrection, supported by Germany and Italy, in a South American country. It thus placed great emphasis on the Caribbean as part of the hemispheric defense plans and already suggested the "Atlantic-first" strategy followed by the U.S. during the war.[113]

The Joint Planning Committee also began working on the five crucial "Rainbow Plans" that were prepared during 1939 and 1940. Rainbow I, the only plan completed during the first phase of war preparations, "envisioned a German-Italian violation of the Monroe Doctrine that would force a direct confrontation with the United States. German and Italian forces presumably would establish 'intermediate bases' in West Africa and Brazil, while American units concentrated in the Caribbean to interdict Axis lines of communication."[114] The lack of naval forces in the Pacific would trigger an attack on the Philippines and Guam. The U.S. would concentrate on the unilateral defense of its territory, the Eastern Pacific and South Atlantic, and Latin America to latitude 10 degrees South (i.e., the Quarter Sphere concept). Yerxa quotes a Navy officer who claimed that "the crucial point in the Rainbow I concept is the Caribbean."[115] Rainbow IV was similar to Rainbow I, except that the U.S. would defend the entire hemisphere, while Rainbow V included the projection of military power to Africa and Europe.[116] Rainbow IV was approved by FDR in mid August of 1940, and a revised version of Rainbow V was ready by November 1941.[117] During this period most existing war plans for the occupation of Latin American countries were abandoned, with the significant exceptions of Mexico ("Green" War Plan) and Brazil ("Purple" War Plan).[118]

Understandably, defense planning for Puerto Rico gathered momentum during 1939. In July 1938, the Commanding General of the II Corps Area of the Army ordered the preparation of a defense plan for Puerto Rico. The Puerto Rico Defense Plan (code named "Orange") was submitted on October 27, 1938. It provided only for the defense of the main island of Puerto Rico, excluding outlying islands. Immediately after the Fleet XX maneuvers (in May 1939), the Joint Planning Committee submitted to the Joint Board a statement on the Puerto Rico-Virgin Islands area that placed great emphasis on its strategic value. It also recommended assigning this area the following missions:

1. Joint Mission: To defend the Puerto Rico-Virgin Islands area as an outlying base; to support the naval forces in controlling the Caribbean Sea and adjacent waters; and to support operations against shore objectives.

2. Army mission: To hold Puerto Rico and the Virgin Islands against attacks by land, sea and air forces, and against hostile sympathisers; to install and operate required Army base facilities; to support the naval forces in controlling the Caribbean Sea and adjacent waters; and to support operations against shore objectives.

3. Navy Mission: To support the naval forces controlling the Caribbean area and adjacent waters; to control and protect the shipping in the coastal zone; to support the Army in the defense of Puerto Rico and the Virgin islands; and to support operations against shore objectives.[119]

The Joint Planning Committee recommended that the army create a separate overseas department and the navy a new naval district in Puerto Rico. Within these parameters, the Joint Puerto Rico Coastal Frontier Defense Plan, the Puerto Rico Defense Project, and the revision of Plan White (against domestic disturbances) were drafted. This strategic planning process culminated in the comprehensive Puerto Rican Department Basic War Plan, 1941, of February 19, 1941, and the Puerto Rican Defense Project of March 1, 1941.[120]

Fleet Problem XX

Fleet Problem XX was specifically designed to identify naval and military requirements in the Caribbean and the Atlantic. In May 1938, Roosevelt, using New York's World Fair as a pretext, ordered the fleet to travel through the Panama Canal and visit eastern ports to await the incoming maneuvers. The maneuvers were again discussed by FDR and Leahy during a November meeting in the White House.[121]

According to the war hypothesis of Fleet Problem XX, a fascist revolt had occurred in Brazil (Green). Germany (White) dispatched a convoy across the Atlantic to aid the rebels. The United States (Black) issued a diplomatic note of protest, ordered its fleet to go through the Panama

Canal and deploy in the waters between Cuba and Haiti. Black eventually declared war. Vice Admiral Adolphus Andrews was placed in command of the Black Fleet, while the attacking White Fleet was commanded by Admiral Edward C. Kalbfus.[122]

The scenario of the maneuvers was based on discussions on the international and Latin American situation in the State-War-Navy Standing Liaison Committee. The strategic problem had been posed by Under Secretary of State Sumner Welles during the meeting on November 14, 1938. On the same day that Roosevelt asked for a tripling of the Army Air Corps, the Standing Liaison Committee was discussing the latest disquieting news from southern South America. Under Secretary of State Sumner Welles informed his counterparts from the War and Navy Departments, Chief of Staff Malin Craig and Chief of Naval Operations William Leahy, that State Department officers in Brazil were expecting German-instigated rebellions to occur soon in Uruguay, Argentina, and Brazil–all "as part of a large Nazi movement to obtain control of those countries." What Welles wanted to know was, if these fears turned out to be real, would the Navy be capable of heading off any "filibustering" activities on the U.S. East Coast. Leahy thought so, assuming it could use Brazilian ports. For the next month, the administration studied Brazilian developments closely. According to Harold Ickes, the cabinet devoted much of its meeting of December 16 to the "very serious situation in Brazil. The Nazis there are up to mischief, undoubtedly with the encouragement, if not the active backing, of Hitler. They are also very active in Uruguay."[123]

In January 1939, Sumner Welles once again depicted the same scenario during another meeting of that committee.[124]

> The President has directed the preparation of a war plan *PURPLE*, under the following assumptions: Quote- 'GERMANY joined by ITALY has successfully conducted a war against ENGLAND and FRANCE. The British and French fleets have been destroyed or dissipated and are no longer a factor to be considered. British and French colonies and dominions in the Western Hemisphere are no longer under British and French protection and their final disposition is awaiting the action of a peace conference. CANADA, BRITISH and FRENCH GUIANA and NEWFOUNDLAND have proclaimed

their independence and have asked the UNITED STATES for protection under the Monroe Doctrine. The British and French Islands in the Caribbean area are still nominally under British and French control. The 1st and 6th Divisions, U.S. Army (full peace strength) have reinforced the garrison at Porto Rica [sic]... A civil war exists in BRAZIL. Federal Forces (north) are opposed to rebel forces (south) along a general line east and west through SAO PAULO. GERMANY and ITALY have established bases of operations in the CAPE VERDE and CANARY ISLANDS off the African coast. They are reinforcing the rebel front by furnishing men and munitions in such quantities and under such conditions as to constitute a definite economic and political penetration of the SOUTH AMERICAN continent and a violation of the Monroe Doctrine. ARGENTINA has aligned itself with the Rebel forces. Other South American countries are neutral but are sympathetic to the aims and purposes of the United States. JAPAN is intensely engaged in the expansion of her interests in the Western Pacific.'[125]

In 1939 there was much concern in Washington with the stability of the Getulio Vargas government in Brazil because of fascist and German activities in that country. In March, General Pedro Aurelio de Goes Monteiro, considered an ultraconservative officer and former fascist sympathizer, had called for Vargas's resignation. The *Açao Integralista Brasilera*, a fascist party that had backed Vargas's *Estado Novo* in 1937, unsuccessfully attempted to carry out a coup and kill the president on May 10 and 11, 1938. U.S. intelligence sources discovered that Germany had directly assisted in this ploy.

Brazil was considered of particular strategic importance because, among other things, its northeast "bulge" could be reached by air from bases in northwest Africa. A German presence in Brazil was seen as directly threatening to U.S. interests in the Caribbean and the Panama Canal. The Chilean *nacistas*, on the other hand, staged a bloody rebellion in September against the conservative government of Arturo Alessandri. Fascist and Axis activities throughout Latin America became a major source of concern in Washington during this period. The December 1938 Inter-American meeting in Lima, convened at the behest of the United States, had the purpose of counteracting perceived fascist subversion.[126]

Thus, Fleet Problem XX focused strategically on the interrelationship between the "Brazilian bulge" (the Natal area) and the Southern Atlantic, on the one hand, and the Caribbean region, on the other. The maneuvers, though mostly centered in the Puerto Rico-Virgin Islands zone, involved a large maritime area ranging from Cuba to the Lesser Antilles. Exercises took place in the following locations: Marie Galante, Guantánamo, Culebra, Vieques, St. Thomas, St. Croix, Montserrat, Antigua, Mona, Ponce, Guayanilla, Rincón, San Juan, Samaná, and the Bahamas. Several air raids and naval attacks on the San Juan harbor were staged. The Vieques Sound also saw much naval action.

In the Dominican Republic, Samaná Bay was the site for air, naval, submarine and mine-laying exercises.[127] The *Raleigh*, *Reid*, and *Cummins* ships with three other ships and fifty planes were in Samaná in March. The maneuvers also had a political dimension regarding that country, since they were used to strengthen military and political ties to the Trujillo regime. The massacre of thousands of Haitians by Trujillo in the Dominican border in 1937 was no longer an obstacle to warm relations. Trujillo used the presence of the cruiser *Texas* and forty-two USMC planes to rename as "U.S. Marine Corps" a section of Trujillo Avenue (the important waterfront avenue in Santo Domingo). The other section he had previously named "George Washington." This was done in a military ceremony in which two companies of marines, with their music band, participated together with Dominican soldiers.

> At last, on February 1939, Brigadier General Upshur and Colonel Roy S. Geiger could visit Santo Domingo since they were participating in naval maneuvers near Puerto Rico. The cruiser Texas and about 42 planes came to Santo Domingo for the ceremony. A large number of marines were aboard the ship.[128]

Trujillo also decorated FDR's son, Colonel James Roosevelt, with a medal while the maneuvers were taking place.[129]

The Caribbean political situation (in this case the Puerto Rican situation) made itself felt in other ways during Fleet Problem XX. The news summary for February 20 prepared in the *USS Houston*, which carried FDR and Leahy, included the following dispatch as the main news item:

Washington. The Government had a recommendation from the American Civil [Liberties] Union today for investigation of what were called "deplorable conditions" in Colonial Administration.

The Civil Liberties group asked a chance for Puerto Rico to vote on Independence and for both Puerto Rico and Hawaii to vote on Statehood.

A new administration for Puerto Rico, citizenship for the natives of Samoa and Guam, extended native participation in the Virgin Islands Government and Native language schools for Guam, Samoa and Puerto Rico were other recommendations.[130]

FDR received an invitation on February 23 from Governor Winship to visit him in Puerto Rico. Roosevelt politely refused, on the grounds that his itinerary depended on the maneuvers.[131]

The maneuvers ended on February 27 with a "major naval battle" about 100 miles to the north of Puerto Rico. In Culebra, FDR reviewed the results of the maneuvers with admirals Leahy, Bloch, Kalbfus and Andrews. He also observed a USMC landing exercise in Flamingo Beach on that island. Among the conclusions derived from the experience, it: 1) reaffirmed the importance of the Caribbean and the Atlantic, 2) underscored the need to enjoy air supremacy, and 3) emphasized the urgent need to obtain bases in the Caribbean.[132] Admiral Adolphus Andrews, Black Commander, informed the president that "some means... [must] be found to provide fortified and well secured bases in this most important strategic area." He also recommended to Admiral Claude C. Bloch, Commander in Chief of the fleet, that:

> In view of the present world conditions, the importance of the West Indian area to our national defense, and the maintenance of our national policies, and the lack of bases therein, it is high time that corrective measures be taken. Not only should provision be made for suitable bases in areas now under American jurisdiction, but steps should be taken that would insure the availability of certain other harbors and facilities to our planes and vessels.[133]

As if to further validate the national existing security consensus, on February 28 the State Department issued the following statement by Senator Sheppard, Chairman of the Military Affairs Committee, which was received in the *Houston*:

> He declared that to permit Panama, Hawaii, Puerto Rico or Alaska to fall to an enemy would jeopardize the security of the continental United States. He said: " A violation of the Monroe Doctrine would probably not occur as a sudden overt act. It could easily take the form of a step by step movement of a peaceful penetration by foreign nations until definite and powerful minorities would be established with the result that before military force replaced diplomatic negotiations hostile nations might already have a foothold in areas that would threaten the most important link in our entire system of defense, the Panama Canal..."[134]

The urgency for an expanded and strengthened base structure in the Caribbean, including the construction of new facilities in Puerto Rico and the Virgin Islands, had already been expressed in the Hepburn Board Report of December 1938.[135] The Army and Navy would use the juncture of the maneuvers to make demands for additional bases and resources considered vital for the defense of Puerto Rico and the Caribbean. According to Abbazia, Fleet Problem XX placed FDR firmly on the road to the "destroyers-for-bases" agreement with Great Britain.[136] It would be one of Leahy's major tasks as Governor of Puerto Rico to oversee war preparations on the island, considered the hub of the envisaged regional naval and military arrangement, from a military and, particularly, from a political perspective.

The Good Neighbor Policy: From Diplomacy to War Preparations

The first two decades of the century were characterized by a high level of military interventionism in Mexico, Central America and the Caribbean. Military intervention in the region, though also related to expanding investments and commercial interests, was internally legitimized by its vital importance to U.S. national security, as formulated by geo-strategic thinkers such as Mahan. Theodore Roosevelt's reformulation of the Monroe Doctrine, the Roosevelt Corollary, posited that the internal stability of regional societies was a security matter for the U.S., since instability could provoke European intervention. This meant the generalization of the principles contained in the Cuban Platt Amendment to the entire region.

Platt-like provisions were written into the constitutions of Nicaragua and Haiti, and contained in the Canal Treaty with Panamá. Apart from the general principles of the Monroe Doctrine, the U.S. lacked a coherent world or Latin American policy, and its interests and influence in South America were much less significant than in the Caribbean Basin. Even the Monroe Doctrine, as Dexter Perkins has remarked, was essentially a Caribbean policy.[137]

By the mid 1920s, the U.S. began a process of relative military disengagement from the Caribbean. Interventionism had fuelled a growing nationalist response and even armed resistance in some countries, such as Mexico, Nicaragua and the Dominican Republic.[138] It had also poisoned relations with the countries of South America. Additionally, the considerable economic costs of the naval and military presence, and of colonial administration, also became an issue, particularly with the onset of the economic crisis in 1929. The adoption of protectionist policies by the Hoover administration, expressed in the Smoot-Hawley tariff of 1930, had further strained relations with Latin America.[139]

Interventionism in the Caribbean and Central America had become a matter of sharp controversy in Inter-American relations. During the Fifth and Sixth International Conferences of American States held at Santiago de Chile in 1923 and La Habana in 1928, the tensions with Latin America provoked by this policy became evident. According to Gellman, "Latin American leaders used the Fifth and Sixth International Conference of American States... to attack United States imperialism."[140] By 1928, the Under Secretary of State, J. Reuben Clark, had clearly distanced himself from Theodore Roosevelt's interpretation of the Monroe Doctrine, and even Franklin Roosevelt was abandoning his earlier enthusiasm for military intervention in the region.[141]

By the early 1930s, in the midst of the Depression and with international tensions looming both in Asia and Europe, the policy towards the Caribbean —as well as relations generally with Latin America— was perceived as compromising rather than enhancing U.S. security. The broad redefinition of hemispheric policy under the Roosevelt administration during the 1930s, known as the "Good Neighbor Policy," was strongly conditioned by new perceived threats emerging from Japan and Europe, and by the consequent need to remove sources of international tensions, forge a world alliance and create a favorable political and diplomatic environment for defense-related measures. The new administration came to power under the shadow of Japanese intervention in China (1931) and Hitler's rise to power in Germany (1933). Throughout the thirties, conflicts both in Asia and Europe relentlessly escalated to culminate in the Second World War.

The adoption of a "non-interventionist" policy in the Central American-Caribbean region became a crucial ingredient in the "Good Neighbor" objective of forging a world security alliance. The first challenge to Roosevelt's policy was the 1933 revolution in Cuba. Though the U.S. was instrumental, through its Ambassador Sumner Welles, in toppling two governments during this crisis (first Machado and, then, Grau), and the island was encircled by naval forces, Roosevelt did not approve Welles's demands for the landing of troops. Instead, there was economic and political pressure to impose a government acceptable to the U.S. (that of Carlos Mendieta), while a military leader, Fulgencio Batista, was promoted as a guarantee to internal order.[142] Cuban policy in 1933 and 1934 could be considered a paradigm later applied to Latin America. In order to legitimize the new government, the U.S. made a concession to nationalist demands by abrogating the Platt Amendment, while the Jones-Costigan Act of 1934 and the trade agreement signed with Cuba provided the economic underpinnings of the Mendieta-Batista government. The sugar quota system and trade liberalization reactivated the Cuban economy but also tied it firmly to the U.S.[143]

By December 1933, during the Seventh Conference of American States held in Montevideo, Secretary of State Cordell Hull had expressed, though with certain reservations, commitment to a policy of "non-intervention" and liberalization of trade. During that same month, Roosevelt stated that "the definite policy of the United States from now on is one opposed to armed intervention." The military occupations of Haiti and Nicaragua were ended and the Cuban Platt Amendment abrogated in 1934. Also in late 1933, Roosevelt had met the new President of Panama, Harmodio Arias, and accepted a renegotiation of the Canal

Treaty.[144] A new Canal Treaty was signed in March 1936. The U.S. also expressly abandoned in January 1934 the policy of non-recognition that had been previously used against the Grau government in Cuba. With regard to Mexico, Ambassador Josephus Daniels plotted a course carefully designed to prevent a collision with Mexican nationalism under Lázaro Cárdenas.[145]

Military disengagement from the Caribbean and measured concessions to nationalist forces did not mean a political abandonment of the region, as new forms of influence were developed.[146] President Arias of Panamá, for example, was deposed in 1941 in a U.S.-supported coup provoked by his reluctance to negotiate demands for numerous additional bases and installations. In Puerto Rico, the repressive administration of General Blanton Winship was maintained from 1934 to 1939. Military forces and leaders, mainly nurtured during periods of occupation, were propelled to a political caretaker role (as in Cuba, the Dominican Republic, Guatemala and Nicaragua). But the new policy did create, together with Hull's active promotion of reciprocal trade agreements,[147] a favorable atmosphere for the extremely active 1930s diplomacy towards Latin America.

Each of the major diplomatic initiatives of the U.S. towards Latin America took place at a critical juncture of the developing world political and military crises in Europe. The Seventh Conference of American States took place in the context of the rise to power of fascism in Germany. The Inter-American Conference for the Maintenance of Peace in December 1936 in Buenos Aires had as its background the Italian invasion of Abyssinia, the Spanish Civil War, the remilitarization of the Rhineland, and the Anti-Comintern Pact. Adolf A. Berle remarked that Roosevelt's speech during this event was "addressed to Europe more than the Americas." In it Roosevelt emphasized hemispheric collective security against aggression. The Eighth Conference of American States (Lima, December 1938) was overshadowed by the Munich crisis, the first steps of U.S. rearmament, and concern with fascist penetration of Latin American countries. The First Consultative Meeting of Ministers (Panama, September 23-October 3, 1939) was prompted by the intervention in Czechoslovakia (March 15), strategic concern with the vulnerability of Brazil, and the invasion of Poland. Finally, the Second Consultative

Meeting in La Habana (July 1940) responded to the intensification of war in Europe, the invasion of Norway and Denmark (April 9), the German offensive in the Netherlands and France (May 10-June 22), and the concern with a possible defeat of Great Britain. It focused on the fate of European colonies in the Caribbean.[148]

This sustained diplomatic offensive was aimed at establishing U.S. leadership in response to European developments, forging collective security mechanisms and, eventually, obtaining full Latin American collaboration in war preparations. Edgar Furniss has explained the nexus between "Good Neighbor" diplomacy and security concerns by emphasizing that the main objectives of U.S. foreign policy in Latin America were: 1) ending the "profound mistrust" that existed on the part of Latin American countries, 2) having access to strategic raw materials, 3) preventing fascist political activities, and 4) forging close military ties.[149]

Roosevelt's Caribbean and Latin American policy during the 1930s, as Irwin Gellman has argued, permitted the transition from neutrality to engagement in Europe.[150] Haglund has even proposed that it was concern with Western Hemisphere security that eventually made "internationalist" and "Atlanticist" perspectives dominant in U.S. foreign policy.[151]

Though driven by security considerations mainly related to the development of the crisis in Europe, "Good Neighbor" diplomacy towards Latin America did not have important consequences in the sphere of military preparations throughout most of the 1930s. U.S. military links with Latin America were relatively weak during this period, and its military presence remained mainly circumscribed to the Caribbean-Central American region. The U.S. did not begin to take steps towards war preparations until late 1937, with rearmament gradually undertaken the following year, particularly after the Munich Crisis of September, which developed with greater force during 1939 and 1940.

In the late thirties, U.S. strategic concerns with Latin America mainly focused on political and economic penetration by Axis countries, potential threats to Panama Canal security posed by Italian and German owned airlines, activities of European military missions, and air and naval threats in the South Atlantic (mainly to Brazil) and in the Caribbean area. In 1938, a framework of military collaboration was designed. It was actively implemented during 1939 and 1940, and it consisted of an ambitious plan of airport construction undertaken under the cover provided by Pan American Airways, staff discussions with the Latin American militaries, an increase in the number of military missions and arms sales, the training of Latin American officers in U.S. academies, naval agreements for the use of Latin American ports, and security collaboration against Axis activities. This process ran parallel, and was related to, military preparations undertaken in the Caribbean.[152]

By the time war broke out in Europe and the possibility of a German attack on the hemisphere receded, military resources were diverted to European allies and were not available for Latin America. Only two Latin American countries, Mexico and Brazil, participated directly in the conflict, while military preparations mainly focused on the Caribbean and in the "half sphere" delimited by the Galapagos Islands in the Pacific and the Natal region of Brazil in the Southern Atlantic. Ironically, the concept of "hemispheric defense" had very little military importance during the war and really became a means of consolidating the considerable political influence developed during the 1930s, particularly over the Latin American military establishments.[153] In 1941 General George C. Marshall stated: "Our objective does not comprise expectations... of being able to use Latin American forces as effective allies in war."[154]

Under the rubric of "economic defense of the hemisphere," new economic mechanisms were built to foster cooperation with Latin America and enhance U.S. influence. These went beyond the reciprocal trade agreements promoted during the first phase of the "Good Neighbor" policy. The Panama Conference of 1939 created the Inter-American Financial and Advisory Council. This body in turn established the Inter-American Development Commission and the Inter-American Bank. The Export-Import Bank, on the other hand, began financing "development" projects. Various proposals for enhanced economic collaboration were actively considered. In June 1940, Nelson Rockefeller submitted a memorandum to Harry Hopkins which "was really a blueprint for the economic defense of the Western Hemisphere, based on cooperation between the public and private sectors in all concerned countries."[155] The Rockefeller proposal prompted the establishment of the powerful Office for Coordination of

Commercial and Cultural Relations between the American Republics (later, Office of the Coordinator of Inter-American Affairs) and Nelson Rockefeller was named Coordinator.[156] As Adolf A. Berle noted, what was involved in this economic activism toward Latin America was not only short-term "economic warfare," but "American patterns in a post-war world."[157]

NOTES

1. *El Mundo*, February 2, 1939, p. 7.

2. *El Mundo*, February 14, 1939, p. 3. Author's translation.

3. AJAX, "Sensacionales aventuras en 'La Patrulla Submarina', Richard Greene y Nancy Kelly son los protagonistas de esta nueva cinta," *El Mundo*, February 13, 1939, p. 6.

4. *El Mundo*, February 16, 1939, p. 6.

5. Julio Cátala, "Revista de Ciencias: La propaganda de la guerra contra la guerra, donde sucumbe la razón," *El Mundo*, October 22, 1939, p. 8; also, advertisement for "Confessions of a Nazi Spy," *El Mundo*, August 5, 1939, p. 7.

6. *El Mundo*, February 6, 1939, p. 4. That same page included a photo of Republican militia in the defense of Barcelona.

7. *El Mundo*, February 13, 1939, p. 12.

8. An abundant literature exists on the role of Hollywood films during World War II. See, for example, Clayton R. Koppes, *Hollywood Goes to War: How Politics Profits and Propaganda Shaped World War II Movies* (New York: Free Press, 1987); Roy Hoopes, *When the Stars Went to War: Hollywood and World War II* (New York: Random House, 1994); Thomas Patrick Doherty, *Projections of War: Hollywood, American Culture and World War II* (New York: Columbia University Press, 1993); Jeanine Basinger, *The World War II Combat Film: Anatomy of a Genre* (New York: Columbia University Press, 1986); and Roger Manvell, *Films and the Second World War* (South Brunswick: A. S. Barnes, 1974).

9. Commissioner of Education, Circular Letter No. 80, March 12, 1937, Education Department Library. I thank my student José Collazo for the information included in this paragraph.

10. Commissioner of Education, Circular Letter No. 105, October 30, 1939.

11. Commissioner of Education, Circular Letter No. 134, December 14, 1939.

12. "El vigésimo aniversario de los niños escuchas," *El Mundo*, February 8, 1939, p. 8.

13. *El Mundo*, February 1, 1939, p. 7.

14. On popular culture during World War II see, Robert Heide and John Gilman, *Home Front America, Popular Culture of the World War II Era* (San Francisco: Chronicle Books, 1995) also, John M. Blum, *V Was for Victory: Politics and American Culture during World War II* (New York: Harcourt Brace Jovanovich, 1976).

15. See, for example, "Francia coloca en pie de guerra su frontera con España," *El Mundo* February 1, 1939, p. 2; "La ciudad de Vich en poder de los nacionalistas," February 2, 1939, p. 2; "Se desploma anoche la resistencia leal en Cataluña" and "Francia se dispone a establecer relaciones con Franco", February 3, 1939, pp. 2, 3; "Francia establece relaciones con Burgos" and "Los nacionalistas están encima de Gerona," February 4, 1939, pp. 2, 3. Articles and photographs of the Spanish Civil War are too numerous to be all cited here.

16. Romualdo Real was the director of the leading graphic journal *Puerto Rico Ilustrado*. It had been founded in 1910 by Real Hermanos, his enterprise. Many contemporary writers and intellectuals, as Emilio S. Belaval, wrote in his journal.

17. Romualdo Real, "Primo de Rivera, el creador genial," *El Mundo*, February 5, 1939, p. 5.

18. Romualdo Real, "Chamberlain, el caudillo de la paz," *El Mundo*, February 22, 1939, p. 10; "Daladier, la figura de Francia," *El Mundo*, February 21, 1939, p. 3.

19. Romualdo Real, "Desfile de Conquistadores," *El Mundo*, February 25, 1939, p. 10.

20. Romualdo Real, "La verdadera salvación de España," *El Mundo*, February 23, 1939, p. 10. See, also, "El fantasma del separatismo," *El Mundo*, February 27, 1939, p. 8.

21. Emilio S. Belaval, "Figuras Jóvenes de Puerto Rico, Carmencita Durán, una falangista de Puerto Rico", *El Mundo*, February 16, 1939, p. 2. She was the daughter of Alberto Durán and Carmen Hernández Usera and studied in the "Colegio de las Madres", an upper class Catholic school.

22. "La bandera rojo y gualda en la Casa de España", *El Mundo*, February 28, 1939, p. 5.

23. Richard Halliburton, "La ciudad de Shanghai bajo el terror de la guerra", *El Mundo*, February 19, 1939, p. 2.

24. F. Sotomayor Rabat, "La muerte de un gigante," *El Mundo*, February 5, 1939, p. 5.

25. Idem. Author's translation.

26. "Prensa alemana alega que en Puerto Rico hay régimen de terror," *El Mundo*, February 2, 1939, p. 1.

27. Oswald Garrison Villard, "Issues and Men," *The Nation*, February 18, 1939. The translation of the German article is Villard's. He had written in 1937 an article strongly condemning the Palm Sunday Massacre. See, "Liberty and Death in Puerto Rico," *The Nation*, April 3, 1937, pp. 371-73.

28. "La Cámara redacta una protesta contra la prensa alemana", *El Mundo*, February 14, 1939, p. 1.

29. "Roosevelt teme que no pueda evitarse la guerra. Habló ayer en términos de absoluta franqueza al Comité de Asuntos Militares del Senado", *El Mundo*, February 1, 1939, p. 3.

30. *El Mundo*, February 2, 1939, p. 1.

31. "Puerto Rico Senator Assails U.S. Control, Martinez Nadal Charges Washington with Fascist Control," *The New York Times*, March 27, 1939, p. 4. Also "Que Puerto Rico está esclavo dijo ayer Martínez Nadal", *El Mundo*, March 25, 1939, p. 1.

32. The issue of military bases was also constantly in the news during the previous month of January. See, for example, "La construcción en San Juan de bases aéreas y navales recomendada por la junta de expertos de la Marina," *El Mundo*, January 4, 1939, p. 1.

33. "El Vicealmirante Harris inspeccionará el dique de carena," *El Mundo*, February 7, 1939, p. 1. The other officers were commanders J.J. Manning and C.W. Porter.

34. Vito Marcantonio to President Franklin Delano Roosevelt, April 27, 1939, FDR Library, FDR Papers, OF 400, Container 25, Folder P.R.

35. "Puerto (sic) Sees Bright Future as Major Defense Area in Caribbean," *The Economic Review*, Vol. 4, No. 3 (June 1939), p. 61.

36. Ibid., p. 29.

37. Idem.

38 Ibid., p. 25.

39. Apparently, this constituted a rejection of demands for making Puerto Rico an "incorporated territory." The report said that, "The Department of the Navy has studied in detail the situation, including the possible movement to permanently incorporate Puerto Rico as an organized territory of the United States. The Navy's legal experts finally decided that it would be much more simple to formulate a plan to retain naval rights without taking into account whatever political decisions are taken in the island." See, "La Marina resuelta a establecer aquí bases permanentes. El plan está ya redactado sin tener en cuenta la eventual disposición política de la isla", *El Mundo*, February 3, 1939, p. 1. Author's translation.

40. See the following articles in *El Mundo*, Fred Bailey, "La Cámara Baja aprobó ayer el proyecto de defensa. Incluye el establecimiento de bases aéreas y navales en Pto. Rico para proteger el canal," February 16, 1939, p. 1; "Se disponen $9,138,000 para la base naval de San Juan. El proyecto fue informado ayer favorablemente por el Comité de Asuntos Navales", February 18 , 1939, p. 1; Julius

C. Edelstein, "No se ha hecho ninguna objeción a la base naval en la isla. El proyecto será discutido en el 'floor' mañana martes. El viaje del Presidente al Caribe enfoca la atención hacia la defensa nacional", February 21, 1939, p. 1; and, "La Cámara aprobará hoy el proyecto de defensa nacional", February 22, 1939, p. 1.

41. Grattan McGroarty, "Se espera que estas maniobras comprueben la necesidad de establecer bases adicionales en el Caribe, incluyendo la de Puerto Rico," *El Mundo*, February 5, 1939, p. 1.

42. See, for example, "El general Arnold pide una base aérea para Puerto Rico. Es el jefe de los cuerpos de aviación y compareció ayer a informar ante el Comité Militar de la Cámara Baja," *El Mundo*, January 19, 1939, p. 1.

43. "Puerto Rico adquiere cada vez mayor importancia en los programas de defensa nacional de los Estados Unidos", *El Mundo*, February 27, 1939, p. 1.

44. "Iglesias presentó el proyecto de Territorio Incorporado. Pasó a la consideración del Comité de Asuntos Insulares", *El Mundo*, February 27, 1939, p. 1. Since early January it had been reported that a "movement" existed to link the demand for incorporated territory status and defense plans, as this would presumably close the door to independence and provide a guarantee to military operations in Puerto Rico. See, "Hay un movimiento para relacionar con los planes de defensa el proyecto que incorpora a Puerto Rico como Territorio de Estados Unidos," *El Mundo*, January 3, 1939, pp. 1, 3.

45. Blanton Winship, "The Status of Puerto Rico, An Address by Governor Blanton Winship, over Columbia Broadcasting System from Washington, D.C., March 25, 1939," Issued by Puerto Rican Trade Council, Shoreham Bldg., Washington, pp. 1-2, 10.

46. "Hay planes para hacer de Puerto Rico una Fortaleza inexpugnable. El Ejército y la Marina proyectan fortificar la Isla a un coste de no menos de $25,000,000, según se informó ayer en Washington," *El Mundo*, March 1, 1939, p. 1.

47. "El senador Sheppard se refirió a Puerto Rico 'eslabón vital,'" *El Mundo*, March 1, 1939, p. 3.

48. "El Presidente destaca la importancia de una base en Pto. Rico. Manifestó ayer en Charleston que esa ha sido una de las lecciones de estas maniobras," *El Mundo*, March 2, 1939, p. 1; also, "Half Billion for Army Voted; Roosevelt Asks 2 Indies Naval Bases," *Washington Post*, March 4, 1939. Leahy also made a similar statement regarding the need for bases in Puerto Rico and the Virgin Islands. See, "Naval Air Force Held World's Best," *The New York Times*. March 8, 1939.

49. "Llegaron a San Juan cuarenta y siete aviones de guerra para tomar parte en las maniobras que se avecinan, en las cuales Puerto Rico desempeña un papel muy importante. El aereopuerto de Isla Grande base de actividad Militar," *El Mundo*, January 18, 1939, pp. 1, 4.

50. "Las maniobras de la escuadrilla aérea en San Juan," *El Mundo*, January 20, 1939, p. 1.

51. "Ayer llegaron a San Juan cuarenta y ocho aviones más", *El Mundo*, January 24, 1939, p. 1; also, "Los aviones de la Marina hacen maniobras en San Juan," *El Mundo*, January 24, 1939, p. 5.

52. Julius C. Edelstein, "Es probable que la 'flota negra' trate de ocupar a Puerto Rico," *El Mundo*, February 14, 1939, p. 1.

53. "La visita del crucero "Phoenix" a nuestro puerto," *El Mundo*, February 12, 1939, p. 1.

54. "El acorazado Wyoming surto en San Juan," *El Mundo*, February 14, 1939, p. 5.

55. "Pasan muy cerca de San Juan unidades de la flota," *El Mundo*, February 16, 1939, p. 8.

56. Julius C. Edelstein, "Es probable...," *El Mundo*, February 16, 1939, p. 1.

57. The White House, Memorandum: Chronological Record of Contacts and Events, Fleet Problem XX, February 25, 1939, FDR Library, FDR Papers, OF 200, Container 49, Folder 200-MMM.

58. Patrick Abbazia, *Mr. Roosevelt's Navy* (Annapolis: Naval Institute Press, 1975), pp. 44, 45.

59. Thomas B. Buell, *The Quiet Warrior: A Biography of Admiral Raymond A. Spruance* (Boston: Little, Brown and Co., 1979), pp. 80-82.

60. "Resultaron muy lucidas las maniobras aéreas el sábado," *El Mundo*, 13 March 1939, p. 5; also, "Espectaculares maniobras aéreas en San Juan el sábado," *El Mundo*, March 9, 1939, p. 1.

61. "Se le confiere a Esteves el rango de Brigadier General," *El Mundo*, February 11, 1939, p. 1. He was the first Puerto Rican to study at West Point, graduating in 1915. Only eight Puerto Ricans had studied there before 1939. See, Héctor Andrés Negroni, *Historia militar de Puerto Rico* (Madrid: Sociedad Estatal Quinto Centenario, Ediciones Siruela, 1992), p. 404, 476-77.

62. "Suspendidas maniobras proyectadas en conexión con semana de Defensa Nacional," *El Mundo*, February 10, 1939, p. 5.

63. "Puerto Rico celebra la semana de la defensa nacional," *El Mundo*, February 15, 1939, p. 4.

64. E. Combas Guerra, "En torno a la Fortaleza," *El Mundo*, February 7, 1939, p. 5. Translated by the author.

65. See, "Naval Operations Plan between Germany and the USA, 1898-1913, A Study of Strategic Planning in the Age of Imperialism," in Paul Kennedy, ed., *The War Plans of the Great Powers, 1880-1914* (Boston: Allen & Unwin, 1985), pp. 39-74; also, María Eugenia Estades, *La presencia Militar de Estados Unidos en Puerto Rico 1898-1918, intereses estratégicos y dominación colonial* (Río Piedras: Ediciones Huracán, 1988), pp. 65-73.

66. The treaties signed 6 February 1922 established a ratio of 5:5:3, respectively, for US, British and Japanese battleship and carrier tonnage, alloted $1^3/_4$ to France and Italy, prohibited the construction of new battleships for a ten year period, and limited their maximum tonnage. Samuel Eliot Morison, *The Two Ocean War* (Boston: Little, Brown and Co., 1963), p. 6.

67. In 1924, the director of the Navy's War Plans Division concluded that Japan was a more likely enemy that Britain and that strategy should be "Pacific-first". By 1927, the General Board was of the opinion that there almost no possibility of war with Britain. Donald A. Yerxa, "The United States Navy and the Caribbean Sea, 1914-1941," Ph. D. dissertation, University of Maine, 1982, p. 245.

68. Dexter Perkins, *The United States and Latin America* (Baton Rouge: Louisiana State University Press, 1961), p. 24.

69. Ibid., 256-57.

70. Rear Admiral A.J. Hepburn, Senior Member, Rear Admiral E. J. Marquart, Captain James S. Woods, Captain Arthur L. Bristol, Jr., Captain (Civil Engineering Corps) Ralph Withman, Commander William E. Hilbert, Recorder.

71. *Report on the Need of Additional Naval Bases to Defend the Coasts of the United States, its Territories and Possessions*, 76th Congress, 1st Session, House of Representatives, Document No. 65. pp. 4-15.

72. Ibid., p. 16.

73. Idem.

74. Ibid., p. 30.

75. "La Cámara aprobó la base naval para Puerto Rico," *El Mundo*, February 24, 1939, p. 1.

76. Ibid., p. 36.

77. "As early as January 1939, the Panama Canal Department recognized the urgent need for bases in other parts of the Caribbean region. These bases would permit advance warning of an enemy attack and would enable the Army Air Corps to engage hostile aircraft before they could strike the Canal. Nature has favored the Caribbean by providing a chain of islands extending from Cuba southeast to the

northern coast of Venezuela. These islands offered natural sites for air bases to guard the Caribbean approaches to the Panama Canal." Herman Hupperich, "The Caribbean-Vital Link in Western Hemisphere Air Defense During World War II," in Eugene R. Huck and Edward H. Moseley, eds., *Militarists, Merchants and Missionaries, United States Expansion in Middle America* (Alabama: University of Alabama Press, 1970), pp. 131-132.

78. "Puerto [sic] Sees Bright Future as Major Defense Area in Caribbean", op. cit., p. 27.

79. Among the abundant literature that reflected the views of the anti-war movement are, Harry Elmer Barnes, *The Genesis of the World War: An Introduction to the Problem of War Guilt* (New York: Alfred A. Knopf, 1926); C. Hartley Grattan, *Why We Fought* (New York: Vanguard Press, 1929); Harold D. Lasswell, *Propaganda Technique in the World War* (New York: Alfred A. Knopf, 1927); Sir Arthur Ponsonby, *Falsehood in War-Time* (London: Allen and Unwin, 1928); Walter Millis, *The Road to War; America, 1914-1917* (Boston: Houghton Mifflin Co., 1935); Helmut C. Engelbrecht and F.C. Haninghen, *Merchants of Death: A Study of the International Armaments Industry* (New York: Dodd, Mead and Co., 1934); Charles A. Beard, *The Devil Theory of War* (New York: Vanguard Press, 1936); Charles C. Tansill, *America Goes to War* (Boston: Little Brown and Co., 1938); Alice M. Morrisey, *The American Defense of Neutral Rights, 1914-1917* (Cambridge, Mass.: Harvard University Press, 1939); and Horace C. Peterson, *Propaganda for War: The Campaign Against American Neutrality, 1914-1917* (Norman, Okla.: University of Oklahoma Press, 1939).

80. Donald F. Drummond, *The Passing of American Neutrality, 1937-1941* (Ann Arbor: The University of Michigan Press, 1955), Chapter 1.

81. Major George Fielding Eliot, *The Ramparts we Watch: A Study of the Problems of American National Defense* (New York: Reynal & Hitchcock, 1938).

82. R. E Dupuy and George Fielding Eliot, *If War Comes* (New York: Macmillan, 1937); see, also, Eliot's *Defending America*, Foreign Policy Association, World Affairs Pamphlets New Series No. 4, 1939.

83. The notion that rearmament should mainly be based on the massive development of air power was advanced by Roosevelt towards the end of 1938 and opposed by both the navy and the army, who wanted a balanced expansion. Apparently, Roosevelt saw air power as an alternative to a large army, as well as an effective means of supporting the European allies.

84. Eliot, *The Ramparts...*, op. cit., p. 1, 193.

85. Ibid., 154-7.

86. Ibid., p. 148.

87. Ibid., pp. 152-3.

88. Ibid., p. 259.

89. Ibid., pp. 154-55.

90. "America Gets Ready to Fight Germany, Italy and Japan," *Life*, Vol. 5, No. 18 (October 31, 1938).

91. Walter Millis, "Anatomy of National Defense," *Washington Post*, November 13, 1938.

92. Walter Millis, *The Road to War...* op. cit. See, also, *The Martial Spirit* (Cambridge, Mass.: The Literary Guild of America, 1931) on the Spanish-American war; and "Arms and the Men," *Fortune*, IX (March 1934), p. 53. He also published in 1956 a critical appraisal of US military history, *Arms and Men, A Study in American Military History* (New York: G. P. Putnam's Sons, 1956).

93. Joseph S. Edgerton, "Defense of Neighbors Held Essential to Safety of the U.S., Continental Plan Advocated to make sure Enemy Would not Seize Weak Country for Basis of Attack," *Washington Star*, November 27, 1938.

94. *The Ramparts We Watch* was also received in Latin America as an authoritative source ("an eminent military authority") of U.S. military policy and strategic thinking. It is significantly cited as the sole source of U.S. strategic thinking in a 1939 article of Haya de la Torre, the Peruvian politician, regarding the need to internationalize the Panama Canal. The article is reproduced under the title "Should the Panama Canal be Internationalized" in Robert J. Alexander, *Aprismo, The Ideas and Doctrines of Víctor Raúl Haya de la Torre* (Kent: The Kent State University Press, 1973), pp. 335-41.

95. Wilbur Burton, "Panama: Defense Problem No. 1," *Current History* (December 1938), pp. 34-6.

96. Harold Sprout, "Strategic Considerations in Hemisphere Defense," *The Quarterly Journal of Inter-American Relations*, Vol. I (October 1939) pp. 21-29.

97. Norman J. Padleford, "An Atlantic Naval Policy for the United States," *U.S. Naval Institute Proceedings*, Vol. 66, No. 6 (September 1940), p. 1304.

98. Colonel Cary I. Crockett, "Island Bulwarks," *U.S. Naval Institute Proceedings* (March 1940), pp. 372-83.

99. Lieutenant Commander Ephraim R. McLean, Jr., "The Caribbean-An American Lake," *U.S. Naval Institute Proceedings* (July 1941), p. 952.

100. Hanson W. Baldwin, *United We Stand!, Defense of the Western Hemisphere* (New York: Whittlesey House, 1941), pp. 105, 165, 217-18, 328-32; "America Rearms," *Foreign Affairs*, Vol. 16, No. 3 (April 1938), pp. 430-44; "Our New Long Shadow," *Foreign Affairs*, Vol. 17, No. 3 (April 1939), pp. 465-76; and, "The Naval Defense of America," *Harper's Magazine*, Vol. 183 (April 1941), pp. 449-63.

101. He argued that armamentism would take the US down the road of fascism. See, Oswald Garrison Villard, "Wanted: A Sane Defense Policy," *Harper's Magazine*, Vol. 178 (April 1939), pp. 449-56.

102. Catherine A. Lutz and Jane L. Collins, *Reading National Geographic* (Chicago: University of Chicago Press, 1993).

103. E. John Long, "Puerto Rico Watchdog of the Caribbean, Venerable Domain Under American Flag Has New Role as West Indian Stronghold and Sentinel of the Panama Canal," *The National Geographic Magazine*, Vol. 76, No. 6 (December 1939), p. 697.

104. Earle K. James, "Puerto Rico at the Crossroads," *Foreign Policy Reports*, Vol. 13, No. 15 (October 15, 1937), pp. 182-92.

105. Anne Rainey Langley, "British West Indian Interlude," *The National Geographic Magazine*, Vol. 79, No. 1 (January 1941), pp. 1-46.

106. Edward T. Folliard, "Martinique, Caribbean Question Mark," *The National Geographic Magazine*, Vol. 79, No. 1 (January 1941), pp. 47-55.

107. See, for example, "Puerto Rico: Gibraltar or Achilles Heel," *Hemisphere* (February 1940), pp. 3-4; Lawrence and Sylvia Martin, "Outpost No. 2: The West Indies," *Harper's Magazine*, Vol. 182 (March 1941), pp. 359-68; James K. Eyre, "Martinique, a Key Point in Hemisphere Defense," *Inter American-Quarterly* (October 1941), pp. 82-8; Charles Taussig, "The Caribbean," *Survey Graphic* (March 1941), pp. 146-8, 198-200.

108. Carleton Beals, *The Coming Struggle for Latin America* (Philadelphia: J. B. Lippincott Co., 1938); J. Fred Rippy, *Caribbean Danger Zone* (New York: G. P. Putnam's Sons, 1940); Walter A. Roberts, *The Caribbean: Our Sea of Destiny* (Indianapolis: Bobbs Merrill, 1940). Beals also published *America Faces South* (Philadelphia: J. B. Lippincott Co., 1938). For the many books that were published on the Caribbean and Latin America from a security angle, see, Hines Calvin Warner, "United States Diplomacy in the Caribbean During World War II," Ph.D. dissertation, University of Texas at Austin, August, 1968, pp. 431-2.

109. Carleton Beals, *The Coming Struggle. . .*, pp. 239-40.

110. William H. Haas, *The American Empire, A Study of the Outlying Territories of the United States* (Chicago: The University of Chicago Press, 1940).

111. Ibid., p. 378-80.

112. Ibid., p. 90.

113. Yerxa, op. cit., pp. 339-43.

114. Ibid., p. 341.

115. Ibid., p. 342.

116. Ibid., p. 341; also, John Child, "From 'Color' to 'Rainbow': U.S. Strategic Planning for Latin America, 1919-1945", *Journal of Interamerican Studies and World Affairs*, Vol. 21, No. 2 (May 1979), pp. 247-49.

117. Marion D. Francis, *History of the Antilles Department*, Section II: Chapter 1 "War Plans and Defense Measures Prior to Organization of the Caribbean Defense Command (July 1, 1939-May 29, 1941), Historical Section, Adjutant General's Office, Antilles Department, San Juan, Puerto Rico, October 1945. p. xv.

118. John Child, op. cit., pp. 239-47.

119. Marion D. Francis, op. cit., pp. 5-6.

120. Ibid., 9-73.

121. Henry H. Adams, *Witness to Power* (Annapolis: Naval Institute Press, 1985), p. 100.

122. For a general description of the maneuvers, see, Patrick Abbazia, *Mr. Roosevelt's Navy, The Private War of the U.S. Atlantic Fleet, 1939-1942* (Annapolis: Naval Institute Press, 1973), Chapter 3, "A Mirror to War: Fleet Problem XX."

123. David G. Haglund, *Latin America and the Transformation of U.S. Strategic Thought, 1936-1940* (Albuquerque: University of New Mexico Press, 1984), p. 99.

124. John Child, op. cit.., p. 249.

125. Major A. H. Rogers, Inf., "War Plan Purple, Oral Presentation," May 20, 1940, Course at the Army War College, 1939-1940, War Plans, Formulation of War Plans Period, Report of Staff Group No. 3, pp. 6-7, U.S. Military History Institute, Carlysle Barracks, PA.

126. Haglund, op. cit., pp. 82-99; see, also, Alton Frye, *Nazi Germany and the American Hemisphere, 1933-1941* (New Haven: Yale University Press, 1967), Chapters 7, 8.

127. For the itinerary of the maneuvers, see, "Memorandum, Subject: Chronological Record of Contacts and Events," FDR Library, FDR Papers, OF 200, Container 49, Folder 200-MMM; also, "Hostile Planes Raid Puerto Rico," *New York Times*, February 26, 1939.

128. Bernardo Vega, *Trujillo y las fuerzas armadas norteamericanas* (Santo Domingo: Fundación Cultural Dominicana, 1992), p. 228.

129. For the *rapprochement* with Trujillo during *Fleet Problem XX*, see, ibid., pp. 228-30.

130. *USS Houston Evening Press News* (2-20-39), FDR Library, FDR Papers, OF 200, Container 49, Folder 200-MMM.

131. "Naval Aide to the President, to: Blanton Winship," February 25, 1939, FDR Library, FDR Papers, OF 200, Container 48, Folder 200-III.

132. For a more detailed description of the maneuvers see Abbazia, op. cit., Chapter 3; and Yerxa, op. cit., pp. 335-39.

133. Yerxa, op. cit., p. 339.

134. *State Department Bulletin*, No. 48 (28 February 1939), p. 4, FDR Library, FDR Papers, OF 200, Container 49, Folder 200-MMM.

135. Among the priority recommendations of the Hepburn Board were the construction of a secondary naval air base with berthing facilities at San Juan. It also called for an expansion of the St. Thomas naval air base and the retention of a submarine facility there. This was followed by the more ambitious and sweeping recommendations for new base facilities contained in the *Greenslade Report* of January, 1941. Yerxa, op. cit., pp. 336, 355.

136. Patrick Abbazia, op. cit., p. 49.

137. "Speaking in practical terms, the Monroe Doctrine was for the most part a Caribbean doctrine, applying to a relatively restricted part of the Latin American world." Perkins, op. cit., p. 18

138. For the armed resistance in the Dominican Republic see Bruce J. Calder, *The Impact of Intervention, The Dominican Republic during the U.S. Occupation of 1916-1924* (Austin: University of Texas Press, 1984), Chapters 5-9. In Nicaragua, Sandino's armed opposition began in 1927. In 1929, popular protests against the occupation took place in Haiti. See, Pablo González Casanova, ed., *América Latina en los años treinta* (México: Universidad Autónoma de México, 1977); also, David Green, *The Containment of Latin America* (Chicago: Quadrangle Books, 1971), Chapter 1.

139. Ibid., p. 7.

140. Irwin F. Gellman, *Good Neighbor Diplomacy, United States Policies in Latin America, 1933-1945* (Baltimore and London: The Johns Hopkins University Press, 1979), p. 78; also, Dexter Perkins, op. cit., p. 70.

141. Irwin F. Gellman, *Good Neighbor Diplomacy...*, Ibid., pp. 1-12.

142. See Irwin F. Gellman, *Roosevelt and Batista: Good Neighbor Diplomacy in Cuba, 1933-1945* (Albuquerque: University of New Mexico Press, 1973). Also José M. Hernández, *Cuba and the United States, Intervention and Militarism, 1898-1933* (Austin: University of Texas Press, 1993), pp. 178-79.

143. See, Hugh Thomas, *Cuba, the Pursuit of Freedom* (New York: Harper & Row, 1971), pp. 694-5; Julio Le Riverend, *Historia Económica de Cuba* (La Habana: Editorial de Ciencias Sociales, 1985), Chapter 29; Irwin Gellman, op. cit., pp. 36-39.

144. The negotiation was concluded in 1936, with the signing of a new Canal Treaty that incorporated some concessions to Panama. By 1939-1940, the U.S. had launched a new military expansion which, in actual practice, not only canceled whatever gains had been obtained by Panama, but meant the cession by Panama of large portions of its territory for about 100 new installations and an unprecedented high level of military activity.

145. See E. David Cronon, *Josephus Daniels in Mexico* (Madison: The University of Wisconsin Press, 1960).

146. "In actuality, the United States abrogated what was obsolete and retained what it considered vital to the national interest... No intervention was never an absolute reality —only an illusion that was valuable in popularizing the Good Neighbor principle." Irwin F. Gellman, *Good Neighbor Diplomacy...*, pp. 38, 39.

147. Trade between the US and Latin America grew moderately during the thirties. See, Irwin F. Gellman, op. cit., p. 58.

148. See, Hines Calvin Warner, United States Diplomacy in the Caribbean during World War II, Ph. D. dissertation University of Texas at Austin, August, 1969; also, Demetrio Boersner, *Relaciones internacionales de América Latina* (Mexico: Nueva Imagen, 1982), pp. 241-243; Gellman, Good Neighbor Diplomacy..., Chapters 2-8; and Haglund, op. cit.

149. Edgar J. Furniss, Jr., "America's Wartime Objectives in Latin America," *World Politics* (April, 1950), pp. 373-74.

150. "... the president moved toward internationalism through the only available opening. At first he did this casually, almost accidentally, but by the eve of the European war, Latin American actions played an integral part in shaping worldwide strategy." Irwin F. Gellman, *Good Neighbor Diplomacy...*, p. 7.

151. "In sum, I maintain that the decision of the Roosevelt administration to abandon isolationism and to construct a de facto alliance with Great Britain (which occurred in the summer of 1940) simply cannot be understood without analyzing the effect that events below the Rio Grande had on perceptions and actions of America policy makers... It is my argument that Roosevelt and his circle of advisers did indeed perceive a strong actual and potential threat to American physical security –a threat stemming principally from their assessment of Axis (mainly German) activities and intentions in Latin America, the most vulnerable part of the Western Hemisphere." David G. Haglund, op. cit., pp. 9, 16.

152. See, Stetson Conn, *The Western Hemisphere, The Framework for Hemisphere Defense* (Washington, D.C.: Office of the Chief of Military History, 1960), pp. 42-49,

and Chapter 8; J. Lloyd Mechan, *The United States and Inter-American Security, 1889-1960* (Austin: University of Texas Press, 1967), pp. 191-200.

153. Thus, its logic during the war increasingly responded to post-war relations with Latin America. See Furniss, op. cit.; also Stetson Conn and Byron Fairchild, op. cit.; and J. Lloyd Mecham, op. cit.

154. Cited in Hines Calvin Warner, op. cit., p. 51.

155. David Green, op. cit., p. 48.

156. Ibid., Chapter 2.

157. Adolf A. Berle, *New Directions in the New World* (New York: Harper & Brothers Publishers, 1940). The quote is the title of his first chapter.

CHAPTER 4

ICKES'S POWDER KEG

Gen. Blanton Winship. U.S. Army.

ICKES'S POWDER KEG

In 1938, after four years of Governor Winship's "mailed fist" policies (to use Harold Ickes's expression) and despite a decisive electoral victory of the *Coalición* in the 1936 elections,[1] Puerto Rican politics continued to be characterized by turmoil and instability. In 1938, the U.S. had begun to move decisively toward rearmament and war preparations. The defense of outlying possessions such as Puerto Rico, and of the Caribbean in general, became a high priority in strategic planning. Consequently, the pacification of Puerto Rico and the promotion of a political environment more favorable to the implementation of defense measures also gained growing importance.

In Puerto Rico, 1938 began with the most serious labor strike since that of the sugar workers from 1933 to 1934. More than seven thousand port workers went on strike on January 3. They paralyzed shipping activities for 37 days, leaving 95,000 other workers temporarily unemployed. The strike was led by new trade unions sponsored by the Congress of Industrial Organizations (CIO), which in the late 1930s had begun to challenge the dominant influence of the American Federation of Labor (AFL) and its affiliated trade unions organized in the *Federación Libre de Trabajadores* (FLT).

The success of the CIO in organizing non-sugar groups of workers such as port and construction workers and public car drivers demonstrated the erosion of support for the AFL-FLT (the organizational backbone of the *Partido Socialista*) among the working class. The crisis in the tobacco industry and the weakening of the traditional leadership provided by the cigar-makers to the working class movement were important factors in this change. Thus, the port strike demonstrated the diminished capacity of the *Partido Socialista* and FLT components of the *Coalición* to guarantee "social peace." Opposition parties such as the

Partido Comunista and *Afirmación Socialista* actively helped to organize the strike and supported the port workers. Strike activity, measured in number of strikers and man-days lost, began rapidly to climb in 1938 and 1939, after a significant drop in the mid-1930s, reaching very high levels in the 1940s.[2]

Significantly, port workers did not budge in the face of the government's threats to break the strike with the National Guard or the regular Army by "federalizing" it, a course demanded by big industrial and commercial interests. Thus, the strike laid bare the limits of the repressive tactics of the Winship government to deal with the new forms of popular mobilization, while exacerbating political differences within his cabinet. Attorney General Benigno Fernández García threw a wrench in the repressive machinery by issuing an opinion that there were no legal grounds for declaring an "emergency." He had been named to his post against the wishes of Governor Winship and the *Coalición*, and with the backing of Ickes and Ernest Gruening when they were still united in support of reformist measures.[3] Fernández García had been the *Partido Liberal* candidate for the post of Resident Commissioner in the 1932 elections and was reputed to be ideologically close to Luis Muñoz Marín.

The Winship administration had to confront another crisis of significant political repercussions in July 1938. It decided to celebrate the anniversary of the U.S. invasion of Puerto Rico on July 25 with a military parade in Ponce. This city had been the site of the "Palm Sunday Massacre" of Nationalists on March 21, 1937. The decision was clearly designed to demonstrate the success of Winship's "law and order" measures in suppressing the Nationalist Party.

Albizu Campos and the top Nationalist leaders had been jailed in 1936, and party activities had been practically banned. Repression against the Nationalists had reached a high point with the 1937 Ponce Massacre. Demands for a thorough official investigation of this dramatic event had been successfully resisted by Winship, Ernest Gruening and the *Coalición*. However, the repercussions of the Ponce massacre had continued to plague Winship, as in February 1938 a jury entirely composed of *coalicionistas* had declared eleven Nationalists not guilty of charges related to the bloody events in Ponce, while the American Civil Liberties Union (ACLU) and other U.S. groups and personalities continued to actively denounce the responsibility of government authorities in the Ponce events, particularly the governor himself. No major acts of political violence had taken place since 1937; however, in June of that year an assassination attempt against Federal Judge Robert A. Cooper had failed and several bombs were placed in homes of government functionaries. The last major incident had been another failed attempt on the life of Resident Commissioner Santiago Iglesias. It had left him slightly wounded.[4]

The July 25 parade in Ponce was abruptly interrupted by a hail of bullets. Most of these were directed at the reviewing stand where Winship stood surrounded by the leading *Coalición* politicians and other dignitaries. Miguel Ángel García Méndez, Speaker of the House, Senators Pedro Juan Serrallés and Alfonso Valdés, and Francisco López Domínguez, Commissioner of Agriculture, among others, were reported to have been slightly wounded. A total of thirty-six persons, both in the grandstand and in the crowd, were wounded. Rafael Martínez Nadal, President of the Senate and of the *Partido Unión Republicana*, was also present in the stand. Detective Juan R. Colón was shot when he leaped to shield the governor from the attack. National Guard Colonel Luis Irizarry, who stood next to Winship, was killed, as well as Nationalist Ángel Esteban Antongiorgi. Several Nationalists in the crowd were arrested and, eventually, nine were accused of participating in the attack. Since the parade was being broadcast by radio, the shooting was heard by radio listeners throughout the island.[5]

The attack on Winship, the first against any governor of Puerto Rico, was prominently covered by the U.S. press, particularly by *The New York Times*. Harwood Hull,[6] author of the dispatch published by the *Times* on July 26, wrote that the governor "did not depart from his prepared address, evidently finding nothing in the attempt on his life to alter the sentiments expressed in his introduction." With evident irony he went on to quote a part of Winship's speech which said, among other things, that "the Puerto Rican people have seen fit to celebrate so enthusiastically the fortieth anniversary of the arrival of the American flag on these shores."[7] The report was accompanied by another one entitled "Winship's Tenure Stormy, Nationalist Uprisings and Labor Troubles Have Beset Him." It stated that Winship had struggled with these problems "during almost his entire tenure" and that in 1935 he had been received from a trip to the U.S. by two parades: one in his honor and another which "marching to funeral music, demanded that he retire."[8]

On July 30, a *New York Times* editorial poked fun at Winship's claim to have detected the culprits among the crowd by using paraffin tests: "The process may be new to the general public, but not to the readers of detective fiction." It also mentioned that although Sherlock Holmes did not know of this technique, certainly Agatha Christie's Hercule Poirot and other fictional detectives "are fully informed of the method."[9] The process against the Nationalists was followed by the prominent newspaper in August. The news item on the beginning of the trial against Elifaz Escobar for the murder of Colonel Irizarry was accompanied by a large photograph of an elegantly dressed Winship in front of a group of poor children with the PRRA-constructed Falansterio housing project of Puerta de Tierra in the background. The text said that "The Governor of Puerto Rico Has a Popular Following."[10] This public relations ploy, whose origin is not difficult to imagine, is understandable in view of the clearly negative coverage Winship was receiving.

Army intelligence, which had been following labor unrest related to the port workers' strike, also filed on July 27 a very detailed report on the attack on Winship. It included a partial list of the wounded, an extensive narration of the incident, and even a sketch of the scene. The investigation of the incident was described in two subsequent weekly reports in August. The documents reflect the gravity ascribed to the attack by the military authorities, as no other event during 1938 was so minutely analyzed in the intelligence reports. It was a major security catastrophe. Although Winship had escaped unscathed, several high government functionaries had been wounded (the Secretary of Agriculture shot through the nose), a National Guard colonel killed and another U.S. officer, and Captain Marshal N. Darby of the Ordnance Department was also wounded. The only mitigating event mentioned was that the action had been very broadly repudiated, to a much greater extent than previous acts of violence by the Nationalists.[11]

The Ponce attack also meant considerable political embarrassment to Winship since one of his few credible claims to success in the Roosevelt administration was his tough policy to counter the challenge to internal security posed by the Nationalist Party. The incident shattered the official argument that the repression unleashed during the three previous years had effectively pacified the country. Ironically, the failed attempt also served to bring into perspective the weakening and political isolation of the Nationalist Party, a force of considerable weight during the first half of the 1930s.

The Nationalist Party officially distanced itself from the attack and claimed it had been the act of an isolated individual. The lawyers that had defended Nationalists in 1936 and 1937, many of them Liberals close to Luis Muñoz Marín, refused to represent the accused on this occasion. The former *muñocista* wing of the Liberal Party, which had begun to register a new party precisely during July 1938, the *Partido Popular Democrático*, did not want to identify itself with Nationalist violence.[12] Repression had also made the Nationalist Party pay a high political price as Pedro Albizu Campos and other important leaders were imprisoned in Atlanta, leaving their embattled followers in Puerto Rico bereft of political direction during a crucial political juncture. It is not surprising that in these circumstances the more moderate Muñoz Marín would attract the considerable pro-independence feeling that had accumulated during the 1930s. In short, the Nationalist Party was condemned to be overtaken by the momentous political events of the late 1930s.

But Winship's political difficulties were not limited to the events involving the labor movement and the Nationalist Party. Less visible developments loomed large as political threats to his "stormy governorship." Both parties in the *Coalición*, the *Partido Socialista* and the *Partido Unión Republicana*, were already profoundly divided by leadership and factional disputes. In the *Partido Socialista*, the succession of the aging Santiago Iglesias and control over the party was being disputed by Senator Bolívar Pagán and Prudencio Rivera Martínez, Commissioner of Labor. Well-defined factions had already formed around these two leaders by 1938. Similarly, the *Partido Unión Republicana* was in the midst of a simmering conflict between the most prominent leader of the *Coalición*, Senate President Rafael Martínez Nadal, and House Speaker García Méndez. Martínez Nadal had been ill with cancer since 1935 and his succession was also a bone of contention amongst Republicans.[13] These divisions would provoke fractures in both *Coalición* parties during 1939 and 1940.

In late 1938, serious charges of corruption made by maverick Socialist legislator Epifanio Fiz Jiménez (in what became known as the "Capitol Racket") against leading *Coalición* politicians such as Bolivar Pagán, were a clear manifestation of these internal disputes.[14] This scandal began to unfold on April 8, 1938, when Francisco Ramírez Pabón complained that an employee of Pagán, Gloria Quintana, held simultaneously another post in Mayagüez and was registered as a student of the University of Puerto Rico. Socialist Senator Sixto Pacheco was arrested on November 5 on eleven charges of fraud. Government authorities promised that it would be the first of "many arrests."[15] The report on the investigation, signed by Assistant Attorney General Enrique Campos del Toro, was made public on February 14, 1939. It revealed numerous irregularities and involved major *Coalición* leaders such as Alfonso Valdés.[16] The issue of corruption by the *Coalición*, and even by Winship himself, continued to plague the government in 1939. It was vehemently denounced in Washington by Representative Vito Marcantonio.[17]

The internal political equation also included Muñoz and his former Liberal Party faction. Though expelled from the party and ostracized from Washington, Muñoz remained an important factor in Puerto Rican politics. The real political weight of the *muñocista* grouping was then an unknown quantity, dismissed by other political actors as of marginal importance. Muñoz, however, had already formulated in 1938 a clear strategy toward participation in the 1940 elections and was feverishly organizing his new party.

Finally, this volatile political situation was further compounded and expressed by a clear break between two of the main policy-makers for Puerto Rico in Washington: Harold Ickes and Ernest Gruening. By 1938, they were clearly working at cross-purposes, the former against Winship and his allies and the latter in a firm alliance with them. This bitter power struggle reflected the existence of divisions between different factions within the administration. In Washington it revealed the existence of power circles regarding policy toward Puerto Rico.

Puerto Rico's economy was plummeting. After a slight economic improvement during 1937, the island went into a recession in 1938. An official economic study conducted by the U.S. Department of Commerce stated that "during the year 1938 there was a considerable falling off of business. Overseas trade decreased 38.4 million dollars to 175.4 million, with imports exceeding exports by 11.2 million, resulting in the first unfavorable balance in 8 years. Shipments of unrefined sugar dropped 38.8% and all sugar 26%."[18] There seemed to be no lasting respite to the prolonged economic crisis that had begun in the early 1930s.

Sugar and Crisis, 1898-1938

As in other newly acquired possessions and protectorates, U.S. control over Puerto Rico provoked, during the first three decades of the century, a relatively rapid process of economic and social transformation. This process was characterized by the decay of the traditional coffee and food-producing agriculture (based on *haciendas* and medium and small landholding) centered in the central mountain towns. In its place, an export oriented agrarian capitalist agriculture, mainly revolving around sugar production in coastal plantations and, to a lesser extent, on tobacco production and manufacture,[19] gradually arose. Sugar not only regained its place as the main export commodity, but forcefully imposed itself as the organizing axis of Puerto Rican economy.

The expansion of the sugar and tobacco industries was based on the large influx of foreign investment, mainly U.S., and the shifting of native capital from the traditional sector to these industries and other expanding economic activities. By 1910, 17 mainly U.S.-owned sugar mills controlled 53.7% of production, with the remainder corresponding to 25 native establishments.[20] Though a modest expansion of native sugar capital took place in the 1910s, two long term tendencies were clear: 1) a process of concentration in larger production units (142 *centrales* produced 2.4 thousand tons of sugar in 1910, while 44 produced 19.7 in 1930), and 2) an expansion of the share controlled by foreign capital.[21]

The new economic structure, in its expansive phase, brought about a certain "modernization" of Puerto Rico since it resulted in the partial breakdown of traditional peasant agriculture and the *hacienda* system, internal migration to the coast (as well as external migration), urbanization in the sugar-producing areas, expansion of other economic activities related to the new model, and growth of professional employment in sugar-related activities (engineers, agronomists, administrators, lawyers, accountants, etc.) or in government (e.g., teachers). This transformation, together with other social and institutional changes, such as the expansion of public primary instruction, the weakening of the influence of the Catholic Church and the growth of Protestantism, and the partial extension of certain legal guarantees for the exercise of civil liberties, ensured a degree of internal consensus and stability. The participation of local capitalists as partners in the new economic structure was important in the colonial arrangement.

In addition to this, the agricultural export economy of Puerto Rico experienced a prolonged period of considerable prosperity from 1912 to 1921. The First World War provoked a sharp rise in the prices of sugar and other export commodities –known as the "Dance of the Millions" in Cuba– that benefited both U.S. corporations and local producers. Political responses to U.S. rule during this period were strongly conditioned by the sense of "material progress" that had been achieved.[22] However, the stability of the colonial arrangement was also guaranteed by the exercise of force through the security institutions constructed after 1898. This was mainly directed against the radical manifestations of the labor movement associated to the strength of anarchism among tobacco workers during the first two decades of the century.[23]

The changes that occurred after 1898 gave rise to three main internal political tendencies (with their roots in the pre-1898 pattern of political conflicts) which found organizational expression in diverse parties. The first tendency mainly expressed the outlook and interests of the traditional coffee producing sector, the *hacendado* class, and sectors of the Puerto Rican sugar-mill owners and of the professional middle class. It expressed itself in the *Partido Federal*, and later the *Partido Unión* and the *Partido Liberal*, and was electorally dominant until 1932.

This political movement became increasingly alienated from the colonial regime and oscillated between requests for territorial autonomy and rhetorical demands for independence. However, it remained within the confines of the political space and institutions of the colonial state. In 1922, a dissident group of pro-independence intellectuals left the *Partido Unión* and founded the *Partido Nacionalista*. The *Partido Unión* fused with the *Partido Republicano Puertorriqueño* in 1924, an alliance which was actively promoted by Governor Horace M. Towner and aimed at containing the ascent of the *Partido Socialista*.

After the *Alianza Puertorriqueña* dissolved, leading to the establishment of the *Partido Liberal* in 1931, the pro-independence forces within that party gained prominence over the more moderate autonomist sector. This lead to the adoption of a platform for the 1932 elections which stated that "its purpose is to demand the immediate recognition of the sovereignty of Puerto Rico and make it effective through the quickest, practical and direct means, thus achieving the absolute Independence of Puerto Rico."[24] After his return to Puerto Rico in that same year, Muñoz joined the *Partido Liberal* as an outspoken leader of its pro-independence wing. The autonomist wing remained in the party and later became an important source of support for Antonio R. Barceló in his struggle against *muñocismo*. An important dimension of this controversy on status was the considerable influence sugar interests, opposed to Muñoz's radicalism, exercised within the party. The *Partido Liberal* became the strongest single party in 1932 when it obtained 170,168 votes.

The second major political tendency was represented by the *Partido Republicano*, founded by mainly middle class professionals who perceived U.S. control as a modernizing force and favored Puerto Rico's annexation as a state. This party gradually became associated to and controlled by the new agricultural, financial, and commercial interests linked to the economic sectors, mainly sugar, that rapidly expanded during the first three decades. Rafael Martínez Nadal and a group of Republicans refused to join the *Alianza Puertorriqueña* and founded the *Partido Republicano Puro* that established a loose coalition with the *Partido Socialista*. In 1930, a group known as *Grupo de Buen Gobierno* made up of *Aliancistas*, *Republicanos Puros* and *Socialistas* formed the new majority block in both chambers of the legislature. The *Grupo de Buen Gobierno* thus became the dominant political formation and the basic nucleus for the *Coalición*, which successfully contested the 1932 elections.[25]

In 1931 and 1932 the *Republicanos Puros* fused with the political remnants of the *Alianza Puertorriqueña* that had not followed Antonio R. Barcelo's *unionistas* in their break with the *Alianza*. García Méndez, who would later play a crucial role in political conflicts during the late 1930s, was one of the *aliancista* Republicans. The new political party was renamed *Partido Unión Republicana* (PUR). Several of its top leaders were *centralistas*, like Alfonso Valdés, or prominent representatives of the sugar industry, like García Méndez. In 1932, the PUR entered into an electoral alliance with the *Partido Socialista* to contest the 1932 elections. PUR's greater electoral strength (it had obtained 110,794 votes to the Socialists' 97,438), its strong links to corporate interests, the control it had over the presidencies of both chambers of the legislature, and the absence of Socialist leader Santiago Iglesias from Puerto Rico due to his post as Resident Commissioner in Washington, made the PUR the dominant party in the *Coalición* and Martínez Nadal its leading spokesman.[26]

Finally, the expanding working class, whose largest component was composed by the sugar workers, became organized in the *Federación Libre de Trabajadores* (FLT), strongly associated with the American Federation of Labor (AFL). Tobacco workers were an important working class group that played a crucial role in trade union and political organization. By 1915, in the context of an upsurge of labor mobilization and strike activity, the organized labor movement created its own party, the *Partido Socialista* (PS). This occurred after the more radical anarchist leadership had been severely weakened by persecution mainly under Colonel Colton's governorship. The PS rapidly grew, obtaining 24% of the vote in 1920, and control over 8 municipalities out of a total of 76.[27]

Electoral and party politics developed within the severely constrained space defined by the colonial state, which meant that, though the internal political forces could obtain a share of political influence in certain spheres, they could not govern. The Foraker Act of 1900, which ended direct military rule, had centralized power in the executive branch, and placed the governorship and other key cabinet posts under the control of the U.S. president. The Jones Act of 1917, though expanding somewhat the sphere of representation of internal political forces and extending U.S. citizenship to Puerto Ricans, did not significantly depart from the existing political arrangement. This made the metropolitan state a major factor in internal politics. It had considerable power resources, which it used at times to promote the *Partido Republicano*, or even to sponsor alliances between traditional antagonists, as with the *Alianza Puertorriqueña* of 1924-1932 between *Republicanos* and *Unionistas* designed to contain the emerging "red menace" represented by the *Partido Socialista*.

Despite its promising beginnings, this economic and political pattern began to show cracks and weaknesses even before the onset of the financial crisis of 1929 and the ensuing depression. Immediately after the First World War, Puerto Rico's economy suffered its first serious downturn as a result of the contraction of its external market, with concomitant manifestations of political unrest. Charles P. Kindleberger has stressed that the depression of the 1930s was preceded by a crisis in agricultural prices and production in the 1920s. The international price of sugar fell constantly since the early 1920s until the early 1930s, when it finally leveled out at a much reduced price than that of the war and post-war period.[28]

Thus, by the mid 1920s, a process of deterioration of Puerto Rico's terms of trade (i.e. a sustained decline of the prices of its main exports) had emerged as a long-term economic tendency. Also, between 1926 and 1928 the amount of tobacco exported dropped by 67%. This contraction occurred before hurricanes San Felipe (1928) and San Ciprián (1932), and cannot be attributed to them, though they further damaged the island's economy. It was in this context of agricultural crisis that U.S. sugar corporations rapidly expanded their control over production. By 1934, Puerto Rican *centralistas* controlled only 27% of total sugar production.[29]

The deterioration of the terms of trade meant that, by 1937, Puerto Rico had to export 36.7% more than in the 1910-1914 period in order to obtain the same income. Thus, though tobacco exports increased 9% from 1921 to 1931, its export income contracted by 51.9%. The 1930s depression almost obliterated tobacco production. Employment in tobacco declined from 5,483 in 1919 and 1920, to 539 in 1939 and 1940.[30] Coffee production and exports, also affected by a severe drop at the beginning of the century and by the hurricanes of 1928 and 1932, practically disappeared, with exports declining 66.7% from 1926 to 1928, and its value decreasing by 89.4% from 1931 to 1935. John A. Dalton described the critical state of the Puerto Rican economy even before the onset of the Depression in the following terms:

> The livelihood of these people was precarious long before the sugar depression. With hurricane damage, a destroyed coffee industry, and falling sugar prices, conditions became desperate,

and it was fitting as well as necessary that some program to offset insular unemployment be undertaken along with adjustment of sugar production. Of course the cost of the scheme for reconstruction, like the cost of sustaining the sugar industry, has been met by the consumer and the taxpayer in the United States.[31]

Non-sugar manufacture, mainly consisting of a domestic needlework industry for export based on female labor, was also affected and its wages were miserable (even as low as $1\frac{1}{8}$ cents an hour).[32] This industry, which was structurally linked to sugar production as it provided a meager additional income to many impoverished families of peasants and sugar workers, became the second most important source of export earnings in the 1930s.[33] It represented 16.2% of the value of exports in 1933 (compared to tobacco's 5.8%) and had grown to 18.5% in 1935.[34]

Only sugar, through a constant expansion of production, was able to remain profitable, consequently strengthening its grip on the insular economy, which was becoming increasingly monocultural. Sugar, however, could not absorb the labor force expelled from other sectors, as the increase in production, at least until 1934, was largely obtained through higher productivity both in the agricultural phase (new varieties of cane) and in the industrial phase.[35] Therefore, even before the onset of the depression, the Puerto Rican economy exhibited signs of stagnation, growing unemployment, and elements of a profound social crisis.

It is not surprising that widespread discontent with the consequences of the consolidation of the sugar plantation economy and the colonial political arrangement associated with it already existed before the depression. In late 1929, journalist Andrés Rodríguez Vera published a pamphlet containing a strong indictment of the sugar economy and of the domestic needlework industry, which he said had imposed a new form of slavery and feudalism. The prologue was written by Vicente Géigel Polanco, who would later become a leading member of the *Partido Popular Democrático* and possibly the most prominent of its pro-independence leaders. Géigel's views are worth quoting at length since they already contained themes that would be further developed by other members of the *trentista* generation of intellectuals, mainly by Antonio S. Pedreira in his influential 1934 book *Insularismo*.[36]

The fertility of the soil, political colonialism imposed on the island, and tariff protection of our sugar cane, are all factors fully utilized by the yankee capitalist. He begins large scale cultivation on the basis of *latifundio*. Agrarian concentration supposes, firstly, the displacement of the small landowner and his proletarization. The transit from owner to wage earner provokes evident moral, economic and political disturbances that generally culminate in the imposition of a XXth century style of industrial feudalism.

The hegemony of sugar cane over other products becomes so accentuated that it eventually mortally wounds them -as happens with coffee- or reduces them to an insignificant volume. Our food production [*frutos menores*] constitutes eloquent evidence. The reduction or elimination of genuinely Puerto Rican crops is a severe blow to the table of the poor, who are deprived of valuable native products and, at the same time, forced to import basic foodstuff from the North American market at the high price imposed by the tariff.

The constant emigration of capital –accumulated labor, according to the classical Marxian expression– that prevailing absenteeism makes inevitable, contributes to impress on our people a seal of apparent progress and prosperity that, in justice, is only a disguise of the growing poverty of the laboring classes and of our condition as a U.S. sugar factory. To state that under the present regime the yankee prospers and the native is ruined, [only] takes note of an evident fact.[37]

Similar views could also be found in Cuban thinker Ramiro Guerra's *Azúcar y población en las Antillas* (1927).[38] In addition to this, in 1931 Bailey and Justine Diffie published *Porto Rico: A Broken Pledge*, which contained a similarly strong critique-in this case from the perspective of U.S. socialist intellectuals-of the wretched social conditions created by the sugar plantation economy even before the onset of the Depression.[39]

The Depression made the economic situation even worse, provoking a sharp drop of per capita income, from around $122 in 1930 to $85 in 1933. The level of 1930 was not restored until 1940.[40] But these figures do not reflect the full impact of the crisis on the majority of the population, as a simultaneous upward redistribution of income occurred.[41] From 1933 to 1935, 42% of the population was receiving federal relief funds, compared to 8% in Alaska and 7% in Hawaii.[42] In 1937, a U.S. economic expert on sugar noted that if rehabilitation failed, which was "not unthinkable," then "the continued expenditures for productive purposes of all kinds from $5,000,000 to $10,000,000 a year may be necessary in order to keep the marginal of the ever increasing population from privation."[43] By 1938, a government study estimated the number of unemployed and their dependents in 1,121,035, approximately 60% of the total population. A report issued by the University of Puerto Rico indicated that 43.8% of its 1929 graduates were unemployed, and that this would increase to 55.6% for its 1931 and 1932 graduates.[44]

The capacity of the sugar industry to make a significant impact on unemployment through further expansion of production, however limited, was further constrained in 1934 with the inclusion of Puerto Rico in the U.S. sugar quota system by the Jones-Costigan Act. This responded both to the trade preferences extended to Cuba during that same year, aimed at stabilizing the government of Carlos Mendieta, and the attempts of the Roosevelt administration to bring order to the domestic sugar market through the Agricultural Adjustment Act. The quota for Puerto Rico was fixed at 37% less than the large 1934 sugar harvest, and froze any further expansion of the industry.

The large sugar corporations organized in the *Asociación de Productores de Azúcar* attempted to retain the largest share of the quota, making the cuts fall mainly on the production of middle and small sugar cane farmers (*colonos*), thus alienating these traditional allies. They formed the *Asociación de Colonos* under the leadership of Jesús T. Piñero, who eventually became an important source of support to the *Partido Popular Democrático*. In general, the quota system meant that the sugar industry could no longer perform the role of the dynamic organizing axis of Puerto Rico's economy and marked the beginning of its eventual demise.[45]

The Roosevelt administration named Robert Gore to the governorship of Puerto Rico in 1933. Gore was a wealthy Florida newspaper owner who had supported Roosevelt's campaign. He could not be suspected of the slightest previous knowledge of Puerto Rico, untactfully referring to Puerto Ricans as "those poor devils down there" before even arriving on the island. He promptly aligned himself with the *Coalición*, becoming the target of *Nacionalista*[46] and *Partido Liberal* attacks. Gore succumbed in a few months in the whirlpool of Puerto Rican politics, with public credit mainly going to Muñoz's incessant public criticism and political scheming.[47]

The atmosphere of intense political turmoil and crisis created during Gore's governorship in the Depression's worst period prompted calls for his replacement by a "strong" governor, preferably a military officer who could stabilize the situation. Labor unrest had risen sharply from 1931 to 1934, with only 6,566 workers involved in strikes, controversies and lockouts during the first period, compared to 72,168 during the second.[48] The level of workers involved in strikes remained high (at about 66 to 68 thousand) during the following two years.

An additional source of concern in government circles was the radical anti-imperialist course the *Partido Nacionalista*, under the leadership of Pedro Albizu Campos, had followed since 1930. Though small and electorally weak,[49] its political importance was magnified by widespread social discontent, growing anti-colonial sentiments, and the labor unrest of the early 1930s. The decision of striking sugar workers to seek the assistance of Albizu Campos on January 12, 1934 further enhanced the perceived threat represented by Nationalism.[50] In was in this context that Roosevelt named General Blanton Winship governor in early 1934.[51]

In 1933, the Federal Emergency Relief Administration (FERA) responded to the deteriorating social situation by setting up the Puerto Rican Emergency Relief Administration (PRERA) and placing it under the direction of James and Dorothy Bourne. This was the first step in the creation of a massive federal welfare structure which, by 1936, generated the equivalent of 50% (about 60,000 workers) of the employment in sugar companies. The PRERA was absorbed in 1934 by a new agency, the Puerto Rico Reconstruction Administration (PRRA) under the direction of Ernest Gruening, who simultaneously held the post of director of the Division of Territories and Island Possessions in the Department of the Interior. As head of PRRA, he reported directly to the President and not to the Secretary of the Interior. The total expenditures of these agencies during the 1933-1938 period ($142 million) was larger than the budget of the Government of Puerto Rico (only $15.8 million in 1938-1939), making them a "parallel government" with considerable power.

The operation of this welfare structure significantly expanded govern-ment employment.[52] It also meant a major restructuring of the state ap-paratus that made control over this federal bureaucracy a major bone of contention among internal political forces.

Governor Blanton Winship, like Gore before him, soon established a relationship of close political collaboration with the *Coalición* and sought to forcefully repress the more radical expression of political discontent, particularly the *Partido Nacionalista*. After the 1932 elections, this party adopted a policy of electoral boycott, organized a paramilitary wing named *Cadetes de la República*, and expanded its political influence. Albizu absolutely rejected any legitimacy of the exercise of U.S. power in Puerto Rico, sought to distance Nationalism from the restrained pro-indepen-dence rhetoric of the *liberales*, and built his politics on militant resistance and non-participation in existing political institutions. The *Partido Nacionalista*, however, did not openly take armed action until after a bloody confrontation with the police in late 1935.

The Nationalist Challenge

Winship sought to deal with the Nationalist challenge through po-lice measures. The police force, which was under the direction of Colo-nel Francis E. Riggs, a close personal friend of Senator Millard Tydings of Maryland, Chairman of the Committee of Territories and Insular Pos-sessions, had been strengthened to deal with internal security. The re-pression of the Nationalists was to be kept strictly a police operation, as involvement of the National Guard or the 65th Infantry Regiment would have created the impression that colonial war was being waged in Puerto Rico.[53] Some doubts also existed regarding the loyalty of these forces.[54] However, the National Guard was used to train the police in the use of machine guns.[55] Thus, under Winship, U.S. policy combined repression with welfare measures in order to contain social and political unrest. The reformist proposals in the 1934 Chardón Plan were never imple-mented due to the close political alignment of Winship with the *Coalición*.[56] Earl Parker Hanson, a key player in the political situation of the 1930s, noted Winship's emphasis on police measures.

The military man, however, demanded discipline for its own sake. He enlarged the force, bought it tear gas, machine guns, and what not, procured a fleet of shining red automobiles for mobility, and sent it to summer camps for intensive training. There can be no doubt that he did it largely for the sole purpose of strengthening the police and making it more effective as a civic organization-simply because his military training had taught him that that was the thing to do. However, in view of the tragic events which followed Riggs' assassination, he came to be widely charged with having militarized and brutalized the police and having transformed it from an arm of the insular government into a tool of the federal government's most reactionary officials.[57]

The first major confrontation between the police and the *nacionalistas*, the "Río Piedras Massacre," took place on October 24, 1935, leaving four members of the party and a bystander dead and forty others injured. This event provoked a serious heightening of political tensions and unleashed a spiral of political violence that lasted, as we have seen, until 1938. The situation was considered so serious in late 1935 that Ernest Gruening requested an opinion of the U.S. Army Commander in San Juan regarding the possibility of doubling the size of the 65th Infantry Regiment, thus bringing it to brigade size. In his answer to Gruening the officer stated that, "in the event of any invasion this force is inadequate. Also in case of serious domestic disturbances there is some doubt as to the sufficiency of such a force to effectively cope with the situation."[58]

After the "Río Piedras Massacre," Riggs issued a statement promising to wage "war, unceasing war" against criminals.[59] The Nationalist Party responded with their own belligerent statement: "War against Yankee imperialism." On February 23, 1936, two Nationalist youths, Elias Beauchamp and Hiram Rosado, killed Colonel Riggs. They, in turn, were killed by the police while under arrest in a police station. The death of Riggs and his attackers triggered off a major political crisis. General Winship declared: "I am going to govern this island. If anybody gets in my way, I'll go over him."[60] For all practical purposes, Puerto Rico was subjected to an undeclared martial law during 1936 and 1937.

As a response to the assassination of Riggs, the Tydings Bill was drafted in Washington under Gruening's supervision and presented by Senator Millard Tydings. It provided for a plebiscite on independence to be held during the 1936 elections.[61] This legislation was clearly punitive, as its economic provisions meant certain economic disaster for an independent Puerto Rico. It was meant to provoke division between radical and moderate independence supporters, and to exarcebate anti-independence feelings.[62] In fact, Socialist leader Santiago Iglesias stressed the "threat" of independence during the 1936 campaign.

Riggs's death had provoked a definitive break between Gruening and Muñoz.[63] The Tydings Bill was accompanied by the persecution of *muñocista* Liberals, designed to deepen existing divisions in the Liberal Party, and by a strong alignment of the Roosevelt administration with the *Coalición*.[64] Under these adverse circumstances, Muñoz thought the Liberal Party was condemned to lose the 1936 elections, consequently adopting a posture of non-participation (*retraimiento*). This set the stage for a definitive break between *muñocismo* and the more conservative wing of the party under Antonio R. Barceló.

Several nationalist leaders were arrested in April 1936. They were sentenced to prison after a second trial in June. However, political violence did not abate, with numerous incidents occurring in 1936 and 1937.[65] On March 21, 1937, a police attack on an unarmed Nationalist march in Ponce left 19 dead and more that 100 wounded. This incident, known as the "Ponce Massacre" or the "Palm Sunday Massacre," was the bloodiest act of political violence in Puerto Rico's recent history. An American Civil Liberties Union (ACLU) report issued shortly after the event placed the blame on Winship's administration, particularly on the governor himself. It was prepared by a commission headed by Arthur Garfield Hays and composed of leading Puerto Rican personalities.[66]

After the July 25, 1938 attack on Winship, a Puerto Rican student at the University of Chicago, Jaime Benítez –who would soon become Chancellor of the University of Puerto Rico– wrote a short essay that, while carefully distancing himself from Nationalism, contained the following indictment of Winship's war on the Nationalist Party. It was sent by his professor, Charles Merriam, to Harold Ickes, and was read by President Roosevelt.

> The point I am to make is that the Governor himself, through his military approach to things, has helped to keep Puerto Rico in an unnecessary state of turmoil. He seems to think that the political problem of Puerto Rico limits itself to a fight between himself and the Nationalists, that no holds are barred in that fight and that everybody else should keep out. As a matter of fact he has played the Nationalist game and they have played his. Rationality, Democracy and Puerto Rico have been the losers.[67]

The essay also accused Winship of pro-Franco sympathies and the *Coalición's* top leadership of being thoroughly corrupt.

Winship's repressive policies against the Nationalists, and Gruening's drive against the *muñocista* Liberals, were perceived by some sectors of the Roosevelt administration and influential U.S. liberal personalities as destabilizing Puerto Rican politics. The Winship-Gruening-*Coalición* alliance was also considered a major obstacle to the implementation of New Deal reformist measures. The 1937 "Palm Sunday Massacre" provoked a major clash between Harold Ickes and Ernest Gruening. Liberal journals such as *Atlantic Monthly, The Nation* and *The Republic* were critical of U.S. policy in Puerto Rico. By 1938, as we have seen, *The New York Times* had become an additional source of criticism. Books such as Arthur Gayer's *The Sugar Economy of Puerto Rico* and Trumbull White's *Puerto Rico and Its People*, both published in 1938, were aimed at neutralizing the increasingly negative perception of U.S. colonial policy and the Winship government.[68]

The American Civil Liberties Union (ACLU) and the Committee for Fair Play to Puerto Rico, headed by Oswald Garrison Villard, were also very active in Puerto Rican issues.[69] Prominent liberal personalities such as Villard,[70] Editor of *The Nation*, Arthur Garfield Hays, Ruby Black, John Franklin Carter, Roger Baldwin, Carleton Beals, painter Rockwell Kent,[72] James and Dorothy Bourne, Earl Parker Hanson, and New York Representative Vito Marcantonio, among others, were outspoken opponents of Winship, and some of them had access to administration power circles. Their arguments were very similar to those expressed by Benítez, who was already politically aligned with Muñoz Marín. Less conspicuous, but no less important, were the New Deal figures who, together with Eleanor Roosevelt, had unsuccessfully tried to implement reformist policies in 1934 under the banner of the Chardón Plan. These were, among others, Rexford Guy Tugwell, Charles Taussig, and John Franklin Carter. This heterogeneous constellation of forces had one common element by the late 1930s: they wanted Winship and the *Coalición* out of power in Puerto Rico.

Cracks in the *Coalición*

The violent confrontation with the *Partido Nacionalista* was not the only manifestation of internal political instability in Puerto Rico. The traditional party system was subjected to great stress, with factional and leadership struggles provoking divisions in all major parties. The politics of "social peace" followed by the PS and FLT weakened their influence over the labor movement, creating a political space for the emergence of more radical political organizations and trade unions.[73]

Important sugar workers strikes outside the control of the FLT took place in 1933 and 1934. The port workers' strike of 1938 was also a serious blow to FLT hegemony. Non-sugar groups of workers, such as drivers and construction workers, sought to organize outside of FLT. The Congress of Industrial Organizations (CIO) was instrumental in organizing new trade unions outside of PS-FLT influence. The emergence of new political groups such as *Afirmación Socialista* and the *Partido Comunista*, which sought to attract the Socialists' working class base, were also evidence of the political costs the PS had to pay for its participation in the *Coalición*. Perhaps more importantly, the *Partido Popular Democrático* strongly supported the new trade union movement and sought to exploit the tensions that existed between the PS-FLT leadership and its working class base. In 1939, Muñoz visited the picket line of striking port workers and declared that he was prepared to have himself arrested in order to uphold their right to picket.[74]

Additionally, after the 1936 elections, a bitter power struggle developed within the PS leadership. Broadly, it reflected a conflict between the historical trade union leadership that had founded the FLT and the PS political leadership in control of legislative and other political posts, as well as the party structure. The most important leaders of the competing factions were Prudencio Rivera Martínez, Secretary of Labor and power-ful FLT leader, and Bolívar Pagán, Vice President of the Senate. Rivera Martínez came from a background as a tobacco worker of anarchist sym-pathies, and as a trade union organizer. Bolívar Pagán was a lawyer, professional politician, and the son-in-law of Socialist leader Santiago Iglesias. Pagán was also Treasurer of San Juan and interim President of the PS, substituting for Iglesias, who was in Washington.[75]

Dissension between Pagán and Rivera Martínez regarding key de-tails of the electoral pact with the PUR surfaced during the August 14, 1936 party convention in Caguas.[76] Santiago Iglesias sided with Pagán in this controversy. By the summer of 1937, factions had coalesced around the two leaders. After the death of Secretary General of the Party Alfonso Torres in late 1937, Pagán and Rivera Martínez supported competing candidates for this post. The former's candidate, Santiago Carreras, won the post on November 28, 1937 by obtaining the support of seven sena-torial districts. Epifanio Fiz Jiménez, a pro-Rivera Martínez senator, was defeated.[77] It was Fiz Jiménez who later denounced the "Capitol Racket" which involved Bolívar Pagán and his supporters.

Attempts by Santiago Iglesias to prevent an open break in the party were unsuccessful. By early 1939, with the "Capitol Racket" in the back-ground, tensions had escalated even further. Epifanio Fiz Jiménez was expelled from the PS in March 1939. That same month the Rivera Martínez faction, *Oposición Socialista*, met and decided to decree a "truce" with Pagán until the following June. Gonzalo Córdova characterized the situ-ation in the PS in the following manner: "Harmony and discipline be-gan to erode alarmingly as the numerous attacks among the various lead-ers began to wreck the Free Federation and the Socialist Party."[78]

News of the removal of Governor Winship and his replacement by Admiral Leahy, based on a declaration issued by Roosevelt on May 11, further complicated the political situation on the island. According to Pagán, this was a time of "constant political intrigue" as the leading po-litical figures (with the exception of Muñoz, who had decided on a policy of no alliances) sought to position themselves and establish pacts with a view toward the 1940 elections. The anti-*muñocista* Liberals, under the presidency of José Ramírez Santibáñez,[79] first approached Pagán to woo him away from the Republicans and also met with PUR leader Rafael

Martínez Nadal. Rebuffed, Ramírez Santibáñez approached the dissident Secretary of Labor, who proved more amenable to an alliance.

According to Pagán, Rivera Martínez was openly using his post as Secretary of Labor to organize his faction and to launch attacks on his leadership.[80] By June 1939, Santiago Iglesias had given up in his efforts at mediation and sided with Pagán. Two months later, Pagán presided over a party convention that "dishonorably" expelled Rivera Martínez.

Thus, when Admiral Leahy was inaugurated on September 11, the first major political break in the *Coalición* had already occurred, and an important Socialist faction had formed a tacit alliance with the official leadership of the Liberal Party. The maverick Socialist Prudencio Rivera Martínez was a member of his cabinet and the official *Coalición* leadership was demanding his removal. Therefore, the governor could hardly stand aloof from this conflict. The *Partido Laborista Puro* was founded on December 3, 1939 by the Socialist followers of Rivera Martínez.

Similarly, the *Partido Unión Republicana* was undergoing an internal power struggle between Rafael Martínez Nadal, President of the Senate and main leader of the party, and Miguel Ángel García Méndez, Speaker of the House. The former was seriously ill with cancer since 1935, making the issue of his succession, among other things, a source of friction and division among Republican factions. Differences existed between these two leaders since that year, as Martínez Nadal was inclined to prefer Senator Alfonso Valdés as his successor.[81] By 1938, the Martínez Nadal-García Méndez feud had intensified.

On July 4, 1939, García Méndez gave an important speech calling for the "union of the Puerto Rican family." It was interpreted as an expression of support for the incipient political formation that was emerging in negotiations between the anti-*muñocistas* in the *Partido Liberal* and the dissident wing of the *Partido Socialista*, led by Prudencio Rivera Martínez. An accusation against García Méndez that he "had made a pact with Mr. Ramírez Santibáñez and Mr. Rivera Martínez to topple the government," was considered by the Central Committee of the PUR on July 18. However, he was exonerated as his expulsion would have precipitated a split in the party.[82] Neither could he openly break with the party at this early juncture as he would have been immediately removed from his post as Speaker by Martínez Nadal and Pagán's supporters in the House of Representatives.

A political commentary written by Sergio Romanecce in *El Mundo* ironically stated that:

> The speech of the Speaker Don Miguel Angel García Méndez
> . . . has had the great virtue of moving the hearts and wills of
> ninety nine percent of the Puerto Rican citizens . . . The true
> and certain fact is that the country is is tired, rather, revolted
> with the present indecent state of affairs . . .
>
> The certain truth is that the constitution of a new political
> party is imminent. It is public knowledge who will form part
> of this powerful organization and what will be its ideological
> postulates.[83]

The press also claimed that the new political formation, already known as *Tripartismo*, had been created as a result of efforts by powerful Roosevelt administration functionaries, particularly in the Department of the Interior. According to these reports, "these high functionaries feel a very friendly inclination toward the proposal of the new party."[84] Jesús T. Piñero, in a letter dated August 30, 1939, noted that the "Winship removal has broken the coalition and made tripartism possible." He credited Vito Marcantonio for this feat and remarked that he now was after Auditor Leslie A. McLeod and a functionary named E. G. Sturn.[85]

On July 18, Muñoz commemorated the anniversary of the birth of his father, Luis Muñoz Rivera, with a speech significantly entitled "The Old Alliance, the Coalition and the New Alliance Are the Same Thing." In this speech he called the leadership of the *Partido Liberal* merchants who trafficked with the name of his father and the symbols of the party, but had no popular following. He said that he had driven them out of the temple of Muñoz Rivera's sepulchre to the "market" of petty politics.[86]

Just before Leahy's arrival in Puerto Rico, activities toward the formation of the new political alliance became hectic. On July 22, it was reported that the three leaders of *Tripartismo* (Santibáñez, García Méndez and Rivera Martínez) would be traveling to Washington in early August.[87] Their platform for the 1940 elections was being drafted with the purpose of informing the "National Administration" of its content. This had the aim of demonstrating "that there was a party in Puerto Rico favorable to the policy of the Federal Government." Republican leaders close to García Méndez had allegedly participated in the process.[88] On August 19, García Méndez forcefully denied that he had "fled" from the new movement. Its leaders also claimed that they were in constant communication with their friends in Puerto Rico and with "high functionaries of the Federal administration."[89]

By the summer of 1940, the cracks in the *Coalición* had led, on the one hand, to the formation of the *Unificación Puertorriqueña Tripartita* among the García Méndez Republicans, significantly renamed the *Partido Republicano Reformista*, the *Partido Laborista Puro*, and the remnants of the *Partido Liberal*, while, on the other hand, Martínez Nadal and Bolívar Pagán renewed the *Coalición* pact.

A New Party Emerges: the *Partido Popular Democrático*

Muñoz had played a very prominent role in Puerto Rican politics during the first *Coalición* administration (1932-1936). His successful campaign for the removal of Governor Robert Gore (1933) had gained him notoriety. Within the *Partido Liberal*, he became the recognized leader of the younger generation of pro-independence and reformist members. He effectively used his post as senator during this period to forcefully campaign for the application of the 500 Acre Law and other reform measures contained in the Chardón Plan, of which he had been an important architect. His strategy was designed to drive a wedge between the *Partido Socialista*, which had made a programmatic commitment for the application of the law, and the more conservative *Partido Unión Republicana*, which adamantly opposed any measure that could injure the interests of the sugar industry.[90] As director of *La Democracia*, the newspaper founded by his father, he also controlled the main organ of the *Partido Liberal*. Muñoz also used his pedigree (heir to the legacy of Luis Muñoz Rivera) as an important symbolic asset of his political capital. His star rose rapidly in the party and by the mid 1930s he was in a position to dispute the leadership of the party's founder Antonio R. Barceló.

Muñoz had also constructed, during his long sojourn in the U.S., an important network of contacts among liberals and influential New Deal personalities.[91] His marriage to writer Muna Lee facilitated his entry into

U.S. progressive intellectual and political circles. Once Franklin Roosevelt won the 1932 elections, several of his friends came to occupy important posts in the administration, while others were in key positions in the press, academia, or influential institutions as the American Civil Liberties Union. Muñoz always placed great emphasis on his lobbying and public relations efforts in U.S. and Washington power circles. His abundant communications during this period constantly stressed that he was the authentic representative of the pro-New Deal forces in Puerto Rico.[92]

His faithful and effective "Washington correspondent" of *La Democracia*, Ruby Black, was a key player in this network. She not only performed the role of newspaper correspondent, but also provided Muñoz with a constant flow of inside information, both public and confidential, on political developments in Washington and U.S. policy toward Puerto Rico. Additionally, Black acted as a lobbyist on Muñoz's behalf, and served as a conduit to Washington functionaries. Her personal friendship with Eleanor Roosevelt was particularly useful in this regard. Thus, Muñoz could bypass the official *Partido Liberal* representative in Washington, Walter Mc K Jones, either through Ruby Black or through his own frequent trips.[93]

The controversy over participation in the 1936 elections provides an indication of the influence of Muñoz's leadership within the party. His call for *retraimiento* (non-participation), which ran against the grain of a party oriented toward electoral participation, split the party down the middle. In a party convention held on July 25, 1936, the supporters of Muñoz and the proponents of electoral participation obtained exactly the same number of votes, with Antonio R. Barceló's vote deciding the issue in favor of participation. This confrontation, together with Muñoz's dramatic break with Gruening and the consequent difficulties with the Roosevelt administration, set the stage for a final break between Barceló and Muñoz, and their respective factions. Barceló blamed Muñoz's radicalism for the defeat in the 1936 elections. The Liberal Party received 45.9% of the vote to the *Coalición*'s 54.05%. On the other hand, in 1936 Muñoz formally organized in 1936 his faction under the name of *Acción Social Independentista* (ASI).[94]

On May 31, 1937, Muñoz and his supporters were formally expelled from the *Partido Liberal*. He soon renamed his grouping *Partido Liberal*

Neto, Auténtico y Completo, practically another name for ASI, but he was in no position to challenge the control Barceló exercised over the formal party structure and governing bodies. Only a minority of elected officials still supported the expelled leader. In fact, everything indicated that Muñoz's political career was on the wane in 1936. He no longer held a seat in the Senate. He led a party that existed only in name and that was really the loosely organized faction that had been expelled from the *Partido Liberal.* His supporters were being singled out for persecution and removed from government posts, as in the PRRA, by Ernest Gruening and with the enthusiastic support of the *Coalición.* His break with Gruening, and Roosevelt's decision to back the hard-line policies of his subordinates, had severely diminished Muñoz's influence in Washington. In 1937, Roosevelt told Santiago Iglesias that Muñoz had been an "educator in the wrong way" and that henceforth he would only consult the Resident Commissioner.[95]

From 1936 to 1940, Muñoz could hardly be considered a leader anointed by the metropolitan power. Subsequent events would demonstrate that he had not been permanently excommunicated. But regaining his role as interlocutor with Washington presupposed the construction of a strong political force in Puerto Rico. A close collaborator and biographer of Muñoz noted that "it was said that Muñoz Marín was politically dead."[96] His chauffeur and secretary from this period, Lieban Córdova, commented on the desperate economic circumstances of *La Democracia* and Muñoz's relative political isolation.[97] Earl Parker Hanson, another of his sympathizers, also described his situation.

> It was to those people [the peasantry] that Muñoz, rejected by Washington and his own political party, written off by nearly all the politically wise as being politically dead beyond chance of resurrection, was now to address himself-without a cent for purchasing votes, without hardly a dollar with which to support himself and his family. Early in 1937 he was forced to give up his home in the Condado section of San Juan and move into the crowded old walled city, in the building of *La Democracia*, to eke out an existence for himself, wife, and two children on the few dollars per month that the paper managed to pay him, on contributions from his few remaining friends, plus Muna Lee's small salary at the university.

Crisis had narrowed down his open friends to a small number of those who were held to him by qualities of integrity and personal dedication which are the essence of leadership.[98]

Thus, Muñoz's assets were few in mid 1937. He still controlled *La Democracia*, an indebted newspaper with limited circulation. He retained the loyalty of the younger generation of liberal leaders –which included some distinguished intellectuals and professionals– and of a few legislators. His contacts in the U.S. and Washington, though adversely affected, were still important. He consciously sought to retain them through a constant flow of letters and memoranda to policy-makers and political allies.[99] These contacts proved useful, for example, in mobilizing the ACLU to investigate the "Palm Sunday Massacre" in Ponce. And, he also counted on an asset of significant symbolic value: he was still the son of Luis Muñoz Rivera.

It was under these circumstances that Muñoz set out to organize a new party. His potential constituency was the large segment of the population, composed of diverse classes and groups adversely affected by the Depression (impoverished peasants, sugar workers, unemployed professional groups, university intellectuals, bankrupt *hacendados*, sugar *colonos* and tobacco growers, new working class sectors, etc.), that felt alienated from the traditional parties. They increasingly identified the sugar corporations, the *Coalición* and U.S. colonial administration, personified by Winship, as the source of the country's ills. In the cultural sphere the *trentista* generation of intellectuals (Vicente Géigel Polanco, Tomás Blanco, Antonio S. Pedreira, Emilio S. Belaval, among others) articulated a critique of the existing economic and political arrangement that provided an intellectual basis to the emerging populist movement. This "available mass," together with a large portion of the *Partido Liberal*, encapsulated in the concept of the "Puerto Rican people," would provide the basis for the movement led by Muñoz. The notion of "constructing democracy" through the action of the "people" themselves would occupy a central position in the populist political project.

The split in the *Partido Liberal* and the eventual foundation of the *Partido Popular* meant that all the major political parties were in the midst of internal upheavals during the late 1930s that, taken as a whole, provoked a radical realignment of political forces before the 1940 elections. This process is summarized in Figure 4.1.

FIGURE 4.1.
REALIGNMENT OF POLITICAL FORCES, 1936-1940

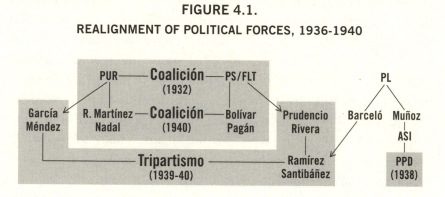

Military intelligence tried to grapple with this convoluted political situation in a report dated January 1940. It considered a possible, but still unlikely, political coalition between a "Liberal-Labor Party" and the Popular Party and a repetition of the majority *Coalición*. The report even depicted the political splits and possible realignments in an elaborate diagram entitled "Puerto Rico - Political," which, it said, "may serve to give a picture of the Political Set-Up in Puerto Rico, which is complicated at best."[100]

Gruening versus Ickes: Mailed Fist and Velvet Glove

The existence of different factions in the Roosevelt administration regarding Puerto Rican policy became obvious in the bitter personal and political feud that developed between Ickes, Secretary of the Interior, and Gruening, Chief of the Division of Territories and Island Possessions and Head of the Puerto Rico Reconstruction Administration (PRRA). The political significance of General Winship's removal from the governorship cannot be fully grasped without reference to this dimension.

In May 1934, the transfer of Puerto Rico from the War to the Interior Department, and the creation of the Division of Territories had placed the coordination of Puerto Rican policy under the authority of

Ickes, Gruening, and other functionaries of the Department of the Interior, among whom was Assistant Secretary Oscar Chapman. Roosevelt's subsequent decision in May 1935 to name Gruening director of the huge PRRA bureaucracy (53,000 people or about five times the size of the government of Puerto Rico) and place him under his direct supervision, thus bypassing Ickes's authority, further strengthened Gruening's role in Puerto Rican policy-making. This decision was apparently supported by Muñoz, who considered Gruening a valuable ally. Gruening thus became the most powerful Washington functionary and architect of colonial policy during a period of great internal political turmoil in Puerto Rico. Gonzalo Córdova has remarked that, "He, so to speak, became the metropolitan proconsul of Washington in San Juan."[101]

According to Gruening's account, conflicts with Ickes began soon after taking up his post in Interior. A controversy over the former's recommendation of Robert Herrick, a retired literature professor, to a post in the Virgin Islands, persuaded Gruening that "it would be impossible to trust him [Ickes]."[102] Ickes, on the other hand, strongly resented Roosevelt's nomination of Gruening as director of PRRA and his direct access to the president. He interpreted this decision as undermining his authority as Secretary of the Interior and his influence over Puerto Rican policy. Ickes was extremely jealous of his prerogatives and authority, which he always strongly defended.[103] When he presented his resignation to Roosevelt in May 1936 (which was not accepted), Ickes mentioned the president's decision to place PRRA under Gruening as an example of an Executive Order that had diminished his control over a subordinate.

> I pointed out to him that there was no check on Gruening unless the President was checking on him, a suggestion that he promptly negatived, and that there might be a first-class blowout one of these days in Puerto Rico for which he and I would be held responsible, when I had no authority in the matter.[104]

During the period from 1934 to early 1936, however, despite existing personal differences, Ickes and Gruening maintained a generally similar approach to Puerto Rican political issues. It consisted of supporting

Winship's hard line attitude toward Pedro Albizu Campos and the Nationalist Party, while simultaneously pushing for the reformist proposals contained in the Chardón Plan.

The most controversial of these was the application of the provisions in the Jones Act, forbidding ownership of land above 500 acres in order to break up sugar *latifundia* and thus promote small and medium peasant ownership geared to food production. Sugar interests represented in the *Coalición*, particularly in the *Partido Republicano*, were adamantly opposed to an agrarian reform through this mechanism. Support for the Chardón Plan became obvious when Carlos Chardón himself was nominated for regional administrator of PRRA. This gave the Liberal Party, particularly its *muñocista* wing, dominant political influence over the PRRA bureaucracy as, according to Gruening, Liberal Party members came to control five of the six key administrative posts. In addition to this, Ickes and Gruening forced the resignation of Attorney General Benjamin Horton, who had shown no enthusiasm in applying the 500-acre provision, and named Benigno Fernández García in Horton's place, and lawyer Miguel Guerra Mondragón as director of the Justice Department unit entrusted with its enforcement.

Support for the Chardón Plan, political control over PRRA, and enforcement of the 500 Acre Law became contentious issues and created friction between the Roosevelt administration and the *Coalición*-controlled legislature. Winship, however, lacking any of the liberal or New Deal reformist pretentions of Ickes and Gruening, pursued a course of political collaboration with the legislative majority. When Ickes visited Puerto Rico in January 7, 1936, he left no doubt regarding his political sympathies for the Puerto Rican political forces. He noted that Governor Winship was "highly conservative," while "the Puerto Rican legislature is in control of a coalition group which is conservative." Chardón, on the other hand, was defined as a "liberal." Liberals, Ickes said, "are strongly opposed to Winship and want him recalled." Urban and rural poverty and widespread illiteracy were starkly described in his account of the visit. These dramatic social conditions were defined as reflecting negatively on the Puerto Rican and U.S. governments. To him the dominant political issue was "the failure of the Puerto Rican government to break up the big sugar estates into five-acre holdings."[105] During his visit, he publicly blamed the *Coalición* legislature for lack of action in the 500-acre issue and accused it of being controlled by big sugar interests, a charge that provoked political attacks on Ickes from the coalitionist leadership, particularly from Rafael Martínez Nadal and Bolívar Pagán.[106] Finally, Ickes remarked, significantly, "the expectation is that the Liberals will win the next election."[107]

Gruening, however, was apparently already moving in early 1936 in the direction of a better political understanding with the *Coalición*, and therefore toward Winship's policy of complete collaboration with the legislative majority. He complains in his memoirs of the constant communications he received from Muñoz and Ruby Black regarding Puerto Rican appointments, but argues that he was forced to support Winship's (i.e., the *Coalición's*) candidates out of loyalty to Roosevelt.

> I did not see how I could impose my choices of appointees on Winship. After all, Winship had to deal with a majority which controlled the Puerto Rican legislature, even if by coalition. In any event, President Roosevelt approved of Winship and it was my duty to work with him as best I could. He had been called to Washington so that we could brief him on our reconstruction program, and there was no evidence that he would not cooperate to the best of his ability.[108]

The death of Colonel Francis E. Riggs provoked a dramatic and definitive break between Gruening and Muñoz. It firmly aligned Gruening with the hard line and conservative policies of Governor Winship and the *Coalición*, further weakened Ickes's role in Puerto Rican policy-making during the period from 1936 to 1938, and set Gruening and Ickes on a collision course that deepened their mutual distrust and resulted in constant dissension.

The Roosevelt administration's response to the assassination of Riggs initially appeared to unify the diverse sectors in Puerto Rico and Washington. Ickes gave his support to the Tydings Bill "because of the quieting effect that I anticipated it might have on Puerto Rican public opinion."[109] Although martial law was not imposed, Winship moved to impose a *de facto* illegalization of the Nationalist Party. Repressive measures during this period of great turmoil were directed not only toward the Nationalist Party, but to independence supporters in general.

Muñoz's refusal of Gruening's demand that he issue a public condemnation of Riggs's assassination served as a pretext to launch an attack on Muñoz's Liberal Party supporters. [110]

Thus, in 1936 police repression against the Nationalist Party was paralleled by a political onslaught on Muñoz and moderate *independentistas* affiliated to the Liberal Party. The Tydings Bill for Puerto Rican independence, drafted under Gruening's supervision, as Muñoz correctly saw at the time, was designed not to satisfy existing pro-independence demands, but to provoke an anti-independence response through its draconian economic provisions. Gruening also forced Carlos Chardón's resignation from PRRA and conducted a purging of *muñocista* supporters in that agency, thus satisfying the *Coalición's* longstanding demands against liberal influence.[111] On the other hand, Liberal Party demands for a new registration of voters before the 1936 elections, which had been submitted as legislation together with the Tydings Bill, went unheeded.

Clearly, Gruening and Winship aimed at punishing the *muñocista* and *independentista* wing of the Liberal Party to make it pay politically for Nationalist Party radicalism and the death of Riggs. It was a policy aimed not only at electorally weakening the Liberal Party in the upcoming 1936 elections, but also at provoking an internal rift in the party between the autonomist and pro-independence wings, and between the traditional leadership of Antonio R. Barceló and the *muñocista* Young Turks, in order to isolate Muñoz. Bereft of Washington support and internally weakened by dissension in his own party, Muñoz's considerable political clout would be eradicated, according to Gruening's expectations. Earl Parker Hanson explained the situation in the following terms:

> In 1936, when I once insisted to Ickes that Muñoz was one hope of the United States in Puerto Rico, the one man who could hold the island together and prevent an American debacle, I had the distinct impression that the Secretary of the Interior was inclined to agree with me but was powerless to do much about the matter. Gruening had many staunch supporters in the Department, and seemed, moreover, to have President Roosevelt's ear. After 1937, of course, it was impossible for Ickes to give support to a Puerto Rican leader who had been ousted by his own party and apparently (until the 1940 elections proved otherwise) had no political following whatever.[112]

By mid November 1936, in the matter of Gruening's decision to oust Carlos Chardón, Ickes had become critical of Gruening's approach to Puerto Rican affairs. He particularly resented the fact that approval to Chardón's removal and his being replaced by Miles H. Fairbanks had been obtained in a "whispered recommendation" to Roosevelt. He also criticized as "an extreme measure" Gruening's additional recommendation, which Roosevelt heeded, that the president should issue instructions for a renewed emphasis on English language instruction. That presidential message and the nomination of José Gallardo as Secretary of Instruction were additional political blows to the *Partido Liberal*. Ickes concluded that Gruening thought "that he is entirely independent of me" and that he had undergone a radical ideological transformation.

> Gruening, from being a liberal, has apparently decided that the mailed fist is the proper policy in dealing with these subject people. He has gone completely in reverse. He is on the outs with all his former liberal friends in Puerto Rico. Formerly he used to damn Governor Winship up hill and down dale for his militaristic point of view. He wanted him ousted as Governor, but now apparently he and Governor Winship see eye to eye and are in perfect accord on questions of policy.[113]

This observation closely parallels Muñoz's comment to Laurence Duggan in February 1937 regarding "An unrelenting attack on friendly and peaceful independence feeling by Director Gruening, originating in the very peculiar state of mind developed in the Director with regard to Puerto Rico as a result of the Riggs assassination by two Nationalist fanatics who were subsequently killed by the Police."[114] He carefully excludes Ickes from any responsibility regarding the flawed Puerto Rican policy.

The "first-class blowout" predicted by Ickes in 1936 came in the form of the March 1937 "Palm Sunday Massacre" in Ponce. The event, a direct result of the "mailed fist" policy, broadened the rift between Ickes and Gruening. While the latter justified the action of the Winship government and joined *Coalición* efforts to cover up and play down the incident,[115] the former redoubled his efforts at removing Winship from the governorship. Ickes had kept open lines of communication to ACLU liberals such as Roger Baldwin, Arthur Garfield Hays, and Oswald Garrison Villard, and was duly informed of the findings of the Hays commission. Representative Vito Marcantonio and former Representative John T. Bernard also visited Ickes and provided him with photographic evidence on the Ponce shooting.[116]

Ickes fully shared the main conclusion of the Hays commission, remarking in March 1938 that he had "always believed this was a cold-blooded shooting by the Ponce police and that those that were killed were shot by the policemen themselves. Of course, Governor Winship and Gruening have been on the other side."[117]

Ickes tried to persuade the President that he was being misinformed by Gruening and Winship. On May 21, he showed Roosevelt photographic evidence used by the Hays commission and asked him to permit him to conduct "an independent investigation of my own."[118] According to Gruening, this investigation was a ruse to remove Winship.

> Ickes had, in fact, already picked out his commission and he was boiling mad that he could not send it. He wanted to use it to get rid of Winship, but that in my view was hardly the time or the way to do it.[119]

Gruening and Winship persuaded Roosevelt to veto any investigation by Ickes. An investigation, Gruening argued, would be interpreted as "lack of confidence" in Winship and would increase political instability in Puerto Rico. They also maneuvered to prevent a Congressional inquiry that was being demanded by some congressmen such as Marcantonio and John T. Bernard of Minnesota. But Ickes sought other means to undermine his subordinate and the governor. Gruening claimed that the Secretary of the Interior sent to Puerto Rico a Walter Flavius McCaleb to "spy" on him, posing as a journalist.[120] In September 1937, Ickes arranged to have two investigators of the General Accounting Office, Herbert R. Pasewalk and Edward V. Colberg, travel to the island to investigate Winship's official expenditures. They found no clear legal violations, but a dramatic increase in Executive Mansion expenditures, which more than doubled the designated amount, this attributed to "an excessive amount due to official entertainment." On December 13, 1937, Ickes informed the president about Winship's "apparent extravagance."[121]

Gruening and Winship were able to weather the 1937 political storm, apparently due in no small measure to Roosevelt's support, but at a considerable political cost. The "Palm Sunday Massacre" and the Hays commission report had substantially damaged the image of U.S. colonial rule in Puerto Rico and of the Winship governorship. It firmly aligned the Secretary of the Interior and a broad spectrum of U.S. liberal institutions and figures opposed to the existing policy. In Puerto Rico, the ostracizing of the *muñocista* liberals had narrowed the base of support of the Roosevelt administration's policies to the conservative *Coalición* legislative majority. In this context, continuing political turmoil, violence and charges of government corruption during 1938 could not bode well for Winship and his allies.

With war rapidly approaching, Roosevelt could hardly have considered the state of affairs in Puerto Rico a favorable political environment to implement the ambitious defense plans that were formulated in late 1938 and early 1939. Thus, the removal of Winship and his replacement by his trusted naval advisor, Admiral Leahy, was a well-calculated move that represented the first major step toward an overall revision of colonial policy. It is not surprising that the nomination of a naval officer was received with great rejoicing by Secretary of the Interior Ickes, an outspoken antimilitarist. Other liberals who opposed Winship were less enthusiastic, and expressed misgivings at the continuation of "military rule."

With the decision on the governorship taken, Ickes's attacks on Winship and the *Coalición* became even more vitriolic. He pointed out to Roosevelt that Winship had become a puppet of Rafael Martínez Nadal,[122] the *Coalición*, and the sugar interests. In his diary, he wrote that Winship was "a perfect militarist and he seems to me to be becoming more dogmatic and sure of himself every day,"[123] and referred to Martínez Nadal as an "s.o.b." García Méndez was "little better than a gangster," and the *Coalición* the "Nadal crowd."[124] He still had to remove Ernest Gruening from Puerto Rican policy-making to reconstruct his influence over insular affairs, but that would not take long.

NOTES

1. The *Coalición* parties obtained 297,033 votes (54.05%) and the *Partido Liberal* 252,467 (45.9%). The *Coalición* won control over 57 municipalities compared to only 19 won by the *liberales*. In the legislature the *Coalición* had 27 representatives to 12 *liberales*, and 14 senators to 5 *liberales*. That gave the *Coalición* a two thirds majority in both houses.

2. See, Juan José Baldrich, "Class and the State, The Origins of Populism in Puerto Rico, 1934-1952," Ph. D. dissertation, Yale University, 1981, Figure 5.1, p. 186.

3. For an account of the port strike, see, Taller de Formación Política, *No estamos pidiendo el cielo: huelga portuaria de 1938* (Río Piedras: Huracán, 1988); also, Ángel Quintero Rivera, "Las bases sociales de la transformación ideológica del Partido Popular Democrático en la década de 1940-1950", unpublished ms, 1975?

4. Sonia Carbonell, "Blanton Winship y el Partido Nacionalista, 1934-1939," Master's dissertation, History Department, University of Puerto Rico, 1984, pp. 237-47.

5. For a very graphic description of the Ponce attack by an eye-witness, see, Eliseo Combas Guerra, *En torno a la Fortaleza, Winship* (San Juan: Biblioteca de Autores Puertorriqueños, 1950), pp. 164-71.

6. The two main U.S. press correspondents in Puerto Rico were Hull, who worked for Associated Press and *The New York Times*, and William O'Riley of United Press. Vito Marcantonio, in August 1939, accused both of being biased in favor of Winship and Gruening and in the payroll of PRRA and the government of Puerto Rico. See, Félix Ojeda Reyes, *Vito Marcantonio y Puerto Rico* (Río Piedras: Ediciones Huracán, 1978), p. 93.

7. Harwood Hull, "Puerto Ricans Fire Upon Gov. Winship, Two Slain as 15 bullets Miss Official, Reviewing Parade Before 40,000 at Ponce," *The New York Times*, July 26, 1938, p. 1.

8. "Winship's Tenure Stormy," op. cit, p. 11.

9. "Fact and Fiction" (Editorial), *The New York Times*, July 30, 1938, p. 12.

10. "Puerto Rican Goes On Trial In Murder, Escobar Accused in Slaying at Anniversary Celebration" and "The Governor of Puerto Rico Has a Popular Following," *The New York Times*, August 30, 1938, p. 11.

11. Col. John W. Wright, "Weekly Summary of Subversive Activities - Puerto Rico Area," July 27, and August 5 and 10, 1938, R.G. 165, MID 1917-41, Box 3112, U.S. National Archives.

12. In 1937, Antonio R. Barceló had accused Muñoz of being an opportunist originally inspired by Albizu: "The man [Muñoz] that, recently converted to an *independentismo* learnt from the radical lips of Pedro Albizu Campos, irrupted in the *Partido Liberal* raising the flag of programmatic radicalism, [but] soon voluntarily toned down the emancipatory ideal during his opulent days as a man agreeable to the Federal Administration." Reece B. Bothwell, *Puerto Rico: Cien Años de Lucha*, Volume III (Río Piedras: Editorial Universitaria, 1979), p. 111. Author's translation. The attempt to identify *muñocismo* with *albizuismo* was also a *Coalición* strategy, a charge vehemently denied in the *Partido Popular*'s newspaper *El Batey*.

13. Gonzalo F. Córdova, "Resident Commissioner Santiago Iglesias and His Times," Ph. D. dissertation, Georgetown University, May 1982, p. 672.

14. Epifanio Fiz Jiménez, *El Racket del Capitolio (Gobierno de la Coalición Repúblico Socialista)* (San Juan: Editorial Esther, 1944).

15. See, "Puerto Rico Asks U.S. Aid To Check Payroll Racket," *The New York Times*, 19 October 1938, p. 11; and "Puerto Rico Leader Held, Socialist Senator Accused of Falsification and Fraud," *The New York Times*, 6 November 1938, p. 30.

16. The full report is included in Epifanio Fiz Jiménez, op. cit., Chapter 5.

17. Félix Ojeda Reyes, op. cit., pp. 44-8, 67-93.

18. Thomas Hibben, "The Industrial Development of Puerto Rico," draft of the report, March 1948, p. 50, in FDR Library, C.W. Taussig Papers, Container 44, Folder Caribbean Commission.

19. On the tobacco industry, see, "Las grandes industrias de Puerto Rico: una visita a la fábrica que posee en Puerta de Tierra la 'Porto Rican American Tobacco Company,'" *Puerto Rico Ilustrado*, 9 March 1912, n.p.; and, Cámara de Comercio de Puerto Rico, "Tobacco Culture," *Boletín Oficial*, Vol. 10, No. 6 (1934), pp. 59-70.

20. See James L. Dietz, *Historia Económica de Puerto Rico* (Río Piedras: Ediciones Huracán, 1989), Chapter 2; also Ángel Quintero Rivera, "La bases sociales de la transformación ideológica del Partido Popular Democrático en la década de 1940-1950," unpublished ms, 1975?.

21. Ángel Quintero Rivera, op. cit., pp. 91-97.

22. Silvia Álvarez Curbelo, "Un discurso ideológico olvidado: los agricultores puertorriqueños (1924-1928)", *Op. Cit., Revista del Centro de Investigaciones Históricas*, Vol. I, No. 2 (1986-1987), pp. 141-160.

23. See, Rubén Dávila Santiago, *El derribo de las murallas, orígenes intelectuales del socialismo en Puerto Rico* (Río Piedras: Editorial Cultural, 1988), Chapter 4. Kelvin Santiago and Myriam Muñiz are also correct in pointing to the also oppressive and authoritarian exercise of state power during the period of consolidation of

the colonial state and the sugar plantation economy, an aspect neglected by other analyses such as that of Angel Quintero Rivera. See, Kelvin Santiago, "Algunos aspectos de la integración de Puerto Rico al interior del Estado metropolitano norteamericano: los orígenes de la nueva estructura estatal colonial: 1898-1929," *Revista de Ciencias Sociales*, Vol XXII, Nos. 3-4 (July-December 1981), pp. 295-348; and Myriam Muñiz Varela, "Análisis del capital monopólico azucarero y el papel del Estado en el proceso de transición al capitalismo en Puerto Rico: 1898-1920," op. cit., pp. 443-96.

24. Cited in Bolivar Pagán, *Historia de los partidos políticos puertorriqueños, 1898-1956*, Volume II (Barcelona: M. Pareja, 1972), p. 23.

25. Bolívar Pagán, *Historia de los partidos políticos puertorriqueños*, Volume I..., pp. 324-8.

26. See, Bolivar Pagán, op. cit., Chapter 1; and, Edgardo Meléndez, *Puerto Rico's Statehood Movement* (New York, Greenwood Press, 1988), Chapter 4.

27. Quintero Rivera has called this pattern of party politics, revolving around three dominant political forces, the "triangular struggle". See. Angel Quintero Rivera, *Conflictos de clase y política* (San Juan: Ediciones Huracán, 1977). If the geometrical metaphor is to be used at all, it would be more accurate to say that politics was, in fact, "quadrangular," due to the role of the metropolitan state.

28. Charles P. Kindleberger, *La crisis económica mundial*, 1929-1939 (Barcelona: Editorial Crítica, 1985), Chapter 4.

29. Ángel Quintero Rivera, "Economía y política en Puerto Rico (1930-1934)", *Revista de Ciencias Sociales*, Vol. 24, Nos. 3-4 (July-December 1985), p. 44.

30. Quintero, "Bases Sociales. . .," pp. 22-23; for an important analysis of the crisis in tobacco and the struggles of the tobacco producers, see, Juan José Baldrich, *Sembraron la no siembra, los cosecheros de tabaco puertorriqueños frente a las corporaciones tabacaleras, 1920-1934* (San Juan: Ediciones Huracán, 1988).

31. John E. Dalton, *Sugar: A Case Study of Government Control* (New York: The Macmillan Company, 1937), p. 228. I thank Argeo Quiñones for pointing out to me Dalton's important study.

32. Quintero, "Bases Sociales. . .," pp. 22-27.

33. For an interesting analysis of the development of the needlework industry, see, Lydia Milagros González García, *Una puntada en la historia: la industria de la aguja en Puerto Rico (1900-1929)* (Santo Domingo: CEREP/CIPAF, 1990).

34. Arthur Gayer and Paul T. Homan, *The Sugar Economy of Puerto Rico* (New York: Columbia University Press, 1938), p. 26.

35. See, J. J. Baldrich, op. cit., Chapter 3.

36. The *treintista* generation of intellectuals coalesced around the journal *Indice* which began appearing in April 1929. Its editors were Antonio S. Pedreira, Vicente Géigel Polanco, Samuel R. Quiñones and A. Collado Martell. It also included other prominent writers as Emilio S. Belaval and Tomás Blanco. For an analysis on the *treintista* generation, see, Pedro Álvarez Ramos, "Memoria histórica y proyecto social: pueblo, raza y esclavitud en el discurso histórico puertorriqueño (1929-1938), Ph. D. dissertation UNAM (México, 1991); also, Silvia Álvarez Curbelo y María Elena Rodríguez Castro, eds., *Del nacionalismo al populismo: Cultura y política en Puerto Rico* (Río Piedras: Ediciones Huracán, 1993), and, *Índice, mensuario de historia, literatura y ciencia* (versión facsimilar), (San Juan: Editorial Universitaria, 1979).

37. Vicente Géigel Polanco, "Prólogo", A. Rodríguez Vera, *Agrarismo por dentro y trabajo a domicilio* (San Juan: La Democracia, January 1929), p. v. Author's translation.

38. Ramiro Guerra y Sánchez, *Azúcar y población en las Antillas* (La Habana: Cultural, 1927).

39. Bailey W. and Justine Diffie, *Porto Rico: A Broken Pledge* (New York: Vanguard Press, 1931).

40. Eliezer Curet Cuevas, *El desarrollo económico de Puerto Rico: 1940 a 1972* (San Juan: Management Aid Center, 1976), p. 17.

41. The share of wages and salaries declined from 74.4% in 1929 to 64.8% in 1935 while income from dividends, interests and rent almost doubled. Another study provided the following figures for 1940: wages and salaries 54.3%, dividends 33%, rent 8.8% and interest 4.0%. See Ángel Quintero, "Bases Sociales. . .," pp. 38-39.

42. John E. Dalton, op. cit., p. 218.

43. Ibid., p. 227.

44. Ibid., pp. 41-54, 67.

45. See Thomas Mathews, *El nuevo trato y la política puertorriqueña* (San Juan: Editorial Universitaria, 1970), pp. 133-144.

46. Albizu Campos scathingly said that "Mister Gore should not feel overwhelmed by his or his country's duties towards the Puerto Ricans. . . The United States has a single duty to perform with Puerto Rico and it is to withdraw immediately its armed forces from our territory." Pedro Albizu Campos, *Obras escogidas* (San Juan: Editorial Jelofe, 1975), p. 272. Author's translation.

47. The documents corresponding to 1933 in the Ruby Black Collection (Centro de Investigaciones Históricas) contain abundant material on Muñoz campaign against Gore.

48. Arthur Gayer, op. cit., p. 232.

49. It obtained 5,257 votes in the 1932 elections and Albizu's at large candidacy to the Senate 11,882.

50. Taller de Formación Política, *¡Huelga en la Caña!, 1933-1934* (Río Piedras, Huracán, 1982).

51. Mathews, op. cit., Chapter 6.

52. New Deal policies during the 1930s were relatively devoid of a reformist thrust, and mainly concentrated in social welfare and employment generating measures. Winship and the *Coalición* successfully blocked attempts at major reforms that may have affected the sugar industry. Welfare versus social and economic reforms was an important parameter of political discourse during the 1930s.

53. The National Guard, however, was garrisoned in 1936 during the arrest of the Nationalist leadership. In May 1936, during a student strike, Company I was deployed behind the Central High School, in Santurce, and Company L, in Río Piedras. In September, all the military forces were garrisoned to prevent a protest organized by the National Congress for the Liberation of Political Prisoners. Vicente Géigel Polanco was president of this group and Jaime Benítez a member. In 1937, during the aftermath of the "Ponce Massacre", the National Guard was again garrisoned in the west. Sonia Carbonell, op. cit., pp. 111-12, 141, 161.

54. Estades, "Colonialismo y Democracia..", op. cit., p. 6.

55. Sonia Carbonell, op. cit., p. 108.

56. For a discussion of the plan, see, Leonardo Santana Rabell, *Planificación y política durante la administración de Luis Muñoz Marín: Un análisis crítico* (Santurce: Análisis, 1984), pp. 43-54.

57. Earl Parker Hanson, *Transformation: The Story of Modern Puerto Rico* (New York: Simon and Schuster, 1955), p. 165.

58. Office of the Post Commander, Headquarters Post of San Juan (no signature) to Mr. Ernest F. Gruening, October 25, 1935, File 9 8 119, R.G. 126, N.A.

59. *La Democracia*, October 26, 1935, cited in Sonia Carbonell. op. cit., p. 53.

60. Cited in Frank Otto Gatell, "Independence Rejected: Puerto Rico and the Tydings Bill of 1936," *Hispanic American Historical Review*, Vol. 38 (February, 1958), p. 29.

61. At this point, an Army intelligence report estimated that independence would obtain an "overwhelming majority" in a plebiscite. María Eugenia Estades, "Colonialismo y Democracia. . .", p. 7.

62. Gatell, op. cit., pp. 25-44.

63. Idem.

64. See, "Memorandum for Laurence Duggan," February 2, 1937, Box 9, Doc. 10, Ruby Black Collection, Historical Research Center.

65. See, Sonia Carbonell, op. cit., pp. 259-61.

66. The investigating commission's report was read at a public gathering held in San Juan on May 22, 1937.

67. Jaime Benítez, "Non-Rational Politics and Waste in Puerto Rico", n.d., sent with a letter of Charles E. Merriam, Dept. of Political Science, University of Chicago to the Secretary of the Interior on November 5, 1938. An attached Memo of Franklin Delano Roosevelt to Harold Ickes, November 27, 1938, said "Please read this and return, It should not be shown to anyone else." FDR Library, FDR Papers, OF 400, Container 24, Folder P.R.

68. Benigno Fernández García claimed that Gayer's book was financed by two sugar corporations to influence public opinion against the application of the 500-acre law. Reece B. Bothwell, *Puerto Rico: Cien años de lucha política*, Volume III (Río Piedras: Editorial Universitaria, 1979), p. 268. See, Arthur Gayer, et. al., op. cit., and Trumbull White, *Puerto Rico and Its People* (New York: Grosset & Dunlap, 1938).

69. Osvald Garrison Villard was President of the Committee of Fair Play to Puerto Rico, Prof. William L. Nunn, Vice-President. The following members signed a May 15, 1939 document: Earl P. Hanson, Carleton Beals, Arthur Garfield Hays, Rep. Vito Marcantonio, Rockwell Kent, Walter Mc K Jones, Viljalmur Stefanson, Charlotte Leeper, David Rein, Gifford Cochran, and Mr. and Mrs. Bourne. Committee for Fair Play to Puerto Rico, "Press Release," May 15, 1939, Box 4, Folder 13, Document 103, Ruby Black Collection, Centro de Investigaciones Históricas.

70. Oswald Garrison Villard wrote in *The Nation*, "The business of putting retired generals into civilian offices usually fails to work. Trained to army routine and red tape, to blind army obedience, without experience in meeting criticism and dissent, they become a danger in a high government post.... There is another example of this in Puerto Rico. Major General Blanton Winship... Personally kind and well-meaning man, he sees dissent for American Policies which is so widespread in the Island as something treacherous and treasonable." (June 4, 1938, p. 644).

71. Writing under the name of Jay Carter, John Franklin Carter demanded, after the "Palm Sunday Massacre" in Ponce, that both Winship and Gruening should resign or be dismissed by Roosevelt. See, Ruby Black Telegram to *La Democracia*, April 3, 1937, Box 3 Document 34, Ruby Black Collection, Historical Research Center.

72. See his two chapters on Puerto Rico in Rockwell Kent, *This Is My Own* (New York: Duell, Sloan and Pearce, 1940), Chapters 33 and 34.

73. Blanca Silvestrini de Pacheco, *Los trabajadores puertorriqueños y el Partido Socialista* (1932-1940) (Río Piedras: Editorial Universitaria, 1979); and, César A. Rey, "Parlamentarismo obrero y coalición, 1932-1940," in Carmen I. Raffucci, Silvia Álvarez Curbelo and Fernando Picó, eds., *Senado de Puerto Rico, Ensayos de historia institucional* (San Juan: Senado de Puerto Rico, 1992), pp. 137-160.

74. See, "Muñoz Marín dice está dispuesto a hacerse arrestar para que se reconozca el derecho de los obreros puertorriqueños a establecer piquetes," *El Mundo*, October 10, 1939, p. 5; and, "Injusticias contra los Trabajadores de los muelles de Ponce", *El Batey*, No. 6 (August 1939), p. 2. Army intelligence reported on this incident that "Muñoz Marin, President of the Popular Democratic Party, made an effort recently to inject himself into the organized labor movement of the island . . ." I also noted that he had been out-maneuvered by the union members and steamship officials. Brig. Gen. Edmund L. Daley, "Weekly Summary of Certain Political Activities," October 14, 1939, R.G. 165, MID 1917-41, Box 3112, U. S. National Archives.

75. For a strong critique of Bolivar Pagán's leadership from the point of view of a Prudencio Rivera Martínez supporter who shared his background as cigar- maker, anarchist and grass-roots labor organizer, see, Epifanio Fiz Jiménez, op. cit., *passim*.

76. Gonzalo Córdova, "Resident Commissioner Santiago Iglesias . . ." pp. 637-9.

77. Bolívar Pagán, op. cit., p. 131.

78. Gonzalo Córdova, "Resident Commissioner Santiago Iglesias. . ." p. 703.

79. The Liberal Party leader, Antonio R. Barceló, had died on October 15, 1938.

80. Bolívar Pagán, op. cit., p. 140. See, also, "Bolívar Pagán afirma que los días de Rivera Martínez, como jefe de Departamento del Trabajo están contados", *El Mundo*, August 1, 1939, pp. 1, 18. In this press report, Pagán is quoted as saying that Prudencio Rivera Martínez would not keep his post much longer.

81. Gonzalo Córdova, "Resident Commissioner Santiago Iglesias . . ." p. 672.

82. Bolívar Pagán, op. cit., Volume II, p. 144. Pagán places this meeting on July 11. However, according to *El Mundo*, it took place on July 18. See, "Desestimada la querella contra García Méndez," *El Mundo*, July 19, 1939, p. 1.

83. Sergio Romanecce, "Es imminente la organización de un nuevo partido político," *El Mundo*, July 7, 1939, p. 5. Author's translation.

84. "Se desarrolla en Washington embrión de nuevo partido, Aunque oficialmente se habla de 'manos afuera', miradas amigas siguen los acontecimientos," *El Mundo*, August 10, 1939, p. 1. Author's translation. See, also, "Tendrá el respaldo de Washington el nuevo partido," *El Mundo*, July 13, 1939, p. 1.

85. Jesús T. Piñero to "Swokeup" [Ruby Black?], August 30, 1939, Box 4, Folder 13, Document 135, Ruby Black Collection, Centro de Investigaciones Históricas.

86. "Vieja Alianza, Coalición y nueva Alianza son la misma cosa," *El Mundo*, July 18, 1939, p. 1.

87. "Representantes del movimiento tripartista volverán a reunirse," *El Mundo*, July 22, 1939, p. 5.

88. "Ya está lista la plataforma del nuevo partido," *El Mundo*, July 25, 1939, p. 1. Author's translation.

89. "Ultiman los detalles del acuerdo para formar nuevo partido, García Méndez se incomodó porque en Nueva York circuló la versión de que él se había huido del movimiento," *El Mundo*, August 19, 1939, p. 1.

90. Silvia Alvarez Curbelo, "La casa de cristal: El ejercicio senatorial de Luis Muñoz Marín, 1932-1936", in Carmen I. Rafucci, Silvia Álvarez Curbelo and Fernando Picó, eds., op. cit., pp. 103-136.

91. In 1910, when his father Luis Muñoz Rivera was elected Resident Commissioner in Washington, Luis Muñoz Marín moved to the US. During the period 1910-1932, he resided for long periods in Washington and New York. See, Carmelo Rosario Natal, *La juventud de Luis Muñoz Marín, vida y pensamiento (1898-1932)* (San Juan: Master Typesetting, 1976). An interesting account of the 1920s intellectual circles in which Muñoz moved appears in Earl Parker Hanson, op. cit., Chapter 4, "Growth of a Leader."

92. "There is in Puerto Rico a generation that is coming to power in all political parties —it is already in power in the Liberal party, and I have the honor to be one of its leaders— that has been educated in the United States . . . This generation, within it own medium, is a very close counterpart of the forces that follow Mr. Roosevelt in the continental United States." Luis Muñoz Marín to Mrs. Franklin D. Roosevelt, December 8, 1933, FDR Library, Eleanor Roosevelt Papers, Series 100, Container 1272, Folder 1933 Mo-Mu.

93. The crucial role played by Ruby Black can be glimpsed from her papers in the Ruby Black Collection, Centro de Investigaciones Históricas.

94. Bolívar Pagán, op. cit., pp. 84-129.

95. Gonzalo Córdova, "Resident Commissioner Santiago Iglesias. . ." p. 662.

96. Enrique Bird Piñero, *Don Luis Muñoz Marín, el poder de la excelencia* (Trujillo Alto: Fundación Luis Muñoz Marín, 1991), p. 70.

97. Lieban Córdova, *7 años con Muñoz Marín (1938-1945)* (Santo Domingo: Editora Corripio, 1989), Chapter 1.

98. Earl Parker Hanson, op. cit., p. 174.

99. See, for example, his "Memorandum to Laurence Duggan," February 2, 1937, Box 2, Folder 11, Document 10, Ruby Black Collection, Centro de Investigaciones Históricas.

100. Brig. Gen. Edmund L. Daley, "Weekly Summary of Certain Political Activities - P.R. Area," January 24, 1940, MID 1917-41, Box 3112, U.S. National Archives.

101. Gonzalo F. Córdova, "Resident Commissioner Santiago Iglesias. . .", p. 575.

102. Ernest Gruening, *Many Battles, The Autobiography of Ernest Gruening* (New York: Liveright, 1973), p. 185.

103. See, Graham White and John Maze, *Harold Ickes of the New Deal, His Private Life and Public Career* (Cambridge, Mass.: Harvard University Press, 1985), Chapter 7.

104. Harold Ickes, *The Secret Diary of Harold L. Ickes, The First Thousand Days, 1933-1936* (New York: Simon and Schuster, 1953), p. 594.

105. Harold Ickes, *The Secret Diary of Harold L. Ickes, The First Thousand Days. . .*, pp. 503-5.

106. Thomas Mathews, op. cit., pp. 236-7.

107. Harold L. Ickes, *The Secret Diary of Harold L. Ickes, The First Thousand Days . . .*, p. 503.

108. Ernest Gruening, op. cit., p. 191.

109. Harold L. Ickes, *The Secret Diaries of Harold L. Ickes, The First Thousand Days. . .*, p. 547.

110. Ernest Gruening, op. cit., pp. 196-98.

111. For a critical account of the anti-*muñocista* purge in the PRRA by a US functionary of that agency, see, Earl Parker Hanson, op. cit., Chapters 8 and 9.

112. Earl Parker Hanson, op. cit., p. 192.

113. Harold L. Ickes, *The Secret Diaries of Harold L. Ickes, The Inside Struggle, 1939-1941*, Volume III (New York: Simon and Schuster, 1955), p. 6.

114. Luis Muñoz Marín, "Memorandum for Laurence Duggan. . ." p. 2. On Muñoz perception of Gruening's transformation, see, also, Luis Muñoz Marín to Mrs. Roosevelt, 9 January 1937, FDR Library, Eleanor Roosevelt Papers, Series 100, Container 717, Folder 1937.

115. Gruening claims that Arthus Garfield Hays produced a "biased report". For his version of the events surrounding the "Palm Sunday Massacre", see, Ernest Gruening, op. cit., pp. 205-08.

116. Félix Ojeda, op. cit., p. 75.

117. Harold Ickes, *The Secret Diary of Harold L. Ickes, The Inside Struggle. . .*, pp. 47, 170, 329.

118. Ibid., pp. 148-49.

119. Ernest Gruening, op. cit., p. 208.

120. Ibid., p. 207.

121. See, Franklin D. Roosevelt to Richard N. Elliot, Acting Comptroller General, 16 September 1937; and, Harold L. Ickes to The President, November 13, 1937, FDR Library, FDR Papers, OF 400, Container 24, Folder P.R.

122. Ickes mentions that in a conversation with the President regarding Leahy's designation he pointed out that "...Senator Nadal really controlled Puerto Rico, and that he and Winship seemed to have an understanding as a result of which each would give the other what he wanted". Harold Ickes, *Secret Diary*, manuscript, Manuscript Division, Library of Congress, entry for March 18, 1939, p. 3308.

123. Ibid., entry for Saturday April 29, 1939, p. 3401.

124. Córdova, op. cit., p. 724.

CHAPTER 5

AN OFFICE FULL
OF GRIEF

*Four governors meet in 1939 at the New York World's Fair:
Winship, Leahy, Winthrop and Roosevelt. El Mundo Collection,
University of Puerto Rico.*

AN OFFICE FULL OF GRIEF

On May 12, 1939, President Roosevelt announced that he would name Admiral William D. Leahy to the governorship of Puerto Rico. The following day *El Mundo* reported the news in bold letters as the main front page story with a photograph of Leahy and a brief biographical sketch. The story mentioned his interest in Puerto Rico's strategic value and that he would be taking office on the following July.[1] In a brief letter to Ruby Black, Jesús T. Piñero, president of the colonos and a follower of Muñoz, claimed that the cablegram was handed to Winship while he was taking a siesta and that the *Coalición* interrupted a legislative caucus to "mourn" the decision with Winship at La Fortaleza.[2]

Winship's "Resignation"

On May 14, 1939, *El Mundo* followed up on the story of Leahy's nomination by announcing that the decision had been based on the "need to eliminate all sources of dissension" due to the "growing importance of Puerto Rico in national defense."[3] It also reported that more than $30 million would be devoted to defense preparations in 1940 and a total of $200 million over the next five years (1940-45). Leahy would "head and coordinate the enormous national defense projects."[4] It was claimed that the base construction program was part of a broader and ambitious plan to "industrialize" Puerto Rico, and for this purpose the staggering amount of one billion dollars would be assigned over the next twenty years.[5] The U.S. press also attributed Leahy's nomination to strategic military considerations regarding defense plans for Puerto Rico and the Caribbean.[6]

As Vito Marcantonio argued,[7] the surprise announcement was the equivalent of destitution to Winship, since he had not resigned despite Ickes's considerable arm-twisting. Winship's letter of resignation, dated

June 3, says that he had been thinking about resigning for about a year but "for different reasons had postponed the request."[8] His letter received a polite reply from the president two days later, thanking him for his "long and distinguished career in the service of your government" and for his "most arduous task" in the governorship of Puerto Rico.[9] Ickes recorded in his diary Winship's stonewalling on the issue of his resignation:

> I cabled on Thursday Governor Winship, asking him to send in his resignation so as to take effect in time for Admiral Leahy to take over as Governor on September 1. I had not received any reply from Governor Winship before I left Washington late Friday afternoon. Neither have I received an acknowledgement of the earlier radiogram that I sent him, telling him that Admiral Leahy would be prepared to take over on September 1.[10]

Ickes had been insistently trying since April 1939 (a month before Roosevelt's announcement of his intention to name Leahy) to obtain Winship's resignation. Ickes met with Winship on April 27 to discuss Puerto Rican affairs. When the issue of his resignation came up, Winship defended his record in "a long recital." He argued that he was willing to resign but still had "to dispose of a large number of bills." Ickes then requested that he should still hand in his resignation effective on the date when he estimated pending matters would be settled. But Winship was adamant and said that he would like to discuss the issue with the President. Winship also attacked Attorney General Benigno Fernández García for his handling of the "Capitol Racket." Consequently, Ickes called the President and asked him to stand firm on Winship's resignation.[11]

On May 3, Roosevelt received a memorandum from his personal secretary about Winship's reluctance to resign and the fact that "Secretary Ickes is very anxious that this be accomplished in this definite manner [i.e., before the governor returned to Puerto Rico]." It also said that Leahy had to be confirmed before Congress adjourned in the summer, in order to be able to draw the governor's salary.[12] Another memorandum of that day said "Secretary Ickes has just phoned me that General Winship is in town. Secretary Ickes told the General that his resignation was desired, and suggested that he resign effective as of a future date at which time he could clear up everything of an urgent nature there."[13]

Winship met with Roosevelt the following day. On that day, Martínez Nadal, García Méndez, and Alfonso Valdés all cabled Roosevelt expressing their support for the governor.[14] Resident Commissioner Santiago Iglesias also wrote praising Winship and requesting that he should continue in his post, to which Roosevelt answered on May 12: "Some time ago I determined to make Admiral Leahy Governor of Puerto Rico when he went on the retired list."[15] During his meeting with Roosevelt, Winship apparently managed to persuade him that it was inopportune for him to resign while under fire from Representative Vito Marcantonio.

In a letter to Roosevelt dated April 27, the same day that Ickes was meeting with Winship, Marcantonio had accused Winship of corruption in the awarding of a $75,000 contract to Frederick R. Graves, a friend of the governor, for the drawing of the plans for the dry dock to be built in San Juan. Marcantonio claimed, among other things, that the plans were practically a copy of a set of plans drawn four years earlier in the office of the Commissioner of the Interior.[16] He also gave a speech at the Confederation of Puerto Rican Societies in New York calling for Winship's immediate removal.[17] Roosevelt referred Marcantonio's letter to Ickes on May 11 instructing him to investigate the charges and proceeded to announce, the following day, that he would be replaced by Leahy.

Ickes was incensed at Roosevelt's inability to extract an immediate resignation from Winship during his meeting of May 4: "I resent the fact that the President authorized me to ask for Winship's resignation and then refused to back me up." He blamed Marcantonio's anti-Winship campaign for Roosevelt's reticence.[18] But he did not let up in his pressure on the governor, making public on May 5 that Puerto Rico had lost $2,735,000 earmarked for the Las Garzas hydroelectric project due to the refusal of the *coalicionista* legislature to approve the required legislation.[19] In his press release, Ickes blamed the legislature for sacrificing social and economic development and the potential employment of thousands of workers.[20]

Winship, on the other hand, felt he had won another round in his fight with Ickes. The day after he met with the Secretary of the Interior, *El Mundo* quoted the governor as saying that rumors on his possible resignation were "foolish."[21] On May 9, *El Mundo* again reported on the issue of the resignation saying that Winship had decided to retain the governorship "indefinitely" and that, consequently, Marcantonio had decided to attack him on the floor of the House.[22] Thus, Roosevelt's statement of May 12 replacing Winship in the governorship with Leahy was generally interpreted as a major victory for Marcantonio's campaign during April and early May. This campaign certainly could have been influential, but Winship's fate had already been sealed at least since the president's conversation with Leahy aboard the *Houston* on March 1, 1939.

The decision, however, was based on broader considerations such as the perceived continued instability of Puerto Rican politics, corruption scandals and the growing political difficulties with the *Coalición*, the negative impact of U.S. policy toward Puerto Rico in U.S. and Latin American public opinion, and the consequently urgent need of revising colonial policy in view of strategic and national defense considerations. The existing arrangement, strongly conditioned by the need to contain Nationalist and pro-independence militancy in the early and mid-thirties, was no longer considered a desirable framework for the implementation of the ambitious defense plans that were being formulated in late 1938 and early 1939.

Winship's close alignment with the *Coalición*, his reputation as a repressive colonial administrator, the insistent accusations of corruption, and his evident reluctance to follow instructions coming from Washington, particularly from Harold Ickes, not only disqualified him as an acceptable agent for a change in policy, but also made him a political liability. To Ickes, who never liked him, the envoy had become too "creolized" and was acting as a "puppet" of the real strongman: Rafael Martínez Nadal.[23] President Roosevelt was fully aware of the Puerto Rican political situation, which he had closely followed since his first term, and of Winship's difficulties, when he offered the governorship to Admiral Leahy.

Reactions to Winship's Removal

Understandably, the leadership of the *Coalición* interpreted Winship's removal as a major political blow engineered by the hated Secretary of the Interior that could foreshadow a major and negative shift in Washington policy. Rafael Martínez Nadal's recent controversial declaration regarding "fascist control" over Puerto Rico by the U.S., published by *The New York Times* on March 27, could have been interpreted not as an outburst against U.S. colonial control in general, but against the undesired meddling by the Secretary of the Interior.[24] It is interesting that in his tirade, which compared U.S. policy to the Russian Czars and the German Nazi government, Martínez Nadal said that it had been the practice of Americans to construct new leaders when the old ones were no longer useful to the colonial regime.[25] Army intelligence took due note both of Martínez Nadal's statement and of the fact that it was extensively quoted in the April 11 Radio Berlin broadcast, a summary of which was published by *El Mundo*.[26]

The displeasure of the *Coalición* was evident. After his return from Washington, Winship, following instructions received during his trip, called an extraordinary session of the legislature just as the White House announced his removal from the governorship. It had the purpose of approving financial aspects of the Las Garzas hydroelectric project, restoring several posts in executive agencies eliminated by the legislative majority as a retaliation for the "Capitol Racket" investigation, and securing cuts of about 10% in the budget.[27] However, only eight senators attended the session, and it was reported that it would conclude without any action.[28]

The large Las Garzas project was part of the restructuring of hydroelectric and power facilities promoted by Ickes since the mid-1930s with the purchase of the Ponce Electric Company. In late 1938, Rafael Martínez Nadal had refused to sign a letter to Ickes making a commitment to approve the required legislation.[29] An important bone of contention was the jurisdiction over the project of a Consultative Board for Emergency Measures (*Junta Consultiva de Medidas de Emergencia*) created by the legislature. In February 1939, in response to a point in Winship's address to the legislature, Martínez Nadal reiterated his refusal to eliminate the Consultative Board from the legislation.[30] Unlike the President of the Senate, Speaker García Méndez signed the letter and the House of Representatives approved legislation in a form acceptable to Ickes. The Senate refused to go along and approved a law without the required provisions. The Las Garzas project was reportedly related to "national defense plans," and Washington functionaries had threatened to have Congress approve a "little TVA in Puerto Rico" in case the Puerto Rican legislature did not approve the required legislation.[31]

On the other hand, on February 14, the Justice Department, under Benigno Fernández García, had concluded its investigation of the "Capitol Racket" and submitted it to Secretary Ickes. The investigation was carried out by Assistant Attorney General Enrique Campos del Toro. Since October 1938 he had to face all sorts of obstacles in the course of his inquiry.[32] After being interrogated by Campos del Toro, Antonio Pomalles, Martínez Nadal's secretary, committed suicide. The report revealed blatant irregularities in the administration of the legislature, among which was the fact that only about 100 of the 356 employees actually worked. The leading Coalición figures (including Bolívar Pagán and Alfonso Valdés) were mentioned in the report as responsible for the scandal, and a Socialist Senator, Sixto A. Pacheco, was charged as liable to criminal prosecution.[33]

The Coalición responded by launching a legislative investigation of the Justice Department and stepping up its attacks on Fernández García and Campos del Toro.[34] During the hearings at the legislature, Campos del Toro refused to submit himself to questioning by Bolívar Pagán. They came close to a fistfight as Pagán charged that the accused legislators were "more decent" than some functionaries in the Justice Department, while Campos del Toro refused to obey Pagán's order to take a seat.[35] Campos del Toro subsequently demanded that Winship take action against "administrative and political immorality" or he would travel to Washington to report on the situation.[36] The liberales decided to boycott the rest of the legislative session, because of the attack on the Justice Department.[37] The scandal continued to attract political attention throughout April 1939 as the Coalición legislature decided not to give out funds for a large number of posts in the Justice Department and even eliminated the post in the Lottery of Puerto Rico occupied by Socialist Senator Epifanio Fiz Jiménez's wife.[38] Fiz had blown the whistle on legislative corruption in 1938.

Parallel to the "Capitol Racket" scandal, Representative Marcantonio continued his attacks on corruption by Winship and Treasurer Leslie A. McLeod even after the announcement of the former's removal. On August 5, in a long speech at the U.S. House of Representatives entitled "Five Years of Tyranny in Puerto Rico," he called the governor the "Nero of the Caribbean." The title possibly made reference to a February speech by Bolivar Pagán entitled "Five Years of Governor Blanton Winship in Puerto Rico" that said, among other things, "Mr. Winship. . . friend No. 1 of our island and our people." It had been inserted in the Congressional Record by Santiago Iglesias.[39] In his speech, Marcantonio denounced Winship's repressive record, reiterated his charges regarding Frederick R. Graves, and claimed that the governor had five official automobiles (compared to one for the Governor of New York) and had used over $225,000 for personal patronage while there were no funds for school lunches.[40]

Government corruption thus became, in 1938 and 1939, a crucial issue that would plague the *Coalición* in the campaign for the 1940 elections. The *Partido Popular* effectively exploited the issue in its campaign, criticizing corrupt electoral practices, particularly the buying of votes. It also insistently pointed out that there was no fundamental difference between the *Coalición* and *Tripartismo*.[41] Speaker García Méndez's speech of July 4, 1939 which called for the "union of the Puerto Rican family" was, among other things, designed to distance himself from charges of corruption and indirectly place the blame on the other leaders of the *Coalición*. Many observers interpreted the emergence of *Tripartismo* (of which García Méndez was already unofficially a key player) as a response to rampant corruption. Muñoz observes in his memoirs that the "stated purpose of what was called *Tripartismo* was to moralize (*adecentar*) Puerto Rican life. The word itself had a certain superficial tone of neat *señoritos* with regard to certain political and administrative procedures, alien to demands for [a] profound social transformation."[42]

On May 17, Martínez Nadal again reacted to the adverse political developments by stating that Puerto Ricans were being treated as "puppets" of U.S. policy.[43] Two days later the *Coalición* bestowed honors on Winship, officially declaring him "adoptive son of Puerto Rico" in a legislative resolution that also emphasized Puerto Rico's strategic importance.[44] The University of Puerto Rico, also controlled by the *Coalición*, decided to grant the outgoing governor an honorary doctorate.[45] San Juan's "high society" honored Winship as a hero in several receptions and cocktail parties: at Col. Manuel Font's residence, the Lion's Club, the Berwind Country Club, the YMCA, etc. Manuel González, who later cultivated a close relationship with Governor Leahy, also organized a farewell party in the Condado Hotel, which he owned.[46]

As a further act of defiance, the legislature approved a resolution demanding statehood, despite the fact that Santiago Iglesias's proposal to make Puerto Rico an incorporated territory had not progressed in Congress.[47] There were also clear signs that the Roosevelt administration did not wish the "status" question to be posed at all in the context of the rapidly deteriorating international situation.[48] On June 26, Santiago Iglesias presented a proposal to Congress entitled "To Enable the People of Puerto Rico to Form a Constitution and State Government and be Admitted into the Union on an Equal Footing with the States."[49] Winship also defiantly joined the chorus in favor of statehood during a meeting of a Statehood Association in the Escambrón Beach Club, one of the many events organized in his honor.[50] He promised to promote "complete membership" of Puerto Rico in the United States.[51]

The official *liberales* and the *populares*, on the other hand, welcomed Winship's removal. José Ramírez Santibañez, Antonio R. Barceló's successor, publicly expressed satisfaction. A change in the governorship would clearly create a more favorable environment for the opposition Tripartista political formation that he was building. Enrique Bird Piñero, a Liberal who subsequently became a close collaborator of Muñoz, described the reception of Leahy's nomination by the *liberales*:

> The best news arrived several months later: Winship had been relieved of the governorship and would return to Washington to await a new assignment to an important post. He would be succeeded in the governorship by Admiral William D. Leahy. . . The implications of the news could not be more positive for us the Liberals: Washington was notifying the *Coalición*, by removing its great crony Winship, that good times were over. With the *Coalición* discarded and Muñoz Marín far afield talking to the peasants [*jíbaros*] about independence, the message was apparently clear: Mr. Ramírez Santibáñez, rally the decent people of the country to the *Partido Liberal*, and you may win the 1940 elections![52]

To Muñoz the change in the governorship ended a long struggle that had begun soon after Winship's inauguration in 1934. The general had proven to be a harder nut to crack than Gore. Although Muñoz's strategy for the 1940 elections did not emphasize obtaining Washington's support or making political pacts at the summit of power, a new governor opened the possibility of discussing crucial electoral issues. In 1937 Muñoz had written to Arthur Garfield Hays that "Little changes in governors or other officials would be simply small change. Little flatteries, such as appointing a Puerto Rican governor, would be like shooting at Madrid with cap pistols. . . Give us sovereign, irrevocable powers, either as a state or an independent republic—and let us make the choice between those two ourselves."[53]

Muñoz carefully framed his reaction to Leahy's inaugural speech of September 11. He said that the message "merits the approval and sympathy of our people. Leahy can not offer more to our people than what he has offered in his inaugural speech. . . an impartial and friendly attitude toward the different points of view regarding Puerto Rican problems that may be presented to him." He noted his disagreement with Leahy's stance on the application of the Fair Labor Standards Act, but added that he was sure that "we will be in agreement with him in many of his objectives," and pledged the support of the Partido Popular.[54] In its October issue, *El Batey*, the Popular biweekly, extensively reported on a meeting between Muñoz Marín and Admiral Leahy.

> Mr. Muñoz Marín said after his interview with Governor Leahy that he felt this governor was a sensible man and had good intentions to improve the conditions of our people.
>
> *El Batey* advises its readers to have a spirit of sympathy and understanding toward the efforts of the new governor to improve the situation of our people and counsels all to give their cooperation to the governor in the efforts he proposes to undertake for the welfare of Puerto Rico.[55]

Two months after Leahy's inauguration, Muna Lee, Muñoz's wife, wrote to Ruby Black that "it is less depressing now that formerly with Governor Leahy . . . really making one feel that he cares about law and order and the Constitution and such things. . . Luis seems to think that so far Leahy is the best governor the Island has ever had."[56] By January 1940, initial support by Muñoz had become enthusiastic praise.

> Let me tell you something about Governor Leahy. I think he has been by far the best governor that has been sent to Puerto

Rico since the beginning of the American Regime. He is the only one that I know who knows how to deal with this situation. . .[57]

However, the U.S. liberals with whom Muñoz had developed a close relationship of collaboration did not receive the nomination of Admiral Leahy with the same enthusiasm. They were glad to be rid of Winship, but had expected a progressive civilian to be named to the post. Instead, to their chagrin, Roosevelt had named a high-ranking naval officer of conservative inclinations. On May 15, the Committee for Fair Play to Puerto Rico, associated with the ACLU, issued a statement criticizing the decision to name a naval officer to a post that dealt with "strictly civilian" matters of "extreme difficulty." The statement also made reference to the exploitation for propaganda purposes of the Puerto Rican situation by the "Nazi press" and the need to name a highly qualified civilian administrator for the governorship.[58] This statement was the only critical reaction to Leahy's nomination that was reported in the U.S. press, and several conservative newspapers editorialized strongly in favor of Roosevelt's decision.[59]

In a letter to Ruby Black, Robert W. Claiborne privately expressed concerns similar to those in the ACLU statement. Claiborne was a labor lawyer entrusted by the Roosevelt administration with enforcement of the Fair Labor Standards Act in Puerto Rico. He was involved in a hostile confrontation with the Winship government. Politically he was close to Luis Muñoz Marín, and Ruby Black had lobbied strongly in favor of his nomination to the post as Administrator of the Wages and Hours Division of the U.S. Department of Labor in Puerto Rico.[60] Shortly before the letter was written, Santiago Iglesias had denounced in the U.S. House of Representatives Claiborne's links to Vito Marcantonio and Muñoz.[61]

Dear Ruby:

Thanks to you and the others Winship is out.

But why the continued "occupation?" A naval Administration is out of the frying pan into the fire.

The Faschists [sic] are celebrating, for "for the sake of peace and military reasons" they will be protected in their exploitations.

Loyalty of a frustrated, unsatisfied people quickly switches to anyone that comes along. You have an Ireland here, which in the next war will be a serious problem to the U.S.

How could Roosevelt have failed to send a liberal thinker, and a young man? Guam is being transferred from Navy to Interior, and we get a Naval Officer for Governor, one who however fine his points is of an older school than even Winship, and a damn right stronger, because not feeble mentally.

Is this only an interim appointment, while Roosevelt can [sic] be looking for a civilian.[62]

Oswald Garrison Villard once again voiced his criticism in an article in *The Nation* meaningfully entitled "Puerto Rico S.O.S." While saying that he had met Leahy and found him "open-minded and eager to learn," he argued that his nomination to the governorship created the impression that Puerto Rico was not part of the U.S. and "merely a military satrapy." He also commented with irony that "the President thought it would do no harm to have it known in Berlin that an admiral has been put in charge of the Island."[63] The meeting with Leahy to which Villard makes reference was not recorded by the former as a happy one.

I also received, during this period, a visitation by Mr. Oswald Garrison Villard, a self-styled "liberal" magazine writer, who told me it was wrong to appoint a military man over liberty loving people who wanted only the privilege of self government, and that his group of Liberals would oppose my appointment.

When I related Governor Winship's account of the assassins he said that much could be said in justification of their being only patriots.

I then assured Mr. Villard that if any of the "patriots" attempted to assassinate me they would have no further trouble in this world because they would be dead before they could move their feet. He expressed horror at this barbarous attitude of mine saying that he did not believe an American could so deliberately dispense with the due process of law. . .[64]

A Sailor's Adventure in Politics

Leahy entitled his brief memoirs on his Puerto Rican governorship "Sailor's Adventure in Politics."[65] They were apparently written in late 1940, before taking up his post as Ambassador to Vichy France. The self-effacing title is characteristic of Leahy's inclination toward understatement. The "sailor" was the highest ranking U.S. naval officer and had been de facto Secretary of the Navy, given Claude Swanson's failing health. The "adventure in politics" was undertaken by someone who had already accumulated considerable political experience as head of one of the largest bureaucracies of the U.S. government and by dealing with the president and the congressional leadership since the mid 1930s.

Later, the man who stood immediately behind Roosevelt, Churchill and Stalin in the official photographs of the Teheran and Yalta conferences, would entitle his Second World War memoirs *I Was There*, as if his role had been that of a mere witness.[66] He honestly cherished this image of faithful and "non-political" servant of the state and *éminence grise*. But it was also a convenient veil for the highly political posts he occupied from the 1930s to the 1950s and for the considerable power he wielded, a measure of power exercised by very few U.S. military officers.

The sailor did not have to disembark in San Juan to begin his adventure in "one of the islands of the Spanish Main," as he referred to Puerto Rico. Soon after the announcement of his nomination, and while still holding the post of CNO, Leahy began dealing with Puerto Rican issues. On May 25, 1939, a delegation representing the Economic Convention visited him to discuss their perspectives on the island's economic problems. The Economic Convention had been created in February 1939 as a broad alliance of 70 non-partisan groups with the purpose of establishing a consensus and making proposals regarding economic policy. It was headed by Filipo de Hostos, President of the Chamber of Commerce, who had designated the members of several committees, mostly drawn from the island's political and business elite.[67] It convened on March 12 in a long and stormy session which was attended by Muñoz as the representative of the unemployed. He had been elected two weeks before in a Congress of the Unemployed as its spokesman.[68] Among the resolutions approved by the Economic Convention, the most controversial was one calling for a plebiscite to decide the island's status, since it was argued that political uncertainty had negative economic repercussions. This decision was supported by Muñoz[69] but severely criticized by the *Coalición* leaders who considered it as an unwarranted "invasion of the political field."[70]

The delegation of the Economic Convention that visited Leahy consisted of Filipo de Hostos, J. A. Roig, Francisco Vizcarrondo, Francisco López Domínguez, and James A. Dickey, lobbyist of the sugar producers association. Leahy refused to discuss his plans with this commission.[71] However, he later stated that he was "very favorably impressed" with their proposals and that he had discussed them with Roosevelt and Ickes.[72] The Roosevelt administration responded favorably to a demand of the Convention to create an inter-agency committee to coordinate policy toward Puerto Rico. Oscar L. Chapman, the Assistant Secretary of the Interior, was named president. The committee also included representatives from the State, Commerce, Agriculture, and Labor departments.[73]

A few days after his meeting with Leahy, Filipo de Hostos appeared before the inter-agency committee and read a statement supposedly containing demands and proposals of the Economic Convention. It provided an indication of the proposals brought earlier to Leahy's attention. According to de Hostos the main economic issues facing Puerto Rico were: 1) the need for a larger sugar quota, 2) a revision of commercial agreements with other countries that negatively affected the Puerto Rican economy, 3) the non-application to Puerto Rico of the minimum wages set by the Fair Labor Standards Act, 4) the rise in the prices of basic commodities, and 5) the delay in the allocation of relief funds.[74] Interestingly, none of the points contemplated major economic reforms or challenged the sugar interests, and they were consistent with the official expressions on the economic policy of Governor Winship and the *Coalición*. Conspicuously absent was any reference to the application of the 500-Acre Law.

On May 30, another delegation met with Leahy. It consisted of Senate President Rafael Martínez Nadal, and senators Juan Bautista García Méndez and Alfonso Valdés, all Republicans and *Coalicionistas*. *El Mundo* reported that Leahy had not revealed his plans to this group.[75] Leahy also welcomed Donald A. Draughon, the Marshal of the Federal Court in Puerto Rico. The U.S. Marshall had been prominently involved in the repression of the Nationalist Party and it is likely that the problems with this organization were brought to his attention during this meeting.[76] A few days later Leahy attended a cocktail party at the Puerto Rico Trade Council where he stated that he would leave Puerto Rico if he failed to do a good job, a statement which could be understood as an indirect reference to Winship's reluctance to resign.[77]

Leahy's taciturn attitude regarding his plans for the governorship was understandable. In late May he wrote to a friend that he had still not heard much regarding the Puerto Rican governorship. He already knew, however, that it was an "office full of grief."

> I have almost no news whatever in regard to the job that the President has been complimentary enough to offer to me. Some of the recent visitors to the Spanish Main assure me that the office is sufficiently full of grief to keep even an old sailor moving rapidly. However, as you and I know so well, old sailors will try anything once, and we will endeavor to survive, if not to enjoy, such incidents as may come to us while trying to administer one of the islands of the Spanish Main.[78]

Furthermore, as CNO, Leahy had to attend to urgent matters related to the deteriorating international situation and the naval rearmament program. The German coup in Czechoslovakia in mid-March 1939 increased concern in Washington regarding the inexorable trend toward war in Europe. Leahy participated during this period in cabinet meetings to discuss the situation in Europe. The naval rearmament program required constant communication with Congress, as well as ongoing secret naval conversations with Britain. Finally, the revision of war plans by the Joint Board, leading to the formal adoption of the five Rainbow Plans, was another dimension of the hectic pace war preparations had already assumed.[79]

In May 1939, Roosevelt apparently considered, even after offering Leahy the Puerto Rican governorship and given the deepening of the European crisis, changing Leahy's assignment and naming him Secretary of the Navy. He also told the CNO that, if the U.S. became involved in the war, he wanted to have him back in Washington as his military advisor. In fact, only a few days after Leahy's inauguration, a list of possible replacements was prepared at the White House under the title

"For Puerto Rico in case Leahy comes back" (due, of course, to events in Europe). The first on the list was Charles Taussig, followed by Francis Michael Shea, the Assistant Attorney General. The last name was that of Colonel John W. Wright, the former commander of the 65th Infantry Regiment. His name was followed by the notation "Commanded the Regiment. . . Suggested by Ernest Gruening."[80] The latter had apparently developed quite an inclination in favor of military officers.[81] Rexford G. Tugwell was not included in the list. In September Ickes tried to have Tugwell accept the post left vacant by Gruening.[82]

The pilgrimage of Puerto Rican politicians to Washington and to Leahy's office continued during June. Rafael Martínez Nadal again met with Leahy on June 13, and the top leadership of the *Coalición* conferred with him two days later.[83] Martínez Nadal, Santiago Iglesias, Bolívar Pagán, Alfonso Valdés, and Fernando J. Géigel, Mayor of San Juan, formed part of that delegation. Significantly, *El Mundo* reported that Leahy had urged the delegation to provide "non-partisan collaboration of all groups." This was followed on June 20 by yet another meeting of the *Coalición* leadership with Ickes, who stated that he was prepared to meet them half-way.[84] On June 24 the press reported that Ickes, Gruening, and Leahy had met to discuss the Puerto Rican situation.[85]

These meetings did not produce any public expression favorable to the *Coalición*. Instead, Leahy made known that he planned to surround himself with "non-partisan" functionaries.[86] The theme of "non-partisanship" would again recur in the inauguration speech. It challenged a basic component of the *Coalición* pact, as it required the collaboration of the governor with regard to nominations to key executive and judicial posts. Without the collaboration that Winship had hitherto provided, the legislative majority could only control the legislative branch. *The New York Times* reported that Leahy's remarks had caused "political ferment" and "immediate consternation" in Puerto Rico. The information placed the adverse reaction in the context of the *Coalición's* factional struggles and Martínez Nadal's opposition to Ickes's "little TVA" plan.[87]

On July 25, Leahy participated in the "Puerto Rican Day" celebrations at New York's World Fair. This event brought together four U.S. governors of Puerto Rico: former governors Beekman Winthrop and Colonel Theodore Roosevelt Jr., the incumbent General Blanton Winship, and incoming governor Leahy. All were former military officers or (in the case of Winthrop) closely linked to the military establishment. Three of them — Winthrop, Roosevelt and Leahy — had held high posts in the naval bureaucracy, either as Assistant Secretaries or as CNO. The celebration provided an opportunity for further discussions on Puerto Rican policy. Resident Commissioner Santiago Iglesias and a high-level representative of the Catholic Church, Mgr. Mariano Vasallo, also participated. The "Puerto Rican Day" was devoted to the commemoration of the landing of U.S. troops in 1898 and the ceremonies were broadcast on the island. In view of the bloody outcome of the 1938 parade, no official local celebration was held in Puerto Rico and a Nationalist Party rally in Yauco was prohibited. Eduardo R. González, the *Coalición*-named Commissioner General of Puerto Rico to the Fair, used his speech to bring up once again the question of statehood, stating that "Today Puerto Rico looks hopefully ahead for a realization of a closer political relationship with the continental nation through being admitted to the sacred national family circle."[88]

An important and politically significant change in personnel was announced in Washington just prior to Leahy's assuming the post of governor: Ernest Gruening's removal from his post in the Department of the Interior and his simultaneous nomination as Governor of Alaska. This decision was reported by *El Mundo* on September 4. The decision was attributed to a recommendation made by the Admiral in a conversation with Roosevelt.[89] The removal of Gruening from the Division of Territories and Island Possessions of the Department of the Interior was also a personal victory for Ickes, who could now name a more cooperative functionary and exercise greater control over Puerto Rican policy. Ickes mentions in his diary that he had been instructed by Roosevelt to offer the governorship of Alaska to Gruening in early June, at which time he began considering Admiral Rossiter as his successor.[90] In mid September, he offered the post to Rexford G. Tugwell, then Chairman of the Planning Board of New York City, who declined for economic reasons. Gruening stayed in his post until late November because a successor had not been named. Ickes laconically consigned in his diary, "Frankly, I am apprehensive of what may happen in Alaska." Rupert Emerson, a Harvard professor with Latin American experience, was chosen in April 1940 to head the Division.[91]

Upon leaving his post in the Department of the Interior, Gruening dealt a final blow to his political opponents in Puerto Rico by issuing a statement where he favored, on anti-colonial grounds, imposing statehood without consulting the people in a plebiscite. His statement was supported by pro-statehood spokesmen.[92] Luis Muñoz Marín, who still favored independence and a plebiscite to settle the status issue, diplomatically applauded Gruening's anti-colonial sentiments, but criticized as un-American and paternalistic the imposition of statehood "from above."[93] With Winship and Gruening's almost simultaneous removal from their posts, the two most visible architects of colonial policy during the 1930s were extracted from Puerto Rican policy-making.

Preparing for the Mission: Leahy's Instructions

The first major meeting with Roosevelt on Puerto Rican matters took place on July 28, 1939.[94] One of the issues discussed at this meeting apparently had to do with Leahy's role in the military construction program underway in Puerto Rico since Roosevelt had issued a letter soon after on September 1, naming him to the post of Territorial Administrator of the Works Progress Administration (WPA).[95] This agency would play a leading role in the construction of military bases and installations and numerous defense-related projects. It would be one of the several posts, in addition to the governorship, placed under Leahy's control.

The President surprised Leahy by conferring him the Distinguished Service Medal during that meeting. The citation issued by Roosevelt stated that "[t]he extraordinary qualities of leadership and administrative ability that have marked his tenure as the highest ranking officer in the Navy have been exemplified throughout his entire naval career."[96] Soon after this meeting, Leahy turned over the post of CNO to Admiral Harold Stark.

The transition in the Navy from Leahy to Stark was part of a broader renewal at the highest levels of the military. On September 1, General George C. Marshall also relieved General Malin Craig as Chief of Staff of the Army. Marshall would lead the army during the war, while Stark would later be replaced by Admiral Ernest J. King (CNO and Commander in Chief, U.S. Fleet). After Leahy's return from Vichy, Roosevelt named him his personal chief of staff (a post of his own creation) and established the Joint Chiefs of Staff with Leahy (chair, Navy), Marshall (Army), King (Navy), and General Henry H. ("Hap") Arnold (Army Air Force) as the four members. Leahy would serve during the war as the liaison of the Joint Chiefs with the President. He would also chair the meetings with the British of the Combined Chiefs of Staff.[97]

Further meetings on Puerto Rico took place in Washington and New York during late August and early September. Leahy held another hour-long meeting with Roosevelt on August 30 (just two days before Germany invaded Poland) where the European situation was discussed. He recorded that meeting in his diary.

> Today I had an hour's talk with the President who discussed at length the prospect of war in Europe and America's possible neutrality action.
>
> He informed me that if the United States becomes seriously involved in the European conflict, it will be necessary for him to recall me from Puerto Rico and assign me to membership on a Four-Man-War Board, with the duty of coordinating the work of the State, War and Navy Departments.[98]

The new governor apparently did not receive detailed written instructions from Roosevelt regarding Puerto Rico, as was the case for his subsequent and extremely delicate assignment as Ambassador to Vichy, France. His account of the president's verbal directive is worth quoting at length.

> In the densely over-populated island containing about two million inhabitants and capable of supporting not more than half that number, the distribution of wealth, resources and opportunity was highly inequitable. Correction of this unfortunate condition was an important part of the task given to me by President Roosevelt.
>
> Practically all of the wealth of the island was in sugar plantations owned by a very small number of native families and by continental corporations.
>
> A considerable number of people employed in servicing the sugar business and residing in the cities were adequately

rewarded and prosperous, but the great mass of the people was illiterate and lived in abject poverty as is not known on the Continent except perhaps among negroes in some of the most distressed areas of our far south . . .

Poor people who had moved in large numbers to the cities lived in unbelievable squalid slums built by the occupants themselves on unused areas that were not fit for human occupation.

All of these appalling conditions were known to President Roosevelt. He gave me oral instructions to do everything within the power of the Governor and the Insular Government to apply corrective measures, and to use the money available for the purpose under the Works Progress Administration to alleviate the distress of under privileged people and to raise their standard of living.

He also gave me oral instructions to keep myself accurately informed in regard to progress on the military installations under construction in the island with the purpose of preserving United States neutrality in the Caribbean Sea, to protect against possible attack by any of the belligerent European nations, and to give such assistance as was available in the territory under my control.[99]

Leahy's description of social and economic conditions in Puerto Rico in 1939 is strikingly similar to the observations made by Ickes during his 1936 trip. It is clearly in contradiction with the optimistic and positive appraisals expressed in official statements and being put forth by authors close to the Winship administration and the sugar corporations. More importantly, the notion of a profound social polarization along class lines, between the "very small number of native families and continental corporations . . . and the people employed in servicing the sugar business," on the one hand, and "the great mass of the people who was illiterate and lived in abject poverty," on the other, was connected in the text to the *Coalición's* oligarchical rule and to Martínez Nadal's caudillismo.

Regarding Martínez Nadal, Leahy wrote that he was ". . . an extremely attractive and able person who was said to have had exclusive influence with preceding governors and who represented the most prosperous part of the population." He was also portrayed as an inflexible politician who sought to exercise absolute control, even over the executive and judicial branches of the Puerto Rican government.

> The legislative branch of the government at this time was completely dominated by Senator Rafael Martínez Nadal, leader of the coalition "Union-Republican" political party. He was generally accepted as the "caudillo" and he found it very difficult to understand how the new governor could fail to accept without question his nomination of officials for appointment to executive and judicial positions regardless of the interest of the people. He learned in time, however, that the new Governor made his nominations on a basis of ability to serve the people regardless of political affiliations. Nominees who were not of Senor [sic] Nadal's political party were usually refused confirmation by the Senate which caused the resulting difficulty to be shared between him and the Governor.[100]

However, Roosevelt also entrusted Leahy with military responsibilities consisting in a supervisory role over defense preparations and operations in Puerto Rico and the entire Caribbean region, and directly supporting the implementation of military construction defense plans in Puerto Rico from the governorship and through his control over the entire federal bureaucracy. Both aspects, the political and the military, were inextricably related as military measures were seen to require redefined political circumstances. Leahy's military tasks were at variance with Ickes's insistence that he would be a civilian functionary with purely civilian tasks. The former was well aware of the criticisms regarding continued military control over Puerto Rico made by the ACLU and the liberal press. Ickes brought the issue up in May during a meeting with Leahy. He made the following observation of the meeting in his diary:

> In our national defense program, Puerto Rico, of course looms big, but the civil affairs of the people of the island are more important than those that relate to national defense. Leahy recognizes this. As a matter of fact, he said that he did not think that, as Governor, he should have anything to do with the defense plans.[101]

Ickes again stressed this point in a statement to the press in early July.[102] It was rather disingenuous on the part of Ickes to claim that

Roosevelt would assign one of his most valuable military cadres to Puerto Rico, where a huge defense program was underway, and not endow him with military responsibilities. But Leahy not only reassured Ickes that he would act as a civil governor. Soon after arriving in Puerto Rico he emphatically denied that he had been named to supervise the construction of naval and air bases, claiming that he was "completely disconnected from his previous activities."[103]

However, Leahy was obviously aware of the crucial military dimension of his duties. He noted that,

> . . . [w]ith Puerto Rico prepared as a major military and naval air base, which is now in process of being accomplished, it will be very difficult for any expedition from overseas to attack the southern coast of the United States, the east coast of Central America, or the north coast of South America, without first occupying Puerto Rico, which latter [sic], when we have completed our present defenses for the island and for an expanded fleet, would be an exceedingly hazardous major military operation.[104]

Leahy related the implementation of the defense plans in Puerto Rico to military measures being planned for the entire Caribbean region. Making reference to "an opinion that has been expressed," he remarked that "sovereignty should be acquired over some other islands in the Caribbean that are now in the possession of European nations."[105] The outright annexation of European colonies had been proposed in 1938 by Major George Fielding Eliot in *The Ramparts We Watch* and had powerful advocates in U.S. military circles.[106] It should be noted that Roosevelt, however, eventually rejected assuming direct administration of European territories. Thus, despite Ickes's admonitions, Leahy would closely follow and intensively involve himself in military developments in Puerto Rico and the Caribbean throughout his governorship. In fact, the entries in his diary for the first ten days after his inauguration as governor dealt exclusively with military matters. These were henceforth frequently recorded.[107]

Roosevelt's decision to name Leahy Territorial Administrator of the Works Progress Administration (WPA) had evident military implications and was related to the strategic aspects of his Puerto Rican assignment. The WPA relief programs, despite congressional scrutiny, began to be secretly used as part of the rearmament program in 1939. The War Department was interested in using relief funds to further national defense. The process of militarization of this agency, which had been an icon of New Deal reformism, gained momentum in the summer of 1939 with Harry Hopkins's nomination as Secretary of Commerce. To replace Hopkins in the post of administrator, the president nominated an active-duty Army officer, Colonel Harrington, to head the agency.[108] This shift occurred amidst a conservative onslaught in Congress against the reformist New Deal policies and agencies, such as the WPA itself.[109]

Military preparations had gathered considerable momentum after the Fleet Problem XX maneuvers held in January and February. During 1939 and early 1940, Puerto Rico was visited by high-ranking military officers (such as George Marshall, "Hap" Arnold and George L. Brett) and several congressional delegations, to oversee military preparations. When Leahy arrived in September to occupy the governorship, defense plans were not only already well under way, but were also being pursued with an added sense of urgency due to the deepening of the European crisis during August and the actual outbreak of war on September 1. This formed part of a military build-up in most U.S. outlying possessions, mainly in Hawaii and Alaska, and in Panama.

The revision of defense plans for Puerto Rico had begun in July 1938, when the commander of the Second Corps Area of the Army ordered the formulation of a new plan, to be code-named Orange, for the Puerto Rico-Virgin Islands area. This plan was submitted in late October 1938, but it only covered the island of Puerto Rico. Another important planning document of this period, in this case of the navy, was the Hepburn Board Report, which recommended the construction of an air and submarine base at Isla Grande. Improvements of the San Juan Harbor (dredging and the construction of a dry dock) and the Isla Grande naval base were the first major projects of military infrastructure undertaken on the island. Their strategic importance was made evident by the inspection visit in April of a large congressional delegation.[110]

In May 1939, only weeks after the annexation of Czechoslovakia and the Fleet Problem XX maneuvers, the Joint Planning Committee submitted to the Joint Board a document entitled "A Study of Puerto Rico and the Virgin Islands." It dealt with the strategic importance of the

Puerto Rico-Virgin Islands area, potential threats in case of war, and the missions it should be assigned. The study recommended a redefinition of the missions and the reinforcement of peacetime garrisons. It also recommended the establishment of a separate overseas department of the Army and a naval district or local naval command encompassing the area.

The Joint Planning Committee proposals were approved, and the President ordered the creation of a new Puerto Rico Department of the Army effective July 1, 1939. It was entrusted with developing joint defense plans without waiting for the completion of the Rainbow Plans and placed under the command of Brigadier General Edmund L. Daley. A Puerto Rico Defense Project, based on new defense plans, was also to be prepared in order to identify necessary military resources. This planning process yielded an extensive list of needs which were only partially approved. The components that were approved consisted of the Army Department Headquarters, additional air corps units, the 65th Infantry at existing strength, and two National Guard regiments. The Tenth Naval District, encompassing Puerto Rico, the Virgin Islands, Guantánamo Naval Station, Cuba, Haiti, Santo Domingo, the Lesser Antilles, and a large portion of the Caribbean Sea, was created in February 1940 and placed under the command of Captain Raymond A. Spruance.[111] Its personnel consisted of 2,961 officers and enlisted men, including 256 aviators.

Air power was a fundamental aspect of military preparations in Puerto Rico. In July 1938, the commander of the Second Corps area pointed out the need to establish Army air forces in Puerto Rico to assist the Navy in the defense of the island. He suggested, "Construct a suitable air base and landing fields in Puerto Rico, but keep the Air Corps garrison to the minimum required for maintenance." During the first half of 1939, five different surveys were carried out to decide on the location of the major air base and other landing fields. On June 22, General Malin Craig, the Army Chief of Staff, approved the recommendation that the main base be built at Punta Borinquen as had been proposed in the document "A Study of Puerto Rico and the Virgin Islands." The Punta Borinquen project was part of a network of air facilities that included another important airfield in Juana Díaz (later named Losey Field), as well as nine auxiliary fields throughout the island. Just before Leahy's arrival, on September 6, the Army had taken possession of a 1,877-acre tract in Punta Borinquen and given residents a peremptory twenty-day period to leave their properties. The construction of Air Base 1 (later Borinquen Field) began in September with 2,000 workers.

The importance of Puerto Rico with regard to army air power went beyond a support role to the navy. Air power projected from Puerto Rico to the Atlantic and the Lesser Antilles had been an important dimension of Fleet Problem XX. The maneuvers had been mainly an air duel, without a round of the battleship guns fired during the six days of the exercise.[112] Air power was considered crucial to the defense of the Panama Canal as military planners had established that the only credible threat to its security from the Atlantic was an air attack.[113] Furthermore, Puerto Rico was to play a role with regard to the defense of the Natal region in Brazil where the U.S. planned to construct another major air base. Two air routes to Natal were considered essential: a Caribbean route via Cuba, Hispaniola, Puerto Rico, the Lesser Antilles, and the north coast of South America, and another Mexican-Central American route via Panama. These routes required the construction of a string of military and civil landing fields. The civilian air fields were to be constructed under the cover of Pan American Airlines projects. The military air bases of McDill in Florida, Río Hato in Panama, and Punta Borinquen in Puerto Rico would form a strategic triangle for the Caribbean region.[114]

Before his departure for Puerto Rico, Leahy held several conferences with Winship. According to Leahy's account of the meetings, the main topics were "the urgent political problems before the island government" and "the existence of a group of self named Nationalists which included some fanatical assassins who had attempted, without success, to kill him and Judge Cooper of the United States District Court." Winship told Leahy that the Nationalists had killed an officer and the Chief of Police and that the "native courts" were so terrorized that they would not convict a political assassin. Leahy noted that "Governor Winship and Judge Cooper were men of superlative courage, and through their personal efforts a number of the Nationalist leaders had been given long prison terms by the United States District Court." It is in this context that he referred to his tense conversation about the Nationalists with Oswald Garrison Villard.[115]

Germany Invades Poland, Leahy Takes Command

Leahy sailed for Puerto Rico with his wife Louise aboard the steamer *SS Coamo* exactly one week after the German invasion of Poland. He stayed in New York during the last two days prior to his departure "where much time was spent discussing Puerto Rican affairs."[116] Ernest Gruening boarded the Coamo to bid Leahy farewell. Lieutenant Commander R. H. Wishard, his naval aide and liaison to the navy, was part of the retinue. The new governor arrived in San Juan on September 11, being driven from the ship in a motorcade directly to the Capitol building to participate in the inauguration ceremonies. He was escorted by Acting Governor Colonel José E. Colom.

Catholic Bishop Edwin V. Byrne opened the ceremony with an invocation, and Colom read a speech. The governor was sworn in by Chief Justice Emilio del Toro Cuebas. Leahy proceeded to read, in English, a six-minute speech, its unusual brevity being duly noted by Harwood Hull of *The New York Times*.[117] A Spanish translation was read by Judge del Toro. The ceremony ended with an hour-long military and civic parade. Brigadier General Edmund L. Daley, commander of the recently created Puerto Rico Department of the Army, accompanied Leahy in reviewing the parading troops. Marine planes from St. Thomas flew in formation low over the reviewing stand. Celebrations continued through the night with a 150 guest reception at La Fortaleza.[118]

The inauguration speech stressed that the governor would devote his energy and talents "exclusively to the task of improving the condition and the opportunities of all the people of Puerto Rico." He also said that he would seek to collaborate with Congress to obtain "a change in the sugar quota, modifications of the local application of the Wages and Hours Act, a correction of the shipping situation as applied to Puerto Rico, the unfavorable trade agreements with foreign nations and the hurricane relief commission debts." These conservative economic proposals did not represent a major departure from the often stated objectives of the Winship-*Coalición* government. In fact, the day before the inauguration, *El Mundo* had published an interview with Winship in which he called for the strengthening of the sugar industry through the liberalization of the sugar quota and the non-application of the Wages and Hours Law.[119] They were also quite similar to the program put forth by the President of the Chamber of Commerce, Filipo de Hostos, on behalf of the Economic Convention. As if it had been timed to coincide with Leahy's inauguration, the Puerto Rican press reported on September 12 that Roosevelt had decided to "temporarily suspend" the sugar quota as a result of increased demand and rising prices provoked by the outbreak of war in Europe.[120] This step had been suggested by Ickes in a September 7 Cabinet meeting with the argument that in Puerto Rico and the Virgin Islands people were "starving because of the strict quota under which sugar is held."[121] The press also informed that a WPA functionary had arrived in San Juan to coordinate the expenditure of ten million dollars in military construction.[122] The message was clear: Leahy's governorship and war preparations promised "a bright future" to the ailing island economy.[123]

Although there was not much new to be glimpsed from the inaugural speech regarding economic policy, Leahy's comments on his approach to Puerto Rican politics were another matter. Leahy used the speech to once again emphasize the "non-partisan" character he planned to impress on his governorship. His comments were clearly targeted at the *Coalición* leadership and meant that the close alignment that had existed under Winship between the governor and the legislative majority would no longer prevail. It also meant that he did not feel bound by the pact established between the majority parties. He devoted a larger portion of his speech to this point than to outlining his economic program.

> Your Governor has no political affiliations and will not become affiliated with any particular group as compared with any other.
>
> He will ask for advice on the conduct of his executive office from the leaders of those groups who hold different views of the local political aspect, and he will respect their counsel and advice to be an expression of their considered opinion as to what is best for the general welfare of the people of Puerto Rico, regardless of any other consideration whatsoever.
>
> We can make no serious errors in the performance of our duties of our office if our only consideration is the welfare of Puerto Rico, and if our official action is taken with the purpose in view.[124]

Political leaders from the *Coalición*, *Tripartismo* and the *Partido Popular* praised the speech.[125] As noted, Luis Muñoz Marín objected to the reference to the Wages and Hours Act but pledged his party's support. Martínez Nadal was hospitalized in the U.S. and his reaction was not reported. The journal Puerto Rico Ilustrado editorialized in favor of the inauguration speech, praising its brevity and lack of empty promises. It pointed out that the crucial issue was that nominations would escape the control of voracious politicians.[126] The weekly Army intelligence report recorded that the speech had met with "the unanimous approval of all parties and groups."[127] However, Leahy's allegedly "nonpartisan" approach to key nominations and other issues would very soon provoke a clash with the *Coalición*, particularly with the President of the Senate.

Leahy's inauguration took place during the outbreak of war in Europe and Roosevelt's response to the crisis, events which accelerated defense preparations. Roosevelt immediately declared a state of "limited emergency" and on September 5 announced the establishment of a 300-mile "neutrality zone" around the entire hemisphere to be enforced by a U.S. naval "neutrality patrol." He had privately argued in August that the zone would have the purpose of preventing "an attack on any European interest in the Western Hemisphere, from Canada to the Guianas." The "neutrality zone" concept received Latin American endorsement in the "Declaration of Panama" on October 2. The British offered the U.S. access for this purpose to base facilities in Bermuda, Trinidad, and Saint Lucia.[128] Plans to reinforce the Puerto Rican regular army garrison by 1,500 men, bringing it to around 2,400, were also announced. *El Mundo* reported that the outbreak of war would hasten existing defense construction plans by six months.[129] During October and November, air, antiaircraft, and engineer units arrived in Puerto Rico, bringing the size of the garrison to just under 3,000 officers and soldiers.[130] This meant that between August and November 1939 the garrison tripled in size. A B-18 bomber squadron was also deployed at Borinquen Field in December.

The creation of the "neutrality zone" and U.S. naval activities in British colonies in the Caribbean immediately increased the naval presence in Puerto Rico. Its enforcement in the Atlantic Ocean was assigned to the

Atlantic Squadron under the command of Admiral Alfred H. Johnson. The squadron had been created in January 1939 and was the initial nucleus of the Atlantic Fleet that was later established on February 1, 1941. The Squadron was divided into eight naval patrols with responsibility over defined geographic areas. The eastern Caribbean south of latitude 23(10' was assigned to Patrols 7 and 8 under the command of Rear Admiral A. C. Pickens. This force consisted of the following ships: *Tuscaloosa, Truxton, Simpson, San Francisco, Patron 33, Lapwing, Broome, Borie, Patron 51, Gannet* and *Trush*.[131]

A destroyer, two seaplane tenders, and twelve scouting planes entered the San Juan harbor on September 12. Leahy had his photograph taken in the garden of La Fortaleza watching a formation of the scouting planes fly over the city. A week later, Rear Admiral Pickens arrived in San Juan aboard his flagship, the heavy cruiser *USS San Francisco*. On September 21, the cruiser *USS Tuscaloosa*, commanded by Captain Harry A. Badt, joined the *San Francisco* and the other ships in the harbor. Leahy met with both Pickens and Badt. A week later the *Sims* and *Hamman* destroyers also arrived in San Juan during "a Caribbean shake-down cruise." By mid October Admiral Pickens and the *San Francisco* were back in San Juan. Thus, immediately following Leahy's arrival, an impressive naval force had assembled at San Juan. He noted that its aim was "to establish an information patrol of the Caribbean Sea, with the purpose of detecting and reporting belligerent activities by the warring European powers."[132]

It should be noted that Roosevelt not only named Leahy to the governorship, but took the unprecedented step of placing all the Federal relief agencies under his direct authority. As noted, he had already been named Territorial Administrator for the WPA, an agency that played a major role in the military construction program. As governor, he also held *ex-officio* the post of President of the Board of Directors of the government-owned Puerto Rico Cement Corporation. Ensuring an adequate supply of low-cost cement to the defense projects was clearly crucial at this juncture, and could become even more crucial with U.S. participation in the war. One of Leahy's first decisions as President of the Board was to raise the price of cement to private clients while keeping it at cost for military agencies and the WPA.[133]

On September 22, Harold D. Smith, Washington's Director of the Budget, informed Leahy that President Roosevelt wanted him to "prepare an organization with three assistant administrators to coordinate all relief agencies in Puerto Rico."[134] The governor wrote to Smith on September 29 with his thoughts on this request. He included a recommendation that he be named Administrator of PRRA, a post held by Ickes. Miles H. Fairbank would be retained as Assistant Administrator. Ickes noted on Leahy's request that he appreciated "this open and frank dealing" and that "so far as I am concerned, the Governor can have the PRRA."[135] His response sharply contrasted his earlier battle to weaken Gruening's control over that key agency. Leahy also pointed out that "the relief efforts of the Civilian Conservation Corps, the Agricultural Extension Service, the Farm Security Administration, the United States Housing Authority and the National Youth Administration, can probably be coordinated with the Works Projects [sic] Administration,"[136] which he directly controlled.

The role of "Federal coordinator" placed under the governor's direct authority practically the entire Federal bureaucracy in Puerto Rico with financial resources much greater that those of the Puerto Rican government. The WPA budget for 1939 was $2.6 million with a further undetermined amount to "employ 10,000 men." The PRRA had a $9 million budget, the Public Works Administration (PWA) $8.4 million, the CCC $1 million, the U.S. Housing Authority $12 million in guaranteed loans and approximately a further $3 million distributed among smaller programs.[137] On November 30, 1939, Roosevelt named Leahy Administrator of PRRA and simultaneously instructed Federal officials of relief agencies to "keep him fully advised as to the status and progress of their relief projects" since there should be "complete cooperation among all officials charged with the expenditure of relief funds in Puerto Rico."[138]

This multiple role of governor, administrator of WPA and PRRA, and coordinator of Federal relief agencies gave Leahy an amount of power never enjoyed by his predecessor. Endowing Winship with such broad powers quite possibly would have provoked a major political firestorm in Puerto Rico. Leahy controlled not only the executive branch of the Puerto Rican government, but also the access to the politically coveted

Federal patronage. In addition to these posts, Leahy had the informal function of military advisor to the president (which he continued to perform throughout his governorship), and the supervisory responsibilities over defense measures in Puerto Rico and the Caribbean that Roosevelt had also assigned him. If the title of proconsul can be applied to a U.S. envoy in Puerto Rico, it would describe Leahy better than Gruening, as can be ascertained in the following table:

TABLE 5.1
POSTS AND INFORMAL ASSIGNMENTS
OF GOVERNOR WILLIAM D. LEAHY, 1939-1940

Government of Puerto Rico	Federal Civil Agencies	Informal tasks
• Governor	• Territorial Administrator WPA	• Military advisor to U.S. President
• President of the Puerto Rican Cement Co. Board	• Administrator PRRA	• Supervisor of P.R.-Caribbean
	• Coordinator: CCC, U.S. Housing Measures Authority, Department Health, National Youth Administration, Farm Security Administration, PWA, Rural Electrification Administration, Agriculture Extension Service, Vocational Education Funds, Department of Interior matching construction funds, etc.	

Leahy had to begin dealing with personnel matters of the government of Puerto Rico long before his inauguration in September. As soon as the removal of Winship was announced, the governor and the *Coalición* began taking steps to ensure the retention of loyal functionaries in key posts. On June 4, Leahy visited Ickes to complain that the legislature had approved, during the extraordinary session, a six-year contract for Colonel William C. Rigby as legal counsel of the government of Puerto Rico.

Rigby was a close associate of Winship, who had brought him to Puerto Rico from the War Department in 1934.[139] Ickes promised to advise the colonel not to sign the contract.[140]

Another controversial official was Auditor Leslie A. McLeod, who had been attacked by Marcantonio for corruption. Leahy told Ickes that McLeod used to go on fishing trips with the governor and "passed favorably upon any request of Winship's."[141] McLeod resigned his post soon after Leahy's inauguration, in early October 1939. An FBI investigation on his conduct had been requested by Ickes, but had not begun. The governor wanted to name Rear Admiral Peoples or Rear Admiral Charles Conard for this job. Ickes strenuously objected in a letter to Roosevelt, pointing out that,

> It would be a mistake to give the impression that either the Army or the Navy is taking over the administration of any of our Island Possessions, especially in view of the fact that you transferred Puerto Rico to this Department at a time when it was within the jurisdiction of the War Department.

Instead, he proposed former Congressman Guy J. Swope, "a New Deal Democrat." Roosevelt wrote back instructing Ickes to take the matter up with Leahy, who "ought to be fully satisfied."[142] Swope was eventually named to replace McLeod.[143]

James J. Lanzetta, who held the post of "advisor" to the Puerto Rican government, survived this initial purge of Winship-named functionaries. Lanzetta was Marcantonio's conservative political opponent for the post of Representative to Congress. Gruening and Winship had rewarded him with a $10,000-a-year Puerto Rican government sinecure for his anti-Marcantonio crusade. In November 1939, Walter Mc K Jones, the Liberal Party representative in the U.S., asked Leahy to remove Lanzetta from his post.[144] A U.S. publication also denounced the scheme, calling Lanzetta "personal lobbyist for Winship" and "a New Yorker who at that time had never set foot in Puerto Rico."[145] Leahy kept Lanzetta in the government payroll but noted in his diary and in public statements his dissatisfaction with what he considered a questionable arrangement. By July 1940 he was finally able to get rid of this embarrasing holdover from Winship's government.[146]

Leahy also had to decide what to do with "inherited" members of his cabinet against whom there were strong objections from the *Coalición* leadership. A case in point was the Commissioner of Labor, Prudencio Rivera Martínez, former Socialist and one of the leaders of the emerging *Tripartista* formation. Bolívar Pagán was actively seeking his removal from the government on the grounds that he had been named to this post as part of the *Coalición* pact but was using it to organize an opposition party. Leahy decided to confirm Prudencio Rivera in his post.[147]

The other cabinet member against whom the majority party had unleashed a bitter campaign was Attorney General Benigno Fernández. He had launched the "Capitol Racket" investigation which had proven to be politically damaging to the *Coalición*. Legal actions related to this investigation were still pending. More importantly, perhaps, was the fact that the Department of Justice had won a major legal victory on July 30, 1938 in the Supreme Court of Puerto Rico against the sugar corporations. In the case of Puerto Rico vs. Rubert Hermanos, Inc., the Supreme Court ordered the effective application of the 500 Acre Law. The government was represented in this case by Miguel Guerra Mondragón, who would later be entrusted with the drafting of key legislation for the *Partido Popular*.[148] This decision, however, did not settle the issue because the law had not been enforced and the sugar corporations appealed to the U.S. District Court of Appeals in Boston, where they obtained a favorable decision on September 27, 1939. The 500 Acre Law case was not finally settled until the government obtained a favorable ruling from the U.S. Supreme Court on March 25, 1940, and a second ruling in 1942.[149]

Leahy made a political concession to the *Coalición* in the case of Benigno Fernández García by replacing him with George A. Malcolm. It should be noted that the military authorities were also opposed to Fernández García. The intelligence report of September 2, 1939, signed by Brigadier General Edmund L. Daley, said that "within his political organization –the Liberal Party– he is considered a pink leftist; having expressed sympathy for the new radical party recently organized by Luis Muñoz Marín."[150] Malcolm, on the other hand, was a "colonial careerist," to use his own expression, with vast experience in the judicial system of the Philippines and who had contacted Ernest Gruening in Washington to obtain a new assignment. Significantly, this important post was not entrusted to a member of the majority party, but to an outsider who was not connected to Puerto Rican politics. The press interpreted this change, together with Gruening's removal from Puerto Rican policy-making, as an effort by Leahy to end political feuding.[151]

Malcolm, however, did not arrive in Puerto Rico until early December, and he informed Leahy that he would not occupy his post for several weeks while he familiarized himself with island affairs. Thus, Fernández García remained as head of the Justice Department until late October.[152] He was succeeded by the Assistant Attorney General, Enrique Campos del Toro, who served as Acting Attorney General until mid January 1940. Campos del Toro was as despised by the *Coalición* as his former boss, since he had directed the "Capitol Racket" investigation. Malcolm's belated assumption of the post did not fully satisfy the *Coalición*, which continued to claim that the agency was "full of Liberals and *Laboristas*."[153] Malcolm eventually obtained Campos del Toro's resignation and moderated the agency's aggressive enforcement of the 500-Acre Law. Significantly, Fernández García, Campos del Toro, and Miguel Guerra Mondragón, three of the ranking functionaries at the Justice Department, soon joined the *Partido Popular*.

The *Coalición* clashed with other high officials in Leahy's cabinet and public corporations, such as Antonio Luchetti, Head of the Water Resources Authority, Treasurer Sancho Bonet, Commissioner of the Interior Colonel José Colom, and even with the Republican Commissioner of Education, José Gallardo. In an editorial published just prior to Leahy's arrival, *El País*, the PUR newspaper, applauded the removal of Ernest Gruening and Benigno Fernández García, but simultaneously demanded that Antonio Luchetti, José M. Gallardo, and Miles H. Fairbank should be also dismissed.[154] The issue of control over nominations to the executive and legislative branches became a major difficulty throughout Leahy's brief governorship. The internal splits in the *Coalición* parties made this issue even more critical during an election year. The governor's commitment to "non-partisanship" meant that the *Coalición* was denied political control over several key agencies, with avowed *anti-coalicionistas* being retained or named in executive positions. The speakership of the House of Representatives was already threatened due to García Mendez's thinly veiled connection to the emerging *Tripartista* formation. Plus, the continued presence of Prudencio Rivera in the Cabinet, and the eventual appointment of Manuel V. Domenech as Treasurer, left the Socialist Party without any important executive position, placing further strains on the *Coalición* pact.

TABLE 5.2
DISTRIBUTION OF MAIN EXECUTIVE POSTS IN LEAHY'S GOVERNMENT

Executive Council

Attorney General:
B. Fernández García (*muñocista* Liberal, until October 31, 1939)
George A. Malcolm (took office on January 13, 1940, "colonial careerist")

Treasurer:
R. Sancho Bonet (maverick Socialist, resigned on May 17, 1940, due to death threat, opposed by Bolívar Pagán)
Manuel V. Domenech (named on May 18, 1940, Republican declared persona non grata by the *Coalición* in 1935, nomination strongly opposed by Socialist Party and Martínez Nadal)

Commissioner of Interior:
Col. José E. Colom (Republican, reappointment opposed by the *Coalición*)

Commissioner of Agriculture:
F. López Domínguez (Republican, until December 27, 1939)
Isidoro Colón (named on December 28, 1939, *Coalición* Republican)

Commissioner of Labor:
Prudencio Rivera Martínez (leader of the *Partido Laborista Puro* and founder of *Tripartismo*, resigned on October 16, just prior to 1940 elections)

Commissioner of Health:
E. Garrido Morales (named in 1933, *Coalición* Republican)

Commissioner of Education:
José M. Gallardo (Republican, accused by *Coalición* of joining *Tripartismo*)

Other important executive posts

Auditor:
Leslie A. Mcleod (Winship's crony, resigned on October 1939)
Guy J. Swope (former Democratic Congressman, named by Leahy on January 29, 1940)

Superintendent of Police:
Col. Enrique de Orbeta (appointed by Winship after Riggs's death, reappointed by Leahy)

Commander National Guard:
Brig. General Luis R. Esteves (as personnel director of PRRA conducted purge of muñocista Liberals, unaffiliated but with family connections to Liberal Party)

Water Resources Authority:
Antonio Luchetti (Republican, reappointment strongly opposed by the *Coalición*)

President of the Board, P.R. Cement Co.:
Governor William D. Leahy

Sources: Leahy's Diary, 1939-1940, op. cit.; "Sailor's Adventure in Politics, Puerto Rico 1939-1940," op. cit.; Thomas Mathews, op. cit.; Honorable William D. Leahy, Fortieth Annual Report of the Governor of Puerto Rico (San Juan: Bureau of Supplies, Printing and Transportation, 1940), p. 57; Honorable Guy J. Swope, Forty-First Annual Report of the Governor of Puerto Rico (San Juan: Bureau of Supplies, Printing and Transportation, 1941), p. 53; *The New York Times* and *El Mundo*; telephone conversation with former Governor Roberto Sánchez Vilella, September 20, 1996.

More broadly, the almost simultaneous removal of Gruening and Winship signified that a major shift in U.S. policy towards Puerto Rico had taken place in 1939.[155] These powerful functionaries had been the agents of the alliance with the *Coalición* and of the campaign against the *muñocista* Liberals. Gruening, however, had eventually fallen from grace with the *Coalición* since he was held responsible of promoting *Tripartismo*. His removal, attributed to Leahy, was applauded by the *Partido Unión Republicana*.[156]

The change confronted the legislative majority with a difficult dilemma. Attacking Ickes or Leahy threatened to broaden the breach with the Roosevelt administration, particularly in the context of a war emergency, while inaction could spell doom in the upcoming elections. For this reason, the attitude of the *coalicionista* leadership oscillated between alternating expressions of loyalty and collaboration, and scathing attacks on their policies. However, the conflict escalated in 1940, with the ill and outspoken Rafael Martínez Nadal playing a leading role in denouncing the new anti-*Coalición* policy. Thus, the nomination of Leahy and the gradual reconstruction of Ickes's influence over Puerto Rican

affairs were clearly adverse developments for the majority party's relations with Washington.

This did not mean that Washington had shifted its support for Muñoz
Marín's emerging political force. He was still considered "unreliable,"
his electoral strength was unknown but generally underestimated, and
the conservative Leahy felt no sympathies for his "radical New Deal"
stance at a time when it was on the wane in the U.S. Leahy's views were
shared by the military authorities in Puerto Rico who closely followed,
in their intelligence reports, the founding of the *Partido Popular* and its
electoral campaign. In June 1938, they referred to the *muñocista* Liberals
as "radicals . . . in favor of immediate independence."[157] In 1940, the
reports still defined the new party as "the most radical," referred to its
"penetration" by Commmunists and Nationalists, noted Muñoz's attempts to "inject himself into the labor movement," and classified the
most prominent leaders as "pink leftists," Nationalists or pro-independence. However, they discounted any possibility of the party obtaining
sufficient electoral support to control either of the legislative chambers.[158]
Tripartismo, or an alliance of *Tripartismo* with the PUR, was Washington's
preferred alternative. This can be glimpsed both from Leahy's account
of his governorship and the anti-*coalicionista* thrust of this policies. The
Coalición insistently accused Leahy of being biased in favor *Tripartismo*
and of even breaking the law to protect García Méndez, one of its main
leaders. After the elections, the adverse results were attributed to
Washington's role.

The pro-*Tripartismo* bias can also be seen in the intelligence reports
filed by the commanding officer of the Puerto Rico Department of the
Army, Brigadier General Edmund L. Daley, in 1939 and 1940. In July
1939, a report said that the new electoral alliance "should be the strongest party in Puerto Rico" and another called it "the proposed new conservative, pro-American party, in process of formation."[159]

However, the change in personnel did remove two major obstacles
to an understanding with the populist movement once it demonstrated
in 1940 its considerable and unexpected electoral strength, while, on
the other hand, the anti-*coalicionista* thrust of colonial policy redefined
the circumstances of the electoral campaign and the elections. With regard to the latter, it opened an opportunity for Muñoz to approach a

generally receptive governor concerning crucial political and electoral issues in the months preceding the decisive 1940 elections.

Additionally, the shared perception among strategic political figures that the *Partido Popular* did not constitute an imminent threat, or that it would become a strong "third force," operated in its favor. This is emphasized by Muñoz in his history of the party and his memoirs.[160] Thus, the decision of the *Coalición*-controlled legislature to grant the new party the status of main party can be understood not merely as an expression of commitment to "democratic principles," but also as a move designed to strengthen a countervailing force to *Tripartismo*. Likewise, Leahy's efforts to ensure "clean and fair" elections were not necessarily designed to open the way for a victory of the "radical" *populares*, but that of the oppositional formation considered the "strongest," i.e. *Tripartismo*. Muñoz deftly maneuvered to penetrate through the cracks in U.S. policy and insular politics.

NOTES

1. "Almirante Leahy Gobdor. de Pto. Rico", *El Mundo*, May 13, 1939, p. 1. Also, "Nombramiento de Leahy relacionado con defensa nacional," *El Mundo*, May 13, 1939, p. 1; and, "Leahy to Succeed Governor Winship," *The New York Times*, May 13, 1939, p. 1.

2. Jesús T. Piñero to Ruby Black, 15 May 1939. Ruby Black Collection, Box 4, Folder 13, Document 105, Centro de Investigaciones Históricas.

3. "Nombramiento de Leahy trata de eliminar fuentes de disensión," *El Mundo*, May 14, 1939, p. 1.

4. "Emplearán en la isla más de $30,000,000 en el próximo año," *El Mundo*, May 15, 1939, p. 1.

5. "Hay planes para industrializar a Puerto Rico," *El Mundo*, May 19, 1939, p. 1.

6. See, press clippings on his nomination in Leahy's scrapbook, William D. Leahy's Papers, Manuscript Division, Library of Congress.

7. "Marcantonio insiste en que Winship fue destituido," *El Mundo*, May 12, 1939, p. 5.

8. Blanton Winship, Governor, to the President, June 3, 1939, FDR Library, FDR Papers, OF 400, Container 25, Folder P.R.

9. Franklin D. Roosevelt to Honorable Blanton Winship, Governor, June 5, 1939. FDR Library, FDR Papers, OF 400, Container 25, Folder P.R.

10. Harold L. Ickes, The Secret of Harold L. Ickes, *The Inside Struggle* 1936-1939, Volume II (New York: Simon and Schuster, 1954), p. 641.

11. Harold L. Ickes, "Secret Diary" (ms), Saturday April 29, 1939, p. 3401, Manuscript Division, Library of Congress. This entry has been deleted in the published version of Ickes' diary, *The Inside Struggle*, 1936-1939, op. cit., p. 623.

12. E.M.W., "Memorandum for the President," May 3, 1939. FDR Library, FDR Papers, OF 400, Container 25, Folder P.R.

13. E.M.W., "Memorandum for the President," May 3, 1939. FDR Library, FDR Papers, OF 400, Container 25, Folder P.R.

14. "Cablegrafían dándole respaldo al gobernador Blanton Winship," *El Mundo*, May 4, 1939, p. 1; "El cablegrama que dirigió Martínez Nadal a Roosevelt," *El Mundo*, May 5, 1939, p.1; also, *The New York Times*, "Winship's Friends Urge His Retention, Believe Sec. Ickes is Trying to Force Him Out," May 5, 1939, p. 8.

15. Franklin D. Roosevelt to Hon. Santiago Iglesias, May 12, 1939. FDR Library, FDR Papers, OF 400, Container 25, Folder P.R. See, also, "Nombramiento de Leahy decidido hace algún tiempo," *El Mundo*, May 15, 1939, p. 1.

16. Vito Marcantonio to Franklin Delano Roosevelt, April 27, 1939. FDR Library, FDR Papers, OF 400, Container 25, Folder P.R.

17. See, Translation of article appearing in "La Voz," May 1, 1939, "Marcantonio Says Winship Should be Removed." FDR Library, FDR Papers, OF 400, Container 25, Folder P.R.

18. Harold L. Ickes, "Secret Diary" (ms), op. cit., p. 3417.

19. "Puerto Rico pierde una asignación de $2,945,000," *El Mundo*, May 6, 1939, p. 1.

20. "Interior Department Press Release," May 5, 1939. Folder 13, Document 97, Ruby Black Collection, Centro de Investigaciones Históricas. The Spanish translation is included in Reece B. Bothwell González, *Puerto Rico: Cien Años de Lucha Política*, Volume III (Río Piedras: Editorial Universitaria, 1979), pp. 195-6.

21. "Blanton Winship calificó de 'tontos' en Nueva York los rumores que circulan en cuanto a que renunciaría como gobernador," *El Mundo*, April 28, 1939, p. 1.

22. "Winship decide retener gobernación indefinidamente," *El Mundo*, May 9, 1939, p. 1. *The New York Times* carried a similar report on that same day (p. 5).

23. It should also be noted that, since 1936, Ickes had been somewhat sidelined in terms of Puerto Rican policy-making as Roosevelt had chosen to support the hard-line course drawn by Gruening and Winship; but a change in the governorship could help him regain a greater degree of control over Puerto Rican policy making.

24. "Sen. Martínez Nadal Charges U.S. with Fascist Control," *The New York Times*, March 27, 1939, p. 4; also, "Que Puerto Rico está esclavo dijo ayer Martínez Nadal", *El Mundo*, March 25, 1939, p. 1.

25. Resident Commissioner Santiago Iglesias inserted Martínez Nadal's controversial speech in the Congressional Record. See *Congressional Record Appendix*, April 10, 1939, pp. 5637-38, Box 4, Folder 13, Document 77, Ruby Black Collection, Centro de Investigaciones Históricas.

26. Col. John W. Wright, Commanding 65th Infantry Regiment, "Weekly Summary of Certain Political Activities," March 29, and April 12, 1939, R.G. 165, Military Intelligence Division (MID) 1917-1941, Box 3112, U.S. National Archives.

27. "El Gobernador trajo instrucciones de Washington," *El Mundo*, May 12, 1939, p. 1.

28. "Hay planes para terminar mañana sesión legislativa," *El Mundo*, May 12, 1939, p. 4.

29. Eliseo Combas Guerra, *En torno a La Fortaleza*, Winship (San Juan: Biblioteca de Autores Puertorriqueños, 1950), pp. 242-4.

30. "Martínez Nadal no contribuirá a aprobar ninguna ley que le arrebate facultades al pueblo de un modo indirecto," *El Mundo*, February 18, 1939, p. 1.

31. "El gobernador trajo instrucciones de Washington," op. cit., p. 1; Eliseo Combas Guerra, op. cit., pp. 243-46; also, footnote 18 above.

32. Eliseo Combas Guerra, op. cit., p. 209.

33. Epifanio Fiz Jiménez, *El Racket del Capitolio (Gobierno de la Coalición Republico-Socialista)* (San Juan: Editorial Esther, 1944); also, "Justicia tiene ya prácticamente decidido acusar," *El Mundo*, April 22, 1939, p. 1.

34. See, for example, "Martínez Nadal le escribe a Gruening que habrá demostraciones si nombran a Fernández García Gobernador interino," *El Mundo*, June 9, 1939, p. 1; and, "Washington quiere retener a Fernández García," *El Mundo*, June 10, 1939, p. 1.

35. "Justicia rechazará hoy ultimátum del Comité legislativo," *El Mundo*, April 12, 1939, p. 1; and, "Se temió un grave encuentro entre Campos y Bolívar Pagán," *El Mundo*, April 13, 1939, p. 1.

36 "Campos del Toro proyecta salir hacia Washington," *El Mundo*, April 14, 1939, p. 1.

37. "Los Liberales se retiran de la legislatura," *El Mundo*, April 14, 1939, p. 1; also, "Winship no logró Liberales volvieran a legislatura," *El Mundo*, April 15, 1939, p. 5.

38. "En el Senado se enmienda presupuesto. . .," *El Mundo*, April 23, 1939, p. 1.

39. See *Congressional Record*, Appendix, February 15, 1939, Box 4, Folder 13, Document 32, Ruby Black Collection, Centro de Investigaciones Históricas.

40. The Spanish version of this important speech is reproduced in Félix Ojeda Reyes, *Vito Marcantonio y Puerto Rico* (Río Piedras: Huracán, 1978), pp. 67-94. See, also, "Marcantonio Hails Winship Dismissal," *The New York Daily Worker*, May 22, 1939, p. 1.

41. "Informe a los campesinos de Puerto Rico sobre el alegado 'racket' –o robalete– del Capitolio," *El Batey*, Year 1, No. 3 (Second fortnight, April 1939), p. 1; also, "La nueva Alianza," *El Batey*, Year 1, NO. 6 (First fortnight, August 1939), p. 6.

42. Luis Muñoz Marín, *Memorias, 1898-1940* (San Juan: Inter-American University Press, 1982), pp. 185-6. Author's translation.

43. "Aquí somos unos muñecos, dice Martínez Nadal," *El Mundo*, May 17, 1939, p. 1.

44. "Winship declarado hijo adoptivo de Puerto Rico," *El Mundo*, May 19, 1939, p. 10.

45. "Winship to Get a Degree, Puerto Rico University Adds Governor to Honors List," *The New York Times*, May 24, 1939, p. 3.

46. *Puerto Rico Ilustrado*, July 1 and 18, 1939, photo section.

47. "La asamblea legislativa acordó solicitar estadidad," *El Mundo*, May 20, 1939, p. 1; also "Estadidad a la mayor brevedad posible y en el interim gobernador electivo", *El Mundo*, June 1, 1939, p. 10.

48. For an analysis of the status proposals presented in Congress during this period, see, José Trías Monge, *Historia Constitucional de Puerto Rico*, Volume II (Río Piedras: Editorial Universitaria, 1981), pp. 218-34. He notes that neither Resident Commissioners Santiago Iglesias nor Bolívar Pagán were able to get any action from Congress apart from some minor amendments to the Jones Act (p. 233).

49. "To Enable the People of Puerto Rico to Form a Constitution and State Government and be Admitted into the Union on an Equal Footing with the States" (HR 6986), House of Representatives, 76th Congress, 1st Session, June 26, 1939. Box 4, Folder 13, Document 119, Ruby Black Collection, Centro de Investigaciones Históricas.

50. A huge banner placed above the stage read "Puerto Rico 49th State," *Puerto Rico Ilustrado*, July 1, 1939, photo section.

51. "Puerto Rico Is Toasted By Winship as 49th State," *The New York Times*, June 20, 1939, p. 44.

52. Enrique Bird Piñero, *Don Luis Muñoz Marín, el poder de la excelencia* (San Juan: Fundación Luis Muñoz Marín, 1991), pp. 78-79. Author's translation.

53. Luis Muñoz Marín to Arthur Garfield Hays, June 14, 1937. Box 3, Folder 11, Document 115, Ruby Black Collection, Centro de Investigaciones Históricas.

54. "Muñoz Marín comenta el discurso de Leahy, la cooperación que ofrece el Partido Popular al gobernador," *El Mundo*, September 12, 1939, p. 6.

55. "Muñoz Marín conferencia con el nuevo gobernador Leahy," *El Batey*, Year I, No. 8 (October 1939), p. 4. Author's translation.

56. Muna Lee to Ruby Black, November 8, 1939. Box 4, Folder 12, Document 151, Ruby Black Collection, Centro de Investigaciones Históricas.

57. Luis Muñoz Marín to Ruby Black, January 8, 1940. Box 5, Folder 14, Document 2, Ruby Black Collection, Centro de Investigaciones Históricas.

58. The statement was signed by Oswald Garrison Villard, President, Prof. William

L. Nunn, Vice-President, Earl P. Hanson, Carleton Beals, Arthur Garfield Hays, Representative Vito Marcantonio, Rockwell Kent, Walter Mc K Jones, Vilhjalmur Stefanson, Charlotte Leeper, David Rein, Gifford Cochran and Mr. and Mrs. Bourne. See, "Press Statement", American Civil Liberties Union, May 15, 1939. Box 4, Folder 13, Document 103, Ruby Black Collection, Centro de Investigaciones Históricas.

59. See, for example, "Governor Leahy," *Providence Bulletin*, May 16, 1939; "Liberties Union Against Leahy" (Editorial), *Miami Herald*, May 16, 1939; and, "Changing Governors in Puerto Rico," *New York Herald Tribune*, May 16, 1939.

60. See, the numerous letters of recommendation for this post, among them those of Ruby Black and Muñoz Marín, in Ruby Black Collection, Box 4, Folder 12, Documents 70-111, Centro de Investigaciones Históricas.

61. See, comments by Santiago Iglesias, May 11, 1939. Box 4, Folder 13, Document 101, Ruby Black Collection, Centro de Investigaciones Históricas.

62. Robert W. Claiborne to Ruby Black, May 13, 1939. Box 4, Folder 13, Document 102, Ruby Black Collection, Centro de Investigaciones Históricas.

63. Oswald Garrison Villard, "Puerto Rico S.O.S.," *The Nation*, June 21, 1939, pp. 728-729.

64. William D. Leahy, "Sailor's Adventure in Politics, Puerto Rico 1939-1940", p. 4. William D. Leahy's Papers, State Historical Society of Wisconsin. I have edited two versions of Leahy's Puerto Rican memoirs in *Las memorias de Leahy, los relatos del Almirante William D. Leahy sobre su gobernación de Puerto Rico (1939-1940)*, (San Juan, Fundación Luis Muñoz Marín, 2002). In this book, however, I cite from the original documents.

65. Ibid.

66 Fleet Admiral William D. Leahy, *I Was There, The Personal Story of the Chief of Staff to Presidents Roosevelt and Truman Based on His Notes and Diaries Made at the Time* (New York: Whittlesey House, McGraw-Hill, 1950).

67. "Nombrados los comités de la Convención Económica", *El Mundo*, 16 February 1939, pp. 1, 15.

68. For Muñoz's account of his role in the "Congress of the Unemployed" see, "Libro, borrador 2, 1970," p. 480, Sección XI, Material de y sobre Luis Muñoz Marín, Material para el libro *Memorias*, Box YY, Luis Muñoz Marín Foundation. This portion of his manuscript was left out of his official memoirs. See, also, "Ustedes mismos deben resolver su propio destino, Eso acordó el congreso económico," *El Batey*, Year 1, No. 2 (April 1939), p. 2.

69. "Muñoz Marín dice que la Convención Económica supo distinguir entre la política y la politiquería al discutir el 'status,'" *El Mundo*, March 14, 1939, p. 4.

70. "Que el Congreso Económico no debió tratar 'status,'" *El Mundo*, March 14, 1939, p. 1; "A que se convierta en ideal solicitud de plebiscito hace objeción el Presidente del Partido Socialista, señor Bolívar Pagán," *El Mundo*, March 15, 1939, p. 5; and, "El speaker García Méndez también opina fue un error plantear 'status' en el reciente Congreso Económico, *El Mundo*, March 15, 1939, p. 4.

71. "Leahy escuchó ayer a una delegación Puertorriqueña," *El Mundo*, May 26, 1939, p. 1.

72. "Leahy habló con el Presidente sobre Puerto Rico," *El Mundo*, June 1, 1939, p. 1.

73. "Roosevelt nombra junta inter departamental para Puerto Rico," *El Mundo*, May 31, 1939, p. 1.

74. "Entró en funciones Junta Interdepartamental," *El Mundo*, June 1, 1939, p. 1.

75. "Leahy mantiene aún en reserva su programa," *El Mundo*, May 30, 1939, p. 1.

76. Thomas Mathews, *La política puertorriqueña y el Nuevo Trato* (Río Piedras: Editorial Universitaria, 1979), pp. 58, 84, 249.

77. "Leahy abandonará Isla si no logra hacer buena labor," *El Mundo*, June 5, 1939, p. 1.

78. William D. Leahy to Admiral Claude Bloch, 17 May 1939, Library of Congress, Manuscript Division, cited in Henry H. Adams, *Witness to Power, The Life of Fleet Admiral William D. Leahy* (Annapolis: Naval Institute Press, 1985), p. 116.

79. Ibid., pp. 112-7.

80 ."For Puerto Rico in case Leahy comes back," September 29, 1939, FDR Library, FDR Papers, OF 400, Container 25, Folder P.R. Wright's post included responsibility for Army intelligence, which closely followed political developments from a politically conservative perspective. See, "Weekly Summary of Subversive Activities - Puerto Rico Area," later entitled "Weekly Summary of Certain Political Activities," for 1938 to the summer 1939, R.G. 165, MID 1917-41, Box 3112, National Archives. After the establishment of the Puerto Rico Department of the Army in mid-1939, weekly intelligence reports were signed by its commanding officer, Brig. General Edmund L. Daley.

81. Gruening had obtained the removal of the brash and hard-drinking Colonel Otis R. Cole as commander of the 65th Infantry Regiment and his replacement by Colonel John Womack Wright. He had a very high opinion of Wright and the *Coalición* requested that he be promoted to the rank of Brigadier General. Ernest Gruening, *Many Battles, The Autobiography of Ernest Gruening* (New York: Livewright, 1973), pp. 194-95, 209.

82. Harold L. Ickes, *The Secret Diary of Harold L. Ickes, The Lowering Clouds, 1939-1941*, Volume III, op. cit., p. 6.

83. "Martínez Nadal conferenció ayer con el Almirante Leahy," *El Mundo*, June 13, 1939; and "Leahy urge cooperación de todos los grupos," *El Mundo*, June 15, 1939, p. 1.

84. "Conferenció Ickes delegación coalicionista," El Mundo, June 20, 1939, p. 1. Rafael Martínez Nadal, who had sharply attacked Ickes, did not form part of this group that included Bolívar Pagán, Santiago Iglesias and Alfonso Valdés. Instead, Rafael Hernández Usera attended.

85. "Ickes, Gruening y Leahy conferencian sobre Puerto Rico," *El Mundo*, June 24, 1939, p. 1.

86. "Leahy inquiere si podría rodearse de funcionarios que no hagan política activa," *El Mundo*, June 21, 1939, p. 1; and, "Leahy se rodeará de grupo puertorriqueño no-partidista," *El Mundo*, July 2, 1939, p. 1.

87. "Puerto Rico Astir Over Leahy Plan," *The New York Times*, July 26, 1939, p. 11.

88. "Winship Asks Aid for Puerto Rico," *The New York Times*, July 26, 1939, p. 6; see, also, "El día dedicado a Puerto Rico en la feria de Nueva York," *El Mundo*, July 30, 1939, p. 1.

89. "Ernest Gruening nombrado gobernador de Alaska, Leahy le dijo a Roosevelt que no quiere continuar los feudos políticos desarrollados en la isla," *El Mundo*, September 4, 1939, p. 1.

90. Harold L. Ickes, *The Secret Diary of Harold L. Ickes, The Inside Struggle, 1936-1939*, Volume II, op. cit., entry for June 4, 1939, p. 641.

91. Harold L. Ickes, *The Secret Diary of Harold L. Ickes, The Lowering Clouds, 1939-1941*, Volume III, op. cit., pp. 6, 33, 70, 160.

92. See, for example, Pedro Juan Barbosa, "El Dr. Ernest Gruening favorece el Estado para Puerto Rico," *El Mundo*, November 27, 1939, p. 13.

93. See, "Muñoz Marín considera que las palabras de Gruening contienen un espíritu de verdadero americanismo y genuino liberalismo," *El Mundo*, November 24, 1939, reproduced in Reece B. Bothwell González, *Puerto Rico: cien años de lucha política*, Volume III (Río Piedras: Editorial Universitaria, 1979), Document No. 65, pp. 212-3; and, "El pueblo mismo deberá decidir su 'status' político, en una elección separada de todo otro 'issue,'" in ibid., Document No. 68, pp. 217-9.

94. "Leahy discute con Roosevelt asuntos de Puerto Rico," *El Mundo*, July 29, 1939, p. 1.

95. See, Roosevelt's letter in "William D. Leahy Diaries, 1939-1940," William D. Leahy's Papers, Manuscript Division, Library of Congress.

96. Ibid.

97. Eric Larrabee, *Commander in Chief, Franklin Delano Roosevelt, His Lieutenants and their War* (New York: Harper & Row, 1987), pp. 20-21.

98. "William Leahy Diaries, 1939-1940," op. cit., p. 3.

99. "Sailor's Adventure in Politics, Puerto Rico 1939-1940," op. cit., p. 14.

100. Ibid., pp. 9, 28. Author's empasis.

101. Harold L. Ickes, *The Secret Diary of Harold L. Ickes, The Inside Struggle, 1936-1939*, Volume II, op. cit., entry for May 20, 1939, p. 615.

102. "Ickes espera que Leahy sea gobernador civil," *El Mundo*, July 7, 1939, p. 1.

103. "Leahy estudiará los problemas económicos de la Isla, dice está completamente desligado de sus actividades anteriores," *El Mundo*, September 14, 1939, p. 1.

104. "Sailor's Adventure in Politics, Puerto Rico 1939-1940," op. cit., p. 8.

105. Idem.

106. Major George Field Eliot, *The Ramparts We Watch: A Study of Problems of American National Defense* (New York: Reynal & Hitchcock, 1938). See, also, Chapter 3.

107. Leahy's Diary, 1939-1940, op. cit., pp. 6-7, *passim*.

108. Robert E. Sherwood, *Roosevelt and Hopkins: An Intimate History* (New York: Harper & Row, 1948), pp. 101-6. Also, Kenneth Davies, *FDR: Into the Storm 1937-1940* (New York: Random House,1993), pp. 378, 380-1, Frank Freidel, *Franklin D. Roosevelt: A Rendezvous with Destiny* (New York: Little Brown, 1990), p. 310.

109. William E. Leuchtenburg, *Franklin D. Roosevelt and the New Deal, 1932-1940* (New York: Harper Torchbooks, 1963), pp. 272-4.

110. It was composed by Melvin J. Maas, George J Bates, Sterling W. Cole, Colgate W. Dardden, William E. Hess, William S. Jacobson, Robert L. Morton and Jed Johnson. See, "Isla Grande inspeccionada por subcomité naval," *El Mundo*, April 4, 1939, p. 1. See, also, on early 1939 military preparations Chapter 3 of this book.

111. E. P. Forrester, *Admiral Raymond A. Spruance, U.S.N.* (Washington, D.C.: GPO, 1966), Chapter 2; also, Marion D. Francis, *History of the Antilles Department*, Section II, Chapter 1, ms, Antilles Department, San Juan, Puerto Rico, October, 1946, pp. 1-12.

112. Patrick Abbazzia, *Mr. Roosevelt's Navy, The Private War of the U.S. Atlantic Fleet, 1939-1932* (Annapolis: Naval Institute Press, 1975), pp. 46-8.

113. An author has recently noted that US military planning for the Caribbean during this early period and the base system developed were "airpower oriented," which later proved to be a limitation during the German submarine campaign. See, Gaylord T.M. Kelshall, *The U-Boat War in the Caribbean* (Annapolis: Naval Institute Press, 1994), p. 7.

114. For a general discussion of military preparations in Puerto Rico and the Caribbean during 1938-1939, see, Stetson Conn and Byron Fairchild, *The Western Hemisphere, The Framework of Hemisphere Defense* (Washington, D.C.: Office of the Chief of Military History, US Army, 1978), pp. 9-25; and, Stetson Conn, Rose C. Engelman and Byron Fairchild, *The Western Hemisphere, Guarding the United States and Its Outposts* (Washington, D.C.: Office of the Chief of Military History, US Army, 1964), Chapters 1-3, 12.

115. "Sailor's Adventure in Politics, Puerto Rico 1939-1940," op. cit., pp. 3-4.

116. Ibid., p. 4.

117. Harwood Hull, "Leahy Takes Over Puerto Rico Post," *The New York Times*, September 12, 1939, p. 17.

118. *Puerto Rico Ilustrado* published the photographs of the inauguration ceremonies amidst a large number of photographs on the outbreak of war in Europe. See, the issues of September 16 and 23, 1939, photo section.

119. "Declaraciones de Winship sobre la situación de la Isla," *El Mundo*, September 10, 1939, p. 1.

120. "Cuota azucarera suspendida temporalmente," *El Mundo*, September 12, 1939, p. 1.

121. Harold L. Ickes, *The Secret Diary of Harold L. Ickes, The Lowering Clouds, 1939-1941*, Volume III, op. cit., entry for September 16, 1939, p. 3.

122. "Llegó en avión alto funcionario de la WPA para cooperar con el gobernador Leahy en el desarrollo del plan de los $10,000,000," *El Mundo*, September 12, 1939, p. 1.

123. See, for example, "Puerto Rico Sees Bright Future As Major Defense Area in Caribbean," *The Economic Review*, Vol. 4, No. 3 (June 1939), pp. 25-32, 65.

124. "Leahy's Inaugural Address," Leahy's Papers, State Historical Society of Wisconsin. A Spanish language version of the speech is included in Antonio Quiñones Calderón, *Pensando a Puerto Rico, un siglo de discursos inaugurales de los gobernadores de Puerto Rico* (San Juan: The Credibility Group, 1996), pp. 190-93.

125. "La reacción al discurso inaugural de Leahy, expresiones expresadas por algunos de los líderes políticos insulares," *El Mundo*, September 12, 1939, p. 5.

126. "Otro morador en La Fortaleza," *Puerto Rico Ilustrado*, September 23, 1939, p. 1.

127. Brig. Gen. Edmund L. Daley, "Weekly Summary of Certain Political Activities," September 16, 1939, R.G. 165, MID 1917-41, Box 3112, U.S. National Archives.

128. See, John Major, "The Navy Plans for War, 1937-1941", in Kenneth J. Hagan, In *Peace and War, Interpretations of American Naval History*, 1775-1978 (Westport, Conn.: Greenwood Press, 1978), pp. 248-9; also, Samuel Eliot Morison, *The Battle of the Atlantic, September 1939-May 1943, History of United States Naval Operations in World War II*, Volume I (Boston: Little, Brown and Co., 1947), pp. 14-5.

129. "El comienzo de las obras de defensa en P.R. ha sido adelantado por seis meses por lo menos debido a los últimos acontecimientos," *El Mundo*, September 17, 1939, p. 1.

130. Caribbean Defense Command, Antilles Department, Historical Section, "A Preliminary Study of Garrisons (Part I)," March, 1946, p. 16.

131. Samuel Eliot Morison, op. cit., p. 15; also, Patrick Abbazzia, op. cit., Chapter 5.

132. Leahy's Diary, 1939-1940, op. cit., pp. 6-8.

133. Leahy's Diaries, 1939-1940, op. cit., entry for December 15, 1939, p. 21.

134. Ibid., p. 7.

135. Harold L. Ickes, *The Secret Diary of Harold L. Ickes, The Lowering Clouds, 1939-1941*, Volume III, op. cit., entry for October 20, 1939, pp. 42-3.

136. Leahy probably refers to the Works Progress Administration (WPA).

137. See, Governor William D. Leahy to Harold D. Smith, Director Bureau of the Budget, September 29, 1939; and, Harold D. Smith, Memorandum for the President, November 25, 1939, FDR Library, FDR Papers, OF 400, Container 25, Folder P.R.

138. See, for example, Franklin D. Roosevelt to Paul V. McNutt, Federal Security Administrator, November 30, 1939, FDR Library, FDR Papers, OF 400, Container 25, Folder P.R.

139. Thomas Mathews, op. cit., p. 151.

140. Harold L. Ickes, *The Secret Diary of Harold L. Ickes, The Inside Struggle 1936-1939*, Volume II, op. cit., entry for June 4, 1939, p. 641.

141. Harold L. Ickes, The Secret Diary of Harold L. Ickes, *The Lowering Clouds 1939-1941*, Volume III, op. cit., entry for January 21, 1940, p. 105.

142. Harold L. Ickes to the President, October 9, 1939, and Memorandum for the Secretary of the Interior from F.D.R., October 10, 1939, FDR Library, FDR Papers, OF 400, Container 25, Folder P.R.

143. "Renunció el auditor de Puerto Rico, Sr. McLeod, para sucederle se informa será nombrado el ex-congresista Guy J. Swope," *El Mundo*, October 24, 1939, p. 1.

144. "Que el gobernador Leahy no debe sostener a Lanzetta, dice en una carta que escribe desde Washington el señor McK Jones," *El Mundo*, Novemeber 27, 1939, p. 12.

145. "Puerto Rico: Gibraltar or Achilles Heel?," *Hemisphere* (February 1940), p. 4.

146. "Leahy acepta la renuncia de Lanzetta," *La Democracia*, July 21, 1940, p. 1.

147. "Leahy dice que ha recibido quejas contra Rivera Martínez, pero agrega no le ha dado seria consideración a cambios en el gabinete", *El Mundo*, October 5, 1939, p. 1.; and, "Bolívar Pagán dice él firmaría lo dicho por Valdés, sostiene Leahy ha pedido opiniones sbre candidatos le han sugerido," *El Mundo*, October 13, 1939, p. 4.

148. Reece B. Bothwell González, Puerto Rico: *Cien años de lucha política*, Volume III, op. cit., document No. 82, p. 265.

149. See, José Trías Monge, op. cit., pp. 327-8.

150. Brig. Gen. Edmund L. Daley, Commander Puerto Rico Department, "Weekly Summary of Certain Political Activities," R.G. 165, MID 1917-41, Box 3112, U. S. National Archives.

151. "Ernest Gruening nombrado gobernador de Alaska, Leahy le dijo a Roosevelt que no quiere continuar los feudos políticos desarrollados en la isla", *El Mundo*, September 4, 1939, p. 1.

152. See, George A. Malcolm, *American Colonial Careerist, Half a Century of Official Life and Personal Experiences in the Philippines and Puerto Rico* (Boston: The Christopher Publishing House, 1957), Chapter 9.

153. See, "Martínez Nadal, Valdés y Malcolm llamados a Fortaleza," *El Mundo*, February 7, 1940, p. 1; and, "Malcolm en conferencia con Leahy," *El Imparcial*, February 4, 1940, p. 1.

154. "Purulencias por extirpar" (Editorial), *El País*, September 7, 1939, p. 4.

155. José Trías Monge overlooks the significance of this change as an expression of revision of policy towards Puerto Rico: "The experience suffered with Winship was not enough to persuade the President of the need to reexamine his policy toward Puerto Rico. His next envoy to the governorship was Admiral William D. Leahy." José Trías Monge, op. cit., p. 198. Author's translation.

156. "Editorial," *El País*, September 7, 1939, p. 4.

157. Co. John W. Wright, "Weekly Summary of Subversive Activities - Puerto Rico Area," June 15, 1938, R.G. 165, MID 1917-41, Box 3112, U. S. National Archives.

158. See the weekly summaries of "subversive" and "certain political" activities for the period 1938-1941, R.G. MID 1917-41, U.S. National Archives.

159.. Brig. Gen. Edmund L. Daley, "Weekly Summary of Certain Political Activities," 18 and 19 July 1939, R.G. 165, MID 1917-41, Box 3112, U.S. National Archives.

160. Luis Muñoz Marín, *La historia del Partido Popular Democrático* (San Juan: Editorial El Batey, 1984), pp. 14-21; and, "Libro, Borrador 2 - 1970", op. cit., pp. 492-3.

CHAPTER 6

LA LIJA: PACIFYING A COLONY FOR WAR

García Méndez greets Leahy on his arrival aboard the SS Coamo.
El Mundo *Collection, UPR.*

LA LIJA:
PACIFYING A COLONY FOR WAR

From September to December 1939, the terse prose of Leahy's diary provides few indications of the looming conflict with the *Coalición*. He recorded, with few comments, some of his official activities. They included, among other things, meetings with military officers, federal functionaries, and visits with congressmen, the coordination of WPA activities, the inspection of PRRA projects and the supervision of its administration, a tour of the island in late October, and official ceremonies and receptions. Brief notes on the progress of the war were also interspersed in this text. However, the paucity of references to Puerto Rican government affairs and political issues is striking. They are mentioned as if no serious controversy or conflict surrounded them.

The *Coalición* had unsuccessfully tried to prevent General Winship's dismissal and had later showered him with honors. But it had been careful not to attack the Admiral. *El País*, the Republican newspaper, had praised Leahy for his alleged part in the removal of Ernest Gruening and Benigno Fernández García, claiming that his "beneficent influence" was being felt before his arrival in Puerto Rico. It also expressed confidence that his stay would "be of great benefit to the interests of our people."[1] Bolívar Pagán, President of the Socialist Party, Alfonso Valdés, Interim President of PUR, and other *coalicionista* leaders publicly complimented Leahy for his inauguration speech and gave him a warm reception.

A brief political honeymoon followed the arrival of the new governor. Senator Alfonso Valdés, after submitting to Leahy a list of economic proposals, commented to the press that "the more I talk to the governor, the more I like him [and] the better the impression he makes in me." Valdés's proposals were broadly aimed at strengthening the sugar industry, but they also contained a extraordinary scheme for the U.S.

government to promote the settlement of 30,000 to 40,000 Puerto Rican families in the Dominican Republic and Venezuela.[2]

However, conflicts between the governor and the *Coalición* did not take long to manifest themselves and escalate into strong attacks by Valdés in November. The disagreements during this period had to do mainly with control over appointments to important executive and judicial posts and access to patronage. At stake was the capacity to dispense government employment both in agencies of the government of Puerto Rico and in the huge bureaucracy and work force created by Federal programs such as WPA and PRRA. This was a crucial political issue, particularly in an election year, since clientelism and the spoils system were important features of the prevalent pattern of party politics. High levels of unemployment, widespread poverty, and the large role played in the economy by government employment enhanced the strategic importance of the spoils system in party competition.[3] Also, the related issue of the budget of the government of Puerto Rico also began to cause dissension between the legislative and the executive branches. After all, the effectiveness of the spoils system depended on the fiscal resources available to generate jobs and dispense favors, while the size of an election-year budget was particularly critical.

This conflict erupted in a constitutional controversy mainly concerning interpretations of the Jones Act, regarding the respective powers of the legislative branch and the governor. The *Coalición* argued that the "advice and consent" attributes of the Senate included an obligation of the governor to name officials from among those recommended by the legislative majority, since "advice" was interpreted as the authority to submit a list of acceptable candidates. If the governor did not comply, then the Senate would not "consent" to their confirmation. This implied that all posts subject to senatorial review had to be occupied by *coalicionistas* or by persons acceptable to the *Coalición*. It also permitted the distribution of important executive posts between the two majority parties as stipulated in the electoral pact.

Furthermore, the *Coalición* argued that the governor should show special deference to budgetary and other actions of the legislative branch since it represented the majority of the Puerto Rican people, while the executive branch was not democratically elected and exercised it power at the will of the U.S. President. That is, the governor should act with circumspection in the exercise of his power due to the colonial character of his post in light of the democratically elected legislature.[4] Moreover, it was stated that, by implication, acting against the will of the legislative branch was tyrannical and would lend credence to attacks on U.S. imperialism.

This *modus operandi*, generally respected by Winship unless otherwise pressed by Washington, clearly clashed with Leahy's stated aim of making "non-partisan" appointments. It also generally diminished his powers. José Trías Monge stated that during the 1930s the legislative branch had successfully encroached on the powers of the governor through several mechanisms.[5] Thus, the governor argued that the senatorial powers of advise and consent included in the Jones Act were analogous to those of the U.S. Constitution, and did not require that nominations be made from a list of candidates provided by the legislative branch.[6] Neither was he too impressed with the argument on democracy since he increasingly perceived the legislature as a collection of wily and self-serving *políticos* under the control of Bolívar Pagán and the *"excelso caudillo"* Martínez Nadal (as his newspaper *El País* called him).[7] His negative perceptions of the *Coalición*-controlled legislature, and particularly of Martínez Nadal, are contained in his memoirs of the governorship. Though less extreme, they are similar to those recorded by Harold Ickes in his diary. In Leahy's memoirs he summarizes the controversy in the following terms:

> For several years political authority in Puerto Rico was exercised by Senator Martínez Nadal of the Union Republican coalition party. . . He maintained that under the Advice and Consent provision of the Organic Act, the Senate had a right to select persons to be nominated by the Governor for public office.

> These appointments, judicial and otherwise, were approved by the Insular Senate exclusively for political advantage to the dominant party. As an example, one recommendation made to me for a municipal judge I found upon investigation to be a person on parole after conviction on a charge of murder.

> My unyielding insistence on basing nominations for public office on merit and regardless of political affiliations was a cause of continued difficulty with the Insular Senate and a persistent irritation to the dominant party.[8]

Battling the *Coalición*

On September 16, Leahy informed the Bar Association that he would aim at establishing an independent judicial branch and that this would be part of an effort to correct "irregularities in the insular government."[9] A few days later he stated that he would not convene the legislature and would retain all incumbents in their post until he informed himself on the functioning of the executive branch.[10] By early October, Lino Padrón Rivera, Vice-President of the House and Socialist supporter of Bolívar Pagán, launched an attack on Prudencio Rivera Martínez claiming that he wanted to exercise control over jobs created with WPA funds despite Leahy's "good intentions."[11] On September 27, the Socialist Party leadership promised to "battle against Leahy" if he did not dismiss Rivera Martínez.[12] The governor responded that he would maintain him in his post regardless of the charges that had been brought against him by the Socialist Party.[13]

A major dispute erupted over the way the large amount of WPA funds — over ten million dollars compared to about fifteen of the entire Puerto Rican budget — would be spent and the role the Secretary of Labor should play in their distribution. One of the problems with WPA funds was that about 14 municipalities had no credit margin with which to finance the 25 per cent in local funds required by WPA.[14] Rivera Martínez and Treasurer Sancho Bonet proposed several solutions to this problem. Rivera suggested convening the legislature, a step which Leahy had already ruled out. Sancho Bonet put forth a plan for an amnesty on tax debts that included using emergency funds in the amount of the estimated additional income.[15] However, Enrique Campos del Toro, interim Attorney General, was of the opinion that Bonet's plan was illegal since emergency funds could not be used for that purpose. The governor decided to go along with this interpretation and, consequently, the Executive Council discarded the plan.

Instead, Leahy considered an alternative plan of transferring funds for municipal roads from solvent municipalities to help those without credit margins and invited the Economic Commission of the legislature to discuss the problem.[16] This commission included the *coalicionista* legislative leadership of both chambers and excluded representation from the Liberal minority.[17] It exercised considerable power over budgetary issues. Campos del Toro had recently expressed an opinion that the commission was illegally constituted and its acts were null and void. This and other adverse legal opinions formulated by Campos del Toro, together with the issue of executive appointments, created considerable tension between Leahy and the *Coalición*. On November 24, Bolívar Pagán accused Campos del Toro of obstructing the legislative process and illegally occupying his post.[18] The following day, *El País* reported in its main headline that "Martínez Nadal informed Leahy that the Senate will not confirm appointments."[19] Alfonso Valdés had made a similar statement just a few days earlier. In what could be construed as a warning, Martínez Nadal also told the governor that his health had improved and that he would soon be back in Puerto Rico. *El Mundo* considered the political confrontation so serious that the *Coalición* could decide to boycott the upcoming legislative session.[20]

Thus, it is not surprising that Leahy's meeting with the Economic Commission on November 25 was, according to *El Mundo*, a stormy one. Leahy angered the legislative leadership by bringing up the issue of the legality of the commission and the absence of minority representation. Bolívar Pagán responded with an attack on Campos del Toro, while another member argued that the Liberals should be excluded.[21] The Speaker of the House, García Méndez, conveniently excused himself from the meeting. *El País* tried to play down the confrontational character of the meeting, but reported that the commission had demanded that Leahy recognize "their rights as the majority."[22]

However, the conflict escalated in December when the Economic Commission, despite the opinion of the Justice Department regarding its illegality, decided to formulate its own plan which consisted in appropriating $240,000 for the insolvent municipalities.[23] Leahy decided to settle the controversy immediately by stating that he would not use those funds or adopt the commission's plan, since that body was unconstitutional.[24] *El País* published this report next to a brief piece on the British Viceroy of India that quoted him as saying that the war emergency meant "that the status of India is something that can not be discussed for a single moment."

The governor refused to remove executive branch officials who were considered objectionable by the legislative majority, such as Rivera

Martínez, Gallardo and Luchetti. He also began to openly challenge the *Coalición's* alleged right to "advise" the governor on all appointments by naming candidates to judicial posts who were not recommended. This was the case with José N. Rivera Barreras, who was named municipal judge in Yauco, and Oliver Frau, appointed to the same post in Ponce. Both were "unrecommended" members of the PUR, and their nomination caused controversy.[25] The governor pointedly told the press regarding these appointments that he asked "for the advice of the leaders of the different parties and of non-political citizens."[26] He also rejected during mid November a pro-statehood scheme concocted by Treasurer Sancho Bonet which consisted of imposing the Federal income tax in Puerto Rico.[27]

The growing conflict between Leahy and the *Coalición* in late 1939 took place amidst the deepening of the leadership crisis in the majority parties. During most of this period Martínez Nadal was critically ill and absent from Puerto Rico. His condition did not improve after his return to San Juan on September 11, 1939, and he had to return to Baltimore in late October to undergo surgery. *El País* followed the course of his illness, reporting even when he was able to take a few steps or eat his first meal of rice and chicken. On November 21 its editorial was entitled "Another Cock will Sing" (he was a passionate supporter of cockfighting and was known as "The Rooster"), referring to how Martínez Nadal would confront the enemies of the *Coalición* (i.e. Leahy's Liberal advisors), once he returned to Puerto Rico. However, his health prevented him from returning until January 15, 1940.

During this period, Nadal's chosen successor, Senator Alfonso Valdés, served as Interim President of the PUR, but his leadership was challenged by the faction of Miguel Ángel García Méndez, Speaker of the House. It was no secret that the latter opposed the repetition of the *Coalición* pact and favored an agreement with the Liberal Party and the dissident faction of the Socialist Party led by Prudencio Rivera Martínez. Both Valdés and García Méndez were directly involved in the sugar industry in the western part of the island. The PUR was the only party that had several legislators who also controlled sugar corporations.[28]

Factionalism was also undermining the unity of the Socialist Party. The *Partido Laborista Puro*, led by Prudencio Rivera Martínez, was formally founded on December 3, 1939 in the *Teatro Tres Banderas* in San Juan during an assembly attended by one thousand delegates. Rivera Martínez had been able to attract some important historical leaders of the Socialist Party and the FLT.[29] As if to stress the leadership crisis of the Socialists, the founder of the party and Resident Commissioner in Washington, Santiago Iglesias Pantín, died only two days later. His son-in-law and chosen successor, Bolívar Pagán, would succeed the labor leader in Washington, leaving the Socialist Party without a strong leader with a constant presence in Puerto Rico. Thus, the main weight of providing leadership to the embattled *Coalición* during the politically turbulent year of 1940 would fall on the shoulders of an ageing man terminally ill with cancer, Martínez Nadal. With the physical decline and death, in quick succession, of Barceló (1938), Iglesias (1939), and, later (1941), Martínez Nadal, biological and political processes seemed to conspire in provoking a rapid renewal of the political leadership.

Amid the tense and unsettled political circumstances, the governor announced that he would be traveling to Washington to discuss matters related to relief funds. He informed the press of his travel plans during the same press conference where he discussed the letter from Martínez Nadal threatening not to confirm his appointments and even to decree a legislative boycott.[30] In late December, before leaving for Washington, Leahy named Bolívar Pagán to succeed his father-in-law in the post of Resident Commissioner. According to Muñoz, he took this step with great reluctance and after consulting him.

> [I visited Leahy] precisely when he had to carry out his function of naming the successor of Santiago Iglesias as Resident Commissioner upon his death. The Socialist Party had recommended Bolívar Pagán. Leahy had formed a very bad opinion of Bolívar Pagán and did not want to name him. I told him that it had to be a Socialist, [that] the party that had elected Santiago Iglesias; that if I were to choose from among the Socialists I would choose Rafael Rivera Zayas. But neither he nor I had the right to use our own judgement in this case. The governor should follow the advice of the Coalition that had elected Santiago Iglesias. Although the Organic Charter Jones [sic] only required that he filled [sic] the post with the advice and consent of the Senate, he accepted my recommendation.[31]

Leahy left for Washington on December 28, 1939 and did not return until a month later. Relations with the *Coalición* and with Rafael Martínez Nadal did not improve in 1940. In fact, they got increasingly worse. The stage had been set for a major political confrontation once the legislative session began in mid February.

According to Leahy's diary, he had a busy schedule in Washington. The first official he met was Ickes for a "discussion of Puerto Rican problems." He met several other times with Ickes and other functionaries of the Department of the Interior.[32] Ickes noted the following observation in his diary: "Governor Leahy came in to see me. He doesn't have any illusions about his job as Governor of Puerto Rico and he gives me the impression of knowing what he is doing and going about it in a self-possessed way."[33] Clearly, the secretary could not disapprove of Leahy's anti-*Coalición* trend, a policy he had long advocated. In January, Leahy also met with President Roosevelt on three occasions. All these meetings were, according to Leahy, to "discuss Puerto Rican problems." Although he gave few hints on what was discussed, it would be reasonable to suppose that the general political situation in Puerto Rico, including the difficulties with the *Coalición*, were an important topic.[34] *El Mundo* reported that, in his last meeting with Roosevelt, Leahy told him that unless "a remedy can be found to the economic conditions in Puerto Rico, the national defense preparations in the island would be endangered."[35]

The rest of his official meetings were with congressmen, federal officials with responsibilities over Puerto Rico, businessmen, and Puerto Rican politicians. Leahy discussed military and naval matters regarding Puerto Rico with the Secretary of the Navy, CNO Admiral Harold Stark and Rear Admirals Pettengill and Nimitz. There was a second meeting with Admiral Stark about "naval affairs in Puerto Rico" and a dinner in Leahy's honor attended by the CNO. Leahy also met with Army Chief of Staff General George C. Marshall about "additional shipping," and with other high-ranking naval officers.[36]

Upon his return to Puerto Rico the governor welcomed leaders of the three contending political forces. Liberal José Ramírez Santibañez brought complaints against the police and PRRA officials; PUR's leader Martínez Nadal paid his respects and offered him the collaboration of the *Coalición*; and Muñoz, accompanied by U.S. District Attorney Cecil

Snyder, denounced illegal political activities by PRRA employees. Muñoz claimed that workers were being charged $2.00 a week to retain their government jobs, which was in violation of the Hatch Act. Snyder concurred that irregularities existed.[37] The next day fifty workers of the PRRA-owned Lafayette sugar-mill submitted affidavits to the governor regarding political discrimination.[38] Leahy apparently believed these charges as he spent an entire day at PRRA headquarters "establishing an office to handle the business of Administrator of PRRA and WPA." He followed up on PRRA and WPA affairs on February 14.[39]

Military affairs required Leahy's simultaneous attention. In early February he was visited by several Army and Navy officers. The most important visit, however, was the inspection visit to Puerto Rico of Army Chief of Staff General George C. Marshall. He visited Leahy at La Fortaleza accompanied by Brigadier General Daley, Commander of the Puerto Rico Department of the Army, General George D. Brett, Assistant Chief of Air Corps, and Colonel Buchanan. An important aspect of Marshall's visit had to do with inspecting the progress of the ambitious air defense plan.[40]

The situation in the Justice Department continued to be an important issue in the relationship between the executive branch and the *Coalición* just prior to the beginning of the 1940 legislative session. Attorney General George Malcolm, in what was reported as the first step in a reorganization of the agency, accepted the resignation of Enrique Campos del Toro. The removal of Campos del Toro was probably designed to mollify the legislative leadership. Leahy also conferred with Valdés, Martínez Nadal, and George Malcolm regarding the budget of the Justice Department. Martínez Nadal told the press that it was "not human" to expect collaboration with an agency that was "full of enemies of the legislature," i.e. *Liberal-Laborista* members.[41]

Governor Leahy inaugurated the legislative session on February 13. The press generally reported that the call for "substantial economies" in the budget was the most important part of his address.[42] With the elections approaching, a policy of fiscal austerity was not precisely the kind of economic policy favored by the *Coalición*. Leahy specifically condemned the practice of hiring "a large number of additional temporary employees in the insular Legislative Assembly" and of financing these jobs with "large supplementary appropriations for both chambers."[43] He said that the tasks of temporary workers should be carried out by regular employees of the legislature or of the executive branch. The "Capitol Racket" investigation revealed numerous irregularities with legislative employees, most of whom did not work at all in an official capacity. Leahy's decision closed an important source of patronage and graft to the *Coalición*. It also made the practice of financing party workers with public funds more difficult to continue.

Military issues were also part of the address. Leahy called for a new Puerto Rican military code in line with most recent U.S. legislation that would facilitate conscription and mobilization. He also requested legislative authorization for a loan to finance the construction of National Guard arsenals by the WPA, and stated that Puerto Rico should cede its rights over the island of Desecheo, off the west coast, to the Federal government for military purposes. This small island was considered vital to the Punta Borinquen air field in Aguadilla.

Various disagreements between Leahy and the *Coalición* would not take long to surface. They initially had to do with the so-called "special budgets." These were permanent agency funds, different from the general government budget submitted to the legislature. They had been previously approved —under Winship— by the Executive Council or reviewed by the Economic Commission of the legislative branch. Without clear control over the Executive Council and with the constitutionality of the Economic Commission questioned by Leahy, Martínez Nadal insisted that all "special budgets" be submitted to the legislature for approval. He threatened to go to the courts "to defend the rights of the Legislature."[44] Leahy nonchalantly agreed with the President of the Senate that he should seek remedy in the courts but denied that he wished to undermine the rights of the legislature.[45] In his memoirs he claims that the legislature paid no attention to his call for fiscal austerity, approving bills "for the benefit of political supporters." According to him, many of these measures were approved "with an expectation that they would not be approved by the Governor who was known to favor no political party."[46]

The controversy over the "special budgets" was interpreted as a major political confrontation. *El Imparcial* published a caricature depicting a stand-off between "*el serrucho*" (the saw, i.e. Martínez Nadal) and "*la lija*" (the sandpaper, i.e. Leahy).[47] Eliseo Combas Guerra also called him "Popeye," the pugnacious sailor with the strong punch. This time the Admiral amply confirmed his perceived abrasiveness in a statement that was generally interpreted as directed at Martínez Nadal.

> Any effort by any individual to make political capital for himself or for his party through attempts at discrediting the Governor constitutes a bad political strategy.[48]

This declaration had considerable impact in the press. A columnist of *La Correspondencia*, E. Colón Baerga, remarked with evident satisfaction, "[t]here is now in the Executive chair a character, a will and a strong force of action. There are no weaknesses that create false impressions convenient for specific interests and ambitious objectives." Colón also contrasted the *Coalición*'s bellicose attitude toward Leahy with its previous subservience toward "Winship, the mummy."[49] Another political columnist, Eliseo Combas Guerra, noted that the silence of Martínez Nadal indicated that he had not found the strength to respond to the blow he had received from "Popeye."[50]

The dust had not settled on the controversy with the "special budgets" when Leahy dropped another political bombshell. He submitted to the Senate the reappointment of the District Attorney for Mayaguez, Enrique Díaz Viera. The *Coalición* had been pushing for the dismissal of this official from the Justice Department as punishment for his participation in the damaging "Capitol Racket" investigation. Díaz Viera was in charge of prosecuting related cases.[51] The press reported that George Malcolm had sought to satisfy the legislative majority by asking him to resign, a step which apparently displeased the governor. Malcolm also dismissed the charges against Senator Sixto Pacheco and others accused in the "Capitol Racket" investigation and instead initiated an investigation against Enrique Campos del Toro, as requested by Bolívar Pagán.[52] Malcolm later made other concessions to the *Coalición* and the sugar corporations regarding the enforcement of the 500 Acre Law, thus provoking an attack by the former Attorney General, Benigno Fernández García.[53] However, the reappointment of Díaz Viera by Leahy was a conscious challenge to the legislative majority and caused a political commotion in the *coalicionista* ranks.[54]

Martínez Nadal, on the other hand, stepped up his attacks on key executive functionaries and Bolívar Pagán returned from Washington to plunge into the political fray.[55] Martínez Nadal claimed that Antonio Luchetti, in charge of the large hydroelectric projects under construction, had "made a mockery of all laws." He submitted to the governor a list of fourteen charges against Luchetti and in March, *El País* published numerous attacks on him. Commissioner of the Interior Colonel José E. Colom also came under *coalicionista* fire for "giving Mr. Luchetti too much authority," and his reconfirmation by the Senate was put in question.[56] The other embattled officials were the Treasurer Sancho Bonet and the Secretary of Labor Prudencio Rivera, whose resignations were being sought by Bolívar Pagán. Both posts "belonged" to the Socialist Party according to the *Coalición* pact. Bonet chose to resign after receiving a death threat, which, according to Leahy, was issued by his own party.[57] On April 15, both chambers of the legislature approved a no-confidence resolution against Education Commissioner José M. Gallardo, who had been named with enthusiastic Republican support.[58] The PUR newspaper kept an unrelenting campaign against him, charging that he did not sufficiently emphasize the teaching of English and tolerated "Communist" teachers.[59]

The case of Luchetti had important ramifications that went beyond personal considerations. He had angered the Senate because he stated, in full agreement with Ickes, that $2.75 million of the Las Garzas project had been lost due to legislative inaction. But, more importantly, the personal attacks on Luchetti were related to efforts by the *Coalición* to stop the "little TVA" legislation for Puerto Rico sponsored by Ickes, then being discussed in Congress. Martínez Nadal was also preparing local legislation for a Water Resources Authority (approved on March 15) to preempt Federal control in this sphere. He was able to block the "little TVA" legislation in Congress by allying himself with anti-New Deal congressmen,[60] but Leahy vetoed the local Water Resources Authority law and reappointed Luchetti.[61] The governor's veto of the bill provoked renewed threats of a legislative strike.[62]

This veto was not an isolated event. The governor also vetoed a large part of the legislation approved during the legislative session, including some bills considered extremely important by the *Coalición*. Among these were the "special budgets," bills that created an intermediate appellate court and the Water Resources Authority, a bill that regulated small loans and another that enabled the creation of the Ports Authority of Arecibo. Carlos J. Benítez, a journalist writing for *El Imparcial*, highlighted the many setbacks suffered by the legislative majority during the session. He estimated that out of a total of 357 projects, Leahy approved 173 and vetoed 184.[63] The situation was depicted in a political cartoon that showed the governor vetoing legislation while a concerned Martínez Nadal looked through a window. Its caption read: "What is useless is thrown away."[64]

Leahy's decision to veto a bill that would support the celebration of a "Santiago Iglesias Day" and another that would celebrate an "Antonio Barceló Day" provoked great controversy. It even reached the pages of *The New York Times*.[65] He argued that it was not a good idea to establish another official holiday. But his unsympathetic description of Iglesias's funeral, which highlighted the long perorations of fifteen speakers and a near riot "to obtain possession of the casket," also indicates there was no love lost for the labor *caudillo*.[66] Muñoz visited Leahy to insist that the founder of the labor movement be honored.[67] The Senate voted to override the veto and Leahy finally signed a bill that represented a compromise: Barceló's day fell on a Sunday, while Iglesias's was made to coincide with the Labor Day holiday.[68]

The *Coalición* countered the governor's uncooperative attitude by not confirming twenty-three (nine rejected, fourteen hold-overs) of his seventy-three appointments.[69] These were mostly for judicial posts. But the governor did not even submit to the legislature the most important appointments and reappointments; he waited until the session closed on April 18 and proceeded to reappoint Luchetti to head the water resources projects and to name Manuel V. Domenech as Treasurer. Domenech was a dissident Republican and former Treasurer strongly opposed by the Socialist Party. The *Coalición* had declared him a *persona non grata* in 1935 amidst accusations of being a "reactionary" and an "enemy of the people."[70] Leahy also reappointed José R. Colom, who was also under attack, as Commissioner of the Interior. The PUR claimed that these appointments were illegal since "the governor is not a creation of the people itself, but a delegate of the President of the United

States."[71] The political cartoonist of *El Imparcial* again illustrated the situation in a cartoon entitled "The Bombs of the Admiral." It showed two explosions labeled Colom and Domenech that threatened to sink the paper boat of the *Coalición*, while Martínez Nadal and Pagán helplessly observed the scene.[72]

The conflicts surrounding the legislative session were also reflected in increasingly abrasive verbal attacks mainly directed against Leahy, his advisors, and Ickes. On April 6, *El País* published an editorial entitled "Debating Club," which argued that the legislature was no more than a university debating club due to the limited powers it enjoyed under the Jones Act. It also said that an informal "Third Chamber" of the legislative branch existed made up of the governor's advisors, whose function was to find fault in any approved legislation. After the "Third Chamber" went over a bill, the "guillotine of the veto" would fall, making the work of the legislature an act of futility.[73] The main headline of that day quoted Martínez Nadal as saying that "it would be best for Puerto Rico to be governed by Mussolini-style decrees." He also stated that he favored "leaving the legislature of Puerto Rico and not return[ing] to legislate on any matter" and that Puerto Rico should then be governed colonially "by a military or civil commission."[74] This outburst was provoked by Leahy's veto of the Water Resources Authority Bill. Martínez Nadal's ill-timed ironic endorsement of fascism coincided with the celebration of the recently established "Army Day," which stressed loyalty, the German invasion of Denmark (April 9), and the landing of German troops in Norway.

The columnist of *El País*'s "The Sentry Box," the "*americano*" C. Leigh Stevenson, openly blamed the "New Dealers" for the crisis in the *Coalición*. He correctly predicted that Muñoz, "the island's outstanding opponent of Americanism," would benefit from it. But he was clearly off the mark when he considered that the legislative role of the Popular Party would be that of a minority "swing group" between the two major political forces: the *Coalición* and *Tripartismo*.

> It is the Coalition that the New Dealers wich [sic] to destroy. . . .
> Any attempt to wreck a safe and well organized party in Puerto
> Rico at the present time represents a type of radicalism that is
> exceedingly dangerous. Puerto Ricans as well as Americans

who get involved in the effort to undermine the influence of the Coalition are playing with fire. Whether they know it or not, they may find themselves working for Luis Muñoz Marín and his communist impregnated popular front party.[75]

Bolívar Pagán and Martínez Nadal appealed to Roosevelt on May 20, claiming that Leahy's interim appointments of Domenech and Colom were "a step to establish in Puerto Rico an intolerable personal rule, undemocratic and un-American." In late June, the President answered that the governor's actions were "in strict conformity with the Organic Act" and that "the power of appointment. . . lies with the Executive." Roosevelt stressed "the utmost confidence in him [Leahy] and in his ability to discharge the responsibilities of the high position to which I have appointed him." He concluded by stating that "we may be assured of a continued sincere and efficient leadership in the Executive branch of the Government of Puerto Rico, and I trust that through the cooperation of the legislative branch and its leadership *as it may be constituted from time to time*, a great opportunity for advancement of the Island will be realized."[76] The President thus informed the *Coalición* in no uncertain terms that he stood firmly by the governor and his policies. It should be noted that he did not request their personal collaboration, suggesting that they might not be in control of the legislative branch after the approaching elections.

The *Coalición* could not have chosen a more inopportune moment to bring their case against Leahy before the president. On May 10, the launching of the German summer offensive through the Ardennes and the Low Countries had brought to an end the so-called "Phoney War." The day the letter was written, May 20, General Guderian's XIX Corps made spectacular gains, and the cities of Amiens and Abbeville were captured. By late May, the French army had practically collapsed, and the British army was caught in the Dunkirk pocket. Paris fell to the Germans on June 14. When Roosevelt answered the letter, the entire strategic situation had rapidly and radically transformed itself, provoking a heightened sense of crisis in the U.S. and additional steps toward rearmament. Among the main concerns were the adverse repercussions in the Caribbean — mainly the question of German control over Dutch, French and even British colonies — of the new military situation. It was under these circumstances that the *Coalición* asked Roosevelt, in the name of "democracy" and "Americanism," to chastise the governor of Puerto Rico, who was also a key player in regional defense plans and measures.

Hell Is Popping in Puerto Rico

The final split in the PUR occurred in May, when Leahy was away on another long trip to Washington. Miguel Ángel García Méndez had sought approval from Martínez Nadal to negotiate a tripartite electoral pact with the Liberals and the *Laboristas* of Prudencio Rivera. The leader of the PUR, however, favored repeating the *Coalición* pact with Bolívar Pagán and consequently refused to allow the talks.[77] The Speaker, whose inclinations toward this opposition group were known since mid 1938, openly disregarded the instructions of the party leader. With the legislative session over, he no longer faced the threat of being voted out of the speakership by Pagán and Martínez Nadal's supporters.

One study on the statehood movement explains the split in the PUR as a result of a long-standing conflict between a petty bourgeois fraction represented by Martínez Nadal and a sugar bourgeois fraction led by García Méndez. The latter supposedly objected to the alliance with the Socialist Party on ideological grounds, since he opposed the social legislation that this party propounded. The study mentions that the sugar bourgeois fraction was also represented by the vice-president of the party, Alfonso Valdés.[78]

However, this interpretation has several flaws. In the first place, Valdés remained not only firmly allied to Martínez Nadal, but was openly mentioned as his successor. Secondly, there seemed to be no major disagreements within the party regarding the decisive issues of the application of the 500-Acre Law or the support to the sugar industry. Also, judging by the weakness of the García Méndez faction, the influence of the sugar bourgeois fraction within the PUR would have been extremely weak. And finally, García Méndez left the party to ally himself with another faction of the Socialist Party that claimed that the official leadership of Bolívar Pagán had abandoned the original social program of the party. His split was apparently motivated by leadership struggles related to the succession to Martínez Nadal, the Speaker's opposition to a new coalition with the Bolívar Pagán faction of the Socialist Party, and his confrontational attitude toward the Roosevelt administration

On May 24, *El País* quoted Martínez Nadal in its main headline as saying "The Speaker or I."[79] The following day a headline read in huge letters: "García Méndez, Disloyal," while another one accused him of leading a "fifth-column" against the PUR and the *Coalición*.[80] During the following weeks a campaign was waged to ensure party loyalty to Martínez Nadal and to reduce the internal impact of García Méndez's defection. By July 14, the *Partido Liberal*, the *Partido Laborista Puro* and the *Unión Republicana Reformista* (García Méndez's Republican faction) held simultaneous assemblies and agreed to form the *Unificación Puertorriqueña Tripartita* .[81]

A serious incident in late September involving García Méndez was used by the *Coalición* as evidence not only of Leahy's political partiality, but of a politically-motivated criminal cover-up. On September 29, during a *Tripartista* rally in Utuado, a group of PUR supporters shouted slogans from a car in favor of the *Coalición* and against García Méndez. His bodyguard and chauffeur approached the group, which was unarmed, killing one and injuring two others. One of the injured men, Jorge Jordán, declared that García Méndez had also used his gun against him. The District Attorney of Arecibo, Ángel Sánchez Fernández, investigated the incident and ordered the arrests of the bodyguard, the chauffeur, and García Méndez on murder charges.[82] The political implications of a murder charge against one of the three main leaders of *Tripartismo* about a month before the elections were potentially devastating.

García Méndez phoned the governor that same day and met with him the following day. His version of the incident was that it represented an attempt on his life planned by his Republican opponents. *The New York Times* and most of the press in Puerto Rico reported the event as a political attempt on García Méndez's life.[83] *El Pueblo*, the Mayagüez *Tripartista* newspaper, openly suggested that the attempt had been the result of a plot hatched by Martínez Nadal.[84] The Republican *El País*, however, presented the report of the District Attorney as the most reliable account. The fact that the alleged attackers were not armed and remained inside the car until members of the Speaker's party intervened suggested that the incident was not a plot to kill the leader but, at most, a provocation. While García Méndez was cleared of the murder charges, his chauffeur was eventually charged for killing one person and wounding another.[85]

According to Leahy's diary, García Méndez had previously reported acts of violence against *Tripartismo*. Orbeta, the Chief of Police, personally took García Méndez's revolver to the governor.[86] Leahy lent credence to the Speaker's account and decided to intervene in the case by removing the District Attorney from the investigation and assigning it to Attorney General George Malcolm. The new investigation exonerated the *tripartista* leader. Ickes noted in his diary the version Leahy gave him of this event about a week later. It seems to place the blame squarely on Martínez Nadal.

> Governor Leahy came in late Friday afternoon. Hell is certainly popping in Puerto Rico, with the usual gunplay that accompanies elections there. Martínez Nadal is more violent than ever, according to Leahy, in his attacks — not only upon me but upon the Governor himself. Already there has been one serious shooting involving the Speaker of the House, who is trying to organize the decent citizens of Puerto Rico into an opposition party. Leahy thinks that there may be an attempt on his own life, but he seems to be prepared for it, and I don't believe that he would hesitate to shoot down anyone who might attack him.[87]

The PUR minced no words in attacking the governor after the Utuado incident. In an editorial entitled "Sailors, to the Ship!" *El País* denounced García Méndez's phone call as a "boast of force and intimacy with the governor." It also made a strong personal indictment of Leahy and Ickes.

> [The incident] will demolish. . . the aura of prestige, wisdom, honesty and independence of character that surrounds the now nebulous figure of the old sailor that resides in "La Fortaleza," as that of another figure of national scale reputed as a champion of North American liberalism, but that for us should look very well in the gallery of tyrants that the American continent has suffered, without excluding the Antilles.[88]

A week later the editorial referred to Leahy again, this time saying that during the forty-two years of "American vassalage," Puerto Rico had experienced good and bad governors. Leahy was among the latter.

A man who has spent all his life on the bridge of a ship, his mental capacity atrophied by naval strategy, accustomed to having his will fulfilled, boxed in by the narrowness of a strict discipline, is not apt to govern a people who possess a civilization a century more mature than his. Hon. William D. Leahy is a prototype of this kind of ruler.[89]

Leahy was accused of "sympathizing and supporting a criminal," i.e. the "pygmy 'ex-speaker.'" Ickes was also considered incompetent to deal with Puerto Rico. Finally, *El País* claimed that "the actions of incompetent [leaders] such as Mr. Leahy and Mr. Ickes have undermined the great sympathies [that exist] for the government of President Roosevelt," and could prevent his reelection.[90]

Socialist leader Lino Padrón Rivera also joined the attacks on the governor by stating that "Puerto Rico merits having governors that represent American democracy and not militarists (*"militarotes"*) who ignore what a civil government is."[91] The columnist of "The Sentry Box" openly accused the governor of having "fixed" García Méndez's case. He called the Speaker "Leahy's baby" and referred to Washington-named officials as "bozos who do not like us and refuse to conform [to] the laws."[92] Many of these articles can be found neatly pasted in Leahy's scrapbook.

The issue of the attitude of Ickes and Leahy toward statehood provoked additional discord with the *Coalición* just before the elections. In mid September *La Correspondencia* published a report signed by Sydney L. Dervan that said that there was strong opposition to Puerto Rican statehood in Washington. It claimed that Leahy had told Roosevelt that it should not be considered for the time being and that Ickes believed the island was not ready for it. Military authorities were said to be firmly against statehood.[93] Leahy denied that he had spoken with the president about statehood and most Puerto Rican newspapers carried articles on his statement.[94]

But the matter resurfaced a few weeks later when Leahy was quoted as saying that there were many more urgent problems in Puerto Rico than statehood.[95] This time *coalicionista* senators Celestino Iriarte and Alfonso Valdés responded to Leahy's statement. The former said that statehood might not be important for the governor but it was "for us, poor and constantly mistreated colonials."[96] On October 30, five days before the elections, *El País* editorially commented that statehood could not be postponed for military reasons and that Leahy had to subordinate his role as naval officer to his role as governor.[97] *La Correspondencia* also argued that the solution to Puerto Rico's colonial status should not be put off for considerations of "national defense." The editorial said that "They can solve the political problem of Puerto Rico in a simultaneous action with the solution of the National Defense problem."[98]

As if this were not enough, in October, Martínez Nadal sought a court injunction against José Colom, claiming that he was illegally occupying the posts of Commissioner of the Interior and Acting Governor since he had been called to active duty in the National Guard.[99] President Roosevelt promptly moved to preempt this legal action by relieving Colom from "active duty in the National Guard during the time he is serving as Acting Governor of Puerto Rico."[100]

After the elections, *El País* bitterly complained that the negative results for the *Coalición* (and in favor of the Popular Party) were due to the message Washington had transmitted to the electorate through Leahy. The editorial commented the Armistice Day celebrations on November 11, during which Muñoz replaced Martínez Nadal as the main Puerto Rican dignitary.

> An executive directs all his scorn against a pro-American grouping, defender of true democracy. American ideals are dealt a stab and the men who repeatedly proclaimed themselves apostles of intransigent separatism, opposed to the strengthening of the English language, achieve a surprising prominence in public affairs by virtue of the results of the last elections. And the Department of the Interior directed by mister Ickes is surprised of the belligerence given to *popularismo* by the electorate. It is not that the Puerto Rican majority personality has retreated ideologically, no . . . *the people respond to the signs of the emerging circumstances.*[101]

Playing Favorites?

The success of *Tripartismo* in the 1940 elections depended on its capacity to attract a large fraction of the leadership and the electorate of the three parties that constituted it and to transform that heterogeneous grouping into a coherent political force. Its electoral appeal hinged mainly on being able to present itself as the only viable political alternative to the *Coalición* and its corrupt political practices, and thus as a credible vehicle for the expression of political discontent. The issue of government corruption and the need to "moralize" or "make decent" (*adecentar*) Puerto Rican politics was very strongly stressed by the new movement. García Méndez had emphasized this issue during his relevant speech on the "union of the Puerto Rican family" of July 1939. It was also brought up by several speakers during the founding assembly of the *Partido Laborista Puro*.[102]

Stressing corruption and offering honest and efficient administration probably provided a political common ground that permitted evading divisive programmatic issues in the ideologically heterogeneous movement. Its political program favored both statehood and "liberal reforms of the existing regime," while its social and economic program consisted of a patchwork of fifty-nine promises that included "the promotion of our sugar wealth."[103] *Tripartismo* also sought to capitalize on the evident dissension between the Roosevelt administration and the majority party by stressing its intention to work harmoniously with Washington and its New Deal policies. The title of "reformist" in García Méndez's new party is meaningful in this context. The Popular Party was dismissed as extremist, disloyal to the U.S. and utopian. An example of *Tripartista* electoral propaganda published in *El Pueblo*, a formerly Republican newspaper controlled by García Méndez which became an organ of the new movement, encapsulates the main issues of its campaign.

HOW TO VOTE IN THE NEXT ELECTIONS

1. If you are a Nationalist as Albizu Campos, a Communist, a member of the Fifth Column, or believe in the stories of Scherazade: Vote for the *populares*.

2. If you believe in the *"plena"* about "Ali Baba and his 40 Thieves," in racketeering, in scandal and misgovernment by irresponsible people: Vote for the *Coalición*.

3. If you are a citizen who loves Law and Order, if you want Puerto Rico to continue being protected by the American Constitution, and the flag of the Stars and Stripes to continue floating

over the Island, if you wish to continue receiving the generous aid of President Roosevelt, if you want to contribute to the formation of a responsible government under the leadership of honest men: Vote for the *Unificación Puertorriqueña*.[104]

Tripartismo, however, faced several political handicaps that proved to be unsurmountable. Two of its main leaders, Prudencio Rivera Martínez and García Méndez, had been associated until very recently with the unpopular policies they now attacked. The former, for example, had actively opposed, as Secretary of Labor, the application of the Federal minimum wage legislation in Puerto Rico. The latter had occupied the post of Speaker of the House until April, thus having to endorse most of the legislative program of the *Coalición*. The third leader, José Ramírez Santibáñez, did not have the political stature of the deceased Liberal *caudillo*, Antonio R. Barceló. The *Coalición* and the Popular Party were able to portray him as an opportunistic politician in desperate search of political alliances, even with erstwhile enemies. In addition to this, many political opponents of the *Coalición* were wary of heterogeneous electoral alliances because of the negative experience with the *Alianza Puertorriqueña* and with the *Coalición* itself. Muñoz capitalized on this widespread dissatisfaction by denouncing agreements made among politicians "behind people's backs" and insisting on a policy of "no alliances."

Additionally, it was not clear how strong these three leaders were in their respective parties. In the case of the Liberal Party, Muñoz had taken with him a large fraction of the leadership and party militants, leaving the extremely weakened remnants to Barceló's group. It should be noted that in 1940, *Tripartismo* polled about 132,000 *fewer* votes than the Liberal Party had obtained *alone* in the 1936 elections, the largest portion of those votes going to the *populares*. It is difficult to ascertain how many Liberal votes *Tripartismo* was able to attract, but it is indicative of the crisis of the official Liberals that they obtained only 38,620 votes in the 1944 elections. Furthermore, since *Tripartismo* also included several thousand Socialist and Republican voters, it would be fair to say that the Popular Party drew substantially more Liberal votes than the 132,000.

Prudencio Rivera, on the other hand, took with him an important portion of the Socialist Party but was unable to break the hold of Bolívar

Pagán over the party structure. Of the two majority parties, it was the Socialist Party that suffered the deepest crisis. It lost about 56,000 of its voters and almost 11% of its share of the total vote between 1936 and 1940. But the dissident Socialist vote was actively contested by the Popular Party, and it is difficult to determine the portions that went to *Tripartismo* and to the *populares*, respectively. The electoral results, however, indicate that Muñoz was successful in wooing a large number of former Socialist voters.

Finally, the PUR, despite factionalism, was the party that maintained the greatest degree of unity. The break in the PUR, though long in gestation, was consummated only five months before the election, and the desertion of García Méndez apparently did not provoke a major split in that party. *El País* calculated that his departure had subtracted no more than 6,000 voters.[105] In fact, the PUR lost in 1940 about 18,000 votes and 4% of the total vote, compared to 1936. Supposing that most of these votes followed García Méndez to *Tripartismo*, it was still a meager contribution. After the elections, a cartoon in *El País* depicted García Méndez lying ill in bed while Santibáñez and Rivera Martínez took his pulse. The caption quoted them as saying that García Méndez was responsible for the electoral disaster.[106] This meant that the base of *Tripartismo* was made up mostly of Liberal and *Laborista* voters. More importantly, rather than adding and subtracting leaders, Muñoz concentrated in a grass-roots campaign designed to retain Liberal support while attracting votes from other parties, mainly Socialists, and winning the support of new voters. There were over 19,000 new voters in 1940 compared to 1936. In a way, instead of an alliance of established political leaders, Muñoz's conception of the party proposed an alliance from below based on the notion of "the people." The Popular Party defined itself as a democratic alliance of voters *against* the unscrupulous alliances (*Coalición* and *Tripartismo*) of unreliable politicians.

Most political commentators considered that the *Coalición* and *Tripartismo* were the two main political forces, with Muñoz's Popular Party occupying a distant third place. For example, a prediction made by a well-known political columnist in February 1940, even before the split in the PUR, saw the Liberal Party and its allies winning the election by a comfortable margin. It gave the *populares* only 90,000 votes, less than half of what they actually obtained.[107] A few days before the elections, Martínez

Nadal predicted that the *Coalición* would win by a margin of 88,250 votes, that its victory in 63 municipalities was assured and that the *populares* could only count on the municipality of Barranquitas.[108] Military intelligence almost underestimated the strength of the *Partido Popular*. Its report of February 1940 categorically stated that "[e]ven though this party may increase considerably from now to November, it is not believed it will win the election, even less control the legislature."[109] The intelligence report on the electoral results had to concede that the "strength shown by the Popular Democratic Party, as well as the weakness of the Unification, which was expected to poll a much larger vote, was surprising."[110] In his history of the Popular Party, Muñoz derides the absurdly inaccurate predictions for the 1940 elections that were made by political pundits.[111]

Despite its surprisingly weak electoral strength (about 130,000 votes), *Tripartismo* played a crucial role in the outcome of the 1940 elections and the rise to power of the Popular Party. It did help to weaken the *Coalición*, which saw its share of the vote drop dramatically from 54.05% in 1936 to 39.10% in 1940. The representatives it elected held the balance of power in the House of Representatives and allowed the Popular Party to control that chamber. Perhaps more importantly, it allowed the Popular Party to articulate an argument after the elections against *coalicionista* pretentions of being treated as the majority party due its slim plurality of votes. The Popular Party answered this claim with the proposition that it was not only the largest single party but the strongest force within massive anti-*Coalición* bloc that included over 60% of the electorate.[112]

TABLE 6.1
ELECTORAL RESULTS, 1932-1944

1932		1936	
(registered: 764,602, voters: 383,722)		(registered: 764,602, voters: 549,500)	
	%		%
PL 170,168	(44.37)	PL 252,467	(45.94)
PS 97,438	(25.39)	PS 144,294	(26.26)
PUR 110,794	(28.87)	PUR 152,739	(27.79)
PN 5,257	(01.37)	—	—

1940		1944	
(registered: 719,960, voters: 568,851)		(registered: 719,759, voters: 591,978)	
	%		%
PPD 214,857	(37.77)	PPD 383,280	(64.47)
PS 87,841	(15.44)	PS 68,107	(11.50)
PUR 134,299	(22.90)	PURP 101,759	(17.19)
UT 130,299	(22.90)	PL 38,630	(06.53)
PAP 1,272	(00.22)	P. Aut. 159	—
—	—	P. Prol. 23	—

Note: PL: Partido Liberal; PS: Partido Socialista; PUR: Partido Unión Republicana; PN: Partido Nacionalista; PPD: Partido Popular Democrático; PAP: Partido Agrícola Puro; UPT: Unificación Puertorriqueña Tripartita ; PURP: Partido Unión Republicana Progresista; P. Aut.: Partido Auténtico; and P. Prol.: Partido Proletario.

It should also be noted that the *Coalición* treated *Tripartismo* as its main antagonist, focusing its attacks on this grouping rather than on the *populares*. Two of the three main leaders of *Tripartismo* were considered "traitors" by the majority parties and were openly seeking to provoke splits in its ranks. If we were to believe *coalicionista* charges, *Tripartismo* practically controlled the executive branch and exercised influence in several federal agencies. Though this may be exaggerated, it did control some agencies, such as the Department of Labor, and, as we have seen, several key executive officials were avowed anti-*coalicionistas*. Furthermore, the legislative majority consistently argued from the outset that *Tripartismo* was a creation of the Roosevelt administration and had the support of Gruening and Ickes. They called the new political group "an outfit controlled from the outside" and "Quislings who love the New Deal more than they do Puerto Rico or America."[113] These charges had to be publicly denied by Leahy in August.[114]

The charge of Washington partiality toward *Tripartismo* is plausible. It has been expounded recently by historian Gonzalo Córdova from a pro-*Coalición* perspective.[115] This new political force, however, was rooted in internal political processes such as the rifts within the leadership of the

PUR and PS, the split in the Liberal Party, and the political space created in the opposition by the erosion of popular support for the *Coalición* and the weakness of the official Liberals. It was this political space that both *Tripartismo* and the *Partido Popular* sought to fill. In this sense, none of the "new" political parties was a "creation" of Washington, as the *Coalición*, and later some pro-independence commentators, had claimed.

However, an anti-*Coalición* consensus had gradually crystallized within the Roosevelt administration beginning in 1938. Ickes's longstanding antagonism toward the legislative majority was well known. The governor's actions and the extremely critical comments in his memoirs regarding Martínez Nadal and the *Coalición* suggest that he shared the secretary's outlook. President Roosevelt did not stand aloof from Puerto Rican political conflicts. He decisively intervened at key junctures in support of Leahy's policies. Army intelligence reports for the period 1939-1940 tended to perceive *Tripartismo* as an acceptable and likely successor to the *Coalición*, although just before the elections they defined both forces as "pro-American" and acceptable. Their main concern, apart from "subversive" groups as the Nationalists, was with the "radicalism" of the *Partido Popular*.[116]

This consensus probably became even more solid in 1939 and 1940 due to what was perceived as an uncooperative — even openly hostile — attitude of the legislative majority. The strong verbal attacks on U.S. policies and rule in Puerto Rico, occasionally used by German propaganda to denounce U.S. tyrannical rule, brought into question the loyalty of what defined itself as the "pro-American" party.[117] Thus, the logic of Leahy's policies, and more broadly of the administration, could be understood as aimed at provoking an electoral defeat, or at least weakening, the *Coalición*.

There is also evidence that *Tripartismo* was considered by Leahy, despite his claim of maintaining a "neutral position," as a more acceptable political force which could take the place of the *Coalición*. The anti-*Coalición* thrust of his policies is indicative of this. The incapacity of the *Coalición* to approve its legislative program, the appointment or reappointment of non-*coalicionista* officials, the limitations imposed on legislative and other forms of patronage, among others, could only have a negative electoral impact. From a political force with a firm hold over the reins of power in the context of a close alignment with the former governor and Ernest Gruening, the majority party had become an embattled political force involved in a running war with the governor and the Roosevelt administration (also represented by Harold Ickes), and torn by internal conflicts.

In this struggle, the *coalicionista* leadership, particularly Martínez Nadal, articulated a radical anti-colonial and anti-militarist discourse which was not far removed from Nationalist rhetoric. It evoked the stance assumed by Martínez Nadal in favor of independence during the controversy provoked by the Tydings Bill of 1937, but his political discourse became increasingly extreme and bitter during 1939 and 1940. German propaganda could, and in fact did, quote the "pro-American" President of the Senate as an authority on U.S. oppression in Puerto Rico.[118] In the context of a war emergency, this could only broaden the rift with the Roosevelt administration.

In his memoirs, Leahy conveniently explains the defeat of the *Coalición* as a result of Martínez Nadal's illness: "It is now my opinion that if Martínez Nadal had been in good health his party under his leadership would have held at least the balance of legislative power." He also notes that the incapacity of the "tripartista party" to "formulate an acceptable platform that would make a strong appeal to the electorate" was the cause of its defeat, and that "a combination . . . of the Union Republicans and Tripartista . . . should have won the election." The possibility of a realignment of political forces that would produce a new alliance embracing the entire Union Republican Party, the Liberals and the dissident Socialists, leaving out the Bolívar Pagán faction, had been predicted in an intelligence report written in 1939:

> In spite of temporary setback to the proposed new conservative, pro-American party, in process of formation, political observers are of the opinion that its possibilities are now greater than ever. It is now believed that not only García Méndez and his Republican followers will join this movement, but that Martínez Nadal and his followers, followed by the whole Republican Party, will do the same. It already has the support of the Liberals and nearly half of the Socialists.[119]

García Méndez had unsuccessfully tried to engineer precisely this combination. It would have blocked the rise to power of the Popular Party.[120] On the other hand, there was not much ideological affinity with Muñoz and the Popular Party. Leahy defined him as "a far left radical" who "advocated subdivision of the great sugar estates to give small land-holders opportunities to become self supporting."[121] Elsewhere in his memoirs, Leahy indicates that the subdivision of the estates was not sound economic policy. He was extremely critical of the PRRA experiment with the Lafayette sugar mill, which distributed "much of the acreage to laborers who had worked on the property." He attributed the purchase of the mill to "'Do Gooders' in the United States," a derogatory expression commonly used to refer to New Deal reformism.[122] The Lafayette project was part of the Chardón plan and strongly supported by Muñoz as part of his scheme for agrarian reform. With regard to the 500-Acre Law, Leahy notes that it was enforced against his best judgement.

> A long neglected Puerto Rican law prescribed a limit of 500 acres of sugar land in the possession of any single owner.

> While on the Island I personally became convinced that 500 acres of sugar land can be made to pay dividends only by close cooperation of several adjacent owners in the cultivation, harvesting and milling of the cane, but we continued our endeavor to enforce the 500 acre law.[123]

Although Leahy noted the glaring gap between the rich and the poor, the appalling social conditions and widespread poverty, and the control over land and wealth exercised by sugar corporations, he did not share Muñoz's critical stance toward the latter. On the contrary, he considered that "sugar proprietors, large and small, have in the past taken adequate care of their workmen judged by standards to which Puerto Rican Labor has been accustomed through the centuries."[124] Neither did he share Muñoz's enthusiasm with the application of Federal minimum wage legislation. He stressed this point in his inauguration speech, and emphasized in his memoirs efforts undertaken to postpone application of the minimum wage.

> Efforts made with some quiet support from President Roosevelt did succeed in postponing action by Labor Union leaders to

impose continental wage scales on employers of the Island. The imposition of continental wages on Puerto Rico at that time would have wrecked such few industries as did exist.[125]

Thus, it is not surprising that Leahy defines Muñoz's campaign as "his political attack on the existing order" and that he expressed mixed feelings regarding the outcome of the election.

> The Popular party underestimated by all the others, obtained a sweeping victory that made Mr. Munos [sic] Marin the real leader replacing Mr. Martinez Nadal as practically a dictator except insofar as restraint is exercised by the governor.

> While not entirely satisfied that results from this election were the best that could have been obtained under competent political leadership, it was a matter of high personal satisfaction to me that I had managed to keep entirely free from association with any political party and to have been able to provide the electorate for the first time with an opportunity to choose their elected representatives freely and without being intimidated.[126]

Leahy's evaluation of the existing political forces suggests that he was closer politically and ideologically to the conservative and pro-sugar outlook of García Méndez than to the reformist program of Muñoz and the Popular Party. Despite his claim of not associating with any political party, his reference to the absence of "competent leadership" clearly refers to the electoral fiasco of *Tripartismo*, while the comment on results that were not the "best" must be read in the context of the surprising electoral strength exhibited by the Popular Party.

In this regard, Ickes's comment that García Méndez was trying to organize the "decent citizens" of Puerto Rico should also be noted. Despite Leahy's negative personal and ideological perceptions of Muñoz, the electoral results had made him the only legitimate alternative interlocutor to the "Nadal crowd." By early December, this is precisely what Ickes recorded as Leahy's position.

> Governor Leahy got back from Puerto Rico on Monday and had a conference with the President that morning about his new duties as Ambassador to France. He came in to see me

Tuesday morning, which gave me an opportunity to tell him how fine a job, in my opinion, he had done as Governor of Puerto Rico. He agreed with me that it would be better to appoint a civilian as governor at this time and he said that if the President came back before he, Leahy, left for France, he would support my recommendation, which was originally his, to appoint Guy Swope. He believes that the defeat of the Nadal crowd on November 5 will be good for the island. He recognizes that Muñoz Marin is unstable but believes that he will be inclined to go along with the administration whenever he can. Muñoz Marin has promised the Governor that he would not raise any issue of independence or even statehood during the next two years.[127]

In sum, Muñoz and his reformist party were the almost unforeseen and to some extent unwelcome beneficiaries of Washington's attempt to redefine Puerto Rican politics with a view to the war, rather than the chosen successors to the *Coalición*. The electoral and political strategy of the Popular Party confronted U.S. policy makers with an unexpected result that was only considered "acceptable." Muñoz was well aware that he could not count on Washington's official "blessings," even after the departure of Ernest Gruening, his old friend, now passionate enemy, from the Puerto Rican scene.

On the other hand, no outright veto was applied against Muñoz's political movement, a step that was possibly considered unnecessary in view of its perceived strength. A veto was also undesirable if the U.S. wanted to clean the tarnished image of its Puerto Rican policy after the turbulent period of Winship's governorship, incorporate the *Partido Popular* as a legitimate and loyal opposition party, and further isolate more radical organizations such as the Nationalists and the Communists. The latter were defined as "security risks," not unlike the *Falange Española*, to be closely watched and repressed.

Consequently, an important component of Muñoz' electoral campaign, and of political decisions and statements immediately following the elections, was clearly designed to assuage metropolitan fears. He explicitly recognized that the war emergency, enhanced concerns with national security, and U.S. geo-strategic interests in Puerto Rico and the Caribbean, required that the populist movement cast itself in the role of a reliable political partner that could ensure internal stability.

NOTES

1. "Purulencias por extirpar" (Editorial), *El País*, September 7; 1939, p. 4.

2. *El Mundo*, October 26, 1939, p. 1.

3. For an interesting social anthropological analysis of the role of the spoils system in politics, see, F.G. Bailey, *Stratagems and Spoils, A Social Anthropology of Politics* (Oxford: Basil Blackwell, 1969).

4. See, for example, "Memorial de presidentes de los partidos coligados planteará a Leahy en derecho de la mayoría a gobernar la isla," *El Mundo*, October 20, 1939, p. 1. These arguments were also constantly expounded in PUR's newspaper *El País* and in public statements of the *Coalición* leadership.

5. José Trías Monge, *Historia constitucional de Puerto Rico*, Vol. II (Río Piedras: Editorial Universitaria, 1981), pp. 214-7.

6. See his statement in "El Gobernador saldrá para Washington en enero para comparecer ante Congreso en gestiones para lograr ayuda de emergencia," *El País*, November 25, 1939, pp. 1, 3.

7. See, for example, "Puerto Rico y la enfermedad de su caudillo," *El País*, 18 September 1939, p. 1.

8. William D. Leahy, "Sailor's Adventure in Politics, Puerto Rico 1939-1940," William D. Leahy's Papers, State Historical Society of Wisconsin, p. 29.

9. "Leahy tratará de establecer judicatura independiente," *El Mundo*, September 16, 1939, p. 1.

10. "Leahy no convocará por ahora a la legislatura," *El Mundo*, September 21, 1939, p. 8.

11. "Es increíble lo que ocurre con los fondos de WPA," *El Mundo*, October 3, 1939, p. 4.

12. "Partido Socialista endosa a Sancho Bonet para Tesorero pero combatirá a Rivera Martínez como Comisionado del Trabajo, se informa que la dirección del partido está dispuesta a dar la batalla al gobernador Leahy si es que no exige la renuncia al actual Comisionado del Trabajo," *El País*, September 27, 1939, p. 1.

13. "Leahy dice ha recibido quejas contra Rivera Martínez, pero agrega no le ha dado seria consideración a cambios en el gabinete," *El Mundo*, October 5, 1939, p. 1.

14. "Díaz Marchand en espera de contestación del gobernador, sobre el problema de los catorce municipios sin margen prestatario," *El Mundo*, October 18, 1939, p. 12.

15. "El problema de los municipios sin margen prestatario habrá de considerarse en la reunión que celebrará el Consejo Ejecutivo," *El Mundo*, October 31, 1939, p. 1.

16. "Plan de Leahy para ayuda de municipios consiste en cambiar el plan aprobado para caminos municipales," *El País*, November 23, 1939, p. 1; also, "Comisión Económica habrá de reunirse hoy con Leahy," *El Mundo*, November 25, 1939, p. 1.

17. This legislative commission should not be confused with the "civic" Economic Commission led by Filipo de Hostos. The members present at the meeting with Leahy were: senators Alfonso Valdés, Leopoldo Figueroa, Bolívar Ochart, Moisés Echeverría, and Bolívar Pagán (substituting Rafael Martínez Nadal); representatives Lino Padrón Rivera, Jorge Gautier, and Pablo J. Aguiar. Miguel Ángel García Méndez, Speaker of the House, did not attend. "Mayoría parlamentaria reclama de Leahy que reconozca su derecho como tal mayoría," *El País*, November 27, 1939, p. 1.

18. "Se presentará memorial al Gobernador atacando opiniones emitidas por el Procurador General Interino," *El País*. November 24, 1939, p. 1.

19. "Martínez Nadal informa Leahy que Senado no confirmará nombramientos," *El País*, November 25, 1939, p. 1.

20. "Grandes probabilidades de huelga legislativa en febrero próximo," *El Mundo*, November 27, 1939, p. 1.

21. "Agitada la reunión de Leahy con la Comisión Económica, La mayoría coalicionista rehúsa dar intervención a la minoría y el Gobernador insiste en discutir con la Comisión en pleno," *El Mundo*, November 27, 1939, p. 4.

22. "Mayoría parlamentaria reclama de Leahy que reconozca su derecho como tal mayoría," *El País*, November 27, 1939, p. 1.

23. "Valdés informa que la mayoría parlamentaria estudia un plan para resolver el problema de municipios sin margen prestatario," *El Mundo*, November 28, 1939, p. 1; "Hoy se hará entrega a Leahy del informe de la Comisión Económica de la Legislatura de Pto. Rico," *El País*, December 16, 1939, p. 1.

24. "Leahy se niega a utilizar fondos asignados por Comisión Económica para ayuda a municipios," *El País*, December 19, 1939, p. 1.

25. "Mis palabras fueron interpretadas erróneamente, no sé si de buena fé o con una dañada intención," *El País*, November 13, 1939, p. 1.

26. "Gobernador define su política sobre nombramientos, dice que siempre suele solicitar consejos a los líderes de los diferentes partidos y a ciudadanos no políticos," *El Mundo*, November 11, 1939, p. 1. Author's translation.

27. "Leahy se niega a gestionar extensión de income-tax federal," *El Mundo*, November 18, 1939, p. 1.

28. Juan José Baldrich, "Class and the State, The Origins of Populism in Puerto Rico, 1934-1952," Ph. D. dissertation, Yale University, May 1981, Table 5.1., p. 160.

29. "Se constituye el Partido Laborista Puro," *El Mundo*, December 4, 1939, p. 5; also, Bolívar Pagán, *Historia de los partidos políticos puertorriqueños*, Volume II (San Juan: M. Pareja, 1959), pp. 145-47.

30. "Martínez Nadal informa Leahy. . .," *El País*, November 25, 1939, p. 1.

31. Luis Muñoz Marín, *Memorias, 1898-1940* (San Juan: Inter-American University Press, 1982), pp. 198-99. Author's translation.

32. William D. Leahy's Diaries, 1939-1940, William D. Leahy's Papers, Manuscript Division, Library of Congress, p. 22.

33. Harold L. Ickes, *The Secret Diary of Harold L. Ickes: The Lowering Clouds, 1939-1941*, Volume III (New York: Simon and Schuster, 1955), p. 106.

34. William D. Leahy's Diaries, op. cit., pp. 25-32.

35. "Leahy conferenció ayer otra vez con el Presidente," *El Mundo*, January 22, 1940, p. 1. Author's translation.

36. Ibid., pp. 23-33.

37. "Muñoz Marín y el fiscal Snyder conferencian ayer extensamente con el Gob. Leahy," *El País*, February 6, 1940, p. 1; "Muñoz Marín y Snyder conferenciaron con Leahy sobre alegadas coacciones políticas de ciertos funcionarios federales," *El Mundo*, February 6, 1940, p. 1; also, Eliseo Combas Guerra, "En torno a la Fortaleza," *El Mundo*, February 6, 1940, p. 5.

38. "Denuncian ante Leahy actividades políticas en central Lafayette," *El Imparcial*, February 7, 1940, p. 1.

39. William D. Leahy's Diaries, op. cit., pp. 38, 40.

40. Ibid., pp. 38-9; also, "Marshall muy satisfecho con las defensas de la isla," *El Mundo*, February 12, 1940, p. 1.

41. "Malcolm decide aceptar renuncia a Campos del Toro," *El Mundo*, February 6, 1940, p. 1; "Martínez Nadal, Valdés y Malcolm llamados a Fortaleza," *El Mundo*, February 7, 1940, p. 1; and, "Leahy, Martínez Nadal y Valdés discutieron presupuesto del Departamento de Justicia," *El País*, February 8, 1940, p. 1.

42. "Leahy recomienda economías sustanciales en el gobierno," *El Mundo*, February 14, 1940, p. 5. The entire text of the speech is reproduced in this same issue.

43. "Gob. Leahy recomienda que sean eliminados los empleados temporeros de la Legislatura Insular," *La Democracia*, February 14, 1940, p. 1.

44. "Martínez Nadal dispuesto a llevar Gobernador a corte, si éste insiste en no enviar a la legislatura los presupuestos especiales," *El Mundo*, February 21, 1940, p. 1.

45. "'Martínez Nadal tiene razón': Leahy," *El País*, March 4, 1940, p. 1; "Presupuestos especiales se enviarán a la Legislatura," *El Mundo*, February 22, 1940, p. 1; and, "He sostenido que no violaré en forma alguna los derechos de la Legislatura," *El País*, February 24, 1940, p. 1.

46. William D. Leahy, "Sailor's Adventure in Politics, Puerto Rico 1939-1940," op. cit., p. 33.

47. "Caricature," *El Imparcial*, February 23, 1940, p. 13.

48. "El Gobernador define su actitud sobre los presupuestos," *El Mundo*, February 24, 1940, p. 1.

49. E. Colón Baerga, "Glosario de la hora," *La Correspondencia*, February 29, 1940. Author's translation.

50. E. Combas Guerra, "En Torno a la Fortaleza," *El Mundo*, February 26, 1940, p. 5.

51. "Díaz Viera no fue a Corte Municipal a acusar a Héctor Landrón Uviñas y a Utílides Rivera," *El País*, March 4, 1940, p. 1.

52. "Jefe Socialista favorece que se ventile y se aclare todo," *El Mundo*, March 1, 1940, p. 1; "Malcolm en entredicho ante la opinión pública," *La Democracia*, March 2, 1940, p. 1; and, "Juzgan tirantes relaciones entre Leahy y Malcolm," *El Imparcial*, March 1, 1940, p. 3.

53. Reece B. Bothwell, *Puerto Rico: Cien años de lucha política*, Volume III (Río Piedras: Editorial Universitaria, 1979), Document 83, pp. 266-9.

54. "Leahy somete Senado nombramiento fiscal Enrique Díaz Viera," *El Imparcial*, February 28, 1940. p. 3.

55. "Al gobernador Leahy no le gustaría decir que opina sobre el retorno de Bolívar Pagán," *El Mundo*, March 3, 1940, p. 1.

56. "Martínez Nadal entrega a Leahy catorce cargos contra Antonio Luchetti," *El Imparcial*, March 8, 1940, p. 3.

57. "At 5 PM. the Treasurer, Mr. Sancho Bonet, came to the office with information that today Mr. Gauthier, a Socialist member of the House, called at his office and informed him that unless he immediately withdraws from the office of Treasurer he will be killed." William D. Leahy, Diaries, 1939-1940, op. cit., p. 47; also, "El gobernador aceptó la renuncia al Tesorero Sancho Bonet," *El Mundo*, March 17, 1940, p. 1.

58. "Legislatura retira confianza al Comisionado Gallardo," *El País*, April 19, 1940,

p. 1; also, "Attacks Education Chief, Puerto Rican Legislature Charges Lax English Teaching Program," *The New York Times*, April 19, 1940, p. 10.

59. See, for example, "Perdiendo la chaveta" (Editorial), *El País*, April 25, 1940, p. 4.

60. The anti-"little TVA" campaign can be followed in the pages of *El País* during the months of March to May 1940. See, for example, "Derrotado proyecto de la TVA, Martínez Nadal gana otra batalla decisiva, no será considerada por el Congreso la legislación sobre Fuentes Fluviales," *El País*, May 22, 1940, p. 1.

61. "Leahy vedó proyecto de Martínez Nadal sobre Fuentes Fluviales," *El Mundo*, April 5, 1940, p. 1.

62. E. Combas Guerra, "En Torno a la Fortaleza," *El Mundo*, April 6, 1940, p. 5.

63. Carlos J. Benítez, "Noticias y comentarios de la capital," *El Imparcial*, April 17, 1940, p. 8.

64. "Lo que no sirve se bota," *El Imparcial*, April 11, 1940, p. 15.

65. "New Holiday for Puerto Rico," *The New York Times*, April 16, 1940, p. 8.

66. William D. Leahy, "A Sailor's Adventure in Politics," op. cit., pp. 20-21.

67. "Iglesias merece que se recuerde como fundador del movimiento obrero," *El Pueblo*, April 13, 1940, p. 1.

68. "Senado aprobó sobre el veto el proyecto declarando 'El Día de Santiago Iglesias,'" *El País*, April 10, 1940, p. 1; and, "Leahy firma proyectos creando días festivos de Barceló e Iglesias", *El Imparcial*, April 19, 1940, p. 3.

69. "50 nombramientos sometidos por el gobernador fueron confirmados ayer por el Senado, se procedió a rechazar nueve nombramientos y se dejaron sobre la mesa [holding over] catorce más," *El País*, April 16, 1940, p. 1.

70. "Domenech Tesorero," *El Imparcial*, May 16, 1940, p. 2.

71. "El nombramiento de Don Manuel V. Domenech para Tesorero de Puerto Rico" (Editorial), *El País*, May 7, 1940, p. 4; and, "The Sentry Box," *El País*, May 20, 1940, p. 8.

72. "Las bombas del almirante," *El Imparcial*, May 22, 1940, p. 11.

73. "Club de Debates," *El País*, April 6, 1940, p. 4.

74. "Lo mejor sería que se gobierne a Puerto Rico por decretos al estilo Mussolini," *El País*, April 6, 1940, p. 1.

75. Stevenson edited the English language page of *El País*, while simultaneously holding a $3,000 a year job in the Department of Health. He often used his column to snipe at Leahy, Ickes and New Deal policies. Soon after this column was published, he was dismissed from his government job, which he blamed on the "persecution" of Ickes. "The Sentry Box," *El País*, August 15, 1940, p. 8.

76. Franklin D. Roosevelt to Bolívar Pagán, Resident Commissioner, and Rafael Martínez Nadal, President of the Senate, June 28, 1940, FDR Library, FDR Papers, OF 400, Container 25, Folder P.R. Emphasis added.

77. Eliseo Combas Guerra, "En Torno a la Fortaleza," *El Mundo*, April 29, 1940, p. 5.

78. Edgardo Meléndez, *Puerto Rico's Statehood Movement* (Westport: Greenwood Press, 1988), pp. 62-71.

79. "'El Speaker o Yo': Martínez Nadal," *El País*, May 24, 1940, p. 1.

80. "El Speaker no ha hecho otra cosa que atacar por la espalda al Partido Unión Republicana y a la Coalición, desde la quinta columna que dirige," idem.

81. Bolívar Pagán, *Historia de los partidos políticos puertorriqueños*, Volume II, op. cit., pp. 148-52.

82. "Speaker García Méndez, su guarda espaldas y su chofer acusados de atentado a la vida y asesinato," *El País*. September 30, 1940, p. 1; and, "'El chófer del Speaker le metió una bala a Quin Pérez y García Méndez me hirió a mí," *El País*, October 1, 1940, p. 1.

83. "Puerto Rico Leader Escapes Assassin, Attacker is Slain by Body-guard of García Méndez, Speaker of the House," *The New York Times*, September 30, 1940, p. 1; "Mendez Held in Death of Puerto Rico Rival, Speaker was First Reported as Target of Assassination," *The New York Times*, October 1, 1940, p. 5.

84. "¿Martínez Nadal dirigió en la sombra el atentado contra el Speaker García Méndez?," *El Pueblo*, October 2, 1940, p. 1; and, "El único obstáculo para el triunfo de la Coalición es García Méndez–Dijo Martínez Nadal antes del atentado," *El Pueblo*, October 4, 1940, p. 1.

85. "García Méndez cleared, Puerto Rico Speaker's Chauffeur Is Held on Murder Charges," *The New York Times*, October 19, 1940, p. 6.

86. "Orbeta llevó al Gobernador Leahy revólver del Speaker García Méndez," *La Correspondencia*, September 30, 1940, p. 1.

87. Harold L. Ickes, *The Secret Diary of Harold L. Ickes, The Lowering Clouds*, Volume III, op. cit., entry for Sunday October 7, 1940, pp. 348-349.

88. "Marineros, al Barco," *El País*, October 1, 1940, p. 4. Author's translation.

89. "Zapatero a tus zapatos" (Editorial), *El País*, October 7, 1940, p. 4. Author's translation.

90. Idem.

91. "El país es digno de tener gobernadores que sean representativos de la democracia americana y no militarotes con desconocimiento de lo que es un gobierno civil," *El País*, October 3, 1940, p. 1. Author's translation.

92. C. Leigh Stevenson, "The Sentry Box", *El País*, October 31, 1940, p. 8.

93. Sydney L. Dervan, "Fuerte oposición contra estadidad en Washington," *La Correspondencia*, September 19, 1940, p. 1.

94. "El Gobernador Leahy niega haber hablado sobre Estadidad para P.R.," *La Democracia*, September 22, 1940, p. 1.

95. "La cuestión de la estadidad no se ha hecho urgente en P.R., hay muchos problemas de immediata urgencia por resolver, dijo el Gobernador Leahy in Washington," *La Correspondencia*, October 10, 1940, p. 1.

96. "Para él no, pero para nosotros, pobres colonos que constantemente somos maltratados sí es urgente la cuestión de la estadidad," *El País*, October 11, 1940, p. 1.

97. "Editorial," *El País*, October 30, 1940, p. 4.

98. "Tema del día - La defensa nacional y el 'status' de Puerto Rico: dos problemas de urgencia," *La Correspondencia*, October 30, 1940, p. 6.

99. "Martínez Nadal impugna a Colom como Gobernador y Comisionado ante Corte," *El Imparcial,* October 17, 1940, p. 3; also, "Comenzó vista del 'injunction' pedido por Martínez Nadal contra el Comisionado del Interior Colom," *La Correspondencia*, October 24, 1940, p. 1.

100. Franklin D. Roosevelt to the Honorable Secretary of War, October 18, 1940, FDR Library, FDR Papers, OF 400, Container 25, Folder P.R.

101. "Contraste" (Editorial), *El País*, November 12, 1940, p. 4. Author's translation, emphasis added.

102. Reece B. Bothwell, *Puerto Rico: cien años de lucha política*, Volume I.1, op. cit., "Se constituye el Partido Laborista Puro," Document 104, pp. 603-24.

103. Unificación Puertorriqueña Tripartita, "Programa Político" and "Programa Económico Social," *El Pueblo*, October 2, 1940, pp. 8-9, 14.

104. "Forma de votar en las próximas elecciones," *El Pueblo*, October 26, 1940, p. 3. Author's translation.

105. "Causa del desaliento" (Editorial), *El País*, August 8, 1940, p. 4.

106. "No es para tanto," *El País*, November 8, 1940, p. 1.

107. E. Combas Guerra, "En torno a la Fortaleza," *El Mundo*, February 1, 1940, p. 5.

108. "'La Coalición ganará por 88,250 votos las elecciones': Lcdo. Rafael Martínez Nadal," *El País*, November 1, 1940, p. 1.

109. Brig. Gen. Edmund L. Daley, "Weekly Summary of Political Activities - P.R. Area," February 28, 1940, R.G. 165, MID 1917-41, Box 4112, U.S. National Archives.

110. Lt. Col. Thomas R Phillips, "Comments on Current Events, election held on November 5, 1940," November 12, 1940, R.G. 165, MID, Box 3896, Entry 65, U.S. National Archives.

111. Luis Muñoz Marín, *La historia del Partido Popular Democrático* (San Juan: Editorial El Batey, 1984), pp. 14, 21.

112. Reece B. Bothwell, *Puerto Rico: cien años de lucha política*, Volume I.1, op. cit., Document 111, "El Partido Popular demandará todo los cargos del gabinete," pp. 636-7.

113. "The Sentry Box", *El País*, August 15, 1940, p. 8.

114. "'No tengo nada que me haga creer que la Administración Nacional esté interesada en ayudar a determinado partido político en la isla' - Gob. Leahy," *El País*, August 8, 1940, p. 1.

115. Gonzalo F. Córdova, "Resident Commissioner Santiago Iglesias and his Times," Ph. D. dissertation, Georgetown University, May 1982, p. 730.

116. Brig. Gen. Edmund L. Daley, "Comments on Current Events No. 1, Period September 5, 1940, to September 30, 1940," October 1, 1940, R.G. 165, MID, Box 3896, Entry 65, U.S. National Archives.

117. See, for example, Joaquín Gallart Mendía and Juan Bautista Pagán, "Así se escribe la historia," *La Correspondencia*, October 18, 1940, p. 2. They stress how German radio had made use of Martínez Nadal's controversy with Leahy.

118. Col. John W. Wright, "Weekly Summary of Certain Political Activities," March 29, and April 12, 1939, R.G. 165, MID 1917-41, Box 3112, U.S. National Archives.

119. Brig. Gen. Edmund L. Daley, "Weekly Summary of Certain Political Activities," July 19, 1939, R.G. 165, MID 1917-41, Box 3112, U.S. National Archives.

120. William D. Leahy, "A Sailor's Adventure in Politics . . .", op. cit., p. 26.

121. Ibid., p. 27.

122. Ibid. p. 36.

123. Ibid., p. 38.

124. Ibid., p. 57.

125. Ibid., p. 25.

126. Ibid., p. 54.

127. Harold L. Ickes, *The Secret Diary of Harold L. Ickes, The Lowering Clouds*, Volume III, op. cit., entry for December 7, 1940, p. 389.

CHAPTER 7

PEACE AND ORDER IN PUERTO RICO

William Leahy, Rupert Emerson, Luis Muñoz Marín.
Armistice Day, San Juan, November, 1940. El Mundo Collection, UPR.

PEACE AND ORDER IN PUERTO RICO

T wo years before the 1940 elections, Muñoz and his followers had not made much visible progress in the task of organizing a new party. Though clearly still an important political force, his influence had substantially waned after his expulsion from the Liberal Party and the ostracism imposed on him by his powerful former friends in the Roosevelt administration, particularly by Gruening. Having lost to party leader Antonio R. Barceló on the issue of non-participation in the 1936 elections, in September of that year, Muñoz organized his Liberal faction under the name *Acción Social Independentista*. Barceló was able to retain control over the party structure and expelled the "radical" dissidents in a meeting held in late May 1937.

The *muñocista* dissidents, under the high-sounding name of *Partido Liberal, Neto, Auténtico y Completo*, met in Arecibo immediately following their expulsion and decided to form a new party. Their leadership consisted mainly of young middle class professionals and intellectuals who, together with Muñoz, had unsuccessfully tried to steer the Liberal Party towards a left course consisting in a more militant commitment to independence and a radical reformist social and economic program. Under Muñoz's charismatic leadership, they rejected proposals aimed at reforming the colonial political arrangement, which they attributed to the conservative wing of the Liberal Party, while upholding the *Plan Chardón* as a blueprint for "social justice" and economic reconstruction. The 1930s generation of intellectuals (known as the *trentista* generation), among whom Antonio S. Pedreira was a leading figure, played a major role in shaping the outlook of the *muñocista* Liberals and was directly represented among the leadership by personalities such as Vicente Géigel Polanco and Samuel R. Quiñones. This group's outlook intertwined political and socio-economic aspects in the view that independence was not viable without a profound social and economic reorganization and a democratization of the political system. Neither could independence obtain mass support without a progressive social program that promised material, cultural, and political betterment for the people.

Unlike the Nationalist Party, Muñoz believed in independence not as a "supreme moral principle," but as instrumental in achieving the "redemption" of the people, since he identified the prevalent political forms of colonial oppression with sugar monoculture, widespread poverty, and the hegemony of "absentee-owned" sugar corporations. Statehood, on the other hand, would only freeze the *status quo* and saddle Puerto Rico with additional economic problems.[1] He also rejected Nationalist calls for armed resistance and, despite his non-participation stance before the 1936 elections, remained firmly committed to an electoral strategy. After Riggs's death and the wave of repression it unleashed, Muñoz made strenuous efforts to distance his pro-independence advocacy ("friendly and peaceful independence") from Nationalism.[2]

Building the New Reformist Party from the Grassroots

In July 1938, the *Partido Popular Democrático* was founded. Its symbol of a peasant or rural worker with a *pava* (the *jíbaro* straw hat) and the slogan "Bread, Land and Liberty" were chosen. The emblem indistinctly represented the peasantry or the rural sugar proletariat. The new party was registered in the municipalities of Barranquitas and Luquillo. By late 1938, it had been registered in no more than a dozen municipalities, and in February 1939, the registration drive had increased that number to only twenty-three, less than a third of the total. Despite the discouraging pace of the process of registration, the leadership rejected joining the emerging opposition that would eventually become the *Unificación Puertorriqueña Tripartita* and, instead, entrusted Jesús T. Piñero with a renewed effort at registration.[3] According to Muñoz, *tripartista* leaders made another approach in the summer of 1940, after the party's convention, but it was also rejected.[4]

This was a daring gamble since the emerging party counted with very few resources. *La Democracia*, Muñoz's newspaper, was in dire financial straits and could hardly pay its employees. The party also rejected, on principle, economic contributions from "corporate interests." Neither were contributions readily forthcoming for a party considered a sure loser and inimical to business interests. The campaign was run with scant financial resources, a fact that Muñoz and other *popular* commentators have stressed. In addition to this, apart from a handful of liberal legislators and local leaders who had followed Muñoz in his split from the party, the *populares*, unlike the *tripartistas*, did not have access to powerful power brokers in the government structure. (see Table 5.2)

The only high official who was politically close to Muñoz was Attorney General Benigno Fernández García, who was a Liberal and a personal friend. However, he thought only *Tripartismo* could unseat the *Coalición* and tried to persuade Muñoz to join. Subsequently he openly endorsed the Popular Party.[5] But he was removed from his post and replaced by the conservative George A. Malcolm. Other *muñocistas* were purged from the Justice Department by Malcolm. By 1940, all important executive posts were held by *tripartistas* or *coalicionistas*. In his account of the 1940 electoral campaign, Muñoz emphasizes that not "one department or agency of the government cooperated [with the party]."[6]

In November 1938, Muñoz wrote a letter to Ruby Black explaining the process of organization of the party that is worth quoting at length.

> Let me give you a general idea of my work here. The Popular Democratic Party progresses and registration is based on the bulk of the liberal electors, with some socialists and republicans. It is a long job, but not a difficult one. After the party is registered completely, I intend to have rural committees in 700 wards, instead of merely in the 77 towns as other parties have. I am not merely trying to organize a party for electoral action: I am trying to organize the people for democracy. We will establish a system of constant consultation in even the remotest wards, to give the people a sense that they are participating in public life instead of being merely herds of election cattle every four years. The three new characteristics of the Popular Democratic Party are: 1) it submits practically everything to the vote of the people in mass; 2) it does not pay a cent for a signature in the registration and does not pay a cent for a vote in the election . . .; 3) it will write the principal legislation, in cooperation with the affected groups, before the election instead of after.[7]

Muñoz also explained that this meant that he would have to personally visit "at least 300 of the 700 rural wards in Puerto Rico" and that the party's financial situation was "horrible." Face-to-face contact of the leader with his potential followers, even in distant and isolated rural communities, and the incorporation of the peasantry and other components of the "people" into the party at the ward level were political innovations that Muñoz later defined as revolutionary. The building of the party was considered tantamount to the "organization of the people for democracy." Unfettered by the "high politics" wheeling and dealing of the *Coalición* and *Tripartismo*, Muñoz and the leadership of the *Partido Popular* could concentrate on organizing the new party from the grassroots.

Another important aspect of the organizational strategy followed by Muñoz in 1938 and 1939 was to concentrate his efforts in the rural districts, later to "encircle" and "penetrate" the towns. In his history of the party, written from 1941 to 1942, he explains the success in organizing the urban areas as a result of the "rumor that was beginning to arrive from the countryside, as the distant sound of a river that is rising . . . The noise that was coming from the mountains had to awaken something in the spirit of the middle class!"[8] In a text written three decades later, he again used the metaphor of springs flowing from the countryside to the towns. The springs formed rivers that, in turn, became cataracts when they reached San Juan. Muñoz defined his role in the campaign as directing the rivers toward San Juan.[9]

In March 1939, Muñoz founded the important biweekly party newspaper *El Batey*. He called it "the rural organ" and had the subtitle "*El Correo del Campesino Puertorriqueño*" (the courier of the Puerto Rican mountain peasant). However, an analysis of its contents indicates that it was targeted not only at the peasantry, but also at the rural and urban working class, the urban unemployed and the middle class. *El Batey* was printed in the facilities of *La Democracia*, which precariously continued circulating but played a less important role in the campaign, and was solely financed through paid advertisements, with the main funds coming from businessman Félix Benítez Rexach, since it was distributed free of charge. It corresponded to an established tradition of party-based journalism, such as *La Democracia* (Liberal Party), *El País* (Union Republicans), and *El Pueblo*

(*Tripartismo*). Nonetheless, *El Batey* also represented, in many ways, a departure from the prevalent character of party newspapers.[10]

The first printing of *El Batey* was massive by Puerto Rican standards: 100,000 copies, compared to the 25,000 of *El Mundo*, the largest commercial newspaper on the island. *El Batey* also encouraged its readers to pass it on once read. The distribution was entrusted to the ward committees, thus ensuring its penetration into all rural communities. *El Batey* was a key instrument of the Popular Party campaign and a mirror of its strategy. Muñoz called it "the main weapon" and explained that the campaign was waged through party meetings, *El Batey*, and the radio, with the latter playing a less important role.[11]

> The campaign was educational. The meetings were the lessons. *El Batey* was the text. The elections were the examination. The people brilliantly approved.[12]

On August 11, 1939, exactly one month before the inauguration of Governor Leahy, the *populares* felt sufficiently strong to hold their first mass rally in San Juan. A large crowd heard Muñoz and other leaders speak at *Parada 22* in Santurce.[13] By then, the process of registration of the party was also well advanced, and Muñoz wanted to have it almost concluded by the time Leahy arrived.[14] The registration of new voters in January 1940 yielded 55,000 registration cards handed in to the party, for a total of about 150,000 sympathizers according to Muñoz's calculations.[15] In addition to the intense campaigning in rural communities, meetings were held in large towns and Muñoz was invited to address groups such as the unemployed and chauffeurs.

Muñoz always stressed that the party "did not seek influence in Washington or La Fortaleza," nor did it receive any help "except that of its truth."[16] He did meet Leahy several times, mostly to bring up matters related to the campaign and the elections, but he apparently did not have the privileged access that García Méndez had. *El Batey* reported a meeting that took place just after Leahy's inauguration. The article stressed the party and Muñoz's support for the new governor.[17] This meeting was not recorded by Leahy in his diary. The first mention of a visit from Muñoz in Leahy's diary is dated February 5, 1940. According to the diary, Muñoz came to complain about "political activity by employees of

PRRA that is detrimental to the interests of his political party." The District Attorney, Cecil Snyder, accompanied Muñoz and apparently concurred with the charges.

This was followed by another meeting on March 14, the topic of which is not mentioned in Leahy's diary.[18] *El País* reported that this time Muñoz brought up a public works loan by the municipality of Utuado that was to be used for the campaign.[19] During this month, Muñoz and other leaders of the Popular Party also requested from Leahy equal electoral representation.[20] Support for an official Santiago Iglesias Day and for the full application of the 500 Acre Law were subjects of another meeting in April.[21]

Apparently, Muñoz did not visit Leahy again until July 22, 1940, the day after the party congress was held at the Sixto Escobar ball park. He was accompanied this time by Benigno Fernández García and Antonio Fernós. The governor was officially informed of the formation and aims of the party.[22] Muñoz stated to the press that they had expressed to the governor, on behalf of the party congress, "the unequivocal and unlimited collaboration of the Popular Democratic Party with the government of the United States for national defense and the defense of democracy in general." The situation of Central Lafayette and PRRA workers was discussed, as well as electoral issues.

The status of Puerto Rico and the party's stance to independence were quite possibly breached during this meeting, since they were dealt with in the party program that had been approved. It should be noted that Fernós had just published a series of articles in *El Mundo* regarding the status question and would later be the leader entrusted by Muñoz to negotiate political reforms. He argued that status should not be an issue at a general election but should be resolved through a plebiscite or a Constituent Assembly at the behest of the U.S. Congress, "our sovereign."[23] After the meeting, Muñoz said that the party congress had not approved a demand for a plebiscite, and had "emphatically declared that political 'status' was not at issue." He also stated that colonial status would only become an issue when the assembly so decided.[24]

The other meetings took place just prior to the elections, on September 24, October 31, and November 1. In the first two, Muñoz asked that electoral laws be fully enforced to ensure clean elections and that measures be taken to prevent the locking up of voters.[25] The request for a letter from District Attorney Snyder to counter charges of anti-Americanism against Muñoz was made during this period. Samuel R. Quiñones participated in the October 31 meeting. The last meeting was called by Leahy and included leaders of all the parties except the *Partido Unión Republicana* (which boycotted the meeting). The impending vote was discussed and Muñoz again brought up the locking up of voters.[26] Muñoz expressed confidence in Leahy's efforts to guarantee voters' rights.[27]

The new party held its programmatic assembly on July 21, 1940 in the Sixto Escobar ball park. It was a show of strength and of broad popular participation as about 4,000 delegates attended -compared to two or three hundred in the case of other parties- and the program was spiritedly debated well into the night. During that same month, the *coalicionista* legislature, in a move that could be interpreted as designed to make the Popular Party a counterweight to *Tripartismo*, approved legislation to accord it official representation in the electoral board.[28] Subsequently, specific legislative measures related to the promises contained in the program were discussed and approved during a meeting convened for that purpose in the Puerto Rico Atheneum. The discussion there dragged on for several days and was derided as childish by other parties. The campaign culminated in a large mass meeting on September 15, broadcasted over the radio, where legislative candidates publicly swore to vote for the legislative projects.[29] Muñoz made a final appeal to voters in a key speech broadcasted on November 4, the day before the elections.[30]

El Catecismo del pueblo: The Strategic Outlook

One of the most important documents on the party's strategy, ideology and program during this initial period is the *Catecismo del pueblo* (the People's Catechism). It was a widely distributed pamphlet published in September 1939 and written by Muñoz.[31] Resorting to religious symbols was not only obvious in the title of the pamphlet, but also in its form. It consisted of sixty-three questions which were answered in a very plain and direct language. Religious metaphors, such as the notion of the "redemption" of the people or the messianic presentation of the role of the party and the leader, and references to religion, abounded in the campaign of the *populares*.[32] The *Catecismo* was not a traditional party program consisting of a list of promises and commitments. In fact, the party's electoral program was not officially framed until July 1940, when the Constituent Assembly met in the Sixto Escobar baseball park.

The *Catecismo* was unique because it placed programmatic promises within a broader analysis of the Puerto Rican situation, consistent with Muñoz's "educational" strategy. The introductory questions (1-9) described the dire social conditions and poverty under which the majority of Puerto Ricans lived: inadequate housing, food, clothing, health, education, elderly security, and even lack of means for a burial. Widespread poverty was attributed to social injustice due to the inequitable distribution of wealth, and this, in turn, was linked to "large corporations and other powerful economic interests that every year take out of Puerto Rico twenty million dollars." The large profits made by the corporations were responsible for prevalent poverty since "the lower the salaries, the lower the retribution to the farmer, the greater the profits extracted by the large corporations"(question 9).

The proposed solution consisted of implementing measures of redistributive justice that would ensure fewer "profits above and less poverty below." These measures are spelled out in the answer to question 10 as: 1) minimum salary laws, 2) protection for agricultural producers, native industry, and commerce "so that they can pay these minimum salaries without risking ruin," 3) lowering taxes on consumption, 4) lowering taxes on poor agricultural producers, 5) controlling the prices of coffee, tobacco and "other products which give life to our people," 6) redistributing the land of "absentee corporations" among thousands of workers who are landless, and 7) increasing taxes on those that "extract millions from Puerto Rico."

The part that followed (questions 12-50) dealt with the political system, both internally and in its colonial dimension, and with the related question of democracy. It posited the general thesis that the undemocratic character of the island's political system, particularly of the electoral process, was the root of the perpetuation of poverty, exploitation, and the dire social conditions. The corruption of the electoral process through the practice of buying votes is proposed as the explanation for the perpetuation of an unjust economic system with the electoral support of the majority of the population.

According to the *Catecismo*, large corporations provide political candidates and leaders with funds to swindle and buy the votes of the people. Therefore, the politicians were committed after the elections, not to the voters, but to the business interests that financed them. Poverty and the deterioration of living conditions supported corrupt electoral practices by making people more susceptible to corruption. Voters, thus, participated in elections as a "herd of votes," while leaders "in order to buy their votes had to sell themselves first to the large interests that extracted millions from their misery." Corruption was not defined as a dishonest act, however prevalent and carried out by politicians once they obtained power (as in the campaign of *tripartismo*, which called for a "cleansing" of Puerto Rican politics through the removal of the *Coalición* leadership). Corruption was inherent in the normal functioning of the political system. It pervaded the political process from top to bottom and had its origins in the economic power of absentee corporations.

The undemocratic and corrupt character of the political system expressed itself in a particular relationship of unaccountability and distance between the "leaders in San Juan" and the people. The former acted "behind your backs, without consulting you, without explaining, without answering your questions." Furthermore, incapable of offering anything concrete to improve the lot of the people, they resorted to "beautiful" speeches and empty rhetoric full of phrases that meant "nothing at all." The prevalent political discourse was consequently denounced as a way "of hiding in words," as a symptom that "he who makes beautiful speeches does not possess a simple and clear truth about you and your relatives's bread and about a life of fullness and dignity for you and your relatives." By implication, the Popular Party was not only the bearer of a new program and a more democratic way of doing politics, but also of a new discourse, devoid of the deviousness and trickery of traditional politicians.

In this context, the *Catecismo* claimed that the vicious circle of poverty-corruption-poverty could only be broken through the electoral system as, in a clear reference to the Nationalist Party, the "people should be absolutely against violence, because in Puerto Rico violence can deepen the problems, make more difficult their solution or prevent the development of democratic customs of a peaceful and orderly government of the people by the people, which are the only salvation and defense that our people have." Rejection of violence was stressed throughout the campaign, while the party claimed that it was an instrument to impose "peace and order." Consequently, the only viable manner of obtaining justice and implementing necessary reforms consisted in "voting against money," voting against the "leaders in San Juan" that did not consult with the people, voting against the leaders that gave "beautiful" speeches. This implied abandoning traditional party loyalties ("feeling as parents and men instead of Republicans, Socialists, or Liberals") and voting for those who would "owe nothing to any large corporation" and would "owe everything to your free votes." In fact, the *Catecismo* articulated a project of a "grassroots *tripartismo*," with the Popular Party embodying an alliance of the people from below, instead of the agreement "from above" of some of the "traditional" politicians it sought to displace.

The contrast between the Popular Party and all other existing parties ("*antiguos partidos*," old parties) was further emphasized in the concluding set of questions (59-63). The *Catecismo* claimed that the *Partido Popular Democrático* acted "by orders of the people, consulting the people about their needs and wishes," and that it was established "by order of the liberal people through its legitimate representatives, and to represent all the people." The distinctive features of the new party were: 1) that it consulted with the people, answered their questions and obeyed their orders, and 2) that it did not buy votes or receive money from large corporations. The "old parties," on the other hand, forgot the people until just before the elections, gave speeches during the campaign, asked money from large corporations to buy the people in order to win the elections, and later legislated in favor of those who finance them.

Having dealt with the internal workings of the political system in these two sections, the pamphlet also focused on the colonial character of the polity. The nexus was established in question 29, with regard to the veto powers of the U.S.-named governor and the consequent capacity of the executive to prevent the implementation of reform legislation. Thus, colonialism was politically personified in the governorship, in opposition to a democratically elected legislative branch. The pamphlet predicted a potential clash between the executive (representing the colonial character of the polity and the "vested interests") and the legislative branch (embodying a democratic mandate for necessary reforms).

> In such a situation, with the legislators approving laws on a people's mandate and a governor annulling them in defense of vested interests, the colonial system could not last much longer. (question 31)

It was in this indirect way and within an extremely circumscribed conception of the colonial system that the stance to colonialism was discussed in the pamphlet. The answer to another question (46) suggested that the colonial system was dictatorial "because the Governor can veto laws against the will of the people." Even then, the clash was not even considered inevitable as "the Governor will be careful not to veto laws that the people ask for, approved by popular mandate in a legislature of men who are free from the money of the corporations." But, if he chose to veto the reform legislation, then the legislators would appeal directly to the people, and the need to democratically end the colonial system through a plebiscite would become evident.

Such a plebiscite should then be held to establish a "sovereign system of government" chosen by the people, and only two options were mentioned: independence or statehood. Both were discussed in the answer to several questions, emphasizing the pros of independence and the cons of statehood. It should be noted that the arguments in favor of independence focused mainly on its economic advantages and compatibility with democratic institutions, steering clear of traditional Nationalist postures regarding the illegality of colonialism. Answers to questions 48 and 49, attributed the cause of dictatorship to "large quantities of armed soldiers" and proposed a demilitarized Republic along Costa Rican lines, a view that obviously clashed with the ongoing U.S. military buildup in Puerto Rico and with the party's support of Roosevelt's defense measures.

The *Catecismo*, unlike other party documents, did not explicitly refer to the international crisis or to the role of Puerto Rico in military preparations. Neither did it contain a clear commitment to independence. Even

the discussion of a plebiscite on status did not imply a definite programmatic promise to promote it. The way the colonial issue was posed, elicited the question (extremely relevant in view of subsequent events) of
what would be the party's policy if no major clash with the governor or
the metropolitan authorities occurred.

Another important part of the document was a set of questions (50-
58) related to the sugar industry. This part clarified some of the party's
(and Muñoz's) notions on the organization of the economy and the class
structure, as well as the content of the concept of the "people." The sugar
industry was described as a pyramidal structure with the "absentee corporations that take millions out of Puerto Rico" at the top. Under these
were placed the sugar mills owned by "residents" of Puerto Rico who
were denied "half of their sugar quota by the absentee sugar mills." A
step below were the cane farmers ("*colonos*"), who paid a high interest
for their *refacción* (crop loans). Their cane was badly paid for and they
often risked losing their land. On the bottom rung of the ladder were the
workers and their children, who suffered from hunger because of the
profits of the "absentee corporations." Justice in the sugar industry meant
inverting the priority of the "Government that until now has worried
more of ensuring the profits about the corporations" rather than "ensuring that the people have decent food and life, that every day there are
more owners of land rather than less."

Consequently, redistributive justice, mainly directed at improving
the lot of *colonos* and sugar workers, was urgently needed in the sugar
industry. This implied, among other things, guaranteeing better economic
conditions for the *colonos* and improving the salaries of the workers. Sugar
workers should also be provided land through the enforcement of the
500 Acre Law, decent housing, and relief from taxation on consumption
articles. In addition to this, larger quotas should be provided to the sugar
mills of "resident owners" and absenteeism should be curtailed (question 55 and 57). The text suggested that these two classes (*colonos* and
sugar workers) form the core of the "people" in the class structure of the
sugar industry. What was proposed, however, went beyond income redistributive measures, as support for an agrarian reform through the
enforcement of the 500 Acre Law suggested. It amounted to a radical
restructuring of the sugar industry since it simultaneously called for a

new organization "under the form of cooperative sugar mills owned by farmers and workers" (question 52).

The *Catecismo* went on to relate the situation in the sugar industry, its control by "absentee corporations," and the extraction of huge profits from Puerto Rico with a negative impact on employment and the prevalent "misery throughout the island." The money exported in the form of profits "is money that does not circulate in Puerto Rico," thus reducing the size of the internal market. Particularly affected were the coffee-producing municipalities of the center of the island since the "exploitation of the coast produces in this way economic inactivity in the interior." In line with the Hobsonian social reformist and underconsumptionist thesis,[33] the pamphlet claimed that the reforms in the sugar industry would serve as an overall stimulus to Puerto Rican economy. Therefore, an expanded internal market would benefit coffee producers, peasants, truck and public cars *(públicos)* drivers, and native merchants and manufacturers. Treaty-making powers and customs protection would afford additional support to coffee production and native industry (question 58).

In this manner, the *Catecismo* identified as the main antagonists the "absentee corporations" and the "old parties." U.S. colonial power, personified in the governor, was seen as part of the prevalent power arrangement, but was dealt with in more ambiguous terms. Likewise, some lip-service was paid to the interest of "resident owners" of sugar-mills, but the thrust of the argument seemed to lump them together with U.S.-owned corporations, outside the realm of the "people." In the late thirties, the resident-owned sugar-mills still controlled a sizeable portion of production. From this perspective, the text can be interpreted as an indictment of the sugar bourgeoisie as a whole.

The Popular Party proposed a broad class-alliance that went beyond traditional party loyalties. At the core of this alliance were the *colonos* and sugar workers, but it also sought to embrace small and medium groups of peasants, coffee producers, merchants, *público* drivers, and "native" manufacturers. The emphasis was clearly on the rural population of the coast and the mountains, though some specific urban social groups were also mentioned.[34] In other texts, Muñoz saw the "suffering and spiritually fearful" urban middle class as being "liberated" by the rural population, the "mass of the people."[35] There were many parallels between the formulations of contemporary Latin American populist thinkers, such as those of the Peruvian Víctor Raúl Haya de la Torre, and Muñoz's analysis of the Puerto Rico situation.[36]

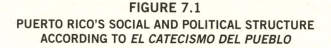

FIGURE 7.1
PUERTO RICO'S SOCIAL AND POLITICAL STRUCTURE
ACCORDING TO *EL CATECISMO DEL PUEBLO*

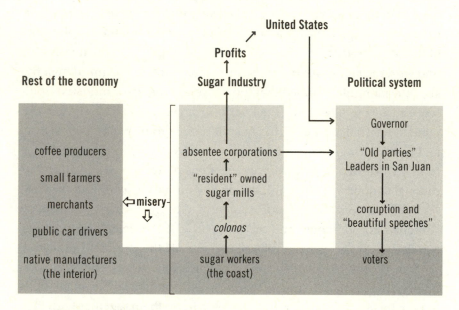

El Batey: The "Main Weapon"

While the *Catecismo* contained the populist strategic blueprint, the newspaper *El Batey* was a mirror of the *populares's* specific campaign strategy and tactics. It aimed at ensuring the support of the bulk of the Liberal vote, attracting discontented new voters, and trying to provoke an electoral rebellion of *Coalición* voters, mainly of the working class base of the *Partido Socialista*. The first issue set the tone of the publication and touched on some of the arguments that it would repeatedly bring up throughout the rest of the campaign.

The article introducing the newspaper defined it as an instrument to teach the *campesino* (peasant or rural worker) how to defend himself and improve his living conditions. In this case, however, the term *campesino* was apparently used to refer specifically to the rural proletariat, rather than the peasantry, since the rest of the article mainly referred to the situation of the sugar workers. The Sugar Agreement was condemned as "treason" to the workers, as it set salaries below the level of the Fair Labor Standards Act (1938) of the Roosevelt administration. It should be noted that the sugar agreements negotiated since 1934 between the *Federación Libre de Trabajadores* and the *Asociación de Productores de Azúcar* had caused great dissension and dissatisfaction within the trade union movement.

The article also commended the work of Robert Claiborne, the federal administrator of the Fair Labor and Standards Act, and contrasted it to the role of "a few [union] leaders in San Juan who lock themselves in a room with the sugar-mill owners and sign an agreement that maintains in misery thousands of workers' households." The Roosevelt administration was defined as favorable to the "popular classes," unlike other U.S. administrations that were "generally . . . not as good as this one."[37]

Support for working class interests and for the policies of the Roosevelt administration was further stressed in other parts of this first issue. In an article entitled "The Popular Democratic Party and the American People," a statement claimed that the new party was "in complete friendship with the American people and in sympathy with the present democratic and popular government, even though it disagrees with some of its actions in Puerto Rico." Violence was also emphatically rejected.[38] This was again broached in the first two points of a text entitled "The Program of *El Batey*," which summarized the party's program.

1. Peace and order in Puerto Rico, and permanent friendship with the people of the United States.

2. On the basis of this peace, order, and this friendship, the freedom of Puerto Rico, so that the people of Puerto Rico may freely struggle against their hunger and misery.[39]

Also included was a brief historical sketch of Muñoz Marín written by Pedro Juan Dumont, identified as a trade union member of the construction industry affiliated to the Congress of Industrial Organizations

(CIO). The CIO was then disputing the hegemony, in the field of trade union organization, of the *Federación Libre de Trabajadores* (FLT), affiliated to the Socialist Party. Both Muñoz and Robert Claiborne had openly sided with the former. Dumont stressed in his article that Muñoz was the leader of the *liberales* "free of the influence of the corporations" and of thousands of Socialists and Republicans who favored a new political movement.[40] Finally, the newspaper highlighted Muñoz's efforts in favor of the unemployed.[41]

Appealing to the working class became an important component of *El Batey* throughout 1939 and 1940. Great emphasis was placed on the efforts of the party in support of the application of federal minimum wage legislation.[42] Actions in favor of Puerto Rican workers by the CIO and Vito Marcantonio were also favorably reported. Problems affecting specific groups of workers, such as construction and dock workers, were denounced.[43] Taxation of popular consumption items-as the salt tax imposed by Winship to support the promotion of tourism-was opposed as contrary to the interests of workers and the rest of the people.[44]

While expressing respect for Santiago Iglesias as a labor leader (not as a politician), *El Batey* hammered at the message that the Socialist Party and the "labor leaders in San Juan" had turned their backs on the workers and the Socialist "people." Singled out for attack was Prudencio Rivera Martínez, Commissioner of Labor and prominent leader of the *Tripartismo*. Although the publication occasionally appealed to Republican voters,[45] its main thrust was clearly in the direction of discontented working class and Socialist Party voters.

The newspaper also specifically addressed messages to other classes and groups such as the peasantry and small landowners, drivers, teachers, the unemployed, women, and Christians. As outlined in the *Catecismo*, it offered a government that would respond to their interests by, among other things, lowering taxes, promoting rural electrification, applying the 500 Acre Law to distribute land, ending corruption and constructing democratic practices, creating jobs, protecting small businesses, preventing government abuse against specific groups, and so on.[46] The case of candidate Norberto Bernacet, a peasant, was used to argue that "many workers and peasants are candidates of the Popular Party."[47] Women were asked to tell men that "hunger and suffering should end," because "if women make men feel ashamed of selling themselves, salvation in social and economic justice will be achieved." They were said to know best the meaning of suffering.[48]

As noted, religious issues and appeals for the support of Christians were an important aspect of the campaign. Muñoz and *El Batey* also had to counter claims that the party was against religion and in favor of Communism. An article entitled "The Meaning of Holy Week for the People" argued that "[t]he mission of the Christian as a citizen is to make the ideal of Christianity real and effective on earth."[49] The title of a front page article noted: "The Bishop of Ponce Defends Social Justice." It expressed support for a homily by Bishop Willinger which called for "making the sugar industry serve the common good instead of a small minority."[50] Willinger was again cited in Muñoz's radio address of November 4, the day before the elections. In this speech Muñoz referred several times to God and argued that the "useless epoch" that the Popular Party was trying to overcome was "clearly contrary to the spirit of Christianity and religion among men" since it did not see the *campesino* and the people as "rational creatures of God."[51] Muñoz entitled a front page article "God Made Bread for all Mouths."[52] Another main article pointed out in its title that "Religion and Justice, [constituted the] Clear Position of the Popular Party in Defense of Both."[53] All this implied that what was being offered was not simply an alternative political program, but "social redemption" from a state that was inherently sinful.

An important controversy during the campaign, involving religion and the party, was provoked by a sermon given by a Dutch priest, Ramón Stadta. It was entitled "Beware of False Prophets" and it was printed and widely distributed as propaganda against the *populares*. In February 1940, *El Batey* published a letter from the priest, as requested by Muñoz, claiming that his sermon had been directed at Communism and not at the Popular Party. The newspaper accused as liars those who had used Stadta's sermon against the party.[54] This was followed up by the publication of a letter of a Father Rivera, clearly a sympathizer of the party and a personal friend of Muñoz. Father Rivera denied that Muñoz was a Communist and emphasized that "he is the only one who dares to speak *en cristiano*," (which is colloquial for clearly).[55] Finally, in an issue that was published just before the elections, the

Catholic journal *El Piloto* was quoted as saying that the party's candidate to the post of Resident Commissioner had been the only one to defend the Church.[56]

Likewise, the newspaper repeatedly countered charges of being "anti-American" and of having connections with the Nationalist Party.[57] As noted, the Roosevelt administration was praised and the first point of *El Batey* program promised "permanent friendship with the people of the United States." Federal legislation –such as the Fair Labor Standards Act, and the Hatch and Wagner Acts– was generally considered as furthering the interests of the people. Their full application was demanded. Muñoz clearly aimed at distancing the party both from Nationalist demands for independence and criticism of U.S. military preparations, and from the increasingly strident anti-Roosevelt and anti-New Deal rhetoric of the *Coalición*.

El Batey placed great emphasis on the fact that the status of Puerto Rico was not considered an issue in the 1940 elections and that the party was not committed to independence.[58] The "freedom" mentioned in the party slogan was defined as "the right of the people to vote on which should be the final destiny of all Puerto Rico."[59] In that same issue, the first meeting between Muñoz and Leahy was favorably reported and the article recommended "sympathy and understanding" towards the new governor.[60] An October 1940 issue further underscored the message by stating that "the Popular Democratic Party is the best defender of American democracy," that most "Americans" in Puerto Rico and Puerto Rican soldiers sympathized with the party, and that the candidate for Cayey-Cidra was the *americano* Elmer Ellsworth.[61] The last issue before the elections quoted a letter by District Attorney A. Cecil Snyder to Muñoz that said: "I firmly believe you are a defender of democracy, and have a profound respect for democratic institutions and for the American attitude towards life."[62]

El Batey also sought to appeal to the electoral base of the Liberal Party with the notion that the Popular Party was the authentic expression of the liberal "people," despite its new name.[63] In 1938 speech at his father's gravesite, Muñoz had promised to "evict from your sepulchre the merchants of your name."[64] During the campaign, the figure of Muñoz was presented as guaranteeing the continuity of the authentic legacy of

Muñoz Rivera, a legacy that had been squandered by the leadership of the Liberal Party. An article entitled "From Muñoz Rivera to Muñoz Marín" claimed that "all politics in Puerto Rico has been lost since Muñoz Rivera died until the popular and democratic forces with which Muñoz Marín is forging a people have entered into action."[65] Muñoz's personality and political pedigree were transformed into important symbolic instruments in the campaign.

Finally, *Tripartismo* was disqualified as a legitimate oppositional option. It was derided as "the same thing" as the *Coalición*, and dubbed "*la mogolla*" (the jumble) and "*tripa(h)artitas*" (full bellies). In August 1939, *El Batey* published the first two articles against "the new alliance."

> The *Coalición* has protected the large exploitative interests that extract millions from the hunger and the misery of the people. The people are tired of the *Coalición*. The large exploitative corporations know it, and want to present the people [with] the old bad habits with a new name. What they pretend with this is that the people, to vote against the *Coalición*, will vote for the new alliance or *mogolla*, which is exactly the same as the *Coalición*.[66]

This argument was reiterated in numerous other articles in 1939 and 1940, while it was claimed that the Popular Party "was not the same."[67] After García Méndez openly broke with the *Partido Unión Republicana* and joined *Tripartismo*, the newspaper argued that the Liberals who had "killed the Liberal Party" had then proceeded to surrender the name to the "*corporacionista*" Republicans of the former.[68] The stated policy of "no agreements or alliances" was mainly aimed at *Tripartismo* and the Nationalist Party.

The issue of corruption was also brought up by *El Batey*, which made reference to the "Capitol Racket."[69] Corruption, however, was defined in broad terms, as in the *Catecismo*, thus including the practice of buying votes or obtaining illegal party contributions. In a text written in 1970 for his memoirs, Muñoz stresses that while the stated aim of *Tripartismo* was to "moralize the government," this only amounted to removing the dust ("*un pasado de plumero*") when the problem was the woodworm that corroded the country.[70]

"The Struggle of Two Great Systems:" The Popular Democratic Party, the War, and U.S. Military preparations

From 1939 to 1941, Luis Muñoz Marín and the Popular Democratic Party professed an increasingly emphatic support for Roosevelt's foreign policy, particularly its anti-fascist expressions, and for ongoing military preparations. Discourse on the international crisis tended to identify the democratic character of the party's reformist program with a continental and global crusade for democracy under Roosevelt's leadership. As the international conflict escalated, Muñoz called for full and unconditional collaboration of Puerto Ricans in the war effort, even at the price of postponing certain democratic demands until the end of the war.

The Popular Party's stance on the war contrasted both with Martínez Nadal's troublesome and sharp criticisms of U.S. rule in Puerto Rico, which were exploited by German radio and press to Washington's embarrassment, and Nationalist Party opposition to U.S. "military penetration" and to any form of Puerto Rican collaboration with defense preparations. During the campaign, both *Tripartismo* and the *Partido Popular* emphasized their commitment to the New Deal and the Roosevelt administration, as well as their support for its foreign policy in a juncture of international crisis.

Muñoz's insistent expressions of support for the internal and foreign policies of the Roosevelt administration, his commitment to political stability and social peace in Puerto Rico, his downplaying of independence and "status" issues in general, and his unequivocal endorsement of U.S. military preparations, were certainly key factors in Washington's eventual *rapprochement* and reconciliation with Muñoz. With the constant worsening of the international crisis, and given the large and crucial role Puerto Rico was playing in U.S. strategic military planning, no political force could realistically expect to share colonial power without a clear expression of loyalty. Muñoz was well aware of how the international situation conditioned U.S. policy towards Puerto Rico. He particularly emphasized, in a text written during the war, the need to muffle the question of status.

. . .before the third month after the foundation of the Popular Democratic Party had elapsed, the forces of Hitler invaded Czechoslovakia, thus initiating the process that would lead to the present war. Later, Roosevelt began to educate world public opinion in the deep and decisive meaning of the looming war. The position of the people of Puerto Rico in the geography of the world and in the geography of justice and hope, could not be obstructive of the United States or the democratic cause. The posing of political "status" under such circumstances, be it independence or statehood, would be embarrassing for the United States, as Congress, the constitutional authority that could decide "status," could lack sufficient maturity in its international outlook to adequately fathom the relevance in America of denying Puerto Rico a formal demand for a solution to its "status."[71]

Muñoz went on to argue that Roosevelt should be spared "this diplomatic risk," particularly since the war was being fought for the "rights of the people," as the Atlantic Charter proved.[72] Spontaneous collaboration would provide the necessary "moral force" to obtain "definitive solutions" once the risks of war were victoriously overcome.[73] He apparently had used this argument (that the U.S. should not be embarrassed) to keep pro-independence leaders in his party under a tight rein during the 1940 campaign.[74]

In an eloquent passage of a manuscript written in 1970 for his memoirs (which was not included in the published version), Muñoz described the development of the European crisis and the war up to late 1940, when Governor Leahy was named Ambassador to Vichy. In his reconstruction of the period, the war was a major dimension of the context within which the Popular Party had risen to power, while the Spanish Civil War was described as the first stage of that "great tragedy."

During those years when I had been totally absorbed in the foundation of the Popular Party, the world was living through its great tragedy. The Spanish Civil War had occurred. Hitler had tested there his new methods and instruments of war, and the rulers of Russia, under Stalin, had done the same. They intervened on both sides of that tragic war as part of its training policy, in one case, or its world strategy, on the other. The expansionist policy of Hitler and the appeasement policy of the European democratic powers had prepared the ground for another great war catastrophe. The Republic had been destroyed in Spain. France had been invaded and defeated, and a government established in the southern part of the French territory with its capital in Vichy by an agreement with the German conquerors. It was the German's way for not having to directly govern a part of France, while they carried on the war with control over Paris and making arrangements to invade England . . . While the world bled and burnt, Puerto Rico had been developing the peaceful revolution of a new democracy.[75]

Muñoz and the Popular Party's attitude towards the war and U.S. military preparations cannot be explained merely as political expediency. It had deep roots in the leadership's anti-dictatorial and anti-fascist persuasion. Since the 1920s, Muñoz had expressed opposition to autocratic and dictatorial regimes in Latin America. For example, as a delegate to the American Federation of Labor's annual convention of 1923, he sponsored a resolution condemning the regime of Juan Vicente Gómez in Venezuela.[76] He later became an ardent opponent of the Trujillo dictatorship in the Dominican Republic.[77]

In addition to this, the impact of the Spanish Civil War among Puerto Rican intellectuals and professionals, many of whom were *muñocistas* and later became leaders of the Popular Party, was a major factor in shaping the party's outlook on the war. In the 1930s, Spain's political and intellectual life remained an important point of reference for Puerto Rico's intellectual elite. "Hispanism", of various hues and versions, became one of the forms of expression of anti-imperialist sentiment. The noted intellectual Antonio S. Pedreira professed that Puerto Rico was no more than a "gesture" of and within Hispanic culture.[78] Tomás Blanco condemned "insular isolation" (i.e. "the exclusive monopoly of U.S. influence") and called for strengthening ties with "the peoples of Hispanic language."[79] Albizu Campos's nationalist discourse also stressed the Spanish cultural legacy. In a speech celebrating the Spanish Republic in June 1931, Antonio J. Colorado, who would later become a prominent leader of the Popular Party, claimed that Puerto Ricans were "Spaniards who have lived for four centuries in Puerto Rico."[80] Muñoz's *La Democracia*, like other Puerto Rican newspapers, had covered the Spanish

Civil War extensively after its outbreak in 1936 with a section entitled *"Crónicas de la Guerra Española"* (Chronicles of the Spanish War) and *"Página de la Revolución Española"* (Page of the Spanish Revolution).[81]

Also, the Hispanic Studies Department at the University of Puerto Rico, established in 1927, maintained strong links with Spanish intellectuals and sponsored visits of leading academic figures such as Giner de los Ríos, Fernando de los Ríos, Tomás Navarro, and Juan Ramón Jiménez. When the Spanish Civil War ended in 1939, this became a stream of refugees that were well received by pro-Republican Puerto Rican intellectuals, among whom was Jaime Benítez, the Chancellor of the University of Puerto Rico. On the other hand, the Spanish community, calculated in about 6,000 persons, including powerful San Juan merchants and financiers, also maintained strong ties with the "mother country" and became an important source of support for Franco and the *Falange*. Its activities were closely monitored by U.S. intelligence.

The Spanish Civil War provoked a differentiation among intellectuals, more generally in the political elite, between Republican and Nationalist supporters. It even precipitated tensions and splits within the Nationalist Party. This party did not express support for the Spanish Republic and sought to remain "neutral" during the civil war.[82] The pro-Republican faction included a large portion of the *intelligentsia*, the leadership of the Socialist Party[83], the small Communist parties and the Popular Party. Pro-Republican sentiment was well represented in the University of Puerto Rico and the Atheneum.[84] The pro-Franco faction included some intellectuals, the newspapers *El Mundo* and *Puerto Rico Ilustrado*, the Catholic Church, and Spanish business circles.[85] Upon the fall of the Republic, the *falangistas* symbolically took over the *Casa de España*, an institution that was already a center of pro-Franco activities. The *muñocista* Jaime Benítez accused Winship of openly supporting the pro-Franco faction.[86] The Chief of Police under Winship and Leahy, Colonel Enrique de Orbeta, was married to a daughter of the leader of the *Falange*, Dionisio Trigo.

Prominent Popular Party leaders such as Gustavo Agrait, Jaime Benítez, Antonio J. Colorado, Salvador Tió, José A. Buitrago, Samuel R. Quiñones, Ernesto Ramos Antonini and Vicente Géigel Polanco, to mention but a few, were outspoken supporters of Republican Spain during the 1930s. Some of them established an "Association for the Defense of the Spanish Popular Front," published the journal *Alerta*, and sponsored a weekly radio program entitled *Acción Democrática*, where the Spanish situation was discussed.[87] Muna Lee, Muñoz's first wife, and Inés Mendoza, his second wife, signed a manifesto of intellectuals in support of the Republic. Opposition to fascism and to expansionist adventures by fascist powers was an important element of consensus within the Popular Party and shaped its conception of democracy. Not surprisingly, the party enthusiastically supported the increasingly hard line of the Roosevelt administration with regard to European fascism.

In January 1937, Muñoz had sought to dismiss the strategic military importance of Puerto Rico to the United States in a memorandum to Ickes arguing that these considerations "play no part in the Puerto Rican problem." This corresponded to his view at this time that the U.S. had no vital interest in Puerto Rico which could justify prolonging colonial rule. He also stressed the difference between his conception of independence and that of the *Partido Nacionalista*. However, he was careful to add in a footnote that "every sensible Puerto Rican will agree that even under independence the United States should have all the naval and military facilities in Puerto Rico that they may require for their national security," as "the security of the whole Caribbean will always be intimately involved with the national security of the United States."[88] If Puerto Rico was so unimportant militarily, why add the footnote? He also wrote another long memorandum to Laurence Duggan, a high-ranking functionary at the Latin American Division of the State Department, stressing his disagreement with the Nationalists, but also pointing to the negative image Gruening's policies were creating in Latin America. In this document no reference was made to military issues, only to the adverse diplomatic implications of Puerto Rican policy.[89]

Muñoz's argument regarding Puerto Rico's marginal military importance may have had some plausibility in early 1937, before the U.S. had launched its process of rearmament. Nevertheless, contemporary international developments already seemed ominous. In March 1936, Germany remilitarized the Rhineland. The following month, Italy culminated the conquest of Ethiopia with the capture of Addis Ababa. By July, the Spanish Civil War had begun. During November 1936 and January 1937, the Anti-Comintern Pact was signed and the Treaty of Versailles was finally repudiated by Hitler. Bitter fighting continued in Spain and China throughout 1937 and 1938, while international tensions mounted in Central Europe.

Historians generally place the beginnings of U.S. rearmament around the Munich Crisis of September 1938. Hitler's aggressive Nuremberg speech of September 12, in particular, prompted Roosevelt to dispatch Harry Hopkins to the West Coast to study the production potential of the aviation industry. The Munich agreement was perceived as extremely threatening to the U.S. since it was interpreted as laying bare Britain and France's lack of resolve to contain Nazi Germany.[90] Defense plans for Puerto Rico were being reviewed since the summer, with the first revised plan ready by late October 1938. In November, Ruby Black wrote to Muna Lee, Muñoz's wife, stressing that the international situation and strategic considerations advised abandoning demands for independence.

> The present international situation is such that Congress would not grant independence to Puerto Rico. It could, and might, if the proper arguments are put, think more of Puerto Rico as the means of keeping the American Continent ONE CONTINENT, of maintaining the continental doctrine, the continental solidarity. But the talk of independence now is, realistically, futile, considering the American Congress. DEFENSE will be the watchword, and Puerto Rico will be considered an important key to Panama, etc. no matter what some militarists say.[91]

Muñoz seemed to heed Ruby Black's prescient words. In June 1938, military intelligence still referred to him as "Mr. Luis Muñoz Marín, leader of the 'Net-Authentic-Complete' Liberal Party (radicals in favor of immediate independence for Puerto Rico)."[92] In his memoirs he explains that he decided to abandon pro-independence advocacy during the campaign because of an incident in Río Grande with a sugar cane worker named Nicanor Guerra. To Muñoz, the latter personified the "terror" with the idea of independence that was based on "what he heard mentioned about the independent republics of Latin America." He also mentions that "the image of the United States was that of a protecting older brother." It is interesting to note that Muñoz chose a man named Guerra (war) to exemplify working class opposition to independence.

Muñoz contrasts Guerra with a Popular Party leader named Cortés, who confronted him during a meeting in San Juan regarding his commitment to independence. According to Muñoz, Cortés was "more respectable" than Guerra, since his attitude was based on courage. However, he argues that a commitment to independence "would have closed the doors to the history of Puerto Rico." It would have made impossible the achievement of social justice, which was unacceptable since he "was a socialist first, and then an *independentista*."[93] As noted, Muñoz also provided an "external" explanation for his abandonment of independence, often overlooked, that is related to the war. But both explanations can be seen as interrelated, as closing "the doors to history" may have been perceived by Muñoz as a result of a combination of internal opposition to independence (represented by Guerra) and U.S. entrenched refusal to consider any change in status under war conditions.

In the 1939-1940 juncture, there was much to gain and little to lose politically in the downplaying of independence. First, the Popular Party was the only available venue for the pro-independence vote, as the two other forces supported statehood. The Nationalist Party was severely weakened, with a large part of its following flocking to the *populares*.[94] In addition, the absence of a commitment to independence made it easier for discontented Republican and, particularly, Socialist voters to heed Muñoz's message. Perhaps most importantly, the muffling of the demand for independence, at least during the war period, was quite possibly a necessary precondition for an understanding with the Roosevelt administration.

By December 1939, the "Weekly Summary of Certain Political Activities" (previously entitled "Subversive Activities") already reported that Muñoz's posture was very different from that of 1936, when he broke with Antonio R. Barceló. The report stated that he now favored a status referendum.[95] It is interesting that military intelligence also took note of Muñoz's discussion with Cortés, as a subsequent report refers to a "mass-meeting" of the Popular Party in Plaza Baldorioty with about 1,000 spectators. According to the military, a spectator, presumably Cortés, asked Muñoz why the speakers had not addressed the issue of independence. The latter used the opportunity to state that status was not an issue in the elections. The intelligence report also notes that Muñoz "was in favor of independence by peaceful means and on friendly terms with the United States," but "status" would have to be settled by the people in a referendum separate from the general elections.[96] The promise of a referendum was later contained in *El Batey*, but without any mention of the party's support for independence.

Nevertheless, Muñoz's shedding of independence did not dispel the political suspicions of the military. His participation in the 1939 May Day celebration was reported under the title "Communist Activities." It is worth quoting what caused so much concern to military intelligence.

> **Communist Activities**. a. May 1st was celebrated in San Juan by a meeting in which the speeches showed decided communistic leanings. The speakers were: Luis Muñoz Marin, President of the "Partido Popular Democrático" or left wing of the Liberal Party; Judge Arjona Siaca, from Humacao, who is a pink leftist; John B. Cadet, CIO representative from New York City. About 500 persons attended this meeting. Some of the speakers strongly eulogized the Soviet Union and its ideal form of government. They advocated: (1) Stopping Hitler and Mussolini in their expansion programs; (2) Restoration of the Spanish and Czechoslovakian republics; (3) Expulsion of the Japanese invaders from China; (4) Liberation of Albania and Ethiopia, without stating how these things would be accomplished. A true pan-Americanism and the defense of the principle of free determination in solving the political status of Puerto Rico were also strongly recommended.[97]

The "status" question was again dealt with in the party's official program approved at the Sixto Escobar Constituent Assembly in July 1940. The program contained, in a more detailed manner, many of the commitments of the *Catecismo del Pueblo*. Muñoz points out that the program was based on a speech he had delivered a few days earlier in Barranquitas during the annual pilgrimage to the gravesite of Muñoz Rivera.[98] Also, in an interview published by *El Mundo* in late June, Muñoz had rejected the possibility of reforming the "colonial regime." He stated that, "Political 'status' is the most serious and most fundamental problem of Puerto Rico." In order to finally resolve the "problem of the colony" and to preclude its utilization by politicians who divided the Puerto Ricans, it was "necessary that our people have the opportunity, as soon as possible, to decide its political status by its own will, democratically expressed within peace and order."[99]

The assembly took place under the shadow of a major military crisis in the European war. On May 10, the Germans had put an end to the "Phony War" period by launching a massive attack in the west through the Low Countries. That same day Leahy noted the following in his diary:

> Radio reports this morning bring information that the German army started an invasion of Holland, Belgium and Luxemburg at daylight today and made rapid progress into Holland.
>
> This serious threat to England must be countered at once by vigorous allied action which up to the present time on other fronts seems to have been impossible. Italy may now very probably join with Germany and any extension of the war to the Dutch West or East Indies may force the United States to take some protective action.[100]

Henceforth, the progress of the German offensive can be followed in Leahy's curt notations in his diary. In about two weeks, Allied resistance had practically collapsed and large forces were trapped in the Dunkirk area. By early June, about 338,000 British and French soldiers had been evacuated and 40,000 were captured. Paris fell to the Germans on June 14, and eight days later the armistice was signed with the new Vichy regime. The following month the decisive "Battle of Britain" was fought in the skies over the British Isles, while Hitler ordered preparations for an invasion. As Leahy foresaw, these developments did have an immediate impact in the Caribbean regarding the future of European colonies and also due to a sharp British-Vichy France confrontation following the armistice.

The party program approved by the assembly promised to end "the system of economic exploitation to which our people is subjected" through the "exercise of democracy." It contained a final part entitled "Political 'Status'," which clearly represented a difficult transaction between tendencies. Political status was declared not to be an issue in the elections and a "solemn promise" made to the people that votes for the party would not be interpreted as favoring a particular "status." This was placed within the context of "this solemn moment of crisis for the world, of the intensification of the defense of the rights of man in democracy, of readjustment in the American hemisphere, and the affirmation of justice for our people."

The party was committed to extending "all its collaboration for the defense of democracy," which expressed itself in the American hemisphere as a "confederation of the free peoples of America." In the "decisive year of 1940," the future of Puerto Rico in the American hemisphere had to do with the "struggle of two great systems," since the country was not "floating in space, untouched by the other regions of the world." Neither independence nor statehood would be possible "if democracy perishes in the American continent."

> The world has changed in the last three months. The liberty of Puerto Rico is now bound up in the liberty of the whole of America, the justice for the people of Puerto Rico is now bound up in the capacity and the right of all America to make, defend and sustain justice for the peoples of America. America is now the refuge of democracy and must jointly defend democracy.

Within this hemispheric defense conception, "status" options became redefined as a matter of deciding whether Puerto Rico should join the hemispheric confederation as a U.S. state, or as "a leading people in the great march towards confederation of all the free peoples of America." The latter option was favored. It was a rather complicated formulation that evaded any direct mention of independence. Immediately after this passage, "status" was declared not to be an issue in the upcoming elections. The need for a plebiscite separate from general elections was mentioned, but no time frame was set.[101]

The intelligence officer who wrote the report on the assembly had to point out that "The political part contains a long and almost unintelligible preamble." He even felt necessary to include a parenthesis clarifying that a passage of the program was referring to "(As a free state by itself, independent)." But the report also indicated that Muñoz had argued against a resolution moved by Antonio Pacheco Padró, "a former Nationalist," to declare independence "as the only aspiration of the Popular

Democratic Party." The report notes that "[Pacheco's] resolution received a good hand when introduced, probably from over fifty per cent of those present." It was withdrawn due to Muñoz's objection.[102] A subsequent intelligence report indicated the following:

> [Muñoz] is silencing any reference to the Island's future po-litical status, although he admits that when [the] time come[s] to decide this matter, he will favor independence. In the last general convention of this party held at San Juan, Prof. Rafael Soltero Peralta, who teaches commercial law at the University of Puerto Rico, moved that a cablegram be sent to the Havana Conference denouncing the United States' regime in Puerto Rico. But Mr. Muñoz Marin himself objected to such a resolution alleging that, in view of the international situation, the United States should not be bothered or embarrassed at the present moment.[103]

This was particularly significant since Muñoz had supported sending Vicente Géigel Polanco and Coll Cuchí to denounce U.S. policy toward Puerto Rico at the Buenos Aires Conference of December 1936.

The war as a crusade for democracy led by President Roosevelt—within which the Popular Democratic Party and the people of Puerto Rico had to make a contribution—became a major theme of Muñoz's speeches in late 1940 and throughout 1941.[104] In the last-minute appeal to the electorate on November 4, 1940, he spoke of "the democracy that President Roosevelt defends in the world and that we must help him defend."[105] He again referred to the war in the speech setting out the objectives of his party delivered a few days after the elections. To him, Puerto Rico was "an example and symbol of the immortal vitality of democracy . . . among a people that never really experimented it be-fore," and at a time when "democracy is under siege in the world." The "creation of democracy" in Puerto Rico was "an example of the enor-mous potential of the democratic spirit and hope for many in far off lands. . . who were losing faith in democracy." He asked for prayers to the Almighty so that "the democratic example of Puerto Rico may be a grain of sand in the barrier that will prevent that democracy is disre-spected in all of America."[106]

On December 16, 1940, Muñoz participated in a Barranquitas celebration entitled "Roosevelt's Day." Military registration was about to start in four days, and a recruitment drive was in full swing. This time Muñoz spoke to a group of children dressed to represent the American Republics. The podium was decorated with a photograph of the President. Behind Muñoz a sign proclaimed "¡Hurrah Roosevelt!" and another stated "The people of Puerto Rico are with you in the defense of democracy." In the speech, the Popular leader claimed that the results of the elections were a homage of the people of Puerto Rico to the "idea symbolized by this man." Roosevelt was an "emblem" and a "symbol" of democracy, which was not a "static structure" but a "force that moves, aspires and grows." What united the entire American continent was not the achievement of democracy, which was unequal, but the "unity in the dream of complete democratic fulfillment."[107] However, to the ever skeptical military intelligence agents, this was no more than "posing" by Muñoz Marín.

> Celebration of President Roosevelt's Day in Pan-America. Puerto Rico enthusiastically joined the rest of Latin America in celebrating President Roosevelt's Day on December 16. There were parades and speeches made about President Roosevelt throughout the island. Of special interest was the participation in the celebration of Luis Munoz Marin (sic), President of the Popular Democratic Party and in all probability the next President of the Puerto Rican Senate. It has been claimed that Munoz Marin (sic) is anti-American and favors independence for Puerto Rico. To counteract these charges, he has insistently stated that the future political status of Puerto Rico is not an issue at present. In the Roosevelt Day celebration, he was pictured greeting Uncle Sam (a boy dressed as Uncle Sam), and he made a speech praising the United States. Apparently Mr. Munoz Marin (sic) is trying to do everything in his power to pose as a friend of the United States and as an advocate of the National Defense program for the island.[108]

There was also a reference to the war and national defense in Muñoz's inaugural speech as President of the Senate on February 10, 1941. He again stressed the democratic character of the Popular Party campaign and related it to "the democracy that our great President Roosevelt is defending in the world, the democracy that we are prepared to defend with our lives." No longer was Puerto Rico's contribution limited to its democratic example. Now it also consisted of the ultimate sacrifice.

Additionally, the governorship, then held by Leahy´s successor Guy J. Swope, no longer personified U.S. colonial rule and a potential source of conflict with a reformist legislative program, as envisaged in the *Catecismo del Pueblo*. On the contrary, Muñoz now claimed that "in the person of the governor come together the democratic policy of the President and the democratic policy of the people of Puerto Rico." Among the "democratic realities" of the President, the governor and the people of Puerto Rico were "the best and most harmonious arrangement." He went on to state that no democratic principle could oppose the rejection of any law by the Governor or the President that could "in any way be prejudicial to the national defense of the United States -which is the same as saying the defense of democracy itself in America and the whole world." U.S. national defense was "the defense of Puerto Rico and many other peoples." It was the "defense of democratic principles," and "Democracy, [a] vital and creative force, does not have the power to commit suicide."[109]

By mid-1941, with the U.S. drawing nearer to formal entry into the war, Muñoz further clarified his position on the war, the colonial question and the Popular Party's program. In a speech at the University of Puerto Rico in early July, he divided the world into the "area of democracy" and the "area that denies democracy." Puerto Rico was part of the former, but its situation was "peculiar" because "it defended and practiced democracy, without fully having it." Puerto Ricans could thus be called the "serfs of democracy" (*serviles de la democracia*), as they defended a liberty that they did not fully enjoy. The country's contribution to democracy consisted in "giving vitality to the democratic reality of our people," and "being prepared to give up our lives." But the most important contribution would be to "end the blindness of the democratic centers to the peculiar situation of Puerto Rico." A victory of the "democratic area" would be equally a victory for all of its parts. Therefore, "complete, unequivocal and unlimited solidarity" was "good," "dignified," "great," "noble," and "redeeming."

In this manner, Muñoz clearly postponed any solution of the "status" question until the end of the war, while defining full collaboration in the military effort as an indirect manner of eventually obtaining "full democracy."[110] Later that same month, Muñoz again called for the postponement of any discussion of "status" when he attacked Bolívar Pagán for having posed the issue. This "encumbered the task of the United States in the life and death struggle of democracy." Thus, it was irresponsible for politicians to bring up "status." "Full collaboration in the defense of democracy" was accelerating "the solution of political 'status' according to the will of the people of Puerto Rico more than petty politicians suspect."[111]

In his 4th of July speech, delivered almost immediately after the one at the university, Muñoz touched on some of these topics. That date was defined as a celebration "of something bigger than nations," of "humble men," "of men of work, of the land, of science and creative spirit." It was an occasion for free men to "rededicate [their] whole being to the purposes of liberty in its moment of greatest siege and danger." The threat was posed by an external enemy: the fascist governments. It was also posed by an internal enemy that was not a "Fifth Column" or capitalism, but the corruption of democracy by the creation "of a cast of politicians more interested in the privilege of its group, of its [political] machinery, than in the responsibilities it has contracted with its people." The democratic struggle demanded the temporary sacrifice of certain rights, i.e. "those that could be used to hinder the cause of democracy in its life and death struggle." As examples he cited the right to strike of workers in defense industries and also "men in democratic countries who wish that democracy may continue expanding and deepening in the life of justice and who could endanger democracy itself if their dissatisfaction with the actual form of democracy in their different countries would move them to actions that might risk the life of democracy itself." To the latter he pointed out that democracy was a "vital" and "expansive force."

The emancipation of the slaves had not been achieved with U.S. independence, but the latter had set in motion the "forces of liberty" that freed the black race eighty years later with the "roar of cannons" during the great civil war. Now, "in the roar of cannons of this war for democracy, the men to whom the next expansion of democratic reality corresponds, already feel the breath of justice." In this manner, Muñoz

attributed an emancipatory character to the war itself that was not unlike contemporary formulations by some U.S. liberals such as Archibald
McLeish.[112] It was a view also shared by Rexford Guy Tugwell.[113] Muñoz
concluded by calling for world unity under a single imaginary flag with
"the single star of the single purpose of democracy" and "the Eagle of
the north and the Condor of the South."[114]

During the hearings held by the Tugwell Commission to study the
application of the 500 Acre Law in July 1941, Muñoz made another significant statement on the relationship between the party's reformist program and U.S. national defense requirements. Tugwell explained that
this crucial statement (which entailed no less than a decision on whether
to collaborate with the approval and implementation of the Land Law,
the capstone of the Popular Party legislative program) was held under
the shadow of war preparations and the President's concern with the
Caribbean.

> It required analysis of the whole Puerto Rican economy. We
> were doing more than that, actually, because the imminence
> of national crisis had led our group into considerations which
> were Caribbean-wide.
>
> The background of this was the President's interest in the area
> as part of our national defense-for that was the phrase we
> used then, the country not being willing to hear the possibil-
> ity of war mentioned even though we were well into an enor-
> mous program of preparation.[115]

In response to Tugwell's questions, Muñoz stated at the hearings
that measures to "keep the people well fed, well dressed and well shel-
tered" were "means" to ensure "national defense." Solving the land issue was also "merely means that lead to that end" (i.e., national defense),
since, according to Muñoz, "Anything that may strengthen the economic
welfare of Puerto Rico will strengthen the wishes of the people to defend what it has."[116] A few days earlier, Rafael Picó, another ranking
Popular Party leader, had also stressed the instrumental character of the
reformist program in almost exactly the same words.[117] This implied a
major discursive shift. No longer did Puerto Rico's contribution to the
global democratic struggle consist mainly of its "creation of democracy"

and its "democratic example." By mid-1941, social reform was predicated as subordinate to national defense, as a means of promoting the people's loyalty to the war effort.

Muñoz gave another important speech about the war on December 21, 1941, about two weeks after Pearl Harbor's attack and the U.S. formal entry into the war.[118] He touched on some of the themes developed in earlier speeches, but this time he used a more martial and warlike language. The war was set apart from previous wars by virtue of the fact that it was not a clash among nations but between opposed systems. This made the people the main actors. The war had been undertaken by the fascist powers as a "totalitarian counterrevolution to destroy the conquests of the democratic revolution." The people of the world were thus faced with a stark choice between liberty and slavery, and Puerto Rico was part of the "democratic area of the world."[119]

To Muñoz, the defense of liberty, however, did not imply the defense of "what exists," of "misery," but "the struggle. . . to continue eliminating that misery from the face of the earth and the slavery that would forever drown the aspiration of its elimination." Thus, the "people of Puerto Rico" were asked by Muñoz to endure the sacrifices demanded by the war effort not only on the basis of their "loyalty to the American nation," or the need to defend the "values of the human spirit," but out of "our imperative need as a people . . . so that the work of democratic justice be not interrupted."[120] In this manner, Muñoz defined the defense of liberty as including the continued implementation of its reform program, while claiming that a fascist victory would destroy both liberty and the possibility of reform and social justice. Democracy could not annul rights in order to defend them. Therefore, "we should not fear that the work of the people towards its justice be paralyzed."[121] War and social reform were thus not in contradiction, a point he stressed several times throughout the speech. The Atlantic Charter was invoked as proof that in war "people are mutually defending their rights."[122]

It should be noted that Muñoz, despite the passing reference to "loyalty to the American nation," did not call upon Puerto Ricans to the war effort as American citizens but as a distinct people joining together with other peoples, including the people of the United States. He defined the Puerto Rican people as courageous and even welcomed their participation in the war, which provided an opportunity for Puerto Rico to use its "force."

> The same harshness of our sacrifice. . . will be a virility tonic for us. It was good that Puerto Rico had to do harsh things in defense of its justice and its hopes. It was not good that it achieved its justice and hopes through a gift, favor or tolerance.[123]

The people of Puerto Rico would not only fight militarily, but had also to maintain "civil discipline." This meant strictly obeying authorities in measures such as the blackouts. In this way, Muñoz obliterated the colonial character of the policy and the fact that Puerto Rico did not possess armed forces of its own to fight the war. However, Puerto Ricans were being massively recruited (about 20,000 by then) into the U.S. armed forces.

> The people of Puerto Rico. . . [are] in the struggle. Our struggle is military as it is civil–we have given twenty thousand volunteers to the army.[124]

Thus, despite postponing the issue of status, Muñoz constructed the notion of a bilateral relationship within which the "people of Puerto Rico" voluntarily participated in the war as an entity in defense of its own interests. Not surprisingly he ended his speech with an exhortation worthy of a Commander-in-Chief.

> Puerto Ricans: At attention and forward! Forward in the march of justice! Forward in the discipline of defense! Forward in the will for victory![125]

NOTES

1. For an illuminating statement of his views on status, see Luis Muñoz Marín to Ruby Black, April 6, 1934, Box 2, Folder VIII-B, Document 103, Ruby Black Collection, Centro de Investigaciones Históricas, UPR. He states that with statehood "we should be forever under the American tariff, forever prevented from industrializing, forever condemned to the bitterness of sugar, forever honored by the privilege of basking under an extra star of the American flag and of starving behind its bars. The full possibilities of fighting our way out of the present mess must not be curtailed by an honor that would probably kill us and disgrace you."

2. See, Luis Muñoz Marín, Memorandum for Laurence Duggan, February 2, 1937. Ruby Black Collection, Box 2, Folder 11, Document 10, Centro de Investigaciones Históricas.

3. Luis Muñoz Marín, *La historia del Partido Popular Democrático* (San Juan: Editorial El Batey, 1984), p. 90.

4. Luis Muñoz Marín, "Libro, Borrador 2–1970," pp. 518-9, Section XI, Material de y sobre Luis Muñoz Marín, Material para el libro *Memorias*, Box YY, Fundación Luis Muñoz Marín.

5. Luis Muñoz Marín, "Libro, Borrador 2–1970", op. cit., pp. 509-10.

6. Luis Muñoz Marín, *La historia* . . ., op. cit., p. 13. Author's translation.

7. Luis Muñoz Marín to Ruby Black, November 16, 1938, Box 4, Folder XII, Document 127, Ruby Black Collection, Centro de Investigaciones Históricas.

8. Luis Muñoz Marín, *La historia* . . ., op. cit., pp. 23-4. Author's translation.

9. Luis Muñoz Marín, "Libro, Borrador 2—1970", op. cit., p. 494.

10. Ibid., pp. 481-2.

11. Luis Muñoz Marín, *La historia* . . ., *op. cit.*, pp. 90, 100. Also, Luis Muñoz Marín, "Libro, Borrador 2—1970", op. cit., p. 481, 521.

12. Luis Muñoz Marín, *La historia* . . ., p. 100. Author's translation.

13. Ibid., pp. 22-3.

14. For the state of organization of the party in August 1939, see, Luis Muñoz Marín to Ruby Black, August 11, 1939, Box 4, Folder 13, Document 130, Ruby Black Collection, Centro de Investigaciones Históricas.

15. Luis Muñoz Marín, "Libro, Borrador 2—1970", op. cit., p. 511.

16. Luis Muñoz Marín, *La historia. . .*, p. 13.

17. "Muñoz Marín conferencia con el nuevo gobernador Leahy," *El Batey*, No. 8 (October, 1939), p. 4. By early January 1940, Muñoz described Leahy in glowing terms in a letter to Ruby Black. Luis Muñoz Marín to Ruby Black, January 8, 1940, Ruby Black Collection, Box 5, 1940, Centro de Investigaciones Históricas.

18. William D. Leahy, Diary, September 11, 1939, to December 5, 1940, Manuscript Division, Library of Congress, p. 37, 45-6.

19. "Muñoz Marín conferenció ayer por la mañana con el gobernador Leahy - Le sometió el caso de la Ordenanza de Utuado que pide dinero para dedicarlo a la campaña política liberal," *El País*, March 15, 1940, p. 1.

20. The other leaders were Samuel R. Quiñones, Jorge Font Saldaña and Urrutia. See, Eliseo Combas Guerra, "En torno a La Fortaleza," *El Mundo*, March 26, 1940, p. 4.

21. "Senado aprobó sobre el veto el proyecto declarando 'El Día de Santiago Iglesias,'" *El País*, April 10, 1940, p. 1.

22. William D. Leahy, Diary, op. cit., p. 77.

23. Dr. A. Fernós Isern, "El nuevo ciclo de 1940 y la voluntad de soberanía", *El Mundo*, April 21 and 22, May 9 and 13, 1940, reproduced in Reece B. Bothwell, *Puerto Rico: Cien Años de Lucha*, Vol. III (Río Piedras: Editorial Universitaria, 1979), Document 74, pp. 233-40.

24. "Comisión Popular saluda al gobernador Leahy", *El Imparcial*, July 24, 1940, p. 1.

25. Muñoz had been insistent on this issue since the early 1930s. See, Silvia Álvarez Curbelo, "La casa de cristal: El ejercicio senatorial de Luis Muñoz Marín (1932-1936)", in Carmen Raffucci, Silvia Álvarez Curbelo y Fernando Picó, eds., Senado de Puerto Rico, 1917-1992 (San Juan: Senado de Puerto Rico, 1992), p. 112.

26. Ibid., pp. 100-1, 115-6. Also, Eliseo Combas Guerra, "En torno a la Fortaleza," *El Mundo*, November 1 and 2,1940, p. 4. The leaders present at the November 1, meeting were: Bolívar Pagán and Ramón Barrios, Socialists; Luis Muñoz Marín and Samuel R. Quiñones, Popular; Adolfo Nogueras Rivera and Francisco Quirós Méndez, *Tripartita*; Julio Morales, *Laborista*, Charles H. Terry, president and other members of the electoral board and Governor Leahy. "La reunión celebrada en Fortaleza sobre el orden de las elecciones -Líderes políticos se comprometieron a empeñar esfuerzos hacia fin indicado", *La Correspondencia*, November 2,1940, p. 1; also, *El Mundo*, November 2, 1940.

27. "Muñoz Marín seguro que Leahy protegerá derechos electores," *El Imparcial*, November 1, 1940.

28. "Cámara de Representantes aprobó proyecto para dar representación al Partido Popular," *El País*, April 18,1940, p. 1.

29. Luis Muñoz Marín, LIBRO, Borrador 2– 1970, pp. 522-3, Fundación Luis Muñoz Marín.

30. "Discurso por la radio la noche del 4 de noviembre de 1940," Discursos de Luis Muñoz Marín, 1932-1948, Fundación Luis Muñoz Marín.

31. Luis Muñoz Marín, *Catecismo del Pueblo, contestaciones a las preguntas que el pueblo hace sobre su vida y su porvenir* (Partido Popular Democrático, 1939). Author's translation of quoted passages.

32. See, for example, Silvia Álvarez Curbelo, "La conflictividad en el discurso político de Luis Muñoz Marín," in Silvia Álvarez Curbelo and María Elena Rodríguez Castro, eds., *Del nacionalismo al populismo, cultura y política en Puerto Rico* (Río Piedras: Ediciones Huracán, 1993), pp. 13-36; also, Luis López Rojas, "Luis Muñoz Marín y las estrategias de poder, 1936-1940," Doctoral dissertation, Centro de Estudios Avanzados de Puerto Rico y el Caribe, 1997, pp. 75-91.

33. See, J. A. Hobson, *Imperialism, A Study* (Michigan: Ann Arbor Paperback, 1972), particularly Chapter 6.

34. In 1940, the rural population still comprised almost 70 per cent of the total population. See, James L. Dietz, *Historia económica de Puerto Rico* (Río Piedras: Ediciones Huracán, 1989), Table 4.5, p. 245.

35. See Luis Muñoz Marín, "Discurso de la victoria, 16 de noviembre de 1940", in *Memorias, 1898-1940* (San Juan: Universidad Interamericana de Puerto Rico, 1982), p. 271-4.

36. See, particularly, Víctor Raúl Haya de la Torre, "Discurso en la Plaza de Acho, 23 de agosto de 1931," in *Textos Apristas, selección de textos No. 2,* mimeo, Universidad Católica de Lima, n.d.; and, *El antimperialismo y el APRA* (Lima: Amauta, 1972). Also, Peter Klaren, *Modernization, Dislocation and Aprismo* (Austin: University of Texas, 1973).

37. See the article presenting the new publication in *El Batey*, No. 1 (second fortnight, March 1939), p. 1.

38. Ibid., "El Partido Popular Democrático y el pueblo americano", p. 2.

39. Ibid.,"Programa 'El Batey,'" pp. 3-4.

40. Ibid., Pedro Juan Dumont, "Historia Breve de Luis Muñoz Marín," p. 3.

41. Ibid.,"Muñoz Marín y los desempleados," p. 4.

42. See, for example, "Última hora," *El Batey*, No. 2 (first fortnight, April 1939), p. 1;

in that same number, "Conspiran para quitar la ley de salario mínimo en el azúcar," p. 3; and, "Los pleitos de salario mínimo en el azúcar, Ramos Antonini y Gutiérrez Franqui defienden a los obreros", No. 4 (first fortnight, June 1939), p. 3.

43. "Mr. John Rogan del CIO", *El Batey*, No. 2 (first fortnight, April 1939), p. 1; "Marcantonio se dirige a trabajadores", No. 4 (first fortnight, June 1939), p. 2; "Miles de obreros sin trabajo y de agricultores sin luz, lo que está pasando en el proyecto de 'Garzas'", No. 5 (second fortnight, June 1939), p. 2; "Injusticias contra los trabajadores de los muelles de Ponce", (first fortnight, August 1939), p. 2; and, "Máquinas excavadoras comiéndose el pan de los hombres", No. 7 (second fortnight, August 1939), p. 3.

44. "Lea esto también sobre la sal del pobre", No. 3 (second fortnight, April 1939), p. 2.

45. "Eusebio Pereira, agricultor republicano – hoy Popular, sus razones", No. 4 (first fortnight, June 1939), p. 2.

46. For example, "Muñoz Marín y los desempleados," No. 1 (second fortnight, March 1939), p. 4; "Lea esto también sobre la sal del pobre," No. 3 (second fortnight, April 1939), p. 2; "Se propone ponerles contribuciones al arroz y al bacalao. . .," No. 4 (first fortnight, June 1939); "La situación de los agricultores, lo que se necesita es eliminar toda contribución a fincas pequeñas," idem.; "Las injusticias contra los choferes, en la ciudad, como en el campo, hay injusticia social," No. 5 (second fortnight, June 1939), p. 1; "El campesino y sus derechos," p. 4; "Las injusticias que se están cometiendo contra el maestro rural," idem.

47. "Muchos trabajadores y agricultores son candidatos del Partido Popular," No. 17 (second fortnight, October 1940), p. 4. The article was accompanied by a photograph of the *jíbaro* Bernacet. After the elections, Muñoz stressed the symbolic importance of the defeat in Ponce of Pedro Juan Serrallés, a Republican and member of a powerful family sugar-owning family, by the Popular candidate who was a worker. According to Juan José Baldrich, however, only a small minority of workers were elected as Popular Party candidates, while there was a strong representation of urban capitalists, large *colonos* and *hacendados*. See, "Class and the State, The Origins of Populism in Puerto Rico, 1934-1952," Doctoral dissertation, Yale University, May 1981, Table 5.1, p. 160.

48. "Lean esto las mujeres del campo," No. 2 (first fortnight, April 1939), p. 4; "A las mujeres," No. 10 (January 1940), p. 4; and, "Mujeres ¡pónganle verguenza a los hombres que no la tengan!," No. 18 (November 1940), p. 2.

49. "Lo que significa la Semana Santa para el pueblo," No. 3 (second fortnight, April 1939), p. 4.

50. "El Obispo de Ponce defiende la justicia social," No. 4 (first fortnight, June 1939), p. 1.

51. Reece B. Bothwell, *Puerto Rico: cien años de lucha política*, Volume III (Río Piedras: Editorial Universitaria, 1979), Document 85, p. 273-6.

52. "Dios hizo el pan para todas las bocas," *El Batey*, No. 6 (first fortnight, August 1939), p. 1.

53. "Religión y justicia, posición clara del Partido Popular en defensa de ambas," *El Batey,* No. 10 (January, 1940), p. 1; see, also, "El Partido Popular Democrático y la religión," No. 15 (September 1940), p. 4.

54. "Carta del Reverendo Padre Stadta a Luis Muñoz Marín," *El Batey*, No. 11 (February 1940), p. 1; and, "Ya el pueblo sabe quiénes son los embusteros," p. 4.

55. "Lea esta carta del Reverendo Padre Rivera a Muñoz Marín, denuncia la mentira de los que dicen que Muñoz Marín es comunista," No. 16 (October 1940), p. 1.

56. "El candidato Popular a Washington fue el único que defendió a la Iglesia, así lo afirma 'El Piloto' periódico católico," No. 18 (November 1940), p. 2.

57. "El Partido Popular no tiene alianzas con nadie," No. 3 (second fortnight, April 1939), p. 2;.

58. "Ni estadidad ni independencia, los votos populares serán votos contra la explotación," No. 15 (September 1940), p. 4.

59. "Qué quiere decir Pan, Tierra y Libertad," No. 8 (October 1939), p. 2.

60. Ibid.,"Muñoz Marín conferencia con el nuevo gobernador Leahy," p. 4.

61. "El Partido Popular Democrático defiende la democracia americana," No. 16 (October 1940), p. 3.

62. "El Fiscal Snyder desbarata otro embuste," No. 18 (November 1940), p. 1. It is interesting that Snyder's letter was in response to a letter from Muñoz dated October 30. Snyder answered on that same day, less than a week before the elections, knowing that his statement would be used in the campaign.

63. "Partido Popular Democrático, ¡Que no es lo mismo!," *El Batey*, No. 2 (first fortnight, April 1939), p. 1; also, "Muñoz Rivera se llamó con los nombres de seis partidos, Barbosa se llamó con los nombres de cinco partidos, eso quiere decir que los nombres de los partidos no tienen importancia", No. 13 (April 1940), p. 2.

64. Luis Muñoz Marín, "Discurso del Día de Muñoz Rivera," Discursos de Luis Muñoz Marín, Fundación Luis Muñoz Marín.

65. "De Muñoz Rivera a Muñoz Marín," *El Batey*, No. 6 (first fortnight, August 1939), p. 1; also, Carlos Román Benítez, "La historia de Muñoz Marín en defensa del pueblo," No. 10 (January 1940), pp. 2-3.

66. "La nueva alianza", No. 6 (first fortnight, August 1939), p. 4.

67. "Partido Popular Democrático ¡Que no es lo mismo!," No. 2 (first fortnight, April 1939), p. 1.

68. "Mataron al 'Partido Liberal', los que se quedaron con el nombre lo entregaron a los Republicanos corporacionistas de García Méndez," No. 15 (September 1940), p. 2.

69. For example, "Senador Coalicionista acusa a la coalición," No. 2 (first fortnight, April 1939), p. 1; and, "Informe a los campesinos de Puerto Rico sobre el alegado 'racket' –o robalete– del Capitolio," No. 3 (second fortnight, April 1939), p. 1.

70. Luis Muñoz Marín, "Libro, Borrador 2–1970", op. cit., p. 518.

71. Luis Muñoz Marín, *La Historia. . .* op. cit., pp. 89-70. Author's translation.

72. It should be noted that here we refer to the post 1940 election period, since the Atlantic Charter was signed by Roosevelt and Churchill on August 14, 1941.

73. Luis Muñoz Marín, *La Historia. . .* op. cit., pp. 89-70.

74. See, Major General E. L. Daley, Commander Puerto Rico Department, "Comments on Current Events No. 1, Period September 5, 1940 to September 30, 1940," October 1, 1940, R.G. 165 (MID), Box 3896, Entry 65, NA.

75. Luis Muñoz Marín, "Libro, Borrador 2—1970. . ." op. cit., pp. 544-5.

76. Carmelo Rosario Natal, *La juventud de Luis Muñoz Marín, Vida y pensamiento 1898-1932* (San Juan: Master Typesetting, 1976), pp. 163-4.

77. I discuss this in "Luis Muñoz Marín y Rafael Leonidas Trujillo, una pugna caribeña (1940-1961), Fernando Picó, ed., *Luis Muñoz Marín. Perfiles de su gobernación* (San Juan: Fundación Luis Muñoz Marín, 2003), pp. 21-62.

78. Antonio S. Pedreira, *Insularismo* (Río Piedras: Editorial Edil, 1973), p. 25.

79. Tomás Blanco, *Prontuario histórico de Puerto Rico* (Río Piedras: Ediciones Huracán, 1981), p. 149.

80. Luis Ángel Ferrao, "Nacionalismo, hispanismo y élite intelectual en el Puerto Rico de la década de 1930", in Silvia Álvarez Curbelo and María Elena Rodríguez Castro, eds., *Del nacionalismo al populismo: cultura y política en Puerto Rico* (Río Piedras: Ediciones Huracán, 1993), pp. 48-9.

81. See, *La Democracia* for the second half of 1936 onwards. The newspaper, however, did not editorialize on the war, at least during this early period.

82. Luis A. Ferrao, *Pedro Albizu Campos y el nacionalismo puertorriqueño* (Río Piedras: Ediciones Cultural, 1990), pp. 185, 229, 245 and 327.

83. See, for example, Bolívar Pagán, "La Guerra Civil Española," in *Ideales en marcha* (San Juan: Biblioteca de Autores Puertorriqueños, 1939), pp. 237-40. Santiago Iglesias also spoke in favor of the Spanish Republic.

84. In 1939-1940, the board of the Atheneum included, among others, Vicente Géigel Polanco, Samuel R. Quiñones, Margot Arce, Nilita Vientós Gastón, Antonio Fernós Isern and Jorge Font Saldaña. See, issues of *Ateneo Puertorriqueño, Revista Trimestral*, for this period.

85. Alfredo Matilla, Matilde Albert, Gabriel Moreno, et al., editors, *Cincuenta años de exilio español en Puerto Rico y el Caribe, 1939-1989* (Coruña: Ediciós do Castro, 1991), p. 22.

86. Refer to footnote 67 of Chapter 4.

87. Matilla, Albert, Moreno, et al., eds., *op. cit.,* p. 23; also, author's conversation with Luis Agrait, October 10, 1997.

88. Luis Muñoz Marín to Secretary Harold L. Ickes, "Memorandum: Political Status of Puerto Rico", January 5, 1937, reproduced in Surendra Bhana, *The U.S. and the Development of the Puerto Rican Status Question, 1936-1968* (Wichita: The University Press of Kansas, 1975), p. 220.

89. Luis Muñoz Marín, "Memorandum for Laurence Duggan," February 2, 1937, Ruby Black Collection, Box 2, Folder XI, Document 10, Centro de Investigaciones Históricas.

90. Stetson Conn and Byron Fairchild, *The Framework of Hemisphere Defense* (Washington, D.C.: Office of the Chief of Military History, US Army, 1960), pp. 4-7.

91. Ruby Black to Muna Lee, November 16, 1938, Box 4, Doc. 126, Ruby Black Collection, Centro de Investigaciones Históricas.

92. Col. John W. Wright, Commanding 65th Infantry, "Weekly Summary of Subversive Activities - Puerto Rico Area", San Juan, June 15, 1938, also, July 6, 1938, R.G. 165, MID, 1917-1941, Box 3112, U.S. National Archives.

93. Luis Muñoz Marín, *Libro, Borrador 2–1970. . .*, op. cit., pp. 481-7.

94. Since mid-1939, military intelligence reported that the trend of public opinion was decidedly pro-American, and that the Nationalist Party was "dormant." In July 1940, it concluded, contrary to Chief of Police Orbeta, that the potential for violence by nationalists was very limited. See, for example, Brig. Gen. E. L. Daley, US Army Commanding, "Weekly. . ." July 16, 1939, op. cit.; and, op. cit., February 28, 1940. The report on the Popular Party's assembly estimated that only 500 Nationalists remained active and that about 10,000 had shifted to the Popular Party. See, op. cit., "Weekly. . .," July 24, 1940.

95. Brig. Edmund L. Daley, "Weekly Summary of Certain Political Activities," December 20, 1939, op. cit.

96. Daley, "Weekly. . .," January 17, 1939, op. cit; see, also, "El Partido Popular Democrático fija su posición," *El Mundo*, January 5, 1939, p. 4.

97. Col. John W. Wright, "Weekly Summary. . .," May 3, 1939, op. cit.

98. Luis Muñoz Marín, "Ante tumba de Muñoz Rivera," July 17, 1940, Speeches, Fundación Luis Muñoz Marín.

99. Bothwell, op. cit., Volume 3, Document 60, pp. 197-8.

100. William D. Leahy, "Diary. . .", op. cit., May 10, 1940, p. 57.

101. "Partido Popular Democrático 1940, Programa económico y social, *Status* político," in Reece B. Bothwell, *Puerto Rico: Cien años de lucha política* (Río Piedras: Editorial Universitaria, 1979), Volume I-1, pp. 613-27. Author's translation.

102. Brig. Gen. E. L. Daley, "Weekly Summary. . .," op. cit., July 24, 1940.

103. Major General E. L. Daley, "Comments on Current Events No. 1. . .," October 1, 1940, op. cit.

104. For the complete text of the most important of his wartime speeches see, Luis Muñoz Marín, *Discursos, 1934-1948* (San Juan: Fundación Luis Muñoz Marín, 1999).

105. Luis Muñoz Marín, "Discurso por la radio la noche del 4 de noviembre de 1940," November 4, 1940, Speeches, Fundación Luis Muñoz Marín. Author's translation.

106. Luis Muñoz Marín, "Luis Muñoz Marín establece las normas de gobierno de su partido," November 16, 1940, Speeches, Fundación Luis Muñoz Marín. Author's translation.

107. Luis Muñoz Marín, "Discurso pronunciado por Luis Muñoz Marín en el Día de Roosevelt," December 16,1940, Speeches, Fundación Luis Muñoz Marín.

108. Lieut. Col. C. S. Ferrin, G.S.C. G-2, "Comments on Current Events," December 31, 1940, op. cit.

109. Reece B. Bothwell, op. cit., "El discurso de Muñoz Marín en el Senado," Document 99, Vol. III, pp. 328-30.

110. Ibid., "El problema de Puerto Rico," Document 106, pp. 346-8. For an analysis of the context of this speech, see, Nereida Rodríguez, *Debate universitario y dominación colonial (1941-1947)* (San Juan: Nereida Rodríguez, 1996), Chapter 3.

111. Reece B. Bothwell, op. cit., "Están entorpeciendo la obra de Estados Unidos," Document 117, p. 375.

112. McLeish was a noted poet who came into government as Librarian of Congress in 1939. He wrote several of FDR's speeches, including the "Four Freedoms" speech of January 1941. In 1944 he became Assistant Secretary of State. James McGregor Burns, *Roosevelt: The Soldier of Freedom* (New York: Harcourt, 1970). Also, Alan Brinkley, "World War II and American Liberalism," in Lewis A. Erenberg and Susan E. Hirsch, *The War in American Culture, Society and Consciousness during World War II* (Chicago and London: The University of Chicago Press, 1966), 313-30.

113. "I was moved by the passage [of Eric Knight's book *This Above All*] in which the survivor of the Dunkerque ordeal asks: 'What are we fighting for? A new world? A better world–or to be the bully of the schoolyard again?' If you ask –and people have asked– you shall be told that 'We shall think of peace when we have won the war!' That isn't good enough–not for me." See, Rexford G. Tugwell, *The Stricken Land, The Story of Puerto Rico* (New York: Doubleday, 1947), p. 106.

114. Luis Muñoz Marín, "Discurso del 4 de julio de 1941," July 4, 1941, Speeches, Fundación Luis Muñoz Marín.

115. Tugwell, op. cit., p. 95.

116. Bothwell, op. cit., Volume 3, Document 113, p. 363. Author's translation.

117. "Democracy should imply security, more welfare. Having here a contented people, a higher living standard, is really the foundation of the island's defense." Ibid., Document 105, p. 342. Author's translation.

118. Luis Muñoz Marín, "Discurso de don Luis Muñoz Marín sobre el significado de la guerra para el pueblo de Puerto Rico," December 21, 1941, Speeches, Fundación Luis Muñoz Marín. All passages translated by the author.

119. Ibid., pp. 1-4.

120. Ibid., p. 6.

121. Ibid., p. 12.

122. Muñoz enumerates three points of the Atlantic Charter declaration signed by Franklin Delano Roosevelt and Winston Churchill at Placentia Bay, Newfoundland, on August 12, 1941.

123. Luis Muñoz Marín, "Discurso. . .," op. cit., p. 13.

124. Ibid., p. 8.

125. Ibid., p. 14.

CHAPTER 8

MOVING MOUNTAINS

Hangar under construction. Borinquen Field, Aguadilla, 1940.
Fundación Luis Muñoz Marín.

MOVING MOUNTAINS

On May 24 1940, nine months into his governorship of Puerto Rico, Admiral Leahy lunched with President Roosevelt to review defense preparations on the island. A few days earlier, on the 10th, the German invasion of the Netherlands, Belgium and Luxembourg had brought the "Phony War" to an end. The crisis of the summer of 1940 had begun. That day Leahy noted the following in his diary:

> Radio reports this morning bring information that the German army started an invasion of Holland, Belgium and Luxemburg at daylight today and made rapid progress into Holland.

> This serious threat to England must be countered at once by vigorous allied action which up to the present time on other fronts seems to have been impossible. Italy may now very probably join with Germany and any extension of the war to the Dutch West or East Indies may force the United States to take some protective action.[1]

The German invasion, indeed, had immediate repercussions in the Caribbean and precisely in the Dutch West Indies. The following day, June 11, British and French forces landed in Aruba and Curaçao to take control over their valuable oil refineries. At stake were vital strategic interests, as both islands formed part of an oil belt in the southern Caribbean and the north coast of South America that also included Venezuela and Trinidad. The refineries in these two Dutch islands were owned by Standard Oil of New Jersey and Royal Dutch Shell, a British-Dutch multinational. The Standard Oil complex at Aruba could refine 250,000 barrels of crude a day, and store over 11 million barrels of crude and other products. The oil produced and refined in this region, including a large portion of high grade airplane fuel produced in Trinidad for the Royal Air Force, was essential for the Allied war effort.[2]

Also, in that region were located the extremely valuable bauxite mines of British Guiana and Surinam, vital for U.S. aluminum production and for Roosevelt's ambitious plans[3] of producing thousands of war planes. Ten days later, on the 21st, German troops had reached the English Channel at Abbeville and encircled the Allied armies. The specter of a total French collapse and eventual defeat of Great Britain hovered over Europe. The evacuation of Allied troops from Dunkirk was completed on June 4. Five days later, the British evacuated Norway, with Italy joining the war against France on the 10. By June 22, the German-French armistice had been signed at Compiegne.

These events transformed, with amazing rapidity, the strategic equation. The U.S. could no longer rely on France and Great Britain to contain the German military machine. The question of the eventual fate of the French and British navies became an inescapable and immediate concern for U.S. strategic planners. A German navy augmented with elements of the French fleet and, perhaps, of the British, or even a neutralized British fleet, would pose a formidable threat for the U.S. in the Atlantic and the Caribbean. The Italian, German and French fleets combined would constitute a force superior to the British Navy. According to a study on naval expansion during the war, "in May and June of 1940, the possible fates of the French and British navies dominated American strategic thinking."[4] Thus, the possibility that the U.S. would have to fight a prolonged war with no allies, at a time when it was hardly prepared militarily to undertake offensive operations against Germany, was for the first time contemplated as likely in the critical juncture of May-June 1940.

In addition, the German summer offensive immediately brought to the fore the issue of European colonial possessions in the Caribbean, as the Allied occupation of Aruba and Curaçao had demonstrated. Would Germany have access to the French territories in the Caribbean? Or to the British? Could it acquire the French airports in Dakar and thence threaten the American continent by air, thus making reality the war hypothesis of the Fleet Problem XX maneuvers? An official War Department history of Caribbean garrisons summarizes well the new strategic situation in the summer of 1940.

By late summer of 1940, Norway, France and the low countries had surrendered. Russia was still an incalculable military weight poised ominously above the scales of the main European conflict, almost certain to plunge into the balance, but unpredictable as to the moment and direction of her impact . . .

Britain had survived Dunkerque only for destruction, vindictive beyond any precedent, to batter down at her from her own skies. The capacity of the English people to endure ordeal by fire had yet to be demonstrated. Their subjection to invasion seemed imminent. The British fleet in the Atlantic could no longer be considered the sure outer defense of the western hemisphere. Suddenly the Antilles and northern South America had become the critical perimeter of defense for the Panama Canal, the Caribbean and southern United States.

The enemy had control of Dakar. Marines of Nazi-dominated France had protective custody of Aruba and Curaçao. Martinique, harboring part of the French fleet, was potentially hostile and actually uncooperative. The flames of Europe, licking toward our own shores threw into relief the need to brace for a conflict which we might have to wage without allies.[5]

After meeting President Roosevelt, Leahy made a statement for the press that was reported by the *New York Times* under the headline "Puerto Rico to Be Our Gibraltar in the Caribbean." His statement was clearly aimed at warning Germany against any incursion in the Caribbean. He said that, "when defense works intended to make Puerto Rico the Gibraltar of the Caribbean are completed it will be impossible for any overseas power to send an expeditionary force to the southern coast of the United States, Central America or the northern coast of South America." He further explained that "no intelligent [enemy] commander" would dare send an expeditionary force past Puerto Rico, "without reducing the island bases first."[6] Such an incursion would be vulnerable to air attack from the island and "there is no way I know of halting a bombing attack." He also used the opportunity to point out the desirability of acquiring bases in the French and British Caribbean.

The brief statement served clearly to explain the strategic rationale for the program of defense preparations that had been launched in 1938-1939. Puerto Rico was to play a key role as the easternmost outpost in the defense of the entire Caribbean and Central American region, and even with regard to the continental United States. However, the important qualification he made, "when defense works . . . are completed," underscored the still vulnerable position of the United States in Puerto Rico, amidst the military crisis of the summer of 1940.

A month later, on the 42nd anniversary of the invasion of Puerto Rico in 1898, Leahy's official speech to commemorate the occasion was broadcasted by radio telephone to the Puerto Rican Exhibit at New York's World Fair. This speech was delivered three days after the German-French armistice had formalized France's surrender and the establishment of a new French government under Henri Pétain and Pierre Laval at the southern city of Vichy. Once again he stressed the importance of Puerto Rico for the defense of "the Panama Canal and the eastern United States." This time, Leahy's rhetoric was full of hyperbole. It evokes passages of Goethe's *Faust*. But his speech did convey the magnitude of military preparations in Puerto Rico, both current and envisaged.

> We are converting our waving cornfields [*canefields,* in the Spanish version] into airplane bases. We are deepening our harbors to accommodate battleships. We are widening our mountain roads to give passage to troop transports. We are moving whole mountains to make room for long-range gun emplacements.
>
> We must now make our island self supporting, to withstand possible long periods of isolation from the mainland. Much can be done along this line if the mainland once realizes that it cannot impose restrictions on the island's industries to survive.[7]

Rupert Emerson, the newly named Director of Territories and Island Possessions at the Department of Interior, was present at the Fair and seconded the governor's speech. He noted that, "never before has there been so urgent a necessity to recognize that Puerto Rico is one of the most essential links in the first line of American Defense." Emerson also stressed that existing differences between "Americans in Puerto and the Continent" had to be openly recognized and resolved. The Director of the Exhibit, E. R. González, also kept to the martial tone of the event remarking that, at that same moment, the Havana Conference was being held to discuss the fate of European possessions in the Caribbean.[8]

Constructing the Gibraltar of the Caribbean

In 1938, the U.S. Army garrison in Puerto Rico was a subcommand, headquartered in San Juan, of the Army II Corps Area. Its mission was to defend the eastern perimeter of the Caribbean, the South Atlantic and the Panama Canal. For this broad mission, the garrison had less than one thousand officers and men of the 65th Infantry Regiment. In addition, there were two Puerto Rican National Guards Regiments, the 295th Infantry and the 296th Infantry, with a total strength of 69 officers and 1410 men, deployed in fifteen sites.[9] Together with an expanded police force, this garrison had been more than adequate for internal security during the 1930s. In fact, though the activities of the Nationalist Party had provoked concern about the capacity of existing security forces to quell an insurrection, neither the National Guard nor regular Army forces had been directly used in the repression of that movement. The regular police, strengthened for that purpose, had sufficed. An entirely different scenario would be an attack by Germany on Puerto Rico or the need to the counter an incursion elsewhere in the Caribbean. The Army garrison was hardly sufficient for such an eventuality.

On the other hand, many of the existing military and naval facilities had been inherited from Spain through the Treaty of Paris and no new major base construction had been undertaken since 1898, despite ambitious plans formulated during the First World War. The only new major naval presence was the naval base in Culebra, acquired in 1899 by presidential decree, and which had not been developed or fortified. Culebra, however, had been used in the late thirties to test the new amphibious landing craft that would later be used in the island-hopping campaign in the Pacific. During the Fleet Landing Exercise Five (Flex 5), 18 different landing craft were tested in Culebra under the supervision of Admiral Richmond Kelly Turner.[10]

Puerto Rico lacked an airport infrastructure that would permit the projection of air power in the region. The main operating airport was the Pan American aerodrome in Isla Grande, which had been in operation since 1928, and was used for international flights. Puerto Rico exhibited many other shortcomings that impinged on the capacity to defend it, let alone use it as the main regional military platform. Endemic infections, such as venereal disease, malaria, and smallpox were prevalent among the population. The road infrastructure, and water and sewer facilities were inadequate for a large garrison. Neither could the existing energy supply sustain major bases.

The revision of defense plans for Puerto Rico had begun in July, 1938, when the commander of the Army II Corps Area ordered the formulation of a new plan for the Puerto Rico-Virgin Islands area to be code-named Orange. This plan was submitted in late October of that same year, but it only covered the island of Puerto Rico. The plan called for bringing up to full strength the Army's 65th Infantry and the National Guard Regiments within 240 days of mobilization.[11] Soon after, as explained in Chapter 3, the Navy's Hepburn Board Report, submitted to CNO Leahy on December 1, 1938, recommended, among other things, expanding the existing naval facilities in Puerto Rico by building an air and submarine base at Isla Grande. This would be the first major defense project begun in 1939 at a cost of $9,138,000. Other lesser defense projects had been launched in 1938. They also centered around the San Juan Harbor and consisted of a dry dock, dredging of the harbor and improvements of the El Morro fortifications, as discussed in a previous chapter. These early projects were merely the modest beginning of the huge investments made in defense construction from 1939 onwards.[12]

Army and Navy planning during 1938 was promptly superceded by more ambitious plans for the defense of Puerto Rico and the Caribbean formulated in the context of the deteriorating international crisis and the outbreak of war in September of 1939. Fleet Problem XX, the maneuvers held in February 1939, revealed the vulnerabilities of U.S. defenses in the region to a German attack. Among other things, it became evident that air power based in Puerto Rico, and in other Caribbean islands, was required to intercept a naval force before it reached the Caribbean. After the maneuvers, Admiral Adolphus Andrews, commander of the "Black" (U.S.) forces, wrote to the President arguing that "some means [must] be found to provide fortified and well secured bases in this most important strategic area."[13]

In May 1939, the Joint Planning Committee, in charge of overall strategic planning, prepared for the Joint (Army-Navy) Board (precursor to the Joint Chiefs of Staff) a analysis of the strategic importance of the Puerto

Rico-Virgin Islands area. The document stressed the vital importance of the area for sea, air and land operations. Its conclusions implied the need for a total revision of defense plans, armed forces missions and garrisons. Among its most important recommendations was that a new overseas Army Department and a new Naval District should be established without delay. Their commanders should participate in the preparation of defense plans and the development of defensive installations. At this time the Joint Planning Committee had begun a major review of war plans that would substitute the color plans, drawn up to deal with "single opponents," with the Rainbow plans that would guide U.S. strategy during the war. Rainbow IV, begun two days after the Dunkirk evacuation, called for "a unilateral defense of the Americas extended to include the area below 10 degrees south latitude and the eastern Atlantic."[14] It was signed by Roosevelt in August 1940 and became the blueprint for strategic planning in the Caribbean. Thus, the review of plans for Puerto Rico was undertaken within a much broader framework of Hemisphere and Caribbean defense.[15]

The Puerto Rican Army Department was created on July 1, 1939, by Presidential Directive. The new Army commander was Brig. Gen. Edmund L. Daley who had arrived in San Juan a few days earlier.[16] Daley was an elderly officer who had been called into active service due to the European military crisis. He remained in Puerto Rico until March 1941, when he was named commander of the V Army Corps based at Camp Beauregard, near Alexandria, Lousiana. The V Corps was deployed in Belfast, Northern Ireland, in early 1942. However, Gen. George Marshall decided to retire all overage officers, including Daley, at the time of the deployment in Europe.[17]

The Tenth Naval District was established January 1, 1940. Its first commander was Captain Raymond A. Spruance, who would later distinguish himself in the Pacific campaign. Spruance had participated in the Fleet Problem XX maneuvers and observed the new experimental landing craft that were being tested in Culebra. The Tenth Naval District would have a budget of $650 million and 10,000 workers for base construction in the Caribbean.[18] It had responsibility for the entire Caribbean Sea. In July 1941, the commander of the Naval District also became the commander of the Caribbean Sea Frontier. With this, "the area of his responsibility as

Sea Frontier Commander was extended to include the entire Caribbean and substantial areas to the north and east of the West Indies."[19]

Daley and Spruance were promoted to two star general and Rear Admiral, respectively, after they assumed their Puerto Rico commands. The island was classified as a Category D coastal frontier, that is, "subject to a major attack." By March 1940, they had produced a Joint Puerto Rican Coastal Frontier Defense Plan (PRCF-1940). Admiral Leahy maintained constant communications with both commanders and, at times, even transmitted Roosevelt's instructions. These organizational changes underscored the enhanced strategic importance attached to Puerto Rico and would facilitate the implementation of the huge defense projects of the 1940s.

In March 1939, an Air Board presided over by General H. H. Arnold was named. Arnold toured the Caribbean, Venezuela and the Panama Canal in May, stopping in Puerto Rico on the 12th.[20] He again visited Puerto Rico together with General Strong on June 2, 1939, to inspect a possible site for a major air base. The press reported that Aguadilla was being considered for this project.[21] The Board submitted a report by late June recommending the construction of four new major air bases, one of them in Puerto Rico. This new base would form a triangle with Panama and the McDill air base in Florida for the control of the Caribbean. It would also constitute a link in a new military island route to the vital region of Natal in the "Brazilian bulge." It also formed part of an alternative transatlantic route to the Far East via Africa. Even before the final report was submitted, the base had been approved.[22] Arnold refers to the large Puerto Rican air base in the northwest corner of the island in his memoirs.

> The purely "Hemisphere Defense" plan mentioned earlier (it was not a plan for defeating Germany), called for 250 airplanes in Hawaii, including one group of B-17's . . . In the Caribbean, we planned for two groups of heavy bombers and two groups of fighters. The big Borinquen base was being built in Puerto Rico. We had gone so far as to make arrangements with the British whereby we would have a group of heavy bombers and a group of fighters in Trinidad.[23]

The German invasion of Poland and the outbreak of war put the Borinquen Field project (originally named Air Base 1) on the fast track. The expropriation of a large tract of land of 1,877 *cuerdas* (a *cuerda* is slightly less than an acre) took place on September 6, a few days prior to Leahy's assumption of the post of governor. The relatively prosperous communities of Maleza Alta and Maleza Baja were forcefully evicted in a matter of hours and in a most callous manner.[24] Two days later preliminary construction work began on the site using Company B of the 65th Infantry Regiment as labor. By October, the work force of the project comprised 2,000 workers of the Works Projects Administration (WPA). The Aguadilla area became a beehive of activity, with a large infux of labor and migrants, which transformed the entire region.[25]

The Borinquen base was the main facility of a network of airfields. Another major airport, the Ponce Air Base (Fort Losey), was constructed in the south. The existing Mercedita airfield was being used by the Marine Corps. Auxiliary regional airfields were built in Salinas, Dorado, Vega Baja, Arecibo and Mayaguez. An additional Army airfield was to be built in St Croix, and the Navy was expected to build its own airfield in Vieques. In the case of the Ponce Air Base, many local landowners and the Ponce Chamber of Commerce donated or sold, at very low prices, large tracts of land.[26] In 1940, the only operational Army airbases were Ponce and Punta Borinquen, Aguadilla. Another important Army project was the construction of Camp Tortuguero in Vega Baja for the expanded National Guard garrison. By October 1940, there were 3,000 WPA workers under Capt. Walter Torres, an engineer, constructing Tortuguero. *El Mundo* reported that the Army had acquired, by late 1940, a total of 26,000 *cuerdas* for military projects.[27]

It soon became evident that the construction of bases was not a localized event, but had broader implications for the infrastructure in Puerto Rico. For example, by early October it was announced that $1,876,000 had been assigned for the development of the road between San Juan and Aguadilla.[28] This road was needed to connect the Navy base of Isla Grande and the improved Army base of Fort Buchanan, in the San Juan area, with the Army airfield at Punta Borinquen.[29] Also, the construction of bases and the enlargement of the garrison in Puerto Rico had sanitary implications, as the military and the civilian authorities sought to control infectious diseases in regions with a large presence of military personnel.[30] Even the establishment in 1939 of a government-owned cement plant, the Puerto Rico Cement Corporation, vital for the construction of defense facilities, responded to the logic of strategic needs. Many of these investments (in roads, improved water supply and sewer facilities, sanitary measures, increased generation of electric power, a larger cement production, communications, and harbor facilities) could be considered of "dual-usage", both military and civilian. Others generated employment and economic prosperity in certain regions

But defense plans sought to strengthen the U.S. military presence not only in Puerto Rico, but in the entire Caribbean area. When the Second World War began, the U.S. base structure in the Caribbean consisted of the bases in the Panama Canal Zone, Guantánamo in Cuba, Puerto Rico, and a Marine Corps airfield known as Bourne Field in the island of St. Thomas.[31] Since 1939, steps were taken to strengthen and expand military facilities in all the "traditional" locations. On the other hand, the U.S. possessed no permanent bases in the Lesser Antilles or near the Caribbean coast of South America, in the oil and mineral rich region of Venezuela and Trinidad. The sea lanes that passed near Trinidad were of vital strategic importance for the oil trade. By late 1939, the garrison of regular troops in the entire region consisted of 21,736 troops, mostly deployed in Panama and to a lesser extent in Puerto Rico.[32] The Marine Corps garrison in Guantánamo was small. Through an agreement with Great Britain, the U.S. military obtained limited access to Bermuda, Saint Lucia and Trinidad. Saint Lucia was deemed vital for the airpower control over the southern accesses to the Caribbean Sea.[33] This arrangement was a precedent for the subsequent "destroyers-for-bases" agreement.

As has been discussed, the need to expand the regional base structure by acquiring bases in European territories had been stressed in U.S. strategic debate, even before the war started. Admiral Leahy, as we have seen, was outspoken in his demand for additional bases. Army Chief of Staff George Marshall proposed in June 1940 the "preventive occupation of the strategic areas in the Western Hemisphere wherein German or Italian bases might be established to menace the Panama Canal or the Continental U.S."[34] Even Rexford Tugwell was an advocate of creating a "Caribbean Protectorate" and putting the French territories under "protective custody."[35]

President Roosevelt, however, rejected the radical proposal of outright annexation of European colonies, with the argument that, with them, the U.S. would also acquire "two million headaches" and economic responsibilities to the civilian population.[36] Instead, he conducted direct negotiations with Churchill for a destroyers-for-bases deal. At least since mid May 1940, the embattled Prime Minister of Britain had been seeking the transfer of First World War vintage U.S. destroyers to employ them to prevent a German invasion or as escorts in the Atlantic. The exchange of correspondence and diplomatic talks bore fruit on September 2, 1940.[37] Churchill would receive 50 old destroyers in exchange for 99 year leases on bases in the Bahamas, Jamaica, Antigua, Saint Lucia, Trinidad and British Guiana, and a gift of bases in Bermuda and Newfoundland.[38]

This agreement required a fresh look at the base infrastructure of the U.S. in the Caribbean that could bring up to date the recommendations of the Hepburn Board Report. Already, naval Commander Lowe had recommended on July 12, 1940, in a "Study of Fleet Base Sites in the West Indies," that Vieques Passage should be developed as a fleet anchorage by building breakwaters, and that facilities in Ensenada Honda, Ceiba, should be developed, including the construction of landing fields.[39] A new naval board under Rear Admiral John W. Greenslade was convened by the President on September 11, 1940, and began inspecting existing and potential sites. In late November, CNO Admiral Harold Stark wrote to Greenslade a memorandum of great relevance for the Navy's regional plans and for Puerto Rico. There he pointed out that,

> In the opinion of the Chief of Naval Operations Puerto Rico should be selected for development as the major operating base area, both because of its superior strategic position, and because of its location in developed territory which will doubtless remain a United States' possession. Puerto Rico, in a central position with respect to the eastern approaches to the Panama Canal and to the ends of the defensive line, completely dominates the Caribbean strategically.[40]

Admiral Stark went on to recommend the construction of a breakwater in the Vieques Passage and a safe anchorage "for an almost unlimited number of vessels of all types", that could be made "practically impregnable" by fortifications and a mobile garrison of troops.

Earlier in November, CNO Stark had submitted to the President the historic "Plan Dog" memorandum, which had set the Europe-first strategy pursued by the U.S. in the war. An Atlantic-centered strategy enhanced the importance of the Caribbean, and of Puerto Rico as the main naval base. Needless to say, Greenslade's report, submitted in early January 1941, contained Stark's recommendations. This clarification of global and regional policy in late 1940, led to the decision to construct a major naval base, to be named Roosevelt Roads in the President's honor, in Ceiba and Vieques. Construction would begin in the early summer of 1941. It would take five years, and a cost of $108 million, to complete.[41] The breakwater in the Vieques Passage, however, a project of pharaonic proportions and vast environmental implications, would never be finished. Stark's momentous decision to make Puerto Rico the main base in the Caribbean almost coincided with the end of Leahy's period as governor.[42]

As discussed, the intensification of defense measures and construction during 1939 explains Roosevelt's unprecedented decision to make Admiral Leahy coordinator of all federal agencies in Puerto Rico. Also, the establishment in Puerto Rico of a new agency, the Works Projects Administration (WPA), coincided with Leahy's arrival as Governor in September of that year. The WPA would be mainly devoted to the construction of new military installations. In 1940 it had a budget of $11 million and employed 18,000 workers. The following year, it was employing 32,615 workers. However, other existing agencies such as the Public Works Administration (PWA) would also play an important role in the development of the necessary infrastructure. PWA was used for large projects such as sewerage, bridges, harbor facilities and public buildings. In 1941 it was employing 1,664 workers a week.[43] In this manner, the large role that the Puerto Rico Reconstruction Administration (PRRA), also directed by an unsympathetic Leahy (who considered it a creature of New Deal "do-gooders"), had performed in rehabilitation programs during the 1930's, began to be eclipsed by defense-related agencies such as the WPA.

The Caribbean Gibraltar also required a larger garrison of regular Army troops. In July 1939, it comprised only 961 officers and men. By the end of that year that number had more than trebled to 2,961. The increase in 1940 was even greater. By June, with the arrival of the Base Detachment of the Headquarters of the 24th Airbase Squad for Borinquen Field, it reached 3,281. Later, the continued arrival of Air Corps personnel and the induction into federal service of the 295th and 296th Regiments of the National Guard brought that figure to 13,280 by December 1940. The National

Guard had been authorized to expand to 239 officers, 2 warrant officers and 3552 enlisted men, more than double its 1939 size. It was inducted into the regular army on October 15, 1940. The decision to use the National Guard to increase the regular Army garrison, instead of bringing more troops from the U.S., was made by Gen. George Marshall, Chief of Staff of the Army.[44] In order to replace the internal security functions of the National Guard, a Home Guard was simultaneously created with 8,000 part-time soldiers organized in 42 companies.[45] By November, the Home Guard had grown to 16,000 men and 98 companies.[46]

Registration of Puerto Ricans for the draft began on November 20, 1940, five weeks later than in the United States and, significantly, after the elections had been held. A total of 240,220 men, between the ages of 21 and 36, registered. The initial quota for the island was fixed at 3,600 white and 1,200 "native". During the course of the war between 45,000 and 50,000 would be drafted into the regular armed forces, including the National Guard troops. They would mainly be assigned to "Puerto Rican service units" and to garrison as "filler replacements" the large base structure the U.S. developed in the Caribbean, thus releasing U.S. troops for use in Europe.[47] By 1941 the Puerto Rican regular Army garrison had reached more than 25,000 troops.

War preparations and the economy

A redefined federal bureaucracy geared to military needs gradually sprang up and became the main source of new jobs in Puerto Rico, dwarfing the modest structure of the government of Puerto Rico. By mid-1941, 28,500 workers were employed by WPA, 25,000 on the payroll of contractors working for the Army and Navy, 30,000 troops were in Army cantonments, while the total personnel of the rest of the civilian federal agencies was 6,250, and all the agencies of the government of Puerto Rico, excluding the municipalities, employed a mere 7,600 persons. The ratio between employment generated by the federal and local structures was almost twelve to one, and between military related and civilian about six to one. A leading publication on Puerto Rican business and the economy commented at the time that defense construction had already surpassed the payroll of the sugar industry. It made the following observation on the astounding rate of growth of the economy.

> Since the fall of 1939, business activity in Puerto Rico has fol-
> lowed an ever ascending graph. Starting at one of the lowest
> points in many years, the summer of 1939, the graph has risen
> steadily, month after month. Following this trend of nearly
> two years, activity in the months if May and June, 1941 regis-
> tered new highs, 25 per cent to 35 per cent better than a year
> ago, depending on the business sector involved...[48]

The steady increase in electric power output since 1938 is an indica-
tor of the upswing of the Puerto Rican economy before the formal entry
of the U.S. in the war. Electric energy output was 129,000 kilowatt-hours
in the period 1937-38. By 1940-41 it had reached 192,000 kilowatt-hours
and 350,000 in 1945-46, the last year of the war. Much of the expansion,
particularly after 1943, was made possible by the Puerto Rico Water Resources Authority.[49]

A Department of Commerce study on the Puerto Rican economy,
submitted by economist Thomas Hibben in 1948, pointed out that, "during 1941 Puerto Rico experienced a period of great prosperity due chiefly
to the Defense program. Construction projects connected with these activities had practically eliminated the Island's unemployment problem."
He also remarked that, in 1942, "employment rose to unusually high
levels due to work on military projects."[50] A 1951 study of the Puerto
Rico Planning Board concurs with Hibben's findings. It argues that,
"during the war years, the increase in output and income was due almost entirely to the tremendous expansion of Federal government activities in connection with defense and war. Thus, insular income derived from these activities increased over six-fold during those years."
The study includes an impressive graph showing the steep growth of
insular and per capita income from 1939, and how it rapidly leveled off
at the end of the war.[51]

A.J. Jaffe has noted that federal expenditures in Puerto Rico during
the period July 1, 1939 to June 30, 1947, amounted to $656 million, cor-
responding $532 to military and just $124 million to civilian purposes.
He compares these figures to the total of $230 million of federal spend-
ing during the years of the Depression, and the $170 million spent dur-
ing the first three decades of U.S. rule. Jaffe argues that in the eight
years 1939-1947 more federal money was spent in Puerto Rico "than the

combined federal and private investment during the preceding 40 years of American occupation of the island." Thus, he concludes that, "the enormous increase in federal spending must still be considered a prime cause of the new prosperity of the island."[52] More recently, a study on the period of the war reached a similar conclusion stressing that the "moving force" for the expansion of Puerto Rico's National Product during the war, from $153.2 to $297.8 million, was U.S. government purchases of goods and services.[53]

The classic study on the Puerto Rican economy by Harvey S. Perloff, *Puerto Rico's Economic Future, A Study in Planned Development,* does not deal historically with the impact of the war. He points out, however, that "federal government contributions have increased steadily since 1934, contributing a large share of the net income of the island (reaching a peak of almost one-quarter of the insular income in 1942-43, 1943-44, and 1944-45)." Perloff includes a table about federal expenditures during the period of the war (1941-46) which shows that expenditures by "war agencies" significantly exceeded, every year, expenditures of civilian agencies. But even his table underestimates military expenditures, as it categorizes the Veterans Administration and the PWA and WPA, involved to a large extent in military related construction, as "civilian" expenditures.[54]

In a sense, the trend in Puerto Rico was not exceptional. With rearmament and war, the entire U.S. economy became highly militarized. Economic historian Alan Milward indicates that military expenditures were only 1.5% of the net product in 1938, rising to 2% in 1939. By 1941, they had reached 10% of the total product, and 40% in 1943. The U.S. Gross National Product grew from 88,600 million in constant prices in 1939, to 135,000 million in 1944. The expansion was so large that civilian consumption also grew by 12% between 1939 and 1944. He remarks that, "the budgetary resources for rearmament in June 1940, together with the expansion of the naval construction program, were beginning to effectively achieve what the New Deal had not been able to produce."[55]

Rafael Picó, who would soon head the Puerto Rico Planning Board under Tugwell, bitterly lamented in 1940 the almost exclusively military character of federal priorities and the dangerous neglect of the needs of the civilian population.

The establishment of powerful naval and army bases in Puerto Rico has lately focused attention on this so-called "Gibraltar of the Caribbean." Lest the strategic position of Puerto Rico, as the key to a continental system of defense, obscure the main problems of the island, it must be kept in mind that Puerto Rico is not merely a military base, but a densely populated island where 1,800,000 Americans dwell . . .

The Government and the people of the United States can not remain indifferent to conditions in Puerto Rico, especially now that island is playing such an important role in national and continental defense. The future attitude of the American people towards the problems indicated above will determine whether the "Gibraltar of the Caribbean" is to be erected on solid rock, or on a treacherous quagmire of political, social and economic ills.[56]

James L. Dietz´s economic history of Puerto Rico devotes a chapter to the Second World War period, which he characterizes as one of "state capitalism". This chapter, however, begins its analysis in 1941 and focuses on the impact of the policies of Governor Rexford G. Tugwell and the *Partido Popular Democrático*. To Dietz, the war provided a "favorable circumstance for Tugwell, Muñoz and the PPD, who were given a freer hand to reform by the President and the Department of the Interior . . ." He does mention that, "fortuitously," "the war did bring significantly higher insular revenues" that helped finance the economic and social program of the PDP.[57]

However, Dietz does not refer to the crucial period 1938-1940, and consequently does not take into account that in 1941, when the *Partido Popular* began enacting its legislative program and Tugwell became governor, Puerto Rico had already begun a war-induced process of economic growth. Neither does he mention that some major institutional reforms, as the establishment of the state-owned Puerto Rican Cement and the Water Resources Authority, entrusted with power generation, predate Tugwell´s governorship. Governor Guy J. Swope's 1941 *Annual Report* already mentioned that "Puerto Rico is at present experiencing a period of great prosperity, due largely to the Defense program, which is now in full swing. Construction projects connected with these activities have, for the time being, virtually done away with the Island's unemployment problem."[58] Thus, Dietz tends to blur the continuities between the two periods, and places almost exclusive emphasis on the reformist thrust of the Tugwell-Muñoz period.

In fact, from an economic point of view, the war had begun to have an impact on Puerto Rico since the second half of 1938. By the summer of 1939, a process of sustained economic growth had begun, mainly induced by increased military expenditures and defense related construction. This process would certainly continue with even greater force, to the electoral benefit of the *Partido Popular*, during the remainder of the war. But it is important to take into account that Muñoz achieved control of the legislature at a very favorable moment, since the economy had already been growing for over a year. It is to his credit that he knew how to capitalize politically from the unprecedented prosperity of the war years in order to "push through a remarkable program of change between 1941 and 1946," as Gordon Lewis characterized it.[59]

Furthermore, to ascribe "state capitalism" mainly to the policies of the Puerto Rican government misses the point that, quite possibly, the largest "state capitalist" structure in the 1940s was the U.S. armed forces. How the local and federal policies related and interacted during the war years is beyond the scope of this book. Nevertheless, it is obvious that the late 30s and 40s still require analysis by economic historians.

The economic boom provoked by the war, and the broad social reforms implemented after 1941, also had sociological and political consequences that would manifest themselves in later years. Tens of thousands of persons were mobilized as construction workers or as soldiers. Women were inducted into the workforce in greater numbers. The service sector grew considerably. New industries were established to supply war needs or war-induced demand (as in the case of rum). The infrastructure was rapidly modernized. Educational opportunities were expanded. Sanitary conditions improved. Puerto Rico resembled less and less the sugar-dominated society depicted in *El Catecismo del Pueblo*. The social subject to which Muñoz referred as "the people," of which the impoverished *jíbaro* and the cane worker were emblematic, was gradually transformed.

Gold, planes and trouble in the Caribbean

As the war approached, conditions in the Caribbean became a major concern for the United States and Great Britain. Not only was Puerto Rico a "powder keg," to use Ickes's phrase, but there was great instability in the British colonies as well. Major strikes had taken place throughout the British West Indies in the period 1935 to 1938, accompanied by social disturbances and bloodshed. In 1937, there was a major strike in the strategically sensitive Trinidad oil fields. Other strikes also broke out in Barbados, British Guiana, St. Lucia and Jamaica. The following year, as in Puerto Rico, the dock workers of Jamaica went on strike. Even in 1939, the year the war began, labor agitation and strikes continued throughout the British Caribbean.

In 1938, the British government named a West India Royal Commission headed by Lord Moyne to investigate political and social conditions in the Caribbean. The Moyne Commission, as it was known, documented the appalling social conditions and the need for urgent social and political reforms. Great Britain faced a similar dilemma as the U.S. in Puerto Rico.[60] Social conditions were not much better in other European territories. Roosevelt also had the benefit of a personal report on social and political conditions in the Caribbean made by Charles W. Taussig and Rexford G. Tugwell after a 1937 trip to the Windward Islands, from St. Thomas to Trinidad. Tugwell mentions that, "we told the President that not only were conditions such that immediate explosions might be expected but that political conditions would be found to be equally contributory."[61]

In November 1940, Roosevelt created a "United States Commission to Study Social and Economic Conditions of the British West Indies." It was headed by Charles W. Taussig and included Col. A.F. Kibler, Lt. Commander W.S. Campbell and Mr. E.R. Pierce as clerk-stenographer. They visited all the British islands of the Lesser Antilles, the U.S. Virgin Islands, and Jamaica.[62] The U.S. was specially concerned with the stability of British colonies where new bases would be built under the destroyers-for-bases agreement. Roosevelt would personally tour the Caribbean in December 1940. The creation in 1942 of the Anglo-American Caribbean Commission was the institutional expression of the intense strategic interest in the viability of British colonies in the Caribbean.[63]

Immediately after the outbreak of war, in September 1939, Roosevelt called for the establishment of a "neutrality zone" comprising the entire American continent. He wanted to prevent a repetition of the highly successful First World War German submarine offensive in the sea lanes around Trinidad, an attack on a European colony, or an armed clash between belligerents and neutrals. The "neutrality zone" included a huge expanse of sea stretching about three hundred miles into both oceans. He ordered the navy to undertake the impossible task of patrolling the zone. Among other things, Fleet Problem XX had shown the urgency of keeping Germany well away from the Caribbean.

Roosevelt also hastily convened an Inter-American Conference in Panama to gain Latin American adherence to the neutrality policy and collaboration in its enforcement. The Panama Conference met from September 23 to October 3, 1939. The "Declaration of Panama" defined a neutrality zone embracing the whole continent, with the exclusion of Canada. The "neutrality zone" served to keep Germany from extending war operations to the Americas until late 1941, in order not to provoke the U.S. to openly enter the war. Also Germany concentrated its initially small submarine force near the British Isles. This shielded the Caribbean from submarine warfare, which tended to concentrate in the North Atlantic, for about two years. The Panama Conference also decided to convene another consultative meeting if "any geographical region of America subject to the jurisdiction of any non-American state . . . be obliged to change its sovereignty and there should result therefrom a danger to the Security of the American continent."[64] This contingency seemed remote in 1939 given the considerable military and naval might of Great Britain and France.

The German offensive of the summer of 1940 radically altered the *status quo* in the Caribbean. The issue of the fate of European territories, particularly the Dutch and French, became urgent. Since a defeat of Britain was not ruled out until the favorable outcome of the aerial "Battle of Britain," decisively settled by the Royal Air Force in September 1940, even eventual German control or access to the numerous British colonies in the Atlantic, Caribbean, and Central and South America, was a concern. The Anglo-French incursion in Curaçao, considered technically a violation of the Monroe Doctrine and the neutrality policy, had brought the war nearer to the United States.

In these circumstances, Secretary of State Cordell Hull called for another Inter-American consultative meeting to be held at La Habana. The first plenary session of the Havana Conference began on July 22. Despite some initial differences with certain Latin American countries, the "Act of Havana," approved by 21 nations on the 30th, allowed emergency unilateral action in case an urgent threat to regional security should arise. It also provided for a territory to be placed afterwards under a collective trusteeship or guardianship by American Republics. An "Inter-American Commission of Territorial Administration" was created. In this way, the U.S. gained a free hand, sanctioned by Latin America, to intervene in any European possession deemed to be a threat.[65] The conference had as its backdrop a major crisis in the French Caribbean territories and U.S. plans to invade Martinique and Guadeloupe. As Governor of Puerto Rico, Admiral Leahy and the naval forces in Puerto Rico would be intensely involved in this crisis.

After the French collapse, on June 16, General De Gaulle, having established his Free French headquarters in London, ordered the freighter *Bourdeaux*, laden with arms and ammunition, to head for the nearest British port. That same day, Admiral Darlan, Pétain's Minister of Marine, ordered the French aircraft carrier *Béarn*, which had just taken aboard 107 planes purchased in the U.S. under the existing "cash-and-carry" provisions, to sail for Martinique. The planes had been bought under the Reynaud government, and would not have been sold to the Vichy regime. The *Béarn* arrived in Fort-de-France on June 24. Two days later it was joined by the modern heavy cruiser *Emile Bertin*. It was carrying $380 million in gold bullion from the Bank of France to buy U.S. armaments. The cruiser *Jeanne d'Arc* and several armed merchant cruisers and patrol vessels were in nearby Guadeloupe. Also at Fort-de-France were six tankers and nine merchant ships. The presence of such an impressive naval force in the Caribbean, combined with the numerous planes the *Béarn* carried, and a treasure in gold bullion, provoked an immediate crisis.

The British were concerned with possible German control of the powerful French fleet under the ambiguous terms of the armistice. The U.S. was alarmed with the presence of such a powerful naval force, with a large number of fighter planes that could operate in a 200 miles radius, in the vicinity of the Panama Canal and its Caribbean bases. According to

Hines Calvin Warner, the French naval contingent at Fort-de-France was the only potentially hostile air-assault force in the entire continent.[66]

On 26 June, the British established a naval blockade of the French islands. Two days later they dispatched Sir Hubert Young, Governor General of Jamaica, with a retinue of advisors, to negotiate with Admiral Georges Robert, French High Commissioner of Martinique and the French Antilles. British control over the military forces was demanded. Young was rebuffed by Robert.[67] A few days later, on July 3, the British Navy attacked and damaged, with Roosevelt's knowledge and approval, French naval vessels at Oran and Mers-el-Kebir, and seized those in British ports. Soon after, the Vichy government ordered Admiral Robert to actively defend the French Antilles from an attack and broke off diplomatic relations with Britain. With five British vessels blockading Martinique, the stage was set for a major armed clash in the vicinity of Puerto Rico.

Leahy was back in Washington in June and conferred with Roosevelt on the 28th on Puerto Rico and "national defense matters." The most urgent matter at that time was the Martinique crisis. It was in this meeting that the President told the Admiral that he should "be ready to return to Washington at any time, in case he should recall me."[68] By July 5, the U.S. issued an ultimatum to the British against armed action in the Caribbean, while beginning to plan its own operation against Robert. It also dispatched a naval force of one cruiser and six destroyers to Martinique.

The Joint Planning Committee hastily prepared Special Plan Three to invade the islands with a task force of one battleship, one aircraft carrier, three cruisers, twenty destroyers, and a landing force of 5,000 soldiers and 2,000 marines.[69] Meanwhile, Secretary of State Cordell Hull attempted to press the Vichy government to turn over the aircraft carrier to the U.S. and the planes to the British. Needless to say, the Germans also intervened to warn the French against such a move.[70] U.S.-Vichy diplomatic talks produced no positive results.

As soon as he returned to Puerto Rico on July 6, Leahy met with the French consul in Puerto Rico to review the situation. He also ordered Federal Marshall Donald Draughon to fly to Martinique to gather information. Draughon was back in San Juan by the 19th with "interesting information."[71] That day Leahy wrote a memorandum to Captain Raymond A. Spruance with the following intelligence.

(a) French airplane carrier *Béarn* has landed 25 fighting planes in Martinique and is supposed to have 150 more on board.
(b) A landing field is being leveled off six miles from Fort de France.
(c) There are in Martinique 1,850 armed native troops with about 150 white officers and petty officers.
(d) The harbor of Port de France is mined.
(e) Admiral Robert appears to be pro-British; Governor Broissellers is pro-Pétain and definitely anti-British.[72]

Unable to obtain results through diplomatic channels, the U.S. decided to begin direct military negotiations with the "local authorities", i. e. Admiral Robert. Consequently, CNO Harold Stark ordered Rear Admiral John W. Greenslade, in early August, to travel to Martinique aboard the aircraft carrier *Ranger*. Greenslade met with Leahy at *La Fortaleza* on August 5, before proceeding that same day to meet Robert.[73] Captain Raymond Spruance, as Commander of the Tenth Naval District, was also actively involved in the negotiations. Robert accepted three of the four U.S. demands, only refusing to hand over the planes. The U.S. agreed to supply the embattled colonies with food and other necessities. By August 8, Greenslade and Spruance were back at *La Fortaleza* reporting to Leahy.

Pierre Laval's meeting with Hitler in Montoire, on October 24, again raised concerns in Washington about the French naval force in the Caribbean. In that meeting, Hitler had demanded the cession of Dakar, dismemberment of the French empire and the use of naval forces in Africa against Great Britain.[74] Secretary of War Frank Knox recommended the immediate invasion of the islands. Invasion plans were once again drafted. This time the Army wanted a force of 25,000 men. The Joint Planning Committee reduced the invasion force to 10,000, but at the time the U.S. did not have even a properly trained force of that size for such an operation. Roosevelt decided, instead, for fresh negotiations.[75] Thus, there was another round of Greenslade-Robert talks on November 2-3, which produced further assurances and concessions. Once again, they included visits by Greenslade and Spruance to the Governor of Puerto Rico.[76] Despite protestations about his "exclusively civilian" role, Leahy was acting as part of the naval team dealing with the Martinique crisis.

The "gentleman's agreement" with Robert, as it was called, prevented armed action by the U.S. It also confirmed in power a Vichy regime in the French Antilles, impeding De Gaulle's Free French movement from obtaining control of the Caribbean territories, as was contemplated in the British-supported Operation Asterisk. Soon after, the Vichy authorities applied draconian legislation to repress all opposition.[77] Even after Operation Torch was launched and Vichy broke diplomatic relations with the U.S. in November 1942, Roosevelt assured Robert that he would not be removed if he cooperated. Robert held on until mid-July 1943, when he was forced out by a strict embargo. He was received in San Juan with great deference by Admiral Hoover, then Commander of the Tenth Naval District, and repatriated to France after three months.[78]

Throughout this period, Leahy would play a key role in U.S. policy towards the French territories and to France more generally, first as Governor of Puerto Rico, later as Ambassador to Vichy France, and, finally, as Roosevelt's Chief of Staff. He proved to be a formidable opponent of General Charles de Gaulle and his Free French movement. Linda McClain, succinctly states, "There is no question that Leahy did not like De Gaulle; most of those in the White House did not."[79]

From San Juan to Vichy

The results of the 1940 elections caused great surprise in Washington and San Juan. They contradicted the predictions of newspaper commentators, military intelligence, and even Leahy's own expectations. *Tripartismo*'s showing was unexpectedly weak, while the *Partido Popular* had obtained an unforeseen strong second place. Governor Leahy had written to Rupert Emerson on November 1, saying that "consensus of opinion here is that there will be three parties in the legislature with Mr Muñoz Marín of the *Partido Popular* holding the balance of power with a small minority."[80] Julius C. Edelstein reported from Washington just after the elections that, "government officials show themselves profoundly surprised at the victory of the *Partido Popular Democrático*."[81]

The day after the elections Leahy wrote to Ickes that the results between the *Coalición* and the PDP had been so close that he had been unable to get "useful results" from the Insular Board of Elections. Still, he informed Washington that Muñoz Marín had achieved "an astounding success" and would probably control the Senate, the House and, even perhaps, the post of Resident Commissioner. He also pointed out that the results implied a "deep division" between the Republican Party and the "radical or at least far leftist element led by Muñoz Marín." Despite this characterization of the Popular Party, his reaction to the electoral outcome appeared to be favorable since, "it will be much better than heretofore if the Union Republican Party does not retain control of the Senate." He also seemed to approve Bolívar Pagán's presumed defeat as Resident Commissioner against "a very promising candidate of the Popular Party."[82] Leahy was once again mistaken.

On November 9, he reported more accurately the results to Ickes, adding that "among those who will be elected are 4 or 5 of the Popular Party who were active in the Nationalist movement of two years ago."[83] The *Coalición* had obtained a slim plurality of the total vote, while Muñoz had obtained control of the Senate. However, he could control the House only by adding *tripartista* votes. Bolívar Pagán finally had turned out to be the victor over Antonio Fernós Isern for the Resident Commissioner post. For Washington, the immediate questions were, whom would it recognize as being in charge and by what political forces would Puerto Rico be governed?

The *Coalición* could point to its plurality of votes and control over the Resident Commissioner post. Control of the latter had been a traditional measure of electoral victory. Muñoz, on the other hand, argued that the PDP had obtained a majority as a single party, had exhibited the most rapid rate of growth, and that the people concurred that it had obtained a "smashing victory."[84] The legal aspects of this issue were discussed in government circles in Washington.[85] There was also concern that, if the *Coalición* were recognized as victor and controlled Executive branch nominations, the candidates could be rejected by the PDP-controlled Senate. From a political point of view, however, it was clear that key offcials as Leahy and Ickes wanted to get rid of the "Nadal crowd," as Ickes referred to the *Coalición*, even at the cost of having to deal with the allegedly "unstable" Muñoz Marín.

Everything indicates that the decision to recognize Muñoz was taken immediately after the election and before November 11, when Armistice

Day was commemorated. In early November, two important federal offcials arrived in Puerto Rico, Secretary of Commerce Henry Morgenthau, Jr., and the recently named Director of the Division of Territories and Island Possessions of the Department of the Interior, Dr. Rupert Emerson. Morgenthau was not only a close collaborator of the President but also a neighbor in Duchess County and "virtually a member of the family." Roosevelt "prized him for his absolute loyalty, his solid convictions, and, perhaps most of all, his fellow feeling for Duchess County, its trees and lands and crops."[86] He arrived accompanied with Commander Donald E. MacKay on a trip to observe the new defenses in Puerto Rico and the Caribbean.[87] Morgenthau was a key participant in Roosevelt's financing of war preparations and military aid to the Allies. He was honored on November 10 by Brig. Gen. Edmund Daley with a military parade.[88]

Representing the Interior Department, Rupert Emerson, a trained Latin America expert with responsibility over Puerto Rico, on the other hand, came to review Puerto Rico's most pressing problems and the post-electoral situation. The press reported that he had been instructed to refrain from traveling to Puerto Rico before the elections in order not to become enmeshed in insular politics. He arrived in the *Borinquen* on November 10, accompanied by Muñoz's confidant, Ruby Black.[89] Emerson was received by a large delegation of officials, and other prominent Puerto Rican figures. According to *La Correspondencia*, "the Administration is anxious that no possible situation develops in the American Gibraltar of the Atlantic that could provide the agents of foreign powers weapons for anti-American agitation in South America." His agenda included reviewing the functioning of PRRA, the educational system (particularly bilingual education), the implementation of the 500 Acre Law, progress of defense construction works and their impact on unemployment, and inspecting the military bases that were being built.[90] Tugwell would be sent the following year at the head of a commission to study the politically sensitive question of the 500 Acre Law and Muñoz Marín's land tenure legislation.

Thus, immediately after the elections, a very high level group consisting of Leahy, Morgenthau and Emerson, Ickes's envoy, assembled in Puerto Rico. They must have dealt with the sensitive issue of the electoral results. We have no evidence of a meeting between Muñoz Marín and Morgenthau. However, Muñoz certainly met Leahy and Emerson. Ickes writes in the entry of December 7, 1940, of his diary, that Leahy told him that, "he recognizes that Muñoz Marín is unstable but believes that he will be inclined to go along with the administration whenever he can. Muñoz Marín has promised the Governor that he would not raise any issue of independence or even statehood during the next two years."

In previous entries, Ickes makes clear that, in his opinion, Muñoz, despite his perceived shortcomings, was preferable to Rafael Martínez Nadal.[91] Also, Leahy had written to Ickes a personal letter on November 16 1940, stating that, "I personally think it will be possible to work with Muñoz Marín in spite of the fact that his party includes among its elective representatives a small number of men who were active in the Nationalist movement of two years ago, and I propose to go along with the expressed will of the electorate insofar as is possible without damage to my conscience."[92]

Armistice Day 1940, held on November 11, 1940, was a martial occasion with great military and political significance. It had been organized as a show of insular military might, patriotism and determination. It also served as the first occasion for a public and official recognition of Luis Muñoz Marín as Puerto Rico's new leader. The parade included the Army, Navy, ROTC, the Police, National Guard, Boy and Girl Scouts, Future Citizens, the American Legion, the Insular Children's Home, the Ladies Auxiliary Legion, Veterans of the 1898 war, armed forces retirees and the Consular corps. The honorary presidents were all military officers: Admiral Leahy, Rear Admiral Spruance, Brigadier General Daley, Colonel Esteves and Colonel Hartle.

Significantly, Luis Muñoz Marín was not among the long list of invited personalities published two days before the parade.[93] However, he did attend, and occupied a position of honor in the reviewing stand next to Emerson and Leahy. The only other prominent politician present at the stand was Prudencio Rivera Martínez, a *Tripartista* leader. The *Coalición* leadership was conspicuously absent. Despite the many prominent civilian and military functionaries on the reviewing stand, it was Muñoz who carried the day. He just nodded and received the longest ovation. Despite the importance that was attached by the press to this martial event, Muñoz does not mention it in his memoirs.[94]

The speeches by Leahy, Spruance, Daley, Col. Miguel A. Muñoz (commander of the Home Guard) and Emerson touched on the need to unite, enhance patriotism, and prepare militarily for hemispheric defense. Col. Muñoz presented to Leahy the recently organized units of the Home Guard. The most belligerent speech was delivered by Emilio del Toro Cuebas, President of Puerto Rico's Supreme Court. He said that "the task of preparation for national defense that is being carried out should progress so rapidly as to become, in itself, a decisive factor in the defeat of Germany and in the victory of England . . ."[95] Rhetorically, at least, the U.S. was at war in Puerto Rico more that a year before it openly declared war on Japan and Germany.

Unable to invade Britain, and before turning on the Soviet Union, Hitler developed a Western strategy that included acquiring Gibraltar, the Canary Islands, Cape Verde and Azores Islands. The plan was known as Operation Felix, and was ready in its details on November 27, 1940. It was designed to prevent a U.S. invasion of North Africa. Control of the Azores would also allow bombing sorties against the continental U.S. with the "Condor" (Focke Wulf 200C) bomber with a reach of 2,500 miles, or a new "Amerika Bomber" that could reach 9,000 miles. To obtain the collaboration of Vichy France and Franco´s Spain, Hitler traveled to France, where he met Pierre Laval at Montoire on October 22. He then traveled to Hendaye, on the Spanish-French border, meeting Franco for nine long hours. Franco was intractable. He refused passage to German troops that would attack Gibraltar. Hitler later remarked that he would much prefer suffering four or five teeth to be pulled than having to talk again to Franco. He then returned to Montoire for a meeting with Pétain, from whom he demanded greater collaboration against Britain. Pétain also resisted Hitler's more extreme demands.[96]

Roosevelt was privy to these maneuvers and wished to maintain the contacts with Vichy that had developed around the Martinique crisis, by naming an Ambassador to the Pétain government. He first considered General John J. Pershing, commander of U.S. forces in Europe during the First World War. Pershing's failing health prevented him from accepting the post. The President's next choice was Admiral Leahy. He thought Leahy could establish a good rapport with Pétain and Admiral Darlan, Minister of Marine. Leahy had met Pétain only once in 1931. Thus, he cabled Leahy on November 27 asking him to accept this crucial mission.

Roosevelt wrote Leahy that, "we need at this time an Ambassador who can gain the confidence of Marshall Pétain" and relate to "the higher officers of the French Navy who are now openly hostile to Great Britain."[97] Leahy replied that he could leave in a week. This time he requested precise written instructions for his Vichy mission. He received detailed instructions signed by Roosevelt on December 20. A major concern was the fate of the French fleet. They also included specific reference to the war vessels and the gold in Martinique and Guadeloupe, and to French Guiana.[98]

Governor Leahy hastily organized his departure from Puerto Rico. According to Ickes, he had accomplished his mission admirably. In Leahy's Puerto Rican memoirs, he says that, on the day of his departure, November 29, "the ride through the streets of San Juan was in the nature of a Triumph. The streets were packed with cheering people. Children and adults lined the approaches to the pier area, and cried and shouted their farewell." The *Coalición* leaders were again absent.

Muñoz was at the pier to bid Leahy farewell and hand him a personal letter to Roosevelt. Among other things, it pledged, "we shall refrain from any action that may in any way-no matter how small-impinge upon your great work as leader of the nation and the American Hemisphere."[99] José M. Gallardo, Secretary of Instruction, would remain as Interim Governor. Later, Ickes and Leahy would concur that it would be better to name as Governor the lackluster former U.S. Representative and Auditor of Puerto Rico Guy J. Swope, rather than Roosevelt's candidate, who was the retired Admiral Reeves. With such a large military presence in Puerto Rico, Ickes considered it unwise to name yet another naval officer to the post of Governor.[100] The President eventually accepted this view.

Asked by journalist Julius C. Edelstein, who would later join the Navy and serve under Leahy during the war, about his opinion on the results of the Puerto Rican elections, Admiral Leahy just said that they were OK. That information would be dutifully transmitted to Muñoz Marín by Ruby Black, who had not been able to approach the Admiral or his wife during the sea journey to New York.[101] It is ironic that this vital piece of information would be transmitted with such nonchalance. On December 16, Roosevelt replied to Muñoz's letter with a brief and carefully phrased message stating that, "The purposes of the Popular Democratic Party as you have outlined them are highly praiseworthy and should result in vastly improved social and economic conditions for the Island."[102] In a matter of a few months, Puerto Rican politics had undergone a major transformation.

NOTES

1. William D. Leahy, "Diary", entry for May 10, 1940, p. 57.

2. In 1938, oil exports of the Venezuela-Aruba-Curaçao complex amounted to 178 million barrels, while Trinidad exported 17 million. Most of the Trinidad oil and high octane fuel went to Great Britain. Venezuela was the main supplier of oil both to Germany and the U.S. when the war began. See, Fitzroy A. Baptiste, "New war technologies, new war resources and the changing United States' politico-strategic assessment of the British and other European colonies in the Caribbean, 1914-1978", paper presented at the Tenth Conference of Caribbean Historians, March 26-April 1, 1978, pp. 31-2. Also, by the same author, War, Cooperation and Conflict, *The European Possessions in the Caribbean, 1939-1945* (New York: Greenwood Press, 1988), pp. 29-34. For a table with the exports of leading commodities from European colonies in the Caribbean in 1938, refer to, A. Randle Elliot, "European Colonies in the Western Hemisphere", *Foreign Policy Reports* (August 15, 1940), p.142-43.

3. H.H. Arnold, *Global Mission* (New York: Harper, 1949), pp. 211, 241, 358.

4. Joel R. Davidson, *The unsinkable fleet, the politics of U.S. Navy expansion in World War II* (Annapolis: Naval Institute Press, 1996), p. 18.

5. War Department Special Staff, Historical Division, *Garrisons under the Antilles Department, Tentative Study of Garrisons Part III*, Caribbean Defense Command, 1946.

6. "Puerto Rico to Be Our Gibraltar in the Caribbean", *New York Times*, May 25, 1940, p. 6.

7. Robert S. Bird, "Canal Zone Safe, Leahy Tells Fair", *New York Times*, July 26, 1940, p. 13.

8. Idem.

9. War Department Special Staff, Historical Division, *A Preliminary Study of Garrisons of the Puerto Rican Department, Part I From the Creation of the Puerto Rican Department to the Activation of the Caribbean Defense Command*, Caribbean Defense Command, 1945.

10. George Carroll Dyer, Vice Admiral USN retired, *The Amphibians Came to Conquer, The Story of Admiral Richmond Kelly Turner* (Washington D.C.: GPO, 1972), p. 205.

11. Marion D. Francis, *History of the Antilles Department*, Section II, Chapter 1 (War Plans and Defense Measures of the Caribbean Defense Command Prior to the Organization of the Caribbean Defense Command), Antilles Department, San Juan, Puerto Rico, October, 1946, pp. 1-12.

12. They are reported in, "Puerto Rico Sees Bright Future as Major Defense Area in the Caribbean," *The Economic Review*, Vol. 4 No. 3 (June 1940), pp. 23-32, 65. For a comprehensive study of Navy building in Puerto Rico during the Second World War, refer to, *Building the Navy's Bases in World War II, History of the Bureau of Yards and Docks and the Civil Engineering Corps, 1940-1946*, Two Volumes (Washington D.C.: GPO, 1947).

13. Donald A. Yerxa, "The United States Navy and the Caribbean Sea, 1914-1941," Ph.D. dissertation, University of Maine, 1982, p. 339.

14. John Major, "The Navy Plans for War," in Kenneth J. Kagan, ed., *In Peace and War, Interpretations of American Naval History, 1775-1978* (Westport, Conn.: Greenwood Press, 1978), pp. 245-46.

15. For a detailed analysis on how Puerto Rico related to the broader Caribbean strategy, refer to, Fitzroy André Baptiste, "Puerto Rico: Headquarters of the Caribbean Sea Frontier, 1940-1945," Paper presented before the Grupo de Trabajo sobre el Impacto de la Segunda Guerra Mundial en Puerto Rico y el Caribe, Río Piedras, November 21, 1997.

16. Samuel Badillo, "Llegó ayer el comandante del departamento militar: en opinión del brigadier general Daley, Puerto Rico es la llave de todo el sistema de defensas costaneras de Estados Unidos en esta parte del Atlántico," *El Mundo*, June 27, 1939, p. 1.

17. "V Corps History-Section II," HYPERLINK "http://www.hq.c5.army.mil/history/phaseii.htm" www.hq.c5.army.mil/history/phaseii.htm.

18. Spruance distinguished himself in the Battle of Midway. He also directed the campaigns that captured the Gilberts, Marianas, Iwo Jima and Okinawa, and defeated the Japanese fleet in the Battle of Philippine Sea in June 1944. Thomas B. Buell, *The Quiet Warrior: A Biography of Admiral A. Spruance* (Boston: Little, Brown, 1974).

19. E.P. Forrestel, Vice Admiral USN, retired, *Admiral Raymond A. Spruance, USN* (Washington D.C.: G.P.O., 1966), Chapter 2, "ComTen and ComCaribSeaFron." Also, Marion D. Francis, op.cit. pp. 1-12.

20. Leahy, "Diary," entry for May 12, 1939.

21. For an analysis of the origins of Borinquen Field, see, Carlos I. Hernández, "Pasión y muerte de la Villa San Antonio . . .," Master's dissertation, Centro de Estudios Avanzados, San Juan 1996.

22. Stetson Conn and Byron Fairchild, *The Western Hemisphere, The Framework of Hemisphere Defense* (Washington D.C., Office of the Chief of Military History, 1960), pp. 17-8.

23. H.H. Arnold, op. cit., pp.203-04.

24. The renowned Puerto Rican novelist Enrique Laguerre wrote a moving novel about the tragedy of these communities. He has a character exclaim "It's the end of the world!" *Infiernos privados* (San Juan: Editorial Cultural, 1986), p. 18.

25. Carlos I. Hernández, "Pasión y muerte de la Villa de San Antonio: la expropiación de los barrios Maleza Alta y Maleza Baja de Aguadilla en el marco de la Segunda Guerra Mundial," Masters's dissertation, Centro de Estudios Avanzados de Puerto Rico y el Caribe, October 1996.

26. "El brigadier Daley y tres oficiales más, ascendidos por el Depto. De la Guerra, El Ejército adquiere 26,000 cuerdas de terreno en la isla para desarrollar grandes planes-Ayer fueron llamados a servicio varios oficiales de la Reserva," *El Mundo*, October 1, 1940, p. 1.

27. "La Guardia Nacional de Puerto Rico será aumentada hasta el máximo en tiempos de paz; tendrá una dotación de 5,548 hombres, Tres mil obreros en el Campamento Tortuguero, El Brigadier General Esteves rechazó la oportunidad de seguir como Ayudante General para servir como oficial de tropa", *El Mundo*, October 9, 1940, p. 1.

28 ."Asignados $1,876,000 para carretera de Aguadilla a San Juan. A mediados de noviembre habrá treinta mil obreros empleados en obras de WPA, anunció ayer Leahy en Washington," *El Mundo*, October 8, 1940, p. 1.

29. "Nueva carretera de Buchanan a Punta Borinquen, Interior explica los propósitos que se persiguen. La subasta del primer trozo se efectuará en noviembre veintidós," *El Mundo,* November 17, 1940, p. 1.

30. In 1942, the Commissioner of Health of Puerto Rico wrote to the U.S. Surgeon General that "over 150,000 persons have been immunized against smallpox and over 60,000 against typhoid fever in the neighborhood of Army and Navy ports during the last four months. Extensive malaria control and rural sanitation are being carried out *to protect the armed forces . . .*" He also mentions the isolation of "venereally infected women" and the division of the island into seven defense districts. E. Garrido Morales to Dr. Thomas Parran, Dec. 21, 1942. C.W. Taussig papers, Container 39, Folder P.R.-Tugwell, FDR Library.

31. For an analysis of the existing base structure in the Caribbean, refer to, Randle Eliot, "U.S. Strategic Bases in the Atlantic," *Foreign Policy Reports*, Vol. XVI, No. 21 (January 15, 1941), pp. 258-68.

32. Major John Baker, "The Caribbean Theatre in the Defense of the Americas," p. 36, in U. S. Army Caribbean, *Ten Studies on Aspects and Problems, 1945-1948*, Vol. 10 in 11, microfilm, Centro de Investigaciones Históricas, University of Puerto Rico.

33. See, Humberto García Muñiz, *La estrategia de Estados Unidos y la militarización del Caribe* (Río Piedras: Instituto de Estudios del Caribe, 1988), p. 50.

34. Statement of June 17 to Standing Liaison Committee cited in David C. Haglund,

Latin America and the Transformation of U.S. Strategic Thought, 1936-1940 (Albuquerque: University of New Mexico Press, 1984), p. 202.

35. R.G. Tugwell to Harold L. Ickes, April 10, 1941, R.G. Tugwell Papers, Container 6, Folder Ickes, F.D.R. Library.

36. FDR to Cordell Hull, January 11, 1940, cited in Lowell T. Young, "Franklin D. Roosevelt and America's Islets: Acquisition of Territory in the Caribbean and the Pacific," *The Historian*, Vol. 35, No. 2 (February 1973), p. 211.

37. Francis L. Lowenheim, Harold D. Langley and Manfred Jonas, eds., *Roosevelt and Churchill, Their Secret Wartime Correspondence* (New York: Da Capo, 1975), particularly Roosevelt's letter to Churchill of August 13, 1940, p. 108. Also, John Major, op. cit., pp. 250-53.

38. John Major, op. cit., pp. 250-53.

39. Commander Lowe, "A Study of Fleet Base Sites in the West Indies," Box 96-NB-Naval bases 8/36-7/41, Records of the Strategic Plans Division, Office of the Chief of Naval Operations, Operational Archives, U.S. Naval Historical Center, Navy Yard.

40. From: Chief of Naval Operations to Rear Admiral John W. Greenslade, Suggestion as to Certain Policy and Strategic Factors of the Problem of the Location and Development of Naval Bases, November 29, 1940. Box 96-NB-Naval bases 8/36-7/41, Records of the Strategic Plans Division, Office of the Chief of Naval Operations, Operational Archives, U.S. Naval Historical Center, Navy Yard.

41. *Building the Navy's Bases* . . ., op. cit., Volume II, p. 8.

42. For a history of the Roosevelt Roads Naval base, refer to, Gerardo Piñero Cádiz, "La Segunda Guerra Mundial, Puerto Rico y la base Roosevelt Roads," Doctoral dissertation, Centro de Estudios Avanzados de Puerto Rico y el Caribe, 2004.

43. Thomas Hibben, U.S. Department of Comerce, The Industrial Development of Puerto Rico, March 1948, FDR Library, C.W. Taussig Papers, Container 44, Folder Caribbean Commission.

44. Marion D. Francis, op. cit., pp. 109-123.

45. "Ocho mil puertorriqueños alistados ya para formar en Guardia Local, Cuarenta y dos compañías están debidamente constituidas", *El Mundo*, October 16, 1940, p. 4.

46. "La Home Guard será entregada mañana a Leahy," *El Mundo*, November 10, 1940, p, 1.

47. Marion D. Francis, op. cit., pp. 114-120; War Department Special Staffs, Historical Division, "A Preliminary Study of Garrisons of the Puerto Rican Department", pp. 24-26.

48. "Government is Island's Biggest Business, Defense Construction Has Created Greatest Business Boom in Puerto Rico's History; Payrolls Surpass Sugar Industry," Puerto Rican Trade Review (August-September, 1941), p. 1.

49. Oficina de Investigaciones Económicas, *Anuario Estadístico, Puerto Rico 1950-51* (San Juan: Administración de Fomento Económico, 1952), Table 96, p. 160.

50. Thomas Hibben, op. cit., pp. 53-66.

51. Puerto Rico Planning Board, *Economic Development of Puerto Rico, 1940-1950, 1951-1960* (San Juan; Planning Board, February 1951), p. 18 and Chart 3, p. 11. Emphasis added by the author.

52. A.J. Jaffe, People, *Jobs and Economic Development, A Case History of Puerto Rico Supplemented by Recent Mexican Experiences* (Illinois: The Free Press, 1959), p. 43.

53. Jorge L. Acosta León, "Cambio y transformación en Puerto Rico durante la Segunda Guerra Mundial: el caso de Puerto Rico en 1939-1945," paper presented in the course SOCI 6116, University of Puerto Rico, December 1998, p. 22.

54. Harvey S. Perloff, *Puerto Rico's Economic Future, A Study in Planned Development* (Chicago: The University of Chicago Press, 1950), p. 113-16, Table 35.

55. Alan S. Milward, *La Segunda Guerra Mundial, 1939-1945* (Barcelona: Editorial Crítica, 1986), pp. 60-81. Published originally under the title *War, Economy and Society, 1939-1945.*

56. Rafael Picó, "Puerto Rico: Economic Sore Spot", *Inter-American Quarterly*, Vol. 2, No. 2 (April 1940), pp. 62, 67.

57. James L. Dietz, *Economic History of Puerto Rico: Institutional Change and Capitalist Development* (Princeton, New Jersey: Princeton University Press, 1986), p. 185.

58. Guy J. Swope, *Forty-First Annual Report of the Governor of Puerto Rico* (San Juan: Bureau of Supplies Printing and Transportation, 1941), p. 10.

59. Gordon K. Lewis, *Puerto Rico: Freedom and Power in the Caribbean* (New York: Harper & Row, 1963), p. 97.

60. "West India Royal Commission 1938-39; Recommendations," Parliamentary Papers, Cmd. 6174 (London: H.M. Stationery Office, 1940); also, Bernard L. Poole, *The Caribbean Commission, Background of Cooperation in the West Indies* (Columbia: University of South Carolina Press, 1951), pp. 32-5.

61. Rexford G. Tugwell, *The Stricken Land* (New York: Doubleday 1947), pp. 64-66.

62. "Report of the Chairman, Charles William Taussig, United States Commission to

Study Social and Economic Conditions of the British West Indies, 1940": C.W. Taussig Papers-Container 35, Folder: Caribbean Commission, FDR Library.

63. Poole, op. cit.; also, Mayra Rosario Urrutia, "La Comisión Anglo-Americana del Caribe: una estrategia socioeconómica con fines de seguridad militar," *Avance de Investigación 11*, Centro de Investigaciones Académicas, Universidad del Sagrado Corazón.

64. Hines Calvin Warner, "United States Diplomacy in the Caribbean during World War II," doctoral dissertation, The University of Texas, 1968, p. 95.

65. Ibid., 189-202.

66. Ibid., p. 178.

67. For Robert's account of this visit and his version of the crisis, see Georges Robert, *La France aux Antilles de 1939 à 1943* (Paris: Librairie Plon, Paris), 1950. For another French account, see, Paul Auphan and Jacques Mordal, *The French Navy in World War II* (Westport, Conn.: Greenwood Press), 1976.

68. Leahy, "Diary . . .," entry for June 28, p. 71.

69. Lawrence H. Douglas, "The Martinique Affair: The United States Navy and the French West Indies, 1940-1943", in Williams R. Roberts and Jack Sweetman, *New Interpretations in Naval History* (Annapolis: Naval Institute Press, 1991), pp. 124-39.

70. Hines Calvin Warner, *op. cit.*, Chapters 3 and 4. Also Donald A. Yerxa, op. cit., pp. 361-63.

71. Leahy, "Diary . . .," entries for July 6, 10 and 19, pp. 73, 76.

72. Commandant 10th Naval Distrct, Director of Naval Intelligence, *Military information on the Island of Martinique, F.W.I*, 19 July 1940, Entry 1727, Box 3, Record Group 181, Records of Naval Districts and Shore Establishments, National Archives, cited in, Gerardo Piñero, op. cit.,p. 109.

73. Leahy, "Diary . . .," entry for August 5, p. 82.

74. Lawrence H. Douglas, op. cit., p. 127.

75. Yerxa, op. cit., 365-68.

76. Leahy "Diary . . .", entries for November 2 and 4, pp. 115-16.

77. Fitzroy A. Baptiste, "Le Regime de Vichy en Martinique, Juin 1940-Juin 1943," *Les Cahiers du CERAG*, No. 36, November 1979, pp. 1-39.

78. During his period in San Juan he negotiated not to be arrested upon his return

to France. He was, however, arrested in 1944 and sentenced to 18 months in prison for collaboration with the Germans. In 1946, a high tribunal sentenced him to a further ten year forced labor sentence which he never served. Auphan, op. cit., p. 288; Robert, op. cit., 194.

79. Linda McClain, "The role of Admiral W.D. Leahy in U.S. foreign policy," Ph. D. dissertation, University of Virginia, August, 1984, p. 42.

80. William D. Leahy to Rupert Emerson, November 1, 1940, Interior Department Files, U.S. National Archives.

81. Julius C. Edelstein "Triunfo Popular causa sorpresa en Washington," El Mundo, November 7, 1940, p. 1.

82. William D. Leahy to Harold Ickes, November 6, 1940. Interior Department Files, U.S. National Archives.

83. William D. Leahy to Harold Ickes, November 9, 1940. Interior Department Files, U.S. National Archives.

84. Luis Muñoz Marín, *Memorias, 1898-1940* (San Juan: Universidad Interamericana, 1982), pp.209-10.

85. Julius C. Edelstein, "Funcionarios de Washington cautelosos y reservados sobre las elecciones en Puerto Rico," *El Mundo*, November 10, 1949, p. 2.

86. James MacGregor Burns, *Roosevelt, The Soldier of Freedom* (New York: Harcourt, 1970), p. 8.

87. "Morgenthau in Puerto Rico," *The New York Times*, November 9, 1940, p. 4.

88. "Las tropas de Puerto Rico rinden honores a Morgenthau," El Mundo, November 11, 1940, p. 1.

89. "Leahy pide frente unido", *La Correspondencia*, November 11, 1940, p. 1.

90. Sidney L. Dervan, "Roosevelt preocupado por Puerto Rico, Administración quiere evitar que las condiciones de la Isla den armas para agitación antiamericana en Sur América, El viaje del Dr. Rupert Emerson tiene por objetivo el estudio directo de la situación, Además del sistema escolar y las defensas, examinará el problema de los 500 acres," *La Correspondencia*, November 9, 1940, p. 1. Author's translation.

91. Harold L. Ickes, *The Secret Diary of Harold Ickes, The Lowering Clouds, 1939-1941*, Volume III (New York: Simon and Schuster, 1955), pp. 372, 377, and 389.

92. William D. Leahy to Harold Ickes, November 16,1940, Department of the Interior Papers, U.S. National Archives.

93. "La Home Guard será entregada mañana a Leahy," *El Mundo*, November 10, 1940, p. 1.

94. Luis Muñoz Marín, "Borrador 2–1970," p. 536, Sección XI, Material de y sobre Luis Muñoz Marín, Material para el libro Memorias, Caja YY, Fundación Luis Muñoz Marín.

95. "Puerto Rico conmemoró brillantemente el Armisticio," *El Mundo*, November 12, 1940, p. 3, 16.

96. Holger H. Herwig, *Politics of Frustration, the United States in German Naval Planning, 1889-1941* (Boston: Little, Brown and Co., 1976), p. 211; also, Martin Gilbert, *The Second World War, A Complete History* (New York: Holt, 1989), pp. 133-134.

97. For the complete text, see, Jorge Rodríguez Beruff, ed., *Las memorias de Leahy* (San Juan: Fundación Luis Muñoz Marín, 2002), p. 145.

98. William D. Leahy, *I Was There* (New York: McGraw Hill, 1950), Appendix I.

99. Ibid., pp. 146-50, 218.

100. Ickes, op. cit., pp. 389, 404-05.

101. "Julius Edelstein tells me today that Leahy told him the PR elections were OKAY." December 3, 1940. Box 5, Folder XIV, Document 32, Ruby Black Collection, Centro de Investigaciones Históricas, University of Puerto Rico.

102. Jorge Rodríguez Beruff, op. cit., p. 219.

SELECTED BIBLIOGRAPHY

ARCHIVAL SOURCES

Centro de Investigaciones Históricas, University of Puerto Rico
Ruby Black Collection
Military History Collection of the *Proyecto Caribeño de Justicia y Paz*

Department of State, Washington D.C
Reference Division

***El Mundo* Photographic Collection, University of Puerto Rico**

Franklin D. Roosevelt Library, Hyde Park, New York
Franklin Delano Roosevelt Papers
Eleanor Roosevelt
Adolf Berle
Harry Hopkins
I. Rosenham
Rexford G. Tugwell
Charles W. Taussig

Fundación Luis Muñoz Marín, Trujillo Alto, Puerto Rico
Luis Muñoz Marín
Manuscripts for memoirs
Speeches
President of the Senate
Newspaper *El Batey*
Ruby Black Collection

Library of Congress Manuscript Division
Harold L. Ickes Papers
William D. Leahy's Papers

McKeldin Library, University of Maryland
The Myllard E. Tydings Collection

National Archives, Washington D.C.

Record Groups:
94 Records of the Adjutant General's Office, 1780s-1917
126 Records of the Office of Territories
Relating to Puerto Rico
165 Records of the War Department General and
Special Staffs
Special StaffsRecords of the Military Intelligence Division [MID, G-2]
Records of the War Plans Division [WPD]
Records of the Operations Division [OPD]
168 Records of the National Guard Bureau[NGB]
218 Records of the U.S. Joint Chiefs of Staff [JCS]
226 Records of the Office of Strategic Services [OSS]319
Records of the Army Staff
323 Records of the Puerto Rican Reconstruction Administration [PRRA]
338 Records of the United States Army Commands 1942-
Records of Defense Commands
Records of service commands, departments and base commands
350 Records of the Bureau pf Insular Affairs [BIA]394
Records of the United States Army Continental Commands, 1920-1942
407 Records of the Adjutant General's Office, 1917- [AGO]
National Security Council Collection

Naval Historical Center, Washington Navy Yard

Naval Bases/Stations

U.S. Army Center for Military History, Washington D.C.

U.S. Army Military History Institute, Carlisle Barracks, Pennsylvania

Records of the Army War College

Wisconsin Historical Society

William D. Leahy's Papers

BOOKS

Abbazia, Patrick. *Mr. Roosevelt's Navy: The Private War of the U.S. Atlantic Fleet, 1939-1942* (Annapolis: Naval Institute Press, 1975).

Aboy Benítez, Ramón and Ramón Ramos Casellas. *An Examination into Some of the Utopian Political and Economic Ideas Now Apparently in Vogue in Puerto Rico* (San Juan: Association of Sugar Producers of Puerto Rico, 1939).

Adams, Henry H. *Witness to Power: The Life of Fleet Admiral William D. Leahy* (Annapolis: Naval Institute Press, 1985).

Albi, Julio. *La defensa de las Indias (1764-1799)* (Madrid: Ediciones de Cultura Hispánica, 1987).

Albion, Robert Greenhalgh. *Makers of Naval Policy, 1798-1947* (Annapolis: Naval Institute Press, 1980).

Álvarez Curbelo, Silvia and María Elena Rodríguez. *Del nacionalismo al populismo: cultura y política en Puerto Rico* (Río Piedras: Ediciones Huracán, 1993).

Ambrose, Stephen. *Upton and the Army* (Baton Rouge: Louisiana State University Press, 1964).

American Civil Liberties Union. *Cases: U.S. Foreign Possessions* (New York: ACLU, 1937).

_____. *Civil Liberties in American Colonies* (New York: ACLU, 1939).

American Council on Public Affairs. *Puerto Rican Problems...* (Washington D.C.: American Council on Public Affairs, 1940).

Anthony, Michael. *Port-of-Spain in a World at War, 1939-1945* (Port-of-Spain: Ministry of Sports, Culture and Youth Affairs, n.d.).

Anglin, Douglas George. *The St. Pierre and Miquelon Affair of 1941: A Study in Diplomacy in the North Atlantic Quadrangle* (Toronto: University of Toronto Press, 1966).

Arnold, H.H. *Global Mission* (New York: Harper & Bros., 1949).

Aron, Robert. *The Vichy Regime, 1940-1944* (Boston: Beacon, 1969).

Auphan, Paul and Jacques Mordal. *The French Navy in World War II* (Westport, Conn.: Greenwood Press, 1976).

Baptiste, Fitzroy André. *The United States and West Indian Unrest, 1918-1939*, Working Paper No. 18 (Mona, Jamaica: UWI, 1978).

_____. *War, Cooperation and Conflict: The European Possessions in the Caribbean, 1939-1945* (Westport, Conn.: Greenwood Press, 1988).

Beals, Carleton. *America Faces South* (Philadelphia: J. B. Lippincott, 1938).

_____. *The Coming Struggle for Latin America* (Philadelphia: J.B. Lippincott, 1938).

Beard, Charles A. *American Foreign Policy in the Making, 1932-1940: A Study in Responsibilities* (New Haven: Yale University Press, 1946).

_____. *President Roosevelt and the Coming of War, 1941* (Connecticut: Archon Books, Hamden, 1968).

Bennett, Edward M. *Franklin D. Roosevelt and the Search for Security: American-Soviet Relations, 1933-1939* (Wilmington: Scholarly Resources, 1985).

Berle, Adolf Augustus. *Economic Defense of the Western Hemisphere* (Charlottesville, Va.: 1940).

_____. *New Directions in the New World* (New York: Harper & Bros., 1940).

Bhana, Surendra. *The United States and the Development of the Puerto Rican Status Question, 1936-1968* (Lawrence: University Press of Kansas, 1975).

Bidwell, Percy Wells. *Economic Defense of Latin America* (Boston: World Peace Foundations, 1941).

Bird, Esteban A. *Report on the Sugar Industry in Relation to the Social and Economic System of Puerto Rico* (San Juan: Bureau of Supplies, Printing and Transportation, 1941).

Bird Piñero, Enrique. *Don Luis Muñoz Marín: el poder de la excelencia* (Trujillo Alto: Fundación Luis Muñoz Marín, 1991).

Blair, Clay. *Hitler's U-Boat War* (New York: Random House, 1996).

Blum, John M. *V Was for Victory: Politics and American Culture during World War II* (New York: Harcourt Brace, 1976).

Blumenthal, Henry. *Illusion and Reality in Franco-American Diplomacy, 1914-1945* (Baton Rouge: Louisiana State University Press, 1986).

Boersner, Demetrio. *Relaciones internacionales de América Latina* (Caracas: Nueva Sociedad, 1982).

Bothwell, Reece B. *Puerto Rico: cien años de lucha política* (Río Piedras: Editorial Universitaria, 1979)

Bousquet, Ben and Colin Douglas, eds. *West Indian Women at War: British Racism in World War II* (London: Lawrence and Wishart, 1991).

Brands, H.W. *Bound to Empire: The United States and the Philippines* (New York: Oxford University Press, 1992).

Brown, A.D. *P.R.: A Select List of References* (Washington, D.C.: 1939).

Brown, D. *Dynamite on Our Doorstep: Puerto Rican Paradox* (New York: Greenberg, 1945).

Brune, Lester. *The Origins of American National Security Policy: Sea Power, Air Power and Foreign Policy, 1900-1941* (Kansas: MAIAH Publishing, Kansas State University, 1981).

Buchanan, Albert Russell, ed. *The United States and World War II: Military and Diplomatic Documents* (Columbia: University of South Carolina Press, 1972).

Buell, Thomas B. *The Quiet Warrior: A Biography of Admiral A. Spruance* (Boston: Little, Brown, 1974).

Burns, James H., Walter C. Cole and William D. Leahy. *Industry's Preparation for National Defense* (Washington, D.C.: Chamber of Commerce of the United States, 1939).

Butler, Hugh Alfred. *Expenditures and Commitments by the United States for Latin America* (Washington, D.C.: Government Press Office, 1943).

Cabranes, José A. *Citizenship and the American Empire* (New Haven: Yale University Press, 1979).

Calder, Bruce J. *The Impact of Intervention: The Dominican Republic during the U.S. Occupation of 1916-1924* (Austin: University of Texas Press, 1984).

Calvocoressi, Peter and Guy Wint. *Total War: Causes and Courses of the Second World War* (Harmondsworth: Penguin, 1974).

Cameron Watts, Donald. *How War Came: The Immediate Origins of the Second World War, 1938-1939* (New York: Pantheon Books, 1989).

Carr, E.H. *International Relations between the Two World Wars, 1919-1939* (New York: Harper Torchbooks, 1966)

Challener, Richard D. *Admirals, Generals and American Foreign Policy, 1898-1914* (Princeton: Princeton University Press, 1973).

Chambers, John Whiteclay. *World War II: Film and History* (New York: Oxford University Press, 1996).

_____, and David Culbert, eds. *To Raise an Army: The Draft Comes to Modern America* (New York: Free Press, 1987).

Child, Jack. *Unequal Alliance: The Inter-American Military System, 1938-1978* (Boulder, Colorado: West View Press, 1980).

Clark, Jeanne Nienaber. *Roosevelt's Warrior: Harold L. Ickes and the New Deal* (Baltimore: Johns Hopkins Press, 1996).

Clark, Victor. *Porto Rico and its Problems* (Washington, D.C.: Brookings Institution, 1930).

Cline, Ray S. *Washington Command Post: The Operations Divisions*, United States Army in World War II: The Western Hemisphere, Kent Roberts Greenfield, gen. ed. (Washington: Office of the Chief of Military History, Department of the Army, 1951).

Combas Guerra, Eliseo. *En torno a la Fortaleza: Winship* (San Juan: Biblioteca de Autores Puertorriqueños, 1950).

Commission of Inquiry on Civil Rights in Puerto Rico. *Report on the Events of March 21, 1937), in Ponce* (New York: 1937).

Conn, Stetson and Byron Fairchild. *The Framework of Hemisphere Defense*, United States Army in World War II: The Western Hemisphere, Kent Roberts

Greenfield, gen. ed. (Washington, D.C.: Office of the Chief of Military History, US Army, 1978).

Conn, Stetson, Rose C. Engelman and Byron Fairchild, *Guarding the United States and Its Outposts*, United States Army in World War II: The Western Hemisphere, Kent Roberts Greenfield, gen. ed. (Washington, D.C.: Office of the Chief of Military History, US Army, 1964).

Connery, Robert H. *The Navy and the Industrial Mobilization in World War II* (Princeton: Princeton University Press, 1972).

Córdova, Gonzalo F. *Santiago Iglesias: creador del movimiento obrero de Puerto Rico* (Río Piedras: Editorial Universitaria, 1980).

Córdova, Lieban. *7 años con Muñoz Marín, 1938-1945* (Arecibo: Lieban Córdova, 1989).

Corkran, Herbert, Jr. *Patterns of International Cooperation in the Caribbean, 1942-1969* (Dallas: Southern University Press, 1970).

Cosmas, Graham A. *An Army for Empire: The United States Army in the Spanish-American War* (Columbia, Missouri: University of Missouri Press, 1971).

Council for Pan American Democracy, New York. *Starvation in Puerto Rico: Recommendations for the Immediate Relief of Our Caribbean Gibraltar* (New York: Council for Pan American Democracy, 1943).

Curet Cuevas, Eliezer. *El desarrollo económico de Puerto Rico, 1940-1972* (Hato Rey: Management Aid Center, 1976).

Dallek, Robert. *Franklin D. Roosevelt and American Foreign Policy, 1939-1945* (New York: Oxford University Press, 1979).

_____. *The Roosevelt Diplomacy and World War II* (New York: R.E. Krieger, 1976).

Davidson, Joel R. *The Unsinkable Fleet: The Politics of U.S. Navy Expansion in World War II* (Annapolis: Naval Institute Press, 1996).

Davies, Kenneth. *FDR: Into the Storm, 1937-1940* (New York: Random House, 1993).

Dávila Santiago, Rubén. *El derribo de las murallas: orígenes intelectuales del socialismo en Puerto Rico* (Río Piedras: Editorial Cultural, 1988).

Davis, Forrest. *The Atlantic System: The Story of Anglo-American Control of the Seas* (New York: Reynal & Hitchcock, 1941).

_____ and Ernest K. Lindley. *How War Came* (New York: Simon and Schuster, 1942).

Davis, George T. *A Navy Second to None: The Development of Modern American Naval Policy* (New York: Harcourt Brace, 1940).

De Jesús Toro, Rafael. *Historia económica de Puerto Rico* (Cincinnati: Southern Western Publishing, 1982).

Diedrich, Mari and Dorothea Fischer-Hornung, eds. *Women and War: The Changing Status of American Women from the 1930s to the 1950s* (New York: Berg/St. Martin's Press, 1990).

Dietz, James L. *Historia económica de Puerto Rico* (Río Piedras: Ediciones Huracán, 1989).

Diffie, Bailey W. and Justine Diffey. *Porto Rico: A Broken Pledge* (New York: Vanguard Press, 1931).

Divine, Robert A. *The Reluctant Belligerent: American Entry into World War II* (New York: John Wiley, 1979).

_____. *Roosevelt and World War II* (Baltimore: John Hopkins Press, 1969).

Drummond, Donald F. *The Passing of American Neutrality, 1937-1941* (Ann Arbor: University of Michigan Press, 1955)

Duggan, Laurence. *The Americas: The Search for Hemisphere Security* (New York: Holt, 1949).

Dyer, George Carrollo (Vice Admiral USNR). *Amphibians Came to Conquer: The Story of Admiral Richmond Kelly Turner,* 2 vols., (Washington, D.C.: Department of the Navy, 1972).

Eliot, Major George Fielding. *The Ramparts We Watch: A Study of the Problems of American National Defense* (New York: Reynal & Hitchcock, 1938).

Elmsley, Clive, Arthur Marwick and Wendy Thompson, eds. *War, Peace and Social Change in Twentieth Century Europe* (Philadelphia: Open University Press, 1989).

Erenberg, Lewis A. and Susan E. Hirsch, eds. *The War in American Culture: Society and Culture during World War II* (Chicago: The University of Chicago Press, 1996).

Estades, María Eugenia. *La presencia militar de los Estados Unidos en PuertoRico, 1898-1918* (Río Piedras: Ediciones Huracán, 1988),

Fehrenbach, T.R. *F.D.R.'s Undeclared War, 1939-1941* (New York: D. McKay Co., 1967).

Fiz Jiménez, Epifanio. *El racket del Capitolio: el gobierno de la Coalición Republicana-Socialista, años 1932 al 1940* (San Juan: Editorial Esther, 1944).

Fleming, Thomas. *The New Dealers's War: F.D.R. and the War within World War II* (New York: Basic Books, 2001).

Forrestal, Emmet P. *Admiral Raymond A. Spruance, USN: A Study in Command* (Washington, D.C.: Government Printing Office, 1966).

Friedel, Frank. *Franklin D. Roosevelt: The Apprenticeship* (Boston: Little, Brown, 1952).

Frye, Alton. *Nazi Germany and the American Hemisphere, 1933-1941* (New Haven: Yale University Press, 1967).

García Muñiz, Humberto. *La estrategia de Estados Unidos y la militarización del Caribe* (Río Piedras: Instituto de Estudios del Caribe, 1988).

Gardner, Lloyd C. *Economic Aspects of New Deal Diplomacy* (Madison: University of Wisconsin Press, 1964).

Garland, Jasper Vanderbilt. *War and the Americas* (New York: H.W. Wilson Co., 1941).

Gayer, Arthur, Paul T. Homan and Earle K. James. *The Sugar Economy of Puerto Rico* (New York: Columbia University Press, 1938).

Géigel Polanco, Vicente. *El despertar de un pueblo* (San Juan: Biblioteca de Autores Puertorriqueños, 1942).

_____. *La independencia de Puerto Rico: sus bases históricas, económicas y culturales* (Río Piedras: Imprenta Falcón, 1943).

Gellman, Irwin F. *Good Neighbor Diplomacy: United States Policies in Latin America, 1933-1945* (Baltimore: John Hopkins Press, 1979).

_____. *Roosevelt and Batista: Good Neighbor Diplomacy in Cuba, 1933-1945* (Albuquerque: University of New Mexico Press, 1973).

Gilbert, Martin. *The Second World War* (New York: Henry Holt, 1989).

Glauert, Earl T. and Lester D. Langley. *The United States and Latin America* (Reading: Addison Wesley, 1971).

Gontán, José. *Historia político-social de Puerto Rico* (San Juan: Editorial Esther, 1945).

González Casanova, Pablo y Luis Antezana Ergueta, eds. *América Latina en los años treinta* (Ciudad de México: UNAM, 1977).

Gould, Lyman J. *La Ley Foraker: raíces de la política colonial de los Estados Unidos* (Río Piedras: Editorial Universitaria, 1975).

Green, David. *The Containment of Latin America: A History of the Myths and Realities of the Good Neighbor Policy* (Chicago: Quadrangle Books, 1971).

Gropman, Alan L. *Mobilizing U.S. Industry in World War II: Myth and Reality*, McNair Paper 50 (Washington, D.C., National Defense University, August, 1996).

Gruening, Ernest. *Many Battles: The Autobiography of Ernest Gruening* (New York: Liveright, 1973).

Guerra Mondragón, Miguel. *How Congress Has Treated Puerto Rico* (San Juan: Bureau of Supplies, Printing and Transportation, 1943).

Haas, William H., ed. *The American Empire: A Study of the Outlying Territories of the United States* (Chicago: University of Chicago Press, 1940).

Hagan, Kenneth J. *In Peace and War: Interpretations of American Naval History, 1775-1984* (Westport, Conn.: Greenwood, 1984).

Haglund, David G. *Latin America and the Transformation of U.S. Strategic Thought, 1936-1940* (Albuquerque: University of New Mexico Press, 1984).

Hanson, Earl Parker. *Transformation: The Story of Modern Puerto Rico* (New York: Simon and Schuster, 1955).

Hardach, Gerd. *Historia económica mundial del siglo XX: la Primera Guerra Mundial, 1914-1918* (Barcelona: Crítica, 1986).

Headrick, Daniel R. *Los instrumentos del Imperio* (Madrid: Alianza, 1981).

Healy, David. *Gunboat Diplomacy in the Wilson Era: The U.S. Navy in Haiti, 1915-1916* (Madison: The University of Wisconsin Press, 1976).

_____. *The United States in Cuba, 1898-1902: Generals, Politicians and the Search for Policy* (Madison: The University of Wisconsin Press, 1963).

Heide, Robert and John Gilman. *Home Front America: Popular Culture of the World War II Era* (San Francisco: Chronicle Books, 1995).

Heinrich, Waldo. *Threshold of War: Franklin D. Roosevelt and the American Entry into World War II* (New York: Oxford University Press, 1988).

Herwig, Holger H. *Politics of Frustration: The United States in German Naval Planning, 1889-1941* (Boston: Little, Brown, 1976).

Hill, Howard C. *Roosevelt and the Caribbean* (New York: Russell and Russell, 1965).

Hobson, Harold. *The First Three Years of the War: A Day-by-day Record* (London: Hutchinson, 1942).

Hull, Cordell. *The Memoirs of Cordell Hull*, 2 Vols. (New York: MacMillan, 1984).

Humphreys, R.A. *Latin America and the Second World War* (Atlantic Highlands, NJ.: Athlone Press, 1981).

Ickes, Harold L. *The Secret Diary of Harold L. Ickes*, 4 Vols. (New York: Da Capo Press, 1974).

Janeway, Eliot. *The Struggle for Survival: A Chronicle of Economic Mobilization in World War II* (New Haven: Yale University Press, 1951).

Kelshall, Gaylord T.M. *The U-Boat War in the Caribbean* (Annapolis: Naval Institute Press, 1994).

Kent, Rockwell. *This is My Own* (New Jersey: Duell, Sloan and Pearce, 1940).

Kimball, Warren F. *The Most Unsordid Act: Lend-Lease, 1939-1941* (Baltimore: John Hopkins University Press, 1969).

Kindleberger, Charles P. *Historia económica mundial del siglo XX: la crisis económica, 1929-1939* (Barcelona: Crítica, 1985).

Kinsella, William E. *Leadership in Isolation: F.D.R. and the Origins of the Second World War* (Boston: GK Hall, 1978).

Kirkham, Pat and David Thomas, eds. *War Culture: Social Change and Changing Experience in World War Two* (London: Lawrence and Wishart, 1995).

LaFeber, Walter. *The New Empire: An Interpretation of American Expansion, 1860-1898* (Ithaca: Cornell University Press, 1963).

Langer, William L. *Our Vichy Gamble* (New York: Alfred A. Knopf, 1947).

_____. *The Undeclared War, 1940-1941* (New York: Harper & Row, 1953).

_____ and S. Everett Gleason. *The Challenge to Isolation, 1937-1940* (New York: Harper & Row, 1952).

Larrabee, Eric. *Commander in Chief: Franklin Delano Roosevelt, His Lieutenants and Their War* (New York: Harper & Row, 1987).

Lash, Joseph P. *A World of Love: Eleanor Roosevelt and Her Friends, 1943-1962* (New York: Doubleday, 1984).

Leahy, William D. *I Was There: The Personal Story of the Chief of Staff to Presidents Roosevelt and Truman Based, on His Notes and Diaries Made at the Time* (New York: McGraw-Hill, 1950).

Leuchtenburg, William E. *Franklin D. Roosevelt and the New Deal, 1932-1940* (New York: Harper Torchbooks, 1963).

Leutze, James R. *Bargaining for Supremacy: Anglo-American Naval Collaboration, 1937-1941* (Chapel Hill: University of North Carolina Press, 1977).

Lewis, Gordon K. *Puerto Rico: libertad y poder en el Caribe* (San Juan: Edil, 1969).

Lloyd Jones, Chester, Henry Kittredge Norton and Parker Thomas Moon. *The United States and the Caribbean* (Chicago: University of Chicago, 1934).

Loucheim, Katie and Jonathan Dembo. *The Making of the New Deal: The Insiders Speak* (Cambridge, Mass.: Harvard University Press, 1983).

Louis, William Roger. *Imperialism at Bay, 1941-1945: The United States and the Decolonization of the British Empire* (Oxford: Claredon Press, 1977).

Love, Robert William, ed. *The Chiefs of Naval Operation* (Annapolis: Naval Institute Press, 1980).

Lowenheim, Francis L., Harold D. Langley and Manfred Jonas, eds. *Roosevelt and Churchill: Their Secret Wartime Correspondence* (New York: Da Capo, 1975).

Lugo Silva, Enrique. *Rafael Martínez Nadal: su vida y su obra* (Río Piedras: Departamento de Instrucción Pública, 1979).

MacGregor Burns, James. *Roosevelt: The Lion and the Fox* (New York: Harcourt Brace, 1956).

_____. *Roosevelt: The Soldier of Freedom* (New York: Harcourt, 1970).

Mahan, A. T. *The Gulf and Inland Waters* (New York: Charles Scribner's Sons, 1883).

_____. *The Influence of Sea Power Upon History, 1660-1783* (London: Sampson Low, Marston, Searle & Rivington, 1889).

_____. *Lessons of the War with Spain and Other Articles* (Boston: Little, Brown, 1899)

Malcolm, George Arthur. *American Colonial Careerist: Half Century of Official Life and Personal Experience in the Philippines and Puerto Rico* (Boston: Christopher Publisher House, 1957).

Maldonado, Teófilo. *Rafael Martínez Nadal: su vida* (San Juan: Imprenta Venezuela, 1937).

Matloff, Maurice and Edwin M Snell. *Strategic Planning for Coalition Warfare, 1941-1942*, United States Army in World War II: The Western Hemisphere, Kent Roberts Greenfield, gen. ed. (Washington D.C.: Office of the Chief of Military History, Department of the Army, 1953).

Malone, Dumas and Basil Rauch. *War and Troubled Peace, 1917-1939* (New York: Appleton-Century Crafts, 1960).

Mathews, Thomas. *La política puertorriqueña y el Nuevo Trato* (Río Piedras: Editorial Universitaria, 1970).

Matilla, Alfredo, Matilde Albert, Gabriel Moreno, et al., eds. *Cincuenta años de exilio español en Puerto Rico y el Caribe, 1939-1989* (Coruña: Ediciones do Castro, 1991).

McCann, Frank D. *The Brazilian-American Alliance, 1937-1945* (Princeton: Princeton University Press, 1974).

Mechan, J. Lloyd. *The United States and Inter-American Security, 1889-1960* (Austin: University of Texas Press, 1967).

Meléndez, Edgardo. *Puerto Rico's Statehood Movement* (Westport, Conn.: Greenwood Press, 1988).

Millett, Alan R. *Semper Fidelis: The History of the United States Marine Corps* (New York: Free Press, 1991).

Millis, Walter. *Arms and Men: A Study in American Military History* (New York: G.P. Putnam's Sons, 1956).

_____. *The Martial Spirit* (Cambridge, Mass.: The Literary Guild of America, 1931).

Milton, David. *The Politics of U.S. Labor: From the Great Depression to the New Deal* (New York: Monthly Review, 1982).

Minger, Ralph Eldin. *William Howard Taft and United States Foreign Policy: The Apprenticeship Years, 1900-1908* (Urbana: University of Illinois Press, 1975).

Mintz, Sidney W. *Sweetness and Power: The Place of Sugar in Modern History* (London: Penguin Books, 1985).

Morales Carrión, Arturo. *Puerto Rico: A Political and Cultural History* (New York: W.W. Norton, 1983).

Morison, Samuel E. *The Atlantic Battle Won, May 1943-May 1945,* vol. X of *History of United States Naval Operations in WWII* (Boston: Little, Brown, 1956).

_____. *The Battle of the Atlantic, September 1939-May 1943,* vol. I of *History of United States Naval Operations in WWII* (Boston: Little, Brown, 1947).

Muñoz Marín, Luis. *Catecismo del Pueblo: contestaciones a las preguntas que el pueblo hace sobre su vida y su porvenir* (San Juan: Partido Popular Democrático, 1939).

_____. *Memorias, 1898-1940* (San Juan: Inter American University Press, 1982).

_____. *La historia del Partido Popular Democrático* (San Juan: Editorial Batey, 1984).

Negroni, Héctor Andrés. *Historia militar de Puerto Rico* (San Juan: Comisión Puertorriqueña para la Celebración del Quinto Centenario, 1992).

Nixon, Edgar, B., ed. *Franklin D. Roosevelt and Foreign Affairs*, 3 Vols. (Cambridge, Mass.: Harvard University Press, 1974).

Office of the Adjunt General. *Manual del soldado puertorriqueño* (3ra. edición que incluye los nuevos reglamentos de infantería y nuevas materias de los últimos textos del ejército) Preparado por Luis Raúl Esteves, Brigadier General, G.N.P.R., Ayudante General de Puerto Rico (San Juan, P.R.: Bureau of Supplies, Printing and Transportation, 1939).

Offner, Arnold A., ed. *America and the Origins of World War II, 1933-1941* (Boston: Houghton Mifflin, 1971).

Ojeda Reyes, Félix. *Vito Marcantonio y Puerto Rico* (Río Piedras: Ediciones Huracán, 1978).

Paret, Peter. *Makers of Modern Strategy from Machiavelli to the Nuclear Age* (Princeton: Princeton University Press, 1986).

_____. *Understanding War: Essays on Clausewitz and the History of Military Power* (Princeton: Princeton University Press, 1992).

Pagán, Bolívar. *Historia de los Partidos Políticos, 1898-1956*, 2 vols. (San Juan: Librería Campos, 1959).

_____. *Ideales en marcha* (San Juan: Biblioteca de Autores Puertorriqueños, 1939).

Paolino, Ernest N. *The Foundation of the American Empire: William Henry Seward and U.S. Foreign Policy* (Ithaca: Cornell University Press, 1973).

Perloff, Harvey, S. *Puerto Rico's Economic Future* (New York: Arno Press, 1975).

Perret, Geoffrey. *A Country Made by War* (New York: Vintage Books, 1990).

Picó, Fernando. *1898: La guerra después de la guerra* (Río Piedras: Ediciones Huracán, 1987).

Poole, Bernard. *The Caribbean Commission* (Columbia, South Carolina: University of South Carolina Press, 1951).

Porter, Bruce D. *War and the Rise of the State: The Military Foundations of Modern Politics* (New York: The Free Press, 1994).

Post, Kent. *Strike the Iron: A Colony at War,* 2 vols. (Atlantic Highlands, NJ. & The Hague: The Institute of Social Studies, 1981).

Potter, Elmer Belmont, Roger Fredland and Henry H. Adams. *Sea Power: A Naval History*, 2nd ed. (Annapolis: Naval Institute Press, 1981).

Pratt, Fletcher. *Sea Power and Today's War* (New York: Harrison-Hilton, 1939).

The Puerto Rican Economy during the WarYear of 1942 (Washington, D.C.: Prepared by the Office of Statistics, Office of the Governor, and the Division of Territories and Island Possessions, Department of the Interior, 1943).

Puerto Rico: The Story of a Warbase (San Juan: Office of Publicity and Promotion of Tourism, 1943).

Raffucci, Carmen, Silvia Álvarez Curbelo and Fernando Picó. *Senado de Puerto Rico, 1917-1992: ensayos de historia institucional* (San Juan: Senado de Puerto Rico, 1992).

Rafucci, Carmen. *El gobierno civil y la Ley Foraker* (Río Piedras: Editorial Universitaria, 1981).

Reed, Donald A. *Admiral Leahy at Vichy, France* (Chicago: Adams Press, 1968).

Reynolds, David. *The Creation of the Anglo-American Alliance, 1937-1941: A Study in Competitive Co-operation* (London: Europa Publications, 1981).

Rigdon, William McKinley. *White House Sailor* (New York: Doubleday, 1962).

Rippy, J. Fred. *The Caribbean Danger Zone* (New York: G.P. Putnam's, 1940).

Rivera Ramos, Efrén. *The Legal Construction of Identity* (Washington, D.C.: American Psychological Association), 2001.

Robert, Amiral Georges. *La France aux Antilles de 1939 à 1943* (Paris: Librairie Plon, 1950).

Roberts, Walter Adolphe. *The Caribbean: Our Sea of Destiny* (Indianapolis: Bobbs-Merrill, 1940).

_____. *The French in the West Indies* (Indianapolis: Bobbs-Merrill, 1942).

Rock, David, ed. *Latin America in the 1940s: War and Postwar Transitions* (Berkeley: University of California Press, 1994).

Rodríguez, Nereida. *Debate universitario y dominación colonial (1941-1947)* (San Juan: Nereida Rodríguez, 1996).

Rodríguez Beruff, Jorge, ed. *Las memorias de Leahy: los relatos del Almirante William D. Leahy sobre su gobernación de Puerto Rico (1939-1940)* (San Juan: Fundación Luis Muñoz Marín, 2002).

Roosevelt, Eleanor. *This I Remember* (Westport, Conn.: Greenwood Press, 1975).

Roosevelt, Elliot, ed. *FDR: His Personal Letters, 1928-1945*, 2 vols. (New York: Duell, Sloan and Pearce, 1950).

Rosario Natal, Carmelo. *Luis Muñoz Marín y la independencia de Puerto Rico, 1907-1946* (San Juan: Producciones Históricas, 1994).

Ross, David F. *A Historical Study of Puerto Rico's Program of Economic Development* (San Juan: Edil, 1976).

Rout, Leslie B. *The Shadow War: German Espionage and United States Counterespionage in Latin America during WWII* (Frederick, Md.: University Publications of America, 1986).

Seager, Robert. *Alfred Thayer Mahan: The Man and His Letters* (Annapolis: Naval Institute Press, 1977).

Sempaire, Eliane. *La Guadeloupe en tan Sorin, 1940 à 1943* (Paris: EDCA, 1984).

Sherwood, Robert E. *Roosevelt and Hopkins: An Intimate History* (New York: Harper & Row, 1948).

Shullman, Mark Russell. *Navalism and the Emergence of American Sea Power, 1882-1893* (Annapolis: Naval Institute Press, 1994).

Silvestrini de Pacheco, Blanca. *Los trabajadores puertorriqueños y el Partido Socialista, 1932-1940* (Río Piedras: Editorial Universitaria, 1979).

Smith, Gaddis. *American Diplomacy during the Second World War, 1941-1945* (New York: Wiley, 1965).

Smith, Myson J. *World War II at Sea: A Bibliography of Sources in English* (Metuchen, NJ: Scarecrow Press, 1976).

Snell, John L. *Illusion and Necessity: The Diplomacy of Global War, 1939-1945* (Boston: Houghton Mifflin, 1963).

Spector, Ronald. *Professors of War: The Naval War College and the Development of the Naval Profession* (Newport: Naval War College Press, 1977).

Spykman, Nicholas John. *America's Strategy in World Politics: The United States and the Balance of Power* (New York: Harcourt Brace, 1942).

Steinsher, Bernard. *Rexford Tugwell and the New Deal* (New Brunswick: Rutgers University, 1964).

Taller de Formación Política. *¡Huelga en la caña!, 1933-34* (Río Piedras: Ediciones Huracán, 1982).

_____. *No estamos pidiendo el cielo: huelga portuaria de 1938* (Río Piedras: Ediciones Huracán, 1988).

Tansill, Charles Callan. *Back Door to War: The Roosevelt Foreign Policy, 1933-1941* (Chicago: Henry Reznery, 1952).

Terga, Domingo. *El "modus operandi" de las artes electorales en Puerto Rico* (San Juan: Imprenta Puerto Rico, 1940).

Thomas, R.T. *Britain and Vichy: The Dilemmas of Anglo-French Relations, 1940-42* (New York: St. Martin's Press, 1979).

Tolman, Newton F. *The Search for General Miles* (New York: Putnam's, 1968).

Torregrosa, Angel M. *Miguel Ángel García Méndez* (San Juan: n.p., 1939).

Trías Monge, José. *Historia constitucional de Puerto Rico*, Volume 2 (Río Piedras: Editorial de la Universidad de Puerto Rico, 1981).

Tuchman, Barbara W. *The Proud Tower: A Portrait of the World Before the War, 1890-1914* (New York: Macmillan, 1966).

Tugwell, Rexford Guy. *The Art of Politics* (New York: Doubleday, 1958).

_____. *The Brains Trust* (New York: Viking Press, 1968).

_____. *Changing the Colonial Climate* (New York: Arno Press, 1970).

_____. *F.D.R. Architect of an Era* (New York: Macmillan, 1967).

_____. *In Search of Roosevelt* (Cambridge: Harvard University Press, 1972).

_____. *Roosevelt's Revolution* (New York: Macmillan, 1977).

_____. *The Stricken Land, The Story of Puerto Rico* (New York: Doubleday, 1947).

United States Government. Naval History Division. *United States Naval Chronology, WWII* (Washington, D.C.: Government Printing Office, 1955).

United States Government. Office of Facts and Figures. *Report to the Nation: The American Preparation for War* (Washington, D.C.: Office of Facts and Figures, 1942).

United States Government. Section of the Anglo-American Caribbean Commission. *The Caribbean Islands and the War: A Record of Progress Facing Stern Realities,* U.S. Department of State Publication 2023 (Washington, D.C.: Government Printing Office, 1943).

U.S. Army. Caribbean Defense Command, Historical Section. "French-American military relations in the Caribbean theatre in WWII" (microfilm), Historical manuscript file, Office of the Chief of Military History (Washington, D.C.: U.S. Navy. Bureau of Yards and Docks, 1945)

U.S. Army. *Building the Navy's Bases in World War II* (Washington, D.C.: Government Printing Office, 1947).

U.S. War Department. *Conditions in Porto Rico* (Message from the President of the U.S. transmitting a report made by the Secretary of War.) (Washington, D.C.: Government Printing Office, 1910).

Van der Vat, Dan. *The Atlantic Campaign: World War II's Great Struggle* (New York: Harper & Row, 1988)

Vega, Bernardo. *Nazismo, fascismo y falangismo en la República Dominicana* (Santo Domingo: Fundación Cultural Dominicana, 1985).

_____. *Trujillo y las fuerzas armadas norteamericanas* (Santo Domingo: Fundación Cultural Dominicana, 1992).

Warwick, Arthur. *War and Social Change in the Twentieth Century: A Comparative Study of Britain, France, Germany, Russia and the United States* (London: Macmillan, 1974).

_____, ed. *Total War and Social Change* (New York: St. Martin's Press, 1988).

Watson, Mark Skinner. *Chief of Staff: Prewar Plans and Preparations* (Washington, D.C.: Historical Division, Department of the Army, 1950).

Weigley, Russell F. *The American Way of War: A History of United States Military Strategy and Policy* (Bloomington: Indiana University Press, 1973)

_____. *History of the United States Army* (New York: The Macmillan Company, 1967).

Weinberg, Gerhard. *A World at Arms: A Global History of World War II* (Cambridge: Cambridge University Press, 1994).

Wells, Henry. *La modernización de Puerto Rico* (Río Piedras: Editorial Universitaria, 1972).

Welles, Sumner. *Seven Decisions that Shaped History* (New York: Harper, 1951).

_____. *The Time for Decision* (Cleveland: World Publishing, 1938).

Wheler, Hans-Ulrich. *Der Aufstieg der amerikanischen Imperialismus* (Göttingen: Vandenhoeck & Ruprecht, 1974).

Windt Lavander, César de. *La Segunda Guerra Mundial y los submarinos alemanes en el Caribe* (San Pedro de Macorís: Universidad Central del Este, 1982).

Wood, Bryce. *The Making of the Good Neighbor Policy* (New York: Columbia University Press, 1961).

Wooster, Robert. *Nelson A. Miles and the Twilight of the Frontier Army* (Lincoln & London: University of Nebraska Press, 1993).

ARTICLES

"America's Ireland," *New Republic*, No. 102 (March 4, 1940): 295-296.

"Army Milestone: New Puerto Rican Department Gets Going with General Daley," *Newsweek*, No. 14 (July 10, 1939): 14.

Baldwin, Hanson. "If England Falls, What of the British Fleet?" *Reader's Digest*, (August, 1941).

_____. "The Naval Defense of America," *Harper's Magazine* (April, 1941).

Baptiste, F.A. "The Vichy Regime in Martinique Caught Between the United States and the United Kingdom (June, 1940 -June, 1943)," in Leslie F. Manigat, ed., *The Caribbean Yearbook of International Relations: 1975* (Leiden/ Trinidad: Sijthoff/Institute of International Relations, 1976): 215-253.

_____. "The Anti-Vichyite Movement in French Guiana, June to December 1940," in Leslie F. Manigat, ed., *The Caribbean Yearbook of International Relations: 1976* (Leiden/Trinidad: Sijthoff/Institute of International Relations, 1977): 133-146.

_____. "Le Regime de Vichy en Martinique (Juin 1940 a Juin 1943) L' Apllication des Mesures d'Orde Public," in Rene Acheen, *La Martinique Sons L'amiral Robert*, Les Cahiers du Ceraq Monograph no. 37, vol. 2 (Fort-de-France: Centre d'Etudes Regionales Antilles-Guyane, 1979).

_____. "The United States' Strategic Interest in Brazil, 1914-1939," in *The Caribbean Yearbook of International Relations: 1977*, (Trinidad: Institute of International Relations, University of the West Indies, 1980): 7-15.

_____. "The British Grant of Air and Naval Bases Facilities to the United States in Trinidad, St. Lucia and Bermuda in 1939 (June to December)," *Caribbean Studies,* No.16 (Julio, 1976): 5-43.

Beers, Henry P. "The Development of the Office of the Chief of Naval Operations," 4 part series, *Military Affairs*, Part Two: Vol. 10 (Summer, 1946) pp. 10-38, Part Three:Vol. 11 (Summer, 1947) pp. 88-99, Part Four: Vol. 11 (Winter, 1947): 229-237.

Benner, Thomas E. "American Difficulties in Puerto Rico," *Foreign Affairs*, Vol. 3, No. 4.

Bradford, R.B. "Coaling Stations for the Navy," *Forum*, Vol. 26, No. 6 (February, 1899): 732-47.

Brownback, Annadrug. "Congress Investigates Puerto Rico, 1943-1944," in Eugene R. Huck & Edward H. Moseley, eds. *Militarism, Merchants & Missionaries: U.S. Expansion in Middle America* (Alabama: University of Alabama Press, 1970): 145-158.

Charles, Gerard Pierre. "La segunda guerra mundial y los procesos de cambio en el Caribe: el papel hegemónico de Estados Unidos," *Revista de Ciencias Sociales* (Costa Rica), No. 17-18 (Mar.-Oct., 1979): 135-44.

Child, John. "From 'Color' to 'Rainbow': U.S. Strategic Planning for Latin America, 1919-1945," *Journal of Interamerican Studies and World Affairs*, Vol. 21, No. 2 (May, 1979).

Colby, Elbridge (Capt. U.S. Army). "American Interests in the West Indies," *Proceedings of USNIP*, Vol. 58 (April, 193I): 468-72.

Cronon, E. David. "Interpreting the Good Neighbor Policy: The Cuban Crisis of 1933," *HAHR*, No. 39 (Nov., 1959): 538-567.

Douglas, Lawrence H. "The Martinique Affair: The United States Navy and the French West Indies, 1940-1943," in William R. Roberts and Jack Sweetman, eds., *New Interpretations in Naval History: Selected Papers from the Ninth History Symposium* (Annapolis: Naval Institute Press, 1991).

Earle, Edward Meade. "The Navy's Influence on Our Foreign Relations", *Current History,* Vol. 23, No. 5 (February, 1926).

Emerson, Rupert. "Puerto Rico and American Policy Toward Dependent Areas," *Annals of the American Academy of Political and Social Science,* Vol. 15 (January, 1953): 285-289.

Eyre, James K. "Martinique a Key Point in Hemisphere Defense", *Inter-American Quarterly* Vol. 3, No. 4 (October 1941): 83-84.

Farley, Ena L. "Puerto Rico: Ordeals of an American Dependency during World War II," *Revista Interamericana*, Vol. 6, No. 2 (1976): 202-210.

Foillard, Edward T. "Martinique, Caribbean Question Mark," *National Geographic Magazine* (January, 1944): 47-55.

Furniss, E.J., Jr. "America's Wartime Objectives in Latin America," *World Politics,* Vol. 2 (April, 1950): 373-389.

Gatell, Frank O. "Independence Rejected: Puerto Rico and the Tydings Bill of 1936," *HAHR,* Vol. 38 (February, 1958): 25-44.

Géigel Polanco, Vicente. "El falso derrotero de la estadidad", *Mundo Libre,* No. 1 (June, 1943): 16-21.

_____. "La desorientación de un pueblo," *Índice,* No. 2 (August, 1930): 267-268.

_____. "La independencia: solución de nuestro problema de soberanía," *Mundo Libre,* Vol. 1, No. 4 (August, 1943): 19.

_____. *Mensaje de Puerto Rico a la Conferencia Panamericana de la Paz* (Buenos Aires, 1936).

Gervasi, Frank. "Our Gibraltar on Sand: Building the Most Important Base in our Caribbean Defense System on Puerto Rico," *Collier's,* No. 107 (February 22, 1941): 18-19.

Hays, Arthur Garfield. "Defending Justice in Puerto Rico," *Nation,* No. 144 (June 5, 1937): 647.

Holliday, George L. "Puerto Rico and the War," *Economic Review,* Vol. 6 (Dec., 1941): 1-5; Vol. 7 (Jan., 1942): 1-16; Vol. 7 (First Quarter, 1942): 13.

Hupperich, Herman. "The Caribbean-Vital Link in Western Hemisphere Air Defense During World War II," in Eugene R. Huck and Edward H Moseley, eds., *Militarists, Merchants and Missionaries: U.S. Expansion in Middle America* (Alabama: University of Alabama Press, 1970): 131-144.

"Islands Bulwarks," *USNIP* (March 1940): 372-384.

Johnson, Howard. "The Anglo-American Caribbean Commission and the Extension of American Influence in the British Caribbean, 1942-1945," *The Journal of Commonwealth and Comparative Politics* No. 184 (July, 1984): 180-203.

Landon, Truman H. (Lt. Gen.). "Caribbean Air Command," *Air Force Magazine,* Vol. 42 (Sept. 1959): 194-197.

Langley, Lester D. "The World Crisis and the Good Neighbor Policy in Panama, 1936-1941," *The American,* Vol. 26 (October, 1967): 137-152.

Leahy, William. "Recordemos siempre que una defensa adecuada a la situación mundial demanda una Marina Americana tan fuerte como la de cualquier otra nación", *El Mundo* (October 27, 1939).

Lear, John. "David's Mighty Slingshot Prepared for Invading Goliath," *Sunday Star* (March 24, 1940): c-1.

"Puerto Rico, Key to U.S. Defense, 'Gibraltar' of Western Hemisphere," *Washington Post* (March 24, 1940), section 3: 5.

Long, G. John. "Puerto Rico: Watchdog of the Caribbean, Venerable Domain under American Flag, Has New Role as West Indian Stronghold and Sentinel of the Panama Canal," *National Geographic Magazine* (December, 1939): 697-738.

Lyle, Eugene P., Jr., "Our Experience in Porto Rico," *The World's Work*, Vol. 11, No. 3 (January, 1906): 7082-7094.

Macaulay, N. "Material on Latin America in the United States Marine Corps Archives," *HAHR*, No. XLVI (May, 1966): 179-181.

Magdoff, Harry. "Militarism and Imperialism," *American Economic Review and Procedings*, No. LX (May, 1970): 237-246.

Mahan, A. T. "Remarks to the New York State Chapter of the Colonial Order,"(November, 1898).

_____. "The Relations of the United States to Their New Dependencies," *The Engineering Magazine*, Vol. 16, No. 4 (January, 1899): 523-524.

Martin, Lawrence and Sylvia Martin. "Outpost No. 2: The West Indies, Our New Stake in the Caribbean," *Harper's Magazines* Vol. 182 (December, 1940 / March, 1941).

McIntyre, F. (Major General). "American Territorial Administration," *Foreign Affairs* No. X (January, 1932): 300.

McLean, Ephraim R., Jr. (Lieut. Comm. U.S. Navy). "The Caribbean: An American Lake," *Proceedings of USNIP*, No. LXVIII (July, 1941): 947-952.

Merrill, James M. "Successors of Mahan: A Survey of Writings on American Naval History, 1914-1960," *Mississippi Valley Historical Review*, Vol. 50 (June, 1963): 79-99.

Morales Carrión, Arturo. "Puerto Rico: the fortress or the city?," *InterAmerican Quarterly* (July, 1940): 36-46.

"New Order in Puerto Rico," *New Republic* No. 99 (March 24, 1939): 58.

Olch, Isaiah. "A Resume of National Interests in the Caribbean Area," *Proceedings of the United States Naval Institute*, No. LXVI (September, 1940): 1297-1308.

"Programas políticos de 1940, I :Antecedentes y actualidad de nuestra política," *Isla* No. 2 (February 1940): 13-14.

Pratt, L. "The Anglo-American Naval Conversations of January, 1938," *International Affairs* (July, 1941).

"Puerto Rico," *Fortune* No. 23 (1941): 91-100.

"Puerto Rico: Gibraltar or Achille's Heel?" *Hemisphere* (February, 1940): 3-4.

"Puerto Rico: the economic 'sore spot,'" *Interamerican Quarterly* (April, 1940): 61-70.

"Puerto Rico at the crossroads", *Foreign Policy Reports* (October 15, 1937): 182-192.

Quintero Rivera, Angel G. "La base social de la transformación ideológica del Partido Popular en la década del '40", en *Cambio y Desarrollo en Puerto Rico: la transformación ideológica del Partido Popular Democrático*, Gerardo Navas, ed., (Río Piedras: Escuela Graduada de Planificación, UPR, 1980): 37-119.

Rippy, J. Fred. "German Investments in Latin America", *Journal of Business*, Vol. 21 (April, 1948): 63-73.

Rivera, Rodolfo O. "Puerto Rico Pays," *Nation*, No. 150 (May 25, 1940): 663.

Rodríguez Beruff, Jorge. "Cultura y geopolítica: un acercamiento a la visión de Alfred Thayer Mahan sobre el Caribe", in Antonio Gaztambide, Juan González and Mario Cancel, eds., *Cien años de sociedad: los 98 del Gran Caribe* (San Juan: Ediciones Callejón, 2000): 27-42.

_____. "Puerto Rico and the Caribbean in US Strategic Debate on the Eve of the Second World War," *Revista Mexicana del Caribe*, No. 2 (1996): 55-80.

Sink, Robert F., Lt. General. "U.S. Caribbean Command-Pivot Post of Hemisphere Defense," *Army Information Digest,* Vol. 16 (April, 1961): 10-19.

Sosa Llanos, Pedro Vicente. "La economía venezolana frente a la segunda guerra mundial", *Boletín de la Academia Nacional de la Historia*, Vol. 73, No. 291 (July-September, 1990): 151-160.

Sprout, Harold. "Strategic Considerations in Hemisphere Defense," *The Quarterly Journal of Inter-American Relations*, Vol. I (October, 1939): 21-29.

Stranathan, Leland S., Major General. "Caribbean Air Command," *Air Force Magazine*, Vol. 43, Part 2 (September, 1960): 199-200.

Strange, Susan. "The Four Power Caribbean Commission: Pattern for Colonial Regionalism," *World Affairs,* Vol. I (April, 1947): 171-180.

Taussig, Charles W. "A Four-Power Program in the Caribbean," *Foreign Affairs* (July, 1946): 699-710.

"Teminada la estructura de la base naval de Isla Grande", *Puerto Rico Ilustrado,* No. 33 (January 31, 1942): 100.

"The U.S. is Spending $40 million to Make our Caribbean Possession a Bastion of Defense. But the Island's Sick Economy is Bad Advertising for the Good Neighbor Policy," *Fortune,* No. 23 (February, 1941): 90-100.

Tugwell, Rexford Guy. "The Caribbean Commission: Notes on its Beginnings," in Curtis Wilgus, ed. *The Caribbean: British, Dutch, French, United States* (Gainesville: University of Florida Press, 1958): 262-275.

Tuthill, S. S. "The Insular Police of Porto Rico", *The Independent,* No. 51 (July 20, 1899).

Villard, Oswald Garrison. "Liberty and Death in Puerto Rico," *Nation,* No. 144 (April 3, 1937): 371-373; *Discussion,* No. 144 (May 29, 1937): 630.

_____. "Issues and Men: Nazi Charge that United States is using OCPU Methods," *Nation* No. 148 (February 18, 1939): 205.

_____. "Puerto Rico: Divorce with Alimony?" *Reader's Digest,* No. 45, (September, 1944): 82-86.

_____. "Puerto Rico, S.O.S.", *Nation,* No. 148 (June 24, 1939): 728-729.

Williams, Walter L. "United States' Indian Policy and the Debate over Philippine Annexation: Implications for the Origins of American Imperialism," *Journal of American History* (March, 1980): 810-831.

Winship, Blanton. "The Status of Puerto Rico: An Address by Gen. Blanton Winship over Columbia Broadcasting System from Washington, D.C., March 25, 1939," (Puerto Rico Trade Council, 1939).

Watt, D.C. "American Strategic Interests and Anxieties in the West Indies: A Historical Examination," *Journal of the Royal United Service Institution,* No. CVIII (August, 1963): 224-232.

Wilburn, Burton. "Panama: Defense Problem No. 1," *Current History*, No. XLIX, December, 1938): 34-36.

Young, Lowell T. "Franklin D. Roosevelt and America's Islets: Acquisition of Territory in the Caribbean and in the Pacific," *The Historian,* No. XXXVC (February, 1973): 205-221.

Unpublished Studies

Baldrich, Juan José. "Class and the State: The origins of Populism in Puerto Rico 1934-1952," Ph.D. dissertation, Department of Sociology, Yale University, 1981.

Bucholz, Albert Wallace. "The Liquidation of American Intervention in Certain Countries of the Caribbean Area: 1927-1934," Master's dissertation, University of Florida, 1941.

Burn, North C. "U.S. Base Rights in the British West Indies, 1940-1962," Ph.D. dissertation, Fletcher School of Law and Diplomacy, 1964.

Carbonell Ojeda, Sonia. "Blanton Winship y el Partido Nacionalista", Master's dissertation, History Department, University of Puerto Rico, 1984.

Córdova, Gonzalo F. "Resident Commissioner Santiago Iglesias and his Times", Ph.D. dissertation, Georgetown University, May, 1982.

Estades, María Eugenia. "Colonialismo y democracia: los informes de la División de Inteligencia Militar del Ejército de los Estados Unidos sobre las actividades subversivas en Puerto Rico, 1936-1941," Paper presented at the XVIII International Congress of the Latin American Studies Association, Atlanta, March 10-12, 1994.

Hernández Hernández, Carlos, "Historia y memoria: representaciones de la Segunda Guerra Mundial en la ciudad señorial de Ponce", Ph.D. dissertation, History Department, Universidad de Puerto Rico, 2005.

_____. "Pasión y muerte de la Villa de San Antonio: la expropiación de los barrios Maleza Alta y Maleza Baja de Aguadilla en el marco de la Segunda Guerra Mundial", Master's dissertation, Centro de Estudios Avanzados de Puerto Rico y el Caribe, 1996.

Hines, Calvin Warner. "United States Diplomacy in the Caribbean During World War II," Ph.D. dissertation, University of Texas at Austin, 1968.

Holmes, James Houghton. "Admiral Leahy in Vichy France," Ph.D. dissertation, The George Washington University, 1974.

González Morales, Carlos. "Ramey Air Force Base: su desarrollo y relación con Aguadilla y el Caribe en la prensa puertorriqueña (1939-1973)", Master's dissertation, Centro de Estudios Avanzados de Puerto Rico y el Caribe, 2003.

Karsten, F. D. "The Naval Aristocracy: U. S. Naval Officers from the 1840s to the 1920s: Mahan's Messmates," Ph.D. dissertation, University of Wisconsin, 1968.

Kneer, W.G. "Great Britain and the Caribbean, 1901-1913: A Study of Anglo-American Relations," Ph.D. dissertation, Michigan State University, 1966.

Langley, Lester D. "The United States and Panama, 1933-1941: A Study in Strategy and Diplomacy," Ph.D. dissertation, University of Minnesota, 1965.

Leutze, James R. "If Britain Should Fall: Roosevelt and Churchill and the British-American Naval Relations, 1938-1940," Ph.D. dissertation, Duke University, 1970.

McClain, Linda. "The Role of Admiral Leahy in U.S. Foreign Policy," Ph.D. dissertation, University of Virginia, 1984.

McFarlane, Malcolm R. H. "The Military in the Commonwealth Caribbean: A Study in Comparative Institutionalization," Ph.D. dissertation, University of Western Ontario, 1974.

Piñero Cádiz, Gerardo. "La Segunda Guerra Mundial, Puerto Rico y la base Roosevelt Roads," Ph.D. dissertation, Centro de Estudios Avanzados de Puerto Rico y el Caribe, 2004.

Santiago Caraballo, Josefa. "Guerra, reforma y colonialismo: Luis Muñoz Marín, las reformas del PPD y su vinculación con la militarización de Puerto Rico en el contexto de la Segunda Guerra Mundial," Ph.D. dissertation, Departamento de Historia, Universidad de Puerto Rico, 2004.

Seijo Bruno, María de los Ángeles. "La insurrección nacionalista de 1950," Master's dissertation, Centro de Estudios Avanzados de Puerto Rico y el Caribe, 1985.

Thomas, Gerald Eustis. "William D. Leahy and America's Imperial Years," Ph.D. dissertation, Yale University, 1973.

Torres Ortiz, Benjamín. "Historia del Partido Nacionalista, 1922-1937," Master's dissertation, Centro de Estudios Avanzados de Puerto Rico y el Caribe, 1976.

Yerxa, Donald Allan. "The United States Navy and the Caribbean Sea, 1914-1941," Ph.D. dissertation, University of Maine, 1982.

Newspapers

El Batey
La Correspondencia
La Democracia
El Mundo
The New York Times
El País
El Pueblo (Mayagüez)
Puerto Rico Ilustrado
The Washington Post
The Washington Star

INDEX

1940 elections xi, xii, 166, 181,183,188, 192, 215, 215, 216, 242, 245, 280, 284, 304, 320, 373

500 Acre Law 183, 190, 201, 221, 240, 241, 271, 276, 288, 308, 314, 318, 336, 375

65th Infantry 17, 32-34, 118-120, 176, 177, 223, 231, 247, 251, 345, 355, 356, 359

Abarca, Sucesores de 115

Açao Integralista Brasilera 106, 135

Acción Democrática 326

Acción Social Independentista (ASI) 185, 303

ACLU *see* American Civil Liberties Union

Afirmación Socialista 162, 180

Agrait, Gustavo 325

Agricultural Adjustment Act 174

Agricultural Extension Service 237, 238, 325

Agriculture 101, 167-172, 197, 221, 310

Aguinaldo Rebellion 26, 81, 83

Air bases 93, 117,122, 123, 126, 128, 151, 155, 229-232, 358, 359

Air Base 1 232, 358

Air power 126, 128, 151, 231, 232, 355, 356

Air Forces: 117, 122, 133, 148, 226, 231; Air Corps 124, 134, 150, 231, 269, 362; Royal Air Force 351, 358

Alaska 38, 40, 45, 50, 51, 117, 118, 123, 138, 174, 224, 230, 251, 256

Albizu Campos, Pedro 41, 59, 131, 132, 161, 165, 175, 176, 190, 197, 199, 200, 281, 324, 345

Alerta (journal) 326

Alessandri, Arturo 135

Alger, Russell (Secretary of War) 26

Alianza Puertorriqueña 169, 170, 282

Allen, Charles (P.R.Governor 1900-1904) 27, 35

Álvarez Curbelo, Silvia xiii

American Civil Liberties Union (ACLU) xi, 95, 162, 178, 185, 187, 193, 218, 228, 250, 391

American Federation of Labor (AFL) 36, 39, 161, 170, 324

American Legion 26, 34, 56, 120, 376

American Molasses Company 75, 101

American States, International Conferences of: Fifth and Sixth, 139; Seventh, 140, 141; Eighth, 141

Andrews, Adolphus (Vice Admiral) 109, 134, 137, 356

Anegada passage 7, 11, 15, 126, 127

Anglo-American Caribbean Commission xiii, 368

Antigua 92, 103, 136, 361

Antongiorgi, Ángel Esteban (nationalist) 163

Argentina 134, 135

Arias, Harmodio (President) 75, 140, 141

Arjona Siaca (Judge) 329

Arkansas 90

Army: 4; U.S. Army 14, 15, Army's War Plans Division 16

Army intelligence 125, 164, 200, 202, 213, 251, 286

Army War College 14-16, 50, 51, 56

Arnold, Henry H. "Hap" (General) 117, 148, 226, 230, 358

Aruba 361-353, 380

Asociación de Colonos 174

Asociación de Productores de Azúcar 174, 317

Atlantic Charter 323, 337, 344, 347

Atlantic Squadron 79, 91, 236

Atlantic-first strategy 79, 132

Badt, Harry A. (Captain) 236

Bailey, H.K. (Colonel) 29

Baker, Virgil 76

Baldwin, Hanson W. 129

Bar Association 264

Barbados 126, 127

Barceló, Antonio R. 169, 178, 184, 185, 185, 186, 188, 192, 197, 202, 216, 267, 273, 282, 303, 328

Batista, Fulgencio (General) 75, 92, 101, 106, 107, 140

"Battle of Britain" 330

Bauxite 352

Beals, Carleton 130, 153, 179, 201, 250

Béarn 370, 372

Beauchamp, Elías 177

Beehler, William H. (Captain) 11

Belaval, Emilio S. 113, 146, 187, 199

Benítez, Jaime 95, 178, 179, 200, 325

Benítez Rexach, Félix 116, 306

Berle, Adolf A. 75, 101, 141, 144, 157

Bermuda 92, 129, 235, 360, 361

Bernacet, Norberto 318, 342

Bernard, John T. 194

Berríos, Luis (Assistant Chief of insular Police) 28

Beverley, James R. (Governor of Puerto Rico) 42, 120

Bird Arias, Jorge 42

Bird Piñero, Enrique 216

Black, Ruby 41, 179, 185, 191, 203, 209, 217, 218, 305, 327, 375, 378

Black troops 14, 15, 19, 20, 50, 55, 56

Blanco, Tomás 187, 199, 324

Bloch, Claude C. 109, 137

Bonet, R. Sancho (Treasurer) 241, 242, 264, 266, 272, 291, 294

Borie 236

Borinquen Field 232, 235, 349, 358, 362, 381

Boston 81

Bourdeaux 370

Bourne, James and Dorothy 175, 179, 250

Boxer Rebellion 81, 83, 103

Boy Scouts 113, 376

Bradford, R. B. (Commander) 10, 11, 49

Brazil 92, 106, 126, 127, 132, 133, 134-136, 232

"Brazilian bulge" 127, 136, 358

Breckinridge (General) 94

Brett, George L. (General) 230, 269

Bristol, Arthur L. (Captain) 116, 150

Britain see Great Britain

British possessions 15, 26, 93, 121, 126, 134, 135, 275, 352, 353, 368, 369, 380

British West Indies 130, 368

Brother Rat 112

Brooke, John R. (Major General) 20, 24, 26, 51

Broome 236

Buchanan (Colonel) 269

Buitrago, José A. 325

Burton, Wilbur 128

Butler, Smedley D. 72, 73, 74, 82, 83, 104

Byrne, Edwin V. (Catholic Bishop) 233

Cadet, John B. 329

California 82

Camp Tortuguero in Vega Alta 359, 382

Campbell, W.S. (Liutenant Commander) 368

Campos del Toro, Enrique (Assistant Attorney General) 166, 214, 233, 241, 264, 265, 269, 271

Caperton (Admiral) 72, 83, 84

"Capitol Racket" 181, 210, 213, 214, 240, 241, 321

Cárdenas, Lázaro (President of Mexico) 78, 141

Caribbean Sea Frontier 357

Carreras, Santiago 181

Carter, John Franklin 43, 76, 179, 180, 201

Casa de España 113, 325

Castine 81, 84

Catecismo del pueblo, El 309-313, 315, 316, 318, 321, 329, 334, 367

Catholic Church 168, 224, 325

Chamberlain, Neville 113

Chapman, Oscar L. (Assistant Secretary) 189, 221

Chardón, Carlos 44, 190, 192, 193

Chardón Plan 176, 80, 184, 190, 288, 303

Chief of Naval Operations (CNO) 87, 88

Chilean *Nacistas* 135

China 10, 23, 114, 140, 327, 329

Churchill 93, 97

Citizens Military Training Camps (CMTC) 32

Civil War (U.S.) 3, 5, 19, 20, 22, 52, 79, 90, 335

Civilian Conservation Corps (CCC) 99, 237, 238

Claiborne, Robert W. 218, 317, 318

Clark, Frank S. (Colonel) 131

Clark, J. Reuben (Under Secretary of State) 139

Coalición x, xi, xv, 41, 43, 43, 64, 95, 117, 161, 162, 163, 165, 166, 169, 170, 174, 176, 178, 179, 180, 182, 184, 185, 186, 187, 188, 190, 191, 192, 193, 195, 196, 197, 200, 209, 211, 212-215, 216, 221, 223, 224, 227, 228, 233, 234, 235, 238, 240-242, 243, 244, 251, 261, 262, 263, 264-276, 277, 279, 280, 281, 282-287, 290, 291, 305, 306, 309, 311, 316, 320, 321, 373, 374, 476, 378

Colberg, Edward V. 194

Cold War 89

Coll Cuchí 332

Colom, José E. (Acting Governor Colonel) 28, 233, 241, 242, 272, 273, 274, 275, 280

Colón 80, 82

Colón (Panama) 73

Colón, Juan R. 163

Colonial system 40, 313

Colonialism 6, 173, 312-313

Colorado, Antonio J. 324, 325

Colton, George (Colonel; P.R. Governor 1909-1913) 28, 30, 37, 58

Commissioner of Agriculture 163, 242

Committee for Fair Play to Puerto Rico 218

Communists 275, 281, 290, 319, 325, 329

Conard, Charles (Rear Admiral) 239

Confessions of a Nazi Spy 112

Congress of Industrial Organizations (CIO) 161, 180, 317, 318, 329

Congress of the Unemployed 220

Cooper, Robert A. (Federal Judge) 163, 232

Coordinator of Federal relief agencies 237, 362

Corruption scandals 168, 212-217, 241, 272

Craig, Malin (Army Chief of Staff General) 91, 107, 134, 225, 231

Craven, Thomas T. (Lieutenant Commander) 82

Crenshaw, Russell S. (Captain) 131

Crocket, Carry I. (Colonel) 128

Crowder, Earl (General) 59, 84, 85

Cuba 7, 8, 9, 11, 13, 14, 15, 16, 21, 29, 38, 39, 42, 59, 67, 73, 74-75, 84, 85, 92, 97, 101, 102, 107, 128, 134, 136, 139, 140, 141, 150, 168, 174, 231, 232, 360

Culebra (Island of Culebra, Naval Base) 3, 4, 8, 9, 12, 13, 16, 30, 73, 74, 77-79, 103, 109, 119, 126, 127, 136, 137, 355, 357

Culgoa 84

Cummins 136

Curaçao 126, 351-353, 369, 380

Curzon Howe, L.C.A. (Captain) 93

Czechoslovakia 78, 114, 141, 222, 230, 323, 329

Dakar 127, 352, 353, 372

Daladier, Edouard (French Prime Minister), 113

Daley, Edmund L. (Brigadier General) 112, 231, 233, 240, 251, 255, 256, 257, 269, 357, 358, 375, 376, 377, 381, 382

Daniels, Josephus (Secretary of the Navy) 69, 82, 83, 87, 98, 141

Danish Virgin Islands 3, 73, 74, 100

Darby, Marshall N. (Captain) 164

Darlan (French Minister of Marine Admiral) 370, 377

Davis, George W. (Brigadier General) 20, 23, 24, 25, 26, 28, 51

De Gaulle (General) 370, 373

de Goes Monteiro, Pedro Aurelio (Major General) 92, 135

De Hostos, Filipo (President of the Chamber of Commerce) 76, 220, 221, 234, 292

de los Ríos, Fernando 325

de los Ríos, Giner 325

de Orbeta, Enrique (Colonel) 34, 243, 278, 296, 325, 345

Declaration of Panama 235, 369

del Toro Cuebas, Emilio (Chief Justice of Puerto Rico's Supreme Court) 233, 377

Depression 99, 139, 171, 173, 175, 187, 364

Dern, George (Secretary of War) 41, 44

Destroyers-for-bases 93, 138, 360, 361

Dewey, George (Admiral) 10, 69

Díaz Viera, Enrique 271

Dickey, James A. 221

Dietz, James L. 366-367

Diffie, Bailey and Justine 173

Dolphin 65, 72, 74, 83, 84, 87

Domenech, Manuel V. 242, 273, 274, 275

Dominican Republic 3, 4, 13, 37, 38, 72, 73, 75, 77-78, 79, 82, 84

Douglas, Lewis W. 44

Draft 32, 55, 363

Draughon, Donald A. (Marshall of the Federal Court) 221, 371

Dry dock 17, 115, 211, 230, 356

Duggan, Laurence 193, 326

Dumont, Pedro Juan 317, 318

Dunkirk 275, 330, 352, 357

Durán, Carmecita 113, 146

Dutch possessions 71, 126, 275, 351, 369

Dutch West Indies 330

Economic Commission 264, 270

Economic Convention 220-221, 234

Edelstein, Julius C. 113, 148, 373, 378, 387

El Batey 197, 217, 306-307, 316-321, 329

El Mundo 111, 112, 113, 114, 116, 118, 183, 202, 207, 209, 211, 213, 221, 223, 224, 233, 265, 268, 301, 307, 308, 325, 329

El País 93, 241, 261, 263, 265, 266, 272, 274, 277, 278, 279, 280, 283, 291, 295, 296

El Piloto 320, 343

El Pueblo 277, 281, 306

Eliot, George Fielding 125-128, 229

Ellis, (Vice Admiral) 78

Emerson, Rupert 224, 301, 354, 373, 375, 376, 377, 386

Emile Bertin 370

Escobar, Elifaz 164, 196

Estado Novo (Brazil) 135

Esteves, Luis R. (Colonel, Brigadier General) 34, 120, 149, 243, 376, 382

Ethiopia 90, 326, 329

Export-Import Bank 143

Fascist and Axis activities in Latin America 78, 103, 106, 113, 114, 115, 130, 132, 133, 135, 141, 142, 212, 322, 326, 335, 337

Fairbank, Miles H. 193, 239, 241

Fair Labor Standards Act 217, 218, 221, 320

Falange Española 113, 290, 325

Farley, James A. 40, 42

Federación Libre de Trabajadores 30, 161, 170, 180, 181, 188, 267, 317, 318

Federal Bureau of Intelligence (FBI) 34, 57, 239

Federal Emergency Relief Administration (FERA) 175

Federal Minimum Wage legislation 288

Fernández García, Benigno (Attorney General) 163, 190, 201, 210, 214, 240, 241, 242, 248, 261, 271, 305, 308

Fernós, Antonio 308, 345, 374

Finland 119

Fiske, Bradley A. (Rear Admiral) 69, 87, 98

Fiz Jiménez, Epifanio 166, 181, 214

Fleet Landing Exercises (Flex) 78, 119, 355

Fleet Problem XX 63, 77, 79, 91, 109-144, 230, 232, 352, 356, 357, 369

Fletcher, Frank (Lieutenant) 28

Folliard, Edward T. 130

Foraker Act (1900) 18, 26, 27, 35, 36, 37

Fox, Creed B. 41

France 49, 63, 85, 105, 115, 121, 134, 142, 150, 220, 226, 324, 327, 330, 352, 353, 354, 369, 370, 371, 372, 373, 377, 386

Franco 179, 325, 377

Frau, Oliver 266

Free French Movement 370, 373

French territories in the Caribbean 15, 126, 130, 134, 135, 275, 352, 353, 360, 370-373, 378

Fullam, William F. 69, 98

Gallardo, José M. 112, 193, 241, 266, 272, 378

Gannet 236

García Méndez, Miguel Ángel (Speaker of the House) 163, 165, 169, 170, 182, 183, 184, 188, 195, 211, 213, 215, 241, 244, 265, 266, 276, 277-278, 279, 281, 282, 283, 288, 289, 292, 296, 307, 321, 344

García Menocal, Mario (President) 72

Gardner, Augustus P. 69, 96

Garfield Hays, Arthur 178, 179, 194, 201, 205, 217, 250

Garrison Villard, Oswald 95, 114, 179, 200, 201, 219, 232, 249

Gayer, Arthur 179, 201

Géigel Polanco, Vicente 172, 187, 199, 200, 303, 325, 345

Géigel, Fernando (Mayor of San Juan) 223

Geiger, Roy S. (Colonel) 136

General Board of the Navy 69, 87, 98, 150

German summer offensive 275, 352

Germany 17, 49, 60, 73, 78, 115, 121, 127, 132, 133, 135, 140, 233, 326, 327, 330, 351, 352, 353, 355, 358, 369, 377, 380

Ghormley, Robert L. (Chief of the Navy's War Plans Div. Rear Admiral) 93

Glassford, William A. (Major) 11

González, Eduardo R. 224, 354

Good Neighbor policy and war 140-146

Good Neighbor Policy 68, 75, 77, 138, 140, 142, 143

Gore, Robert (P.R. Governor 1933-1934) 33, 39, 40, 40-42, 56, 59, 76, 174, 175, 176, 184, 199, 216

Grau 74-75, 140, 141

Graves, Frederick R. 115, 211, 215

Great Britain: 90, 92; British monarchs 92; Lindsay (British Ambassador) 92

Green War Plan 132

Greenslade, John W. (Rear Admiral) 94, 361, 362, 372

Gruening, Ernest 41, 42, 43, 44, 95, 162, 166, 175, 178, 179, 185, 186, 188-195, 196, 201, 204, 205, 223-225, 233, 237, 238, 239, 240, 241, 243, 247, 248, 251, 261, 285, 287, 290

Grupo de Buen Gobierno 169

Guam 38, 81, 116, 123, 132, 137, 219

Guantánamo 8, 13, 16 , 72 , 73, 85, 122, 126-128, 136, 231, 360

¡Guardacostas Alertas! 111

Guerra Mondragón, Miguel 190, 240, 241

Guerra, Nicanor 327-328

Guerra y Sánchez, Ramiro 173

Haas, William H. 131

Haba, Amalia de la 113

Haiti 13, 14, 16, 38, 63, 72, 73, 75, 77, 82, 83, 84, 99, 100, 102

Halsey Jr., William F. (Lieutenant) 71

Hamman 236

Harding, Warren G. (Senator; President) 40, 73, 121

Harrington (Colonel) 230

Harris, F.R. (Vice Admiral) 115, 1 47

Hatch Act 269, 320

Havana Conference 323

Hawaii 6, 27, 38, 45, 50, 67, 75, 76, 81, 117, 118, 128, 129, 137, 138, 174, 230, 358

Haya de la Torre, Víctor Raúl 152, 316

Hays, Arthur Garfield 178, 179, 194, 195, 201, 205, 217, 250

Heizen, Ralph 113

Henry Jr., Guy V. (Colonel) 14

Henry, Guy V. (General) 14, 18, 20, 20, 22, 24-26, 29, 35, 51

Hepburn Board 90, 116, 120, 122, 128, 138, 155, 356, 361

Hepburn, A.J. (Admiral) 122, 150

Herrick, Robert 189

Hibben, Thomas 364

Higginson, Francis J. (Captain) 8, 48

Hispanic Studies Department 325

"Hispanism" 324

Hobson, Richmond P. (Congressman) 87, 315

Holmes, Oliver Wendell (Supreme Court Justice) 66, 96

Home Guard 32, 363, 377

Hopkins, Harry 87, 88, 105, 143, 230, 327

Horton, Benjamin (Attorney General) 190

Houston 61, 63, 65, 75, 76, 87, 136, 138, 212

Hull, Cordel (Secretary of the State Department) 77, 92, 107, 140, 141, 370, 371

Hull, Harwood 163, 196, 233

Ickes, Harold (Secretary of the Interior) 43, 44, 64, 87, 88, 95, 105, 130, 134, 159, 161, 162, 166, 178, 179, 188-195, 201, 205, 209, 213, 214, 221, 223, 224, 227, 228, 229, 234, 237, 238, 239, 243, 246, 247, 252, 263, 268, 272, 274, 278, 279, 280, 285, 286, 287, 289, 296, 326, 369, 373, 374, 375, 376, 378

Iglesias Pantín, Santiago 36, 37, 117, 148, 163, 165, 170, 178, 181, 182, 186, 211, 215, 216, 218, 223, 224, 247, 249, 252, 267, 273, 308, 318, 345

Independence 17, 32, 33, 34, 35, 36, 37, 43, 44, 116, 117, 131, 135, 137, 148, 165, 168, 169, 172, 178, 184, 191, 192, 193, 200, 212, 216, 225, 244, 278, 286, 287, 290, 303-304, 308, 313, 320, 323, 326, 327-329, 331, 332, 333, 376

Indian Affairs, Bureau of 19, 22

Indian Wars and Puerto Rico 20, 22

Infanta María Teresa 80

Ingersoll, Royal (Captain) 90

Insular Affairs, Division of 19, 53, 57; Bureau of Insular Affairs (BIA) 16, 19, 30-44, 53, 55-58, 58, 97

Insular Police 24, 25, 29, 34, 36

Insularismo 172

Inter-American Conference for the Maintenance of Peace in Buenos Aires 141, 332

Inter-American Meeting in Lima 135

Inter-American Bank 143

Inter-American Development Commission 143

Iriarte, Celestino 279

Irizarry, Luis (Colonel) 163, 164

Isla Grande (airfield; naval base) 13, 116, 118, 122, 123, 124, 148, 230, 355, 356

Italy 78, 85, 90, 105, 121, 127, 132, 134, 135, 141, 142, 150, 326, 330, 351, 352, 360

Italian invasion of Ethiopia 90, 326

Italian intervention in Spanish Civil War 90

Jaffe, A.J. 364

Jamaica 15, 92, 103, 126, 361, 368, 371

James, Earl K. 129

Japan 11, 49, 69, 78, 81, 85, 90, 91, 96, 98, 105, 114, 121, 124, 125, 127, 131, 135, 140, 150

Japanese expansionism 124-125, 135, 329, 377, 381

Jeanne d'Arc 370

Jiménez, Juan Ramón 325

Johnson, Alfred H. (Admiral) 236

Join the Marines 111

Joint (Army-Navy) Board 91, 98, 131, 132, 222, 230, 356

Joint Chiefs of Staff 226, 356

Joint Planning Committee 131-133, 230, 231, 356, 357, 371, 372

Joint Puerto Rican Coastal Frontier Defense Plan (PRCF-1940) 133, 358

Jones Act (1917) 26, 28, 31, 32, 36, 37, 40, 55, 58, 170, 190, 249, 262, 263, 267, 274

Jones-Costigan Act 43, 60, 140, 174

Jones, Walter Mc K 185, 201, 239, 250

Jordán, Jorge 277

Kalbfus, Edward C. (Admiral) 109, 134, 137

Key West 123

Kibler, A.F. (Colonel) 368

King, Ernest J. (Lieutenant; Admiral) 71, 225, 226

Knox, Frank (Secretary of War) 372

La Democracia 184, 304, 306, 344

Laborista 241, 276

Lafayette sugar-mill 269, 288, 308

Lanzetta, James J. 239

Lapwing 236

Las Garzas hydroelectric project 211, 213, 272

Lathman & Co., E.H. 115

Laval, Pierre 354, 372, 377

Leahy, Michael 79

Leahy, William D. (Admiral; P.R. Governor 1939-1940) 28, 61, 63-66, 70, 72, 74, 79-95, 103, 104, 109, 111, 112, 118, 122, 126, 127, 128, 133, 134, 136, 137, 138, 148, 181, 182, 183, 195, 205, 207-245, 250, 251, 252, 253, 254, 255, 256

Lee, Muna 184, 186, 217, 326, 327

Lewis, Gordon 367

Liberals (voters) 165, 176, 178, 179

Lindsay (British Ambassador) 92

Lodge, Henry Cabot 7, 66, 67, 96, 97

London Naval Conference 85

Long, E. John 129

Long, John D. 8, 11, 48

López Domínguez, Francisco (Commissioner of Agriculture) 221, 242

Los Soldados Mandan 112

Losey Field 231

Luchetti, Antonio 241, 243, 266, 272, 273

Lusitania 70

Lyle, Eugene P. 12

MacKay, Donald E. (Commander) 375

Mahan, Alfred Thayer (Captain) 1, 4, 5-11, 14, 15, 22, 23, 28, 46, 47, 48, 53, 66, 67, 68, 71, 74, 86, 95, 96, 97, 99, 126, 129, 138

Malcolm, George A. (Attorney General) 240, 241, 242, 269, 271, 278, 305

Manchuria 90

Marcantonio, Vito 95, 115, 166, 179, 183, 194, 196, 201, 209, 211, 212, 214, 215, 218, 239, 250, 318

Marshall, George C. (General; Army Chief of Staff) 92, 143, 225, 226, 230, 268, 269, 357, 360, 363

Martin, H.A. 112

Martínez Nadal, Rafael 115, 163, 165, 169, 170, 182, 184, 191, 195, 212, 213, 214, 215, 221, 223, 227, 228, 235, 242, 243, 247, 252, 263, 265, 266, 267, 268, 269, 270, 271, 272, 273, 274, 275, 276-278, 280, 286, 287, 289, 292, 296, 322, 376

Martinique crisis 372-375

Massacre, Palm Sunday Ponce [1937] 35, 114, 146, 162, 178, 179, 187, 193, 195, 200, 201, 205

Mathews, Thomas 58

Mayo, Henry T. (Rear Admiral) 82

McCaleb, Walter Flavius 196

McDill air base 232, 358

McKinley, William (President) 10, 13, 18, 26, 27, 46, 49

McIntyre, Frank (General) 36, 38, 40

McLean, Ephraim (Lieutenant Commander) 129

McLeish, Archibald 336, 347

McLeod, Leslie A. (Treasurer) 183, 214, 239, 242, 256

Mellvile 85

Memphis 84, 118

Men with Wings 111

Mendieta, Carlos (Cuban President) 75, 140, 174

Mendonza, Inés 326

Merriam, Charles 178, 201

Mexico 72, 78, 132, 138, 139, 141, 143

Meyer, George L. (Secretary of the Navy) 87

Miles, Nelson A. (General) 7, 8, 9, 19-20, 21, 22, 48, 51, 52

Military Intelligence Division (MID) 34, 188, 247

Millis, Walter 68, 127, 151

Milward, Alan 365

Mona passage 7, 11, 126, 136

Monroe Doctrine 67, 121, 132, 135, 138, 139, 155, 369

Morales Carrión, Arturo 13, 24, 31, 50, 53-55, 57, 58

Morgan, J.P. 70

Morgenthau Jr., Henry 375, 376

Moyne Commission 368

Munich agreement 91, 113

Munich Crisis 141, 142

Muñoz Rivera, Luis 35, 36, 40, 41, 42, 43, 44, 59, 89, 95

Muñoz Marín, Luis 40, 41, 183, 184, 187, 162, 165, 179, 186, 203, 209, 215, 216-218, 220, 221, 225, 235, 240, 244, 245, 250, 267, 268, 269, 273, 274, 275, 280, 292, 283, 284, 288, 289, 290, 301, 303-310, 314, 315, 316, 317, 318, 319-324, 326-329, 331, 332, 333, 334, 335, 336, 337, 338, 339, 340, 342, 343, 347, 349, 366, 367, 373, 374-376, 378

Muñoz, Miguel A. (Colonel; Commander of the Home Guard) 377

Natal 136, 143, 232, 358

National Guard 15, 17, 19, 28, 30, 31, 33, 34, 56, 112, 113, 119, 120, 162, 163, 163, 176, 200, 231, 243, 280, 355, 356, 359, 363, 376

Nationalist attack on Riggs [1936] 33, 177

Nationalist attack on Winship [1938] 163, 164, 196

Nationalist Party (Puerto Rican) 16, 41, 42, 43, 44, 35, 117, 131, 162, 165, 178, 190, 192, 222, 224, 304, 311, 320-322, 325, 328, 345, 355

Nationalists 44, 114, 130, 162, 163, 164, 165, 176, 179, 232, 244, 286, 290, 326, 245

Nationalist Challenge 176-180

Naval Expansion Act 122

Naval negotiations (U.S-Britain) 90

Naval War College 3, 7, 46, 48, 87

Navarro, Tomás 325

Navy Department reorganization 87

Navy League 70

Nazi movement 134

"neutrality zone" 235

New Deal 71, 89, 91, 179, 184, 185, 200, 230, 244, 272, 274, 281, 288, 296, 320, 322, 363, 365

New York 90

New York's World Fair 79, 133, 207, 223, 354

Newark 81

Newfoundland 92, 134, 347, 361

Nicaragua 4, 13, 16, 20, 38, 67, 82, 83, 92, 104, 106

Nimitz 71, 268

"non-interventionist" policy in Central American-Caribbean region 140

Nordskav 84

North Carolina 90

Office for Coordination of Commercial and Cultural relations between the American Republics 143

Office of Naval Operations 87

Office of Naval Intelligence (ONI) 87

Office of the Coordinator of Inter-American Affairs 144

Oil 55, 78, 90, 351, 360, 368, 380

Olaya Herrera, Enrique (President of Colombia) 75

Oliver, James H. (Rear Admiral) 74, 85

Olney, Richard (Attorney General) 21, 52

Operation Asterisk 373

Operation Felix 377

Operation Torch 373

Oposición Socialista 181

Orbeta (Chief of Police) 34, 243, 278, 325, 345

Oregon 80

Pacheco Padró, Antonio 331, 332

Pacheco, Sixto A. (Senator) 166, 214, 271

Padelford, Norman J. 128

Padrón Rivera, Lino 264, 279, 292

Pagán, Bolívar (senator) 165, 166, 181-182, 184, 188, 191, 202, 214, 215, 223, 240, 249, 252

Pan American Airways 116, 124, 143, 232

Panama 3, 4, 10, 13, 16, 32, 63, 66, 73, 75, 81, 83, 85, 102, 117, 118, 122, 123, 126, 127, 128, 129, 138, 141, 156, 230, 232, 327, 358, 360

Panama Canal 11, 12, 15, 16, 26, 28, 71, 75, 87, 93, 96, 102, 117, 121, 126, 128, 129, 130, 133, 138, 142, 150-151, 232, 353, 354, 355, 360, 361, 370

Panay 90, 125

Partido Agrícola Puro 285

Partido Comunista 162, 180

Partido Federal 35, 168

Partido Laborista Puro 182, 184, 242, 266, 269, 276, 277, 281, 283

Partido Liberal (Liberal Party) x, 41, 44, 162, 165, 166, 168, 169, 175, 178, 182, 183, 184, 185, 186, 187, 188, 190, 192, 193, 196, 202, 203, 216, 239, 240, 243, 266, 269, 277, 282, 283, 285, 286, 303, 306, 320, 321, 327, 329

Partido Liberal, Neto, Auténtico y Completo 185-186, 303

Partido Popular Democrático (Popular Democratic Party) x, xv, 131, 165, 174, 180, 184, 187, 197, 202, 215, 217, 240, 241, 244, 245, 274, 280, 281, 282, 283, 284, 286, 288, 289, 304, 305, 306, 307, 308, 309, 311, 312, 315, 317, 318, 319, 320, 321, 322, 323, 324, 325, 326, 328, 329, 331, 332, 333, 334, 336, 342, 345, 366, 367, 373, 374, 379

Partido Republicano Puertorriqueño 35, 168, 169, 170, 190

Partido Republicano Puro 169

Partido Republicano Reformista 184

Partido Socialista (Socialist Party) x, 161, 165, 169, 170, 182, 184, 242, 261, 264, 266, 267, 272, 273, 276, 282, 283, 316, 318, 325

Partido Unión 168

Partido Unión Republicana (PUR) x, 163, 165, 168, 170, 182, 184, 180, 181, 182, 188, 228, 241, 243, 244, 261, 263, 266, 268, 272, 273, 276, 277, 278, 283, 284, 285, 286, 287, 291, 309, 321, 374

Pasewalk, Herbert R. 194

Patron 33 236

Patron 51 236

Pearl Harbor 94, 337

Pedreira, Antonio S. 172, 187, 199, 303, 324

Peoples (Rear Admiral) 239

Pershing, John, J. (General) 377

Pershing's "Punitive Expedition" 72

Pettengill (Admirals) 268

Philadelphia 77

Philippines 7, 10, 21, 25, 27, 30, 36-39, 44, 47, 50, 57, 59, 60, 68, 81, 126, 132, 240, 256

Phoenix 118

Pickens (Rear Admiral) 236

Picó, Rafael 131, 336, 365

Pierce, E.R. 368

Piñero, Jesús T. 174, 183, 209, 304

Plan Orange 91, 121

Plan White 133

Platt Amendment 139, 140

Plebiscite 178, 221, 225, 308, 313, 314, 331

Poland 93, 141, 226, 233, 358

Pomalles, Antonio 214

Ponce Air Base (Fort Losey) 359

Populares 216, 245, 281, 282, 283, 284, 285, 305, 307, 310, 316, 319, 328, 343

Port strike (1938) 161-162, 164, 166, 180, 196

port workers 161-162, 164, 180

Porto Rico Regiment, U.S. Volunteers Infantry (later Porto Rico Infantry Regiment) 29, 30, 32

Post, Regis H. (P. R. Governor 1907-1909) 35-36, 37

Prairie 84

Pratt, William V. (Admiral) 85, 86

Prieto, Indalecio 113

Primo de Rivera, José Antonio 113

protection of agricultural producers 310

Protestantism 168

Public Works Administration (PWA) 86, 237, 238, 362, 365

Puerto Rican Army Department 357

Puerto Rican Department Basic War Plan, 1941 133

Puerto Rican Economy 27, 43, 45, 124, 166, 167, 168, 171, 172, 173, 174, 198, 221, 234, 262, 314, 315, 316, 336, 363, 364, 365, 367, 384

Puerto Rican garrison 25

Puerto Rican troops 14, 17, 25, 28, 29, 31, 32, 50, 55, 56, 149, 338, 363

Puerto Rico Cement Corporation 235, 259

Puerto Rico Defense Plan 132

Puerto Rico Defense Project 133, 231

Puerto Rico Department of the Army 16, 233, 251, 269

Puerto Rico Reconstruction Administration (PRRA) 43, 164, 175, 186, 188, 189, 190, 192, 196, 204, 237, 238, 243, 261, 262, 268, 269, 288, 308, 362, 375

Puerto Rico Trade Council 222

Pullman strike 21

Punta Borinquen 231, 232, 270, 359

Purple War Plan 132, 134

Quarter Sphere concept 132

Quiñones, Samuel R. 199, 303, 309, 325, 340, 345

Quintana, Gloria 166

Raibow Plans 91, 132, 222, 231, 357

Rainbow I 132

Rainbow IV 132

Rainbow V 132

Raleigh 116, 120

Ramírez Pabón, Francisco 166

Ramírez Santibañez, José 181, 182, 188, 216, 268, 282

Ramos Antonini, Ernesto 325, 342

Ranger 372

Reactionary 177, 273

Ready, Joseph L. (Major) 14, 50

Real, Romualdo 113, 146

Reid 136

Reily, Emmet Montgomery (P.R. Governor 1921-1923) 39, 40

Religion 310, 319

Richards, George 77

Richardson, James O. (Admiral) 94

Rigby, William C. (Colonel) 238, 239

Riggs, Francis E. (Colonel) 33, 34, 44, 106, 176, 177-178, 191, 192, 193, 243, 304

Río Piedras Massacre 177

Rippy, Fred 130

Rivera Martínez, Prudencio 165, 181-182, 183, 202, 240, 242, 256, 264, 266, 267, 283, 291, 318, 376

Rivera Barreras, José N. 266

Robert, Georges (Admiral) 371-373

Roberts, Walter A. 130

Robinson, Edwin Van Dyke 11, 21, 49

Rockefeller, Nelson 143-144

Rodman Board Report 120, 121, 122

Rodríguez Vera, Andrés 172

Roig, J.A. 221

Roosevelt Roads Naval Station 76, 362, 383

Roosevelt, Eleanor 41, 43, 65, 71, 76, 101, 179, 185

Roosevelt, Franklin Delano x, xi, xiv, xv, 17, 27, 35, 40, 41, 42, 43, 44, 45, 59, 60, 63, 64, 65, 66-79, 82, 83, 84, 86, 87, 88, 89, 90, 91, 92, 93, 94, 96, 98, 99, 101, 105, 111, 114,

117, 121, 130, 133, 134, 137, 139,
140, 141, 142, 151, 156, 164, 174,
175, 181, 185, 186, 189, 191, 192,
193, 194, 195, 201, 203, 209, 210,
211, 212, 218, 219, 220, 221, 222,
224, 225, 226, 227, 228, 229, 234,
235, 236, 237, 238, 239, 247, 268,
275, 276, 279, 280, 282, 286, 288,
313, 320, 322, 323, 327, 332, 333,
344, 347, 351, 352, 253, 357, 358,
360, 362, 368, 369, 371, 373, 375,
377, 378

Roosevelt, Henry Latrobe 68, 72, 77, 86,
88, 102

Roosevelt, James (Colonel) 68, 77, 102,
136

Roosevelt, Kermit 77, 102

Roosevelt, Theodore 3, 4, 7, 26, 27, 35,
46, 48, 66, 68, 69, 71, 96, 97, 138,
139

Roosevelt, Theodore Jr. 27, 54, 68, 77,
223

Root, Elihu (Secretary of Defense) 23, 25,
26, 27, 53, 56, 97

Rosado, Hiram 177

Royal Air Force 369

Royal Dutch Shell 351

Russian Revolution 89

Saint Thomas (in Danish Virgin Islands)
3, 7, 8, 9, 11, 13, 73, 78, 101, 119,
126, 136, 155, 233, 368

Samaná Bay (in Dominican Republic) 3,
4, 7, 8, 9, 11, 16, 73, 77, 78, 102,
136

San Francisco 236

San Juan Air Base 119, 123

San Juan Harbor 17, 115, 118, 129,
136, 230, 236

Sánchez Fernández, Ángel 277

Santos Zelaya, José (President of Nicaragua) 82

Satterlee, Herbert 70

Secretary of Agriculture 164

security institutions, creation of new 22,
30-37, 168

Serrallés, Pedro Juan (Senator) 163, 342

Seward, William H. (US Secretary of State
1861-1869) 3, 4, 11, 46

Shawmut 84

Shea, Francis Michael 223

Sheppard, Morris (Senator) 118, 138

Simpson 236

Sims 236

Smith, Harold D. 237

Smoot-Hawley tariff 139

Snyder, Cecil (U.S. District Attorney) 268-
269

Social Darwinisim 4

Soltero Peralta, Rafael (judge) 332

Somoza, Anastasio (General) 92

Sotomayor Rabat, F. 114

Spain 4, 7, 9, 13, 15, 48, 66, 78, 113,
114, 324, 325, 327, 355, 377

Spanish Civil War 113, 141, 146, 323,
325, 326

Special Plan Three to invade islands 371

Sprout, Arnold 96, 128

Spruance, Raymond A. (Captain; Rear
Admiral) 94, 119, 231, 357, 358,
371, 372, 376, 377, 381

St. Lucia 84, 92, 103, 126, 235, 360,
361, 368

Stadta, Ramón (Dutch Priest) 319

Standard Dredging Co. 116

Standard Oil of New Jersey 351

Standley, William S. (Admiral) 86

Stark, Harold R. (Admiral; Lieutenant) 71, 93, 94, 225, 268, 361, 362, 372

Statehood 35, 137, 216, 224, 225, 266, 276, 279, 280, 281, 296, 313, 323, 328, 331, 339, 376

State-War-Navy Standing Liaison Committee 91, 134

Status of Puerto Rico 26, 35, 116, 148, 169, 216, 221, 225, 237, 245, 249, 304, 308, 314, 320, 322, 323, 328-333, 335, 338, 339

Stone, Roy (General) 26

Strategic importance of Puerto Rico 5-19, 75-76, 126-135, 230-234

Sturn, E.G. 183

Submarine Patrol 112

Suez Canal 5, 9, 16

Sugar industry and crisis 169-178

Sugar plantation economy 27, 167, 172-173, 198

Sutherland, W.H.H. (Admiral) 82

Swanson, Claude S. (Secretary of the Navy) 86, 88, 122, 220

Swope, Guy J. (Congressman) 239, 242, 290, 334, 366, 378

system of naval bases 92

Taft, William Howard 25, 27, 34, 36, 37, 57, 69, 81, 82, 87

Taussig, Charlie 43, 75, 76, 101, 180, 223, 368

Teheran (Conference) 220

Tehuantepec 128

Tenth Naval District 357, 372

Territories and Islands Possessions, Division of 44, 175, 188, 375

Texas 90

Thompson, Rober M. (Colonel) 70

Tió, Salvador 325

Tobacco industries 161, 167, 198

Torres, Alfonso 181

Towner, Horace M. (P.R.Governor 1923-1929) 28, 32, 33, 169

Townshend, Orval P. (Lieutenant Colonel) 32

Trentista generation 172, 187, 303

Trías Monge, José 249, 256, 263

Trigo, Dioniso 325

Trinidad 15, 26, 92, 126, 127, 129, 235, 351, 358, 360, 361, 368, 369, 380

Tripartismo 183, 188, 215, 235, 242, 243, 244, 245, 274, 277, 278, 280, 281, 282-283, 284, 285, 286, 289, 305, 306, 307, 309, 311, 312, 318, 321, 322, 373

Tripartismo, support by Leahy 282-292

Trujillo, Rafael Leónidas (General) 77, 92

Trush 236

Truxton 236

Tucaloosa 79

Tuchman, Barbara 6

Tugwell Commission 336

Tugwell, Rexford G. (P.R. Governor 1941-1946) 43, 75, 76, 101, 180, 223, 224, 336, 360, 365, 366, 367, 368, 375

Tuscaloosa 79, 236

Tydings Bill 178, 191, 192, 200, 287

Tydings, Millard (Senator) 176, 178

U.S. Army garrison in Puerto Rico 14, 25, 29, 127, 135, 235, 355-363

U.S. Citizenship xii, 23, 28, 31, 35, 55, 137, 170

U.S. Marine Corps 68, 71, 72, 92, 136, 360

U.S. military in colonial administration 19-47

U.S. strategic thinking towards Caribbean 126-135

Unificación Puertorriqueña Tripartita x, 184, 277, 282, 304

Unión Republicana Reformista 277

"United States Commission to Study Social and Economic Conditions of the British West Indies" 368

White troops 17, 56, 119, 363, 372

University of Puerto Rico 32, 34, 113, 174, 178, 207

Upshur (Brigadier General) 136

Uruguay 134

USSR 89

Valdés, Alfonso (Senator) 163, 166, 170, 182, 211, 214, 221, 223, 252

Van Hook, C.E. (Commander), 16

Vargas, Getulio (Brazil) 135

Vasallo, Mariano (Mgr.) 224

Venezuela 52, 66, 75, 119, 120, 128, 151, 262, 324, 351, 358, 380

Veracruz 38, 59, 72, 83, 84

Vestal, S.C. (Colonel) 14

Vichy, France 63, 220, 226, 323, 324, 330, 354, 370, 371, 373, 377, 378

Vieques 136, 359, 362

Vieques passage 361, 362

Vieques Sound, 15, 16, 29

Vincennes 86

Vincent, Stenio (President of Haiti 1930-1941) 75, 77

Vinson-Trammell Act (1938) 86, 90

Virgin Islands, US 13, 15, 16, 38, 45, 63, 76, 84, 100, 102

Vizcarrondo, Francisco 221

Wages and Hours Act 235

Wagner Acts 320

Waller, L.W.T (Colonel) 83

War and the economy 365-369

War movies 111-112

War preparations, Puerto Rico 120-126, 231-234, 357-365

War, impact in Caribbean 354-356, 370-375

War atmosphere in Puerto Rico 114-122, 238

Washington 90

Washington Naval Conference (1921-1922) 121

Welles, Gideon (Secretary of the Navy in 1866) 3

Welles, Sumner 65, 74, 75, 77, 91, 92, 101, 107, 134, 140

Wells, Henry 12

West Africa 132

White War Plan 133

Williams, John Sharp (Congressman) 40

Wilson, John A. (Major) 34

Wilson, Woodrow 32, 36, 65, 69, 70, 71, 72, 79, 84, 87, 97, 98, 99

Wings of the Navy 112

Winship, Blanton (General; P.R. Governor 1934-1939) 28, 34, 37, 41, 42, 43, 44, 59-60, 63, 64, 85, 95, 102, 114-115, 117, 130, 137, 141, 161, 162-164, 165, 166, 175, 176, 177, 178-179, 180, 181, 183, 187, 188, 190, 191, 192, 193-195, 196, 200, 201, 205, 209-216, 218, 219, 221, 222, 223, 225, 227, 232, 233, 234, 237, 238, 239, 242, 243, 247, 256, 261, 263, 270, 271, 290, 318, 325

Winthrop, Beekman (P.R. Governor 1909-1913) 27, 36, 69, 223, 224

Wishard, R.H. (Liutenant Commander) 233

Wood, Leonard 21, 56, 96, 97, 98

Wood, Philip S. (Lieutenant) 17, 51

Works Progress Administration (WPA) 87, 225, 227, 229, 230, 234, 236, 237, 238, 255, 261, 262, 264, 269, 270, 359, 362, 363, 365

World War I xii, 30, 31, 32, 72, 84, 90, 111, 115, 120, 121, 125, 127-128, 168, 171, 355, 361, 369, 377

Wounded Knee massacre [1890] 20

Wright, John W. (Colonel) 223, 247, 251

Wyoming 118

Yager, Governor 31, 32, 55

Yalta Conference 220

Yorktown 86

Young, Sir Hubert 371